MOON

ROUTE 66

— *Road Trip* —

JESSICA DUNHAM

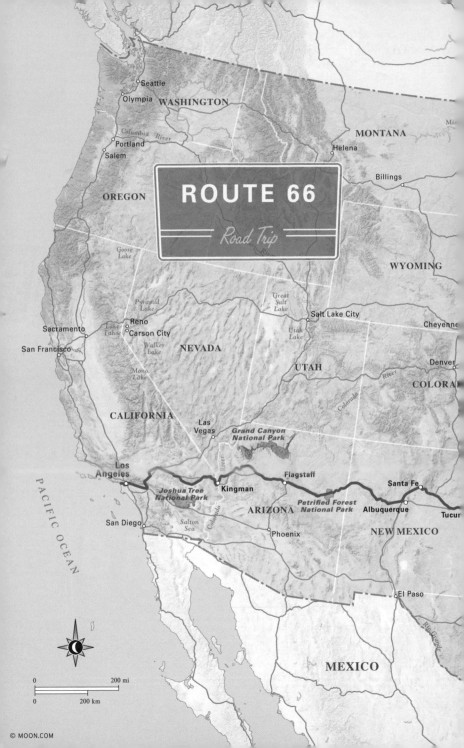

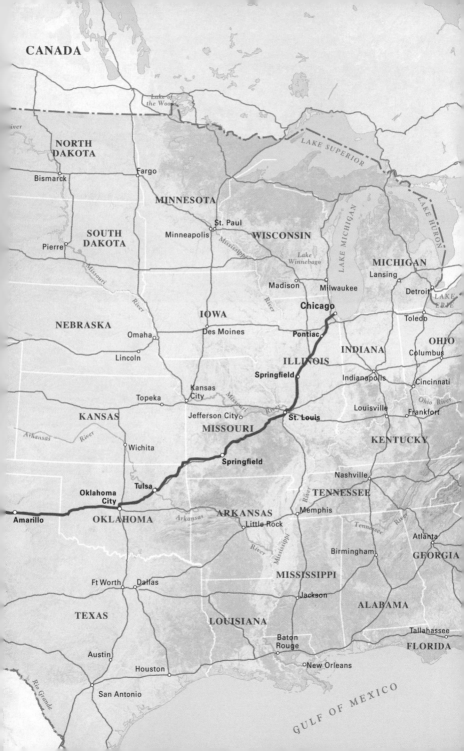

CONTENTS

Although every effort was made to make sure the information in this book was accurate when going to press, research was impacted by the COVID-19 pandemic and things may have changed since the time of writing. Be sure to confirm specific details, like opening hours, closures, and travel guidelines and restrictions, when making your travel plans. For more detailed information, see p. 352.

DISCOVER
Route 66

Road trips are both blessed and burdened by the mythology of the open road. We have high expectations when we pack up the car and hit the pavement. We want to see places that charm, attractions that inspire, oddities that surprise. But more than that, we want to be transformed by the freedom that comes when we feel in charge of our own destiny.

There's a reason that Route 66—a beating heart of blacktop running 2,448 miles (3,939 km) from Chicago to Santa Monica—lands on bucket lists of people from around the world. It's the only journey that lives up to our grandiose vision of a road trip. That's because its spirit was paved by pioneers, risk-takers, disruptors, poets, rule-breakers, and adventurers.

There's Joy Nevin, a woman who trained as a pilot during World War II before traveling Route 66 as a saleswoman in a truck she retrofitted herself. There's Victor Green, who created the *Negro Motorist Green Book,* a travel guide to help Black motorists navigate Route 66 safely during the Jim Crow era. There's writer John Steinbeck, whose novel *The Grapes of Wrath* encapsulated the desperate hope of emigrants who fled west during the Dust Bowl.

From Route 66's birth in 1926 to now, the decades have carved out an identity for the road that shifts depending on where you are. Cosmopolitan cities like Chicago and Los Angeles stand in stark contrast to the laid-back pace of small towns like Seligman, Arizona. A shifting landscape changes with every mile, from rolling prairies to remote deserts to the crashing ocean. And abandoned ghost towns, like Glenrio, Texas, sit as reminders of all that is unknowable about the past.

To travel all of Route 66 requires endurance and grasping its long history necessitates perspective. Meeting the route's residents calls for compassion and slowing down to see each and every sight demands patience. If you don't possess those qualities when you begin your drive, you will by the end. A trip on Route 66 will transform you.

The mythology is real.

PLANNING YOUR TRIP

Where to Go

Route 66 crosses eight states and three time zones. Some of the best-preserved sections of the road include the stretch between Springfield, Missouri, and Tulsa, Oklahoma; the road west of Seligman, Arizona; and the Oatman Highway through the Black Hills of Arizona.

Illinois
Chicago: It's here in America's third-largest city that the Mother Road begins. It snakes southwest through Illinois and into St. Louis, Missouri. Though much of the route has been replaced by I-55, there's still plenty of two-lane blacktop to explore. From Chicago, Route 66 heads to **Pontiac.** Make your first stop the **Route 66 Association Hall of Fame & Museum,** one of the best Route 66 museums on the journey. In **Atlanta,** eat like a local at the **Palms Grill Cafe.** You'll learn about the **1908 Race Riots** on a walking tour in **Springfield,** and in **Funks Grove,** stop for "sirup" at **Funks Grove Pure Maple Sirup.**

Missouri and Kansas
Route 66 through **Missouri** gives you your first glimpse of Ozark country—tree-covered hills that gently rise and dip, and lush valleys that spread before you. This leg of the trip starts in **St. Louis,** where you'll stroll the unusual **Chain of Rocks Bridge,** get interactive at the fun-for-everyone **City Museum,** and taste a custard "concrete" at **Ted Drewes Frozen Custard.** Take a break from the car with a walk around **Laumeier Sculpture Park** in **Kirkwood,** visit the **Trail of Tears Memorial** in **Jerome,** and spend a day in **Springfield,** the official birthplace of Route 66.

The Mother Road only covers 13 miles (20.9 km) through **Kansas,** but you should still make time to visit **Cars on the Route** in **Galena** and stop for sandwiches at **Nelson's Old Riverton Store** in **Riverton.**

Oklahoma
Oklahoma has more drivable miles of Route 66 than any other state. You'll cross **early roadbeds** and one of the **longest bridges** on the Mother Road, plus you'll learn about some of the most significant racial events to shape our country's history. In **Catoosa,** you can check out an oddball roadside attraction, the **Blue Whale.** Spend a few hours in **Tulsa** soaking up the **art deco** architecture before paying a visit to the **Greenwood Cultural Center,** which details the **Tulsa Race Riot.** In **Weatherford,** you can tour real rockets and spacecraft at **Stafford Air & Space Museum.**

Texas
Route 66 runs directly west across the Texas Panhandle, parallel to I-40. The drive is peaceful and solitary, punctuated by rusting grain silos that jut out of the horizon and tiny towns set in the middle of nowhere. Don't miss the art deco marvel, **Tower Station and U-Drop Inn Café** in **Shamrock.** In **Groom,** get pictures of the **Leaning Water Tower** before continuing west to **Amarillo,** where the famed **Cadillac Ranch** shows off 10 vintage Caddies buried nose-deep in a field. A slice of pie at the **MidPoint Café** in **Adrian** marks the halfway point of this road trip and is a must-do.

New Mexico
From Texas, Route 66 crosses into the luminescent landscape of red rocks and eternal sunsets that is New Mexico. **Tucumcari,** a former outlaw town, boasts plenty of **retro neon signage,** while artsy **Santa Fe** beckons travelers to browse the **galleries** and stay for a **traditional New Mexican meal.** The route slides south to **Albuquerque** before winding past **Acoma**

Camera Obscura, Santa Monica, California (top); Wigwam Motel, Holbrook, Arizona (bottom)

Pueblo, which offers a fascinating look at American Indian history and culture. In **Gallup,** you'll meet the nicest townsfolk ever as you traverse the sidewalks on the **Mural Walking Tour.**

Arizona

I-40 is the present-day Route 66 in eastern Arizona. It takes you along the high desert and through quirky Southwest towns such as **Holbrook** (have lunch at **Joe & Aggie's Café)** and **Winslow** (overnight at **La Posada Hotel & Gardens)** before heading into the pine trees of mountainous **Flagstaff** and **Williams.** After reaching the iconic **Delgadillo's Snow Cap Drive-In** in **Seligman,** Route 66 opens up to miles of untouched road

all the way to **Kingman.** Brave the hairpin curves through the Black Mountains on the way to the mining town of **Oatman.**

California

The California stretch of Route 66 is marked by the stark beauty of the desert (**Joshua Tree** and the **Mojave**) and the glitz and glitter of **Los Angeles** before it concludes at the **Santa Monica Pier.** Stop in **Oro Grande** to explore the "forest" at **Elmer Long's Bottle Tree Ranch** and indulge in the big portions at **Emma Jean's Holland Burger** in **Victorville.** Pay a visit to **Fair Oaks Pharmacy,** a 1915 soda fountain in **Pasadena.** And then head west to the Pacific Ocean to mark your journey's end.

Santa Monica Pier

When to Go

The best time for a Route 66 road trip is from **late spring to early summer** and in the **early fall.** The weather is usually temperate and roads are open, as are most Route 66 businesses. Be cautioned, though; Flagstaff, Arizona, sits at an elevation of 7,000 feet (2,134 m), which means the first snowfall can arrive as early as October.

Avoid travel during **August,** when the temperatures can reach 110°F (43°C) or hotter in Texas, Arizona, New Mexico, and the California desert. Though it's a dry heat in the Southwest, the states of Illinois, Missouri, Kansas, and Oklahoma can be oppressively muggy.

July through early September is the monsoon season in New Mexico, Arizona, and California. Heavy rainstorms and heat lightning can occur suddenly—almost every afternoon—and often with freak weather conditions such as hail, high winds, and poor visibility. The storms are spectacular but flash flooding can be deadly, and many roads, especially those in the California desert, become flooded and impassible.

Winter should be avoided altogether. This Route 66 road trip starts in Chicago, which is notorious for cold and brutal winters. Even the western leg of Route 66 is subject to inclement weather. From **November to March,** mountain passes through New Mexico and Arizona (near Flagstaff) may be closed due to snow and ice. Many Route 66 businesses close for the season from **October to April.**

Driving Tips

When Route 66 began in 1926, it was one of the few highways that cut across the country. Today, 15 percent of Route 66 is completely gone. It is no longer possible to follow the route uninterrupted from Chicago to Los Angeles. Since its inception, Route 66 has also been realigned at least three times. Some realignments were major, such as in New Mexico where the road changed direction, while others shifted the asphalt less than one-eighth of a mile (0.2 km).

This road trip outlines the best way to experience Route 66 today, with detailed navigation notes that generally follow the **pre-1930s alignment.** There will be times when freeway driving is unavoidable, and other options explore later alignments that offer the best variety of sights and attractions. Regardless of which alignment you take, avoid following "Historic Route 66" signs if they divert away from the suggested route. These often refer to alignments that lead down rutted dirt paths, dead-ends, or disappointing detours.

HIT THE ROAD

14 Days on Route 66

This two-week itinerary follows the route from Chicago to Santa Monica and includes major highlights as well as hidden gems and the best local eateries. Route 66's diagonal route is unique when compared to the more common north-south or east-west trajectories of most major freeways. Its path cuts a swath through the heart of America. Plan to explore leisurely and meet the locals—a lot of the people who live and work on Route 66 run family-owned businesses that have been in operation for decades. Much of the route was realigned along the interstate highways, so if you need to make up time, you can jump on and off the freeway to reach your next destination quickly. Get ready for an up-close view of many of the cultures, dialects, and traditions that comprise America, from past to present.

Day 1: Chicago
CHICAGO TO PONTIAC:
100 MILES (161 KM)
Day one starts in Chicago (see details and suggestions on page 27). Have lunch at **Giordano's,** then head to **Pontiac** to see the **Route 66 Association Hall of Fame & Museum** and walk across the swinging footbridges, the oldest of which is from 1898. Enjoy dinner at the **Old Log Cabin Restaurant** and spend the night at **Three Roses Bed & Breakfast** in Pontiac.

Day 2: Illinois
PONTIAC TO ST. LOUIS: 200-225
MILES (320-360 KM)
Start the day early and drive southwest about 50 miles (81 km) along Route 66 to **Funks Grove** to pick up some "sirup."

Have lunch at **Ariston Cafe** in **Litchfield** about 1.5 hours away (102 mi/164 km). Head to **Staunton,** about 15 miles (24 km) away, to say hello to the lovable rabbits at **Henry's Rabbit Ranch.** In another 20 miles (32 km), you'll get to **Edwardsville,** where you should have dinner at **Cleveland-Heath.** From there it's only 23 miles (37 km) to **St. Louis.** Check into the **Magnolia Hotel** for the night.

Days 3-4: Missouri
ST. LOUIS TO SPRINGFIELD:
215 MILES (345 KM)
Savor a burger at **Bailey's Range** in **St. Louis.** Ride the tram to the top of **Gateway Arch National Park** or play at the interactive **City Museum.** In the afternoon, drive about 80 miles (129 km) to **Cuba** to see the murals and the **Wagon Wheel Motel.** Stop in Fanning to get a picture of the **World's Second Largest Rocking Chair.** Head to **Springfield,** the birthplace of Route 66, and spend the night at the **Best Western Route 66 Rail Haven.**

SPRINGFIELD THROUGH KANSAS
TO TULSA: 180 MILES (290 KM)
Start the day with a big breakfast at **George's Family Restaurant** before driving about 75 miles (121 km) to the Missouri state line at **Joplin.** Continue for a 13-mile (20.9-km) jaunt through **Kansas,** checking out **Cars on the Route** in **Galena** and ordering sandwiches to go at **Nelson's Old Riverton Store** in **Riverton.** From there, cross into Oklahoma and drive one of the oldest roadbeds on the journey: the **Sidewalk Highway,** between **Miami** and **Afton.** This 3-mile (4.8-km), 9-foot-wide (2.7-meter) stretch—also known as Ribbon Road—pre-dates Route 66 by 15 years. From Afton, it's 40 miles (64 km) to see the **Andy Payne monument** in **Foyil** and then another 30 miles (48 km) to **Tulsa,** where you'll spend the night at **The Mayo Hotel** or **The Campbell Hotel.**

Neon Photo Ops

We live in a digital, high-definition age, which means we don't get to see classic signage illuminated by blinking, flickering neon bulbs anymore. Not so on Route 66. This road trip boasts some of the best retro neon signs, many of them more than half a century old. Each chapter of this guide lists photo-op-worthy signs—for motor courts, diners, gas stations, and more—but here's a quick peek at a few you should build into your itinerary.

Munger Moss Motel in Lebanon, Missouri

♦ **The Berghoff,** Chicago, IL (page 35)

♦ **Dell Rhea's Chicken Basket,** Willowbrook, IL (page 42)

♦ **Munger Moss Motel,** Lebanon, MO (page 106)

♦ **66 Drive-in Theater,** Carthage, MO (page 118)

♦ **Waylan's Ku-Ku,** Miami, OK (page 135)

♦ **Meadow Gold,** Tulsa, OK (page 144)

♦ **Tee Pee Curios,** Tucumcari, NM (page 202)

♦ **Blue Swallow Motel,** Tucumcari, NM (page 204)

♦ **Wigwam Motel,** Holbrook, AZ (page 251)

♦ **The World Famous Sultana Bar,** Williams, AZ (page 282)

♦ **Roy's Motel & Café,** Amboy, CA (page 312)

Day 5: Oklahoma
TULSA TO OKLAHOMA CITY:
100 MILES (161 KM)

Have breakfast at **Corner Cafe,** before visiting the **Greenwood Cultural Center,** where you'll learn about one of the worst incidents of racial violence in U.S. history. Afterward, head west for 106 miles (171 km) to **Arcadia** and the **Round Barn,** which is, well, exactly what it sounds like. In Oklahoma City, check out the **Gold Dome Building** and **Milk Bottle Grocery** before tucking in for the night at **Skirvin Hilton Hotel.** Start your day with coffee and cake doughnuts at **Brown's Bakery,** then check out the 1925 **Lake Overholser Bridge.**

Day 6: Oklahoma and Texas
OKLAHOMA CITY TO AMARILLO:
250-300 MILES (405-485 KM)

Get on the road early to see the **"Pony Bridge"** in **Geary,** then drive about 115 miles (185 km) to the Texas state line. The beautifully restored **Tower Station and U-Drop Inn Café** in **Shamrock** should be your first stop. Drive about 20 miles (32 km) to **McLean** to tour the **Devil's Rope Museum.** Grab lunch at the **Red River Steakhouse.** Head 70 miles (113 km) to **Amarillo** and stay overnight at the **Courtyard by Marriott Amarillo Downtown.** Dinner is right across the street at **Crush Wine Bar & Restaurant.**

Women of the Mother Road

The story of Route 66 isn't complete without the illustrious women who've contributed to the road's growth, success, and preservation. This list highlights the women who made a profound impact on the Mother Road; see each chapter for more in-depth information.

Illinois (page 57)

♦ **Hazel Funk** inherited and ran Funks Grove, the family maple syrup business.

♦ **Sally Rand** was an early pioneer of burlesque and drew fans from all over for her performances along Route 66.

Missouri and Kansas (page 98)

♦ **Julia Chaney** and her husband owned and operated Red's Giant Hamburg, one of the first drive-through restaurants in the country.

♦ **Allyne Earls** owned the (now-demolished) Midway Café, keeping it open 24/7 for Route 66 travelers in need of a bite.

♦ **Elaine Graham Estes** worked at her family's motel and restaurant, the Graham Rib Station, which appeared in the *Negro Motorist Green Book* and welcomed all visitors.

♦ **Alberta Ellis** opened Alberta's Hotel in the early 1950s as a safe place for Black travelers to stay for the night. The hotel was listed in the *Negro Motorist Green Book*.

♦ **Melba Rigg** was one of four women who restored an abandoned gas station that now operates as the popular Cars on the Route.

Oklahoma (page 173)

♦ **Anita Arnold** made milkshakes during the 1950s at the Randolph Drug Store, a business listed in the *Negro Motorist Green Book*. Today, as Executive Director of the Black Liberated Arts Center, she works to preserve Black history and culture in Oklahoma.

♦ **Gladys Cutberth,** aka "Mrs. Route 66," fought to keep Route 66 in small towns.

♦ **Lucille Hamons** was known as "Mother of the Mother Road." She and her husband ran Lucille's Service Station.

♦ **Dawn Welch** is the owner of the popular Rock Cafe; she's also the inspiration for the character Sally Carrera in Pixar's *Cars*.

Day 7: Texas
AMARILLO TO TUCUMCARI:
115 MILES (185 KM)

The next morning, tour **Amarillo's historic district.** Don't miss **Cadillac Ranch,** about 10 miles (16.1 km) west as you leave **Amarillo.** Drive about 40 miles (64 km), then stop for lunch, a slice of pie, and a photo op at **MidPoint Café** in **Adrian**—this marks the halfway point of your Route 66 road trip. Cross the state border in 22 miles (35 km) as you enter **New Mexico.** Drive 40 miles (64 km) to **Tucumcari** and tour the **murals.** Overnight at the iconic **Blue Swallow Motel.**

Texas (page 193)

♦ **Fran Houser** owned the Midpoint Café, welcoming travelers to the halfway point.

New Mexico (page 203)

♦ **Mary Colter** is the famed architect who designed many places along Route 66, including La Posada Hotel in Winslow, Arizona; La Fonda in Santa Fe, New Mexico; and Grand Canyon's Phantom Ranch.

♦ **Lillian Redman** and her husband owned the iconic Blue Swallow Motel.

♦ **Fabiola Cabeza de Baca** was a teacher and activist who traveled Route 66 to teach rural New Mexicans new techniques for agriculture and homemaking.

♦ **Mary Mochimaru Montoya** worked as a Harvey Girl at the El Navajo Harvey House in Gallup before managing the popular Route 66 restaurant Ranch Kitchen for 30 years.

Arizona (page 249)

♦ **Susie Woo** immigrated to Winslow from China in the 1930s and ran a grocery store.

♦ **Andrea Arizaga Limon** was a Harvey Girl, one of many young women hired to meet and greet train travelers at Harvey Houses.

♦ **Luz Delgadillo** performed shows and played live music along Route 66 towns with her brothers in the Delgadillo Family Band.

♦ **Joy Nevin** drove Route 66 countless times as the owner and operator of Stockmen's Supply Service, a traveling sales company.

California (page 313)

♦ **Minerva Hoyt** founded the International Desert Conservation League in 1930.

♦ **Lucia Rodriguez** opened Mitla Café in San Bernardino to support the town's Mexican American residents.

♦ **Cynthia Hare Troup** came up with the catchy title for her husband Bobby's famous song, "(Get Your Kicks on) Route 66."

Days 8-10: New Mexico
TUCUMCARI TO SANTA FE:
120 MILES (193 KM)

Start the day with breakfast at **Comet II Drive-In** in **Santa Rosa,** which is about an hour from Tucumcari. Take the pre-1937 alignment for the beautiful 120-mile (193-km) drive to **Santa Fe.** See the impressive art collection at the **Georgia O'Keeffe Museum** followed by red chile enchiladas at **The Shed.** After lunch, stroll the shops on **The Plaza.** Next, tour the **New Mexico History Museum,** located next to **The Palace of the Governors,** the oldest public building in the United States. Toast a pre-dinner cocktail on the

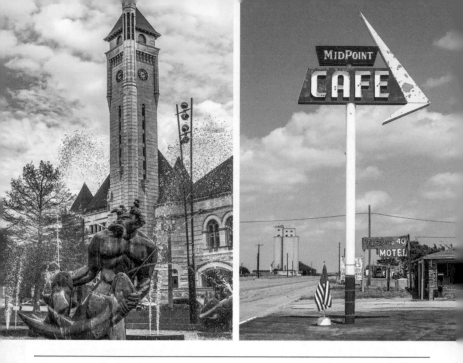

Clockwise from top left: Union Station in St. Louis, Missouri; the MidPoint Café in Adrian, Texas; Cadillac Ranch in Amarillo, Texas

Classic 66 Landmarks

Route 66 includes everything from wacky roadside attractions to important historical and cultural touchstones.

Elmer Long's Bottle Tree Ranch

♦ **"Begin Route 66" sign,** Chicago, IL (page 28)

♦ **Gemini Giant Muffler Man,** Wilmington, IL (page 46)

♦ **Ted Drewes Frozen Custard,** St. Louis, MO (page 89)

♦ **Cars on the Route,** Galena, KS (page 123)

♦ **Blue Whale,** Catoosa, OK (page 143)

♦ **Downtown Tulsa Art Deco,** Tulsa, OK (page 147)

♦ **Round Barn,** Arcadia, OK (page 158)

♦ **Tower Station and U-Drop Inn Café,** Shamrock, TX (page 181)

♦ **Cadillac Ranch,** Amarillo, TX (page 191)

♦ **MidPoint Café,** Adrian, TX (page 193)

♦ **Blue Swallow Motel,** Tucumcari, NM (page 204)

♦ **The Palace of the Governors,** Santa Fe, NM (page 210)

♦ **Wigwam Motel,** Holbrook, AZ (page 251)

♦ **Grand Canyon,** Williams, AZ (page 266)

♦ **Delgadillo's Snow Cap Drive-In,** Seligman, AZ (page 285)

♦ **Elmer Long's Bottle Tree Ranch,** Oro Grande, CA (page 322)

♦ **Santa Monica Pier,** Santa Monica, CA (page 340)

rooftop of the historic **La Fonda on the Plaza** (a former Harvey House), then dine at **El Farol.** Call it a night at **El Rey Court.**

SIDE TRIP TO TAOS: 80 MILES (129 KM)
Breakfast should be at **The Pantry** before you detour north on the High Road for 80 miles (129 km) to Taos. On the way, have a light lunch at **Sugar Nymphs Bistro,** near **Peñasco.** Stop at the **Rio Grand Gorge Bridge** and then head to **Earthship Biotecture** to tour the world's largest off-the-grid community.

Eat dinner at **La Cueva** and stay in an Earthship overnight; if they're fully booked, spend the night at the **El Pueblo Lodge** in Taos.

TAOS TO ALBUQUERQUE: 150 MILES (242 KM)
Drive 150 miles (242 km) south to **Albuquerque** and have lunch at **Loyola's Family Restaurant.** Tour **Old Town,** catch a movie at the historic **KiMo Theatre,** and have dinner at the **Standard Diner.** Spend the night at the

The Origin of the Green Book

The dark underbelly of Route 66's history was that during the era of Jim Crow, Black motorists faced discrimination and even violence when traveling the route. Many businesses wouldn't serve Black people. For a Black motorist, embarking on a journey along the Mother Road involved thoughtful and careful planning. That's why Victor Green, a Black postal worker from Harlem, created the *Negro Motorist Green Book,* an essential and trusted travel guide. Known as the "Green Book," this road companion listed restaurants, motels, garages, gas stations, and other businesses that welcomed and served Black travelers along Route 66 and other roads throughout the country.

Victor Green published the guide from 1936 to 1966; Esso gas stations distributed them. Green's motivation was "to give the Negro traveler information that will keep him from running into difficulties and embarrassments." The Green Book aimed to give Black travelers a means of safe passage, free from harassment, discrimination, and violence.

To learn more about the Green Book and its listings in different states along the route, look to the following sections:

♦ **Illinois (page 65)**

♦ **Missouri (page 121)**

♦ **Oklahoma (page 163)**

♦ **Texas (page 192)**

♦ **New Mexico (page 224)**

♦ **Arizona (page 253)**

♦ **California (page 323)**

lovely **Los Poblanos Inn** or sleep in an Airstream trailer at **Enchanted Trails RV Park.**

Days 11-12: Arizona
ALBUQUERQUE TO WINSLOW:
270 MILES (435 KM)
This day, visit **Acoma Pueblo,** about 70 miles (113 km) west of Albuquerque. Stop in **Gallup** to shop the **trading posts** and explore the city's **murals** before crossing the border into Arizona. About 45 miles from the border, drive through the **Painted Desert and Petrified Forest National Park,** then stop for lunch in **Holbrook** at **Joe & Aggie's Café.** Spend the evening at **La Posada Hotel & Gardens** in **Winslow,** about 30 miles (48 km) west. For an upscale experience, dine at the **Turquoise Room Restaurant;** for something more casual but equally delicious, eat at **E&O Kitchen.**

WINSLOW TO KINGMAN:
200 MILES (320 KM)
Today, drive 60 miles (97 km) toward **Flagstaff.** Walk the picturesque streets of the **historic downtown** and get a bite to eat at **Satchmo's.** Drive 30 miles (48 km) to **Williams.** See the beautiful **Grand Canyon Railway** and snap pics of the retro sign at **The World Famous Sultana Bar** before heading to **Seligman** for lunch at **Delgadillo's Snow Cap Drive-In.** Next up, take the two-lane drive to **Kingman,** passing through **Peach Springs** and **Hackberry.** Spend the night in **Kingman** at **El Trovatore Motel.**

Car Culture

Appealing to our sense of nostalgia, packed with interesting history, and tailor-made for great photo ops, vintage gas stations, car museums, and other quirky automobile attractions dot Route 66, from Chicago to the Pacific Ocean.

♦ **Ambler's Texaco Gas Station,** Dwight, IL: A 1933 cottage-style station that also operates as the Dwight Welcome Center (page 48).

♦ **Bob's Gasoline Alley,** Fanning, MO: An astounding collection of old road signs, retro advertisements, die-cast cars, and more (page 100).

♦ **Cars on the Route,** Galena, KS: The truck that inspired the character of Tow Mater from Pixar's *Cars* sits outside this historic service station (page 123).

♦ **Vickery Phillips 66 Station,** Tulsa, OK: One of only a handful left in the country of service stations designed to look like homes (page 149).

♦ **Cadillac Ranch,** Amarillo, TX: See 10 big-finned Cadillacs sticking straight up from the ground, the Texas horizon looming beyond (page 191).

♦ **New Mexico Route 66 Museum,** Tucumcari, NM: Vintage cars, Route 66 artifacts, and stunning photographs await at this car-centric museum (page 200).

♦ **Old Trails Garage,** Kingman, AZ: This former service station sports meticulously hand-painted automobile logos on the building's exterior and an illuminated neon Packard sign out front (page 288).

Days 13-14: California
KINGMAN TO BARSTOW:
210 MILES (340 KM)

As you leave Kingman, drive the 1926 alignment via **Oatman Highway,** a scenic winding road through the Black Mountains. Take your time—the road has hairpin turns, steep mountain grades, and tight switchbacks. In Oatman, stop at the **General Store,** feed the town **burros,** and do lunch at **The Oatman Hotel & Restaurant,** where the walls are papered with 100,000 one-dollar bills. As you cross the border into **California,** gas up in **Needles** because you'll soon be driving through the desolate **Mojave Desert.** From Needles, it's 140 miles (225 km) west to **Barstow.** If you're up for a side trip, drive about 60 miles (97 km) south to **Joshua Tree** (passing **Roy's Motel & Café** in Amboy with its iconic signage) and spend a peaceful night at **29 Palms Inn.**

BARSTOW TO LOS ANGELES:
130 MILES (209 KM)

In Joshua Tree, have breakfast at **Crossroads Café** and enjoy a driving tour of **Joshua Tree National Park** before hitting the road for the final stretch of your Route 66 journey into Los Angeles. From **Barstow,** it's 75 miles (121 km) to **Fair Oaks Pharmacy** in **Pasadena,** a good place for a lime rickey or to browse the vintage goodies at this 1915 soda fountain.

Time your arrival into downtown LA before 3pm to avoid traffic. The **original Route 66 terminus** is at **7th and Broadway.** Wander the **galleries** and **museums,** nosh on good food at **Grand Central Market,** and stay at **Hotel Figueroa.** If you head to **Santa Monica** on a weekday, try not to leave downtown after 2pm; the 15-mile (24-km) drive to Santa Monica can take 1.5 hours during rush hour. In Santa Monica, greet the end of the Mother Road at the edge of the Pacific Ocean on the **Santa Monica Pier.**

Illinois

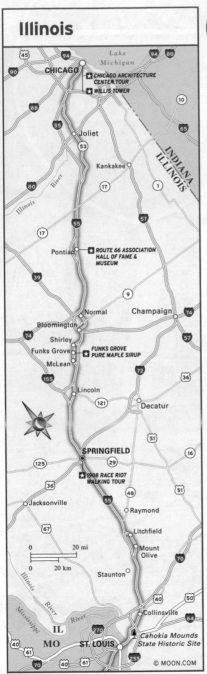

C hicago: Where it all begins. The Windy City's iconic skyline, melting pot of cultures, and rich history make it the perfect starting point for this epic road trip.

On November 11, 1926, the Mother Road was born right here in Chicago. When first built, Route 66 followed Illinois Route 4, also called the Pontiac Trail, the quickest path from Chicago to St. Louis, Missouri. Today, Route 66 runs 300 miles (485 km) through the metropolis of Chicago to the wide-open farms, little factory towns, and coal-mining centers of Joliet, Wilmington, Braidwood, Dwight, Atlanta, Springfield, and Mt. Olive.

Much of Route 66 was replaced with I-55—in some instances, the freeway was built right on top of the Mother Road. For the purposes of this trip, some freeway driving is unavoidable. But don't worry: There are more than 200 miles (320 km) of picturesque two-lane highways ahead.

Planning Your Time

Start your trip on Route 66 by spending the night in **Chicago.** Plan **two days** to travel diagonally across the state, driving 105 miles (169 km; three hours) from Chicago to overnight in Pontiac. The second day, you'll cruise about 200 miles (320 km) south past Litchfield and Staunton and across the border into Missouri, where you'll bed down in St. Louis. If you can swing it, **four days** will allow extra time to explore Chicago, Pontiac, and Atlanta before zooming across the state line.

Highlights

★ **Chicago Architecture Center Tour:** Take a fascinating journey into the city's past by way of its architectural lineage. The center offers boat, bus, train, and walking tours (page 29).

★ **Willis Tower, Chicago:** Head up to the tower's Skydeck, a glass ledge jutting out of the 103rd floor, to soak up 360-degree views of the entire city (page 30).

★ **Route 66 Association Hall of Fame & Museum, Pontiac:** Make a stop at one of the best Route 66 museums on the road (page 52).

★ **Funks Grove Pure Maple Sirup:** Head this way for a Route 66 sweet treat (page 58).

★ **1908 Race Riot Walking Tour, Springfield:** Learn about the violent and chaotic events that led to the founding of the NAACP (page 64).

Best Restaurants

★ **Lou Mitchell's, Chicago:** This diner, a Chicago institution, has been serving people since 1923 (page 34).

★ **The Green Door Tavern, Chicago:** Belly up to the bar at the city's oldest tavern (page 35).

★ **Dell Rhea's Chicken Basket, Willowbrook:** The crispy fried chicken here makes this a must-stop for hungry travelers (page 42).

★ **Palms Grill Cafe, Atlanta:** Dine with the nicest locals you'll ever meet at this 1930s neighborhood restaurant (page 60).

★ **Cleveland-Heath, Edwardsville:** This handsome restaurant in a historic building serves gourmet comfort food (page 71).

Driving Considerations

Traffic may be a factor when leaving Chicago. If time is a concern, take I-55 instead. Plenty of gas stations and auto services line the road until Joliet; gas up here before continuing on to Pontiac.

Chicago is infamous for brutal winters. The best time to travel this section of Route 66 is from **late spring to early fall.** If you must drive during winter, or happen to run into a blizzard, it's best to take the interstate over smaller roads since the larger thoroughfares are generally de-iced first.

Getting There

Starting Points
Car
The **1926 alignment** of Route 66 started at Jackson Boulevard and Michigan Avenue; then in 1933, the start of the route was moved a couple of blocks east to Jackson Boulevard and Lake Shore Drive. Leaving Chicago, head west on Ogden Avenue to join Joliet Road. Drive south on SR-53 through Joliet, Wilmington, and Gardner. West of Gardner, Historic U.S. 66 branches off SR-53 to head south alongside I-55 through Pontiac, Bloomington, Funks Grove, and Atlanta into Springfield.

The 1926-1930 alignment (also Route 4) heads west of Springfield; however, our route follows the **post-1930s alignment** to head south from Springfield toward Litchfield and Mt. Olive. We rejoin the pre-1930s alignment in Staunton. From there, SR-157 heads southwest through Edwardsville and then enters the busy metropolis of St. Louis.

Car Rentals
Most car rental companies are located at **O'Hare International Airport** (ORD, 10000 W. O'Hare Ave., 800/832-6352, www.flychicago.com) and **Midway International Airport** (MDW, 5700 S. Cicero Ave., 773/838-0600, www.flychicago.com). Both airports have about the same number of rental companies, but Midway is easier to navigate than O'Hare. At Midway, **Hertz** (5150 W. 55th St., 800/654-3131, www.hertz.com, 6am-10pm daily) and **National** (5150 W. 55th St., 888/826-6890, www.nationalcar.com, 6am-11pm daily) are good options.

At O'Hare, rental car shuttle service is at the arrival curbside area (located on the lower level outside of baggage claim). **Enterprise** (10255 W. Zemke Blvd., 855/266-9289, www.enterprise.com, 6am-10pm daily) has good rates, while **Avis** (10255 W. Zemke Blvd., 773/825-4600, www.avis.com, 24 hours

Best Accommodations

★ **Kinzie Hotel, Chicago:** This boutique hotel is just a short walk from the Chicago River (page 36).

★ **Acme Hotel Company, Chicago:** Catering to Route 66 travelers, the Acme offers $0.66 treats (page 37).

★ **Palmer House, Chicago:** You'll enjoy the opulent luxury of the longest continually operating hotel in the United States (page 37).

★ **Three Roses Bed & Breakfast, Pontiac:** Charming and intimate, this B&B also serves one of the best breakfasts around (page 54).

★ **Colaw Rooming House, Atlanta:** This spacious 1940s "rooming house" embraces the spirit of Route 66 (page 60).

daily) has a signature class series with Maseratis, BMWs, and Corvette coupes. This road trip crosses eight states, so be sure to select a rental company with a national presence in case you need roadside assistance.

To reach downtown Chicago from O'Hare, take I-190, which turns into I-90 and goes directly into downtown. From Midway Airport, drive north on Cicero Avenue to I-55 north.

Air

O'Hare International Airport (ORD, 10000 W. O'Hare Ave., 800/832-6352, www.flychicago.com) is one of the world's busiest airports, with more than 880,000 flights annually. **Midway International Airport** (MDW, 5700 S. Cicero Ave., 773/838-0600, www. flychicago.com) is a medium-size airport about 8 miles (12.9 km) from Chicago's downtown Loop, served by Allegiant, Delta, North Country, Porter, Southwest Airlines, and Volaris.

Airport Transportation

Since it's difficult and expensive to park downtown (hotels charge $50-100 per night), if you're staying for more than one night, you might want to take a taxi or public transportation from the airport to your hotel and use public transit and cabs

for sightseeing in Chicago. When you're ready to hit the road, you can rent a car downtown.

To reach downtown Chicago from O'Hare, take the **"L,"** Chicago's elevated train system; the Blue Line to downtown takes about 45 minutes. Trains depart from the airport at Terminal 3 (American and Spirit), which is accessible via the pedestrian tunnels at Terminal 1 (United and Lufthansa) and Terminal 2 (Alaska, Delta, Jet Blue, and Air Canada). From Terminal 5 (international airlines), take the ATS (Airport Transit System) to Terminal 3 and follow the signs.

To reach downtown from Midway on the L, take the Orange Line, which arrives downtown in about 25 minutes. As you exit the airport, follow the "Trains to City" signs.

A **taxi** from O'Hare to downtown can take 25-75 minutes, depending on traffic, and costs about $40. A taxi from Midway to downtown can take 15-40 minutes for about $25.

Train and Bus

Union Station (210 S. Canal St., 800/872-7245, www.amtrak.com, 5am-1am daily) is the third-busiest rail station in the United States and operates as a major hub for Amtrak, with service around the country. The *Texas Eagle* follows

26

ILLINOIS

Downtown Chicago

One Day in Chicago

Have an early breakfast at **Lou Mitchell's,** and if the weather permits, take a **Chicago Architecture Center tour** or walk through **Grant Park.** If it's so cold it hurts to breathe, which happens in Chicago, spend the day inside at the **Art Institute of Chicago** or experience the glass viewing platform at the Skydeck at the **Willis Tower.**

For lunch, eat deep-dish pizza at **Giordano's.** Next, visit the **Shedd Aquarium,** wander the luxe lobby of the **Palmer House,** and toast Chicago's cocktail scene with a bevvie at the **Chicago Athletic Association.**

Have dinner at **The Green Door Tavern,** then check out the Chicago music scene with live jazz at the iconic **Green Mill.**

Route 66 in Illinois, passing through Joliet, Pontiac, Bloomington, Lincoln, Springfield, and then St. Louis.

The Chicago **Greyhound Bus Station** (630 W. Harrison St., 312/408-5821 or 800/231-2222, www.greyhound.com) is a few blocks south of Union Station and offers service to all major U.S. cities.

The **Chicago Transit Authority** (CTA, 800/968-7282, www.transitchicago.com) operates the local subway system, or elevated **L train** ($2.50 adults), with bus and train service to 35 suburbs. Most buses ($2.25 adults) arrive every 10-20 minutes. An owl symbol indicates all-night service; these buses run every 30 minutes. Subway train lines run every 10-15 minutes and are color-coded; most trains run daily, except the Purple Line, an express train to downtown.

Chicago

Chicago has everything you'd expect in a great American city—soaring skyscrapers, renowned museums, turn-of-the-20th-century subway platforms with trains that rumble overhead, the tantalizing scent of deep-dish pizza wafting out of busy eateries, and the rush of people on their way to important places.

When Route 66 launched in 1926, Chicago was considered the City of Industry; among other things, it was the birthplace of the Spiegel, Montgomery Ward, and Sears, Roebuck mail-order catalogs. Business was booming—but just a few years later, when the stock market crashed in 1929, the huge workforce that relied on the manufacturing industry took a devastating blow. Chicago was one of the hardest-hit cities in the country, and by 1933 unemployment rates had skyrocketed. Just six years after the start of Route 66, Chicago couldn't afford to meet its payroll, and the emergency relief funds were gone.

It was a dark time in the Windy City, and regardless of race or privilege, no one escaped poverty. In Studs Terkel's *Hard Times*, Louis Banks said,

I'd see 'em floatin' on the river where they would commit suicide because they didn't have anything. They'd steal and kill each other for 50 cents. Black and white, it didn't make any difference because everyone was poor.

People stood in breadlines that wrapped around churches and watched as protesters demanded government intervention. By 1940, one-third of the workers in the manufacturing industry had unionized. When President Franklin D. Roosevelt's New Deal funds came through, Lake Shore Drive, the starting point of Route 66, was built as part of a work relief program. Works Progress Administration (WPA) workers earned $27.50 a month for digging a ditch,

Road Trip Playlist

Curating your road trip playlist is almost as important as mapping the route or booking hotels. Route 66 takes you through vastly different regions of the country, each with its own distinct culture and, yes, music. These song suggestions are tailored to the state you're in.

♦ **"Meet Me in Chicago" by Buddy Guy:** Blues crooner Buddy Guy sings about iconic spots in the city, capturing the live-wire spirit of Chicago with his electric blues melodies.

♦ **"Tonight, Tonight" by Smashing Pumpkins:** Frontman Billy Corgan comes from Chicago—and still lives there today—and this 1990s song was written as an homage to his hometown.

♦ **"Sweet Home Chicago" by Robert Johnson:** This classic blues song has been recorded many times and by many artists, but nothing sounds better than the original. It doesn't get more Chicago blues than Johnson's soulful voice and guitar riffs.

♦ **"Surrender" by Cheap Trick:** While this isn't a song about Route 66 per se, Cheap Trick hails from Illinois, and the 1970s tune is an energetic anthem seemingly made for road trips.

which was great money at the time. The New Deal put thousands to work building, improving, and maintaining roads. Although much of Route 66 in Illinois was paved in 1926, the entire length was paved by 1938.

Today, Chicago is home to more than 70 diverse neighborhoods. Bronzeville is a historically Black neighborhood with public art and beautiful buildings by Mies van der Rohe; Lakeview/Boystown is a thriving gay community; Lincoln Square, traditionally a German neighborhood, has quaint shops on cobblestone streets. The University of Chicago in Hyde Park is a vibrant neighborhood that was home to Barack Obama. The Pilsen area is one of the largest Latino neighborhoods, and Little Village is dubbed "The Mexico of the Midwest."

◈ Route 66 in Chicago

The starting point for Route 66 has moved several times. The 1926 alignment was at Jackson Boulevard and Michigan Avenue, near the Art Institute of Chicago. In 1933, the start of Route 66 moved a couple of blocks east to Jackson Boulevard and Lake Shore Drive, near the World's Fair. Then, in 1955, Jackson became a one-way street heading eastbound; Adams Street, one block north, became the new westbound starting point for Route 66.

Across the street from the Art Institute, at Michigan Avenue and Adams, you can spot the historic **"Begin Route 66" sign.**

Sights
Millennium Park

Millennium Park (201 E. Randolph St., 312/742-1168, www.millenniumpark. org, 8am-9pm daily, free) is a green-space oasis in the middle of a bustling metropolis. Among the walkways and lawns, you'll find the gigantic outdoor **Pritzker Pavilion**, which plays host to many a free concert, as well as the **BP Bridge;** both were designed by renowned architect Frank Gehry. **Crown Fountain**—designed by Spanish artist Jaume Plensa—features two 50-foot-high (15-meter) towers facing one another, upon which are projected images of everyday Chicagoans. Linger when the weather is warm and watch as water shoots from each tower, transforming the area into a cooling center.

Cloud Gate, sculpted by Mumbai's Anish Kapoor, looks like a giant polished-chrome jellybean, but that description doesn't do it justice. The curves of the distinctive sculpture reflect the sky and the groups of people gathered around it. The images are distorted in surprisingly beautiful ways as you approach and pass through the gate. *Cloud Gate* has become one of the city's most popular photo ops.

Art Institute of Chicago
Located in the heart of Millennium Park, the **Art Institute of Chicago** (111 S. Michigan Ave., 312/443-3600, www.artic. edu, 11am-6pm daily, $25) is one of the most impressive and respected art museums in the country. More than 300,000 pieces of ancient and contemporary art are housed in eight buildings totaling 1 million square feet (92,903 sq m). You'll see famous works of art including Grant Wood's *American Gothic,* Vincent van Gogh's *The Bedroom,* and *Nighthawks* by Edward Hopper, a painting of people sitting in a diner at night, as viewed from the street.

★ Chicago Architecture Center Tour
Chicago is the birthplace of the skyscraper and boasts some of the most innovative architecture in the world. On a **Chicago Architecture Center tour** (111 E. Wacker Dr., 312/922-3432, www. architecture.org, 9am-6pm daily, $26-52), you can explore art deco masterpieces, turn-of-the-20th-century skyscrapers, America's most iconic buildings by Frank Lloyd Wright, or Mies van der Rohe's Farnsworth House. There are dozens of tours via bus, boat, and subway; tourists and locals alike agree this is the best way to see the city. Check the website for the

Top to bottom: start of Route 66 in Chicago; Millennium Park; Art Institute of Chicago

Fun Chicago Festivals

Chicago is a great festival city. Many events are free, making them popular draws for locals and visitors. No matter what time of year you're visiting, there's bound to be a reason to get festive.

In June, join blues aficionados and music fans from all over the country for the **Chicago Blues Festival** in Millennium Park. Foodies will love July's **Taste of Chicago** in Grant Park, which lets you nosh on yummy provisions at food booths set up along the lakeshore, visit pop-up restaurants, and attend celebrity chef demos. The **Chicago Jazz Festival** takes place at the end of August at the Chicago Cultural Center and Millennium Park.

The citywide, 11-day **World Music Festival** goes down in September and showcases more than 650 artists. **Oktoberfest Chicago** at the end of September is a raucous event that celebrates Chicago's heritage, German-style.

schedules. Book early: Some of the popular options, like the Frank Lloyd Wright, Riverfront, and Downtown Deco tours, sell out quickly.

The Chicago Architecture Center also has highly popular 90-minute architecture tours on **The Chicago First Lady Cruises** (112 E. Wacker Dr., 312/922-3432, www. architecture.org, 10am-7:30pm daily Apr.-Nov., $47-52). Learn about the design and creation of 50 buildings as you relax on an elegant ship that cruises right through the middle of the city. The boat has an open-air upper deck, a climate-controlled main deck, bistro seating, and a full bar.

Money Museum

Learn how the Federal Reserve System works at the **Money Museum** (230 S. LaSalle St., 312/322-2400, www. chicagofed.org, 8:30am-5pm Mon.-Fri., free). Perhaps that doesn't sound exciting, but this mighty museum is a fascinating exploration of the history of U.S. currency. There are interactive exhibits that show you how to detect counterfeit dollars and even an exhibit that is related to the popular musical *Hamilton* and describes Alexander Hamilton's integral role in creating the Federal Reserve System. If you ever wanted to know what a million bucks looks like, a cube built of one million one-dollar bills puts things into perspective.

★ Willis Tower

Willis Tower (formerly Sears Tower, 233 S. Wacker Dr., 312/875-9447, http:// theskydeck.com, 9am-5pm daily) is the reigning champion of the Chicago skyline. Designed by the firm Skidmore, Owings & Merrill and completed in 1973, the tower scratches the stratosphere with its awe-inspiring 1,450 feet (442 m). It is so tall that on certain days the weather at the 110th floor is different from the weather on the ground. Staring up at the structure is simply not enough: Everyone should ascend to the **Skydeck** (103rd floor, 9am-10pm daily Apr.-Sept., 10am-8pm daily Oct.-Mar., $26 adults, $18 children), the highest public viewing area in the United States. On a clear day, the observation deck shows you 50 miles (80 km) of land, taking in all of Chicago's other, suddenly small-looking buildings, much of massive Lake Michigan, and sometimes parts of other states. Tip: Arrive about 40 minutes before sunset to watch the sun sink below the horizon while the twinkling lights of the city begin to sparkle.

Grant Park

Grant Park (bounded by E. Randolph St. Michigan Ave., Roosevelt Rd., and Lake Michigan St.) is one of the oldest parks in Chicago, home to several attractions, world-class museums, and some of the best public art in the country. In 1893, Grant Park hosted the World's Columbian Exposition, and fairgoers were introduced to diet soda, Aunt Jemima's syrup, Cracker Jacks, and Pabst Blue Ribbon.

Buckingham Fountain (301 S. Columbus Dr.) sits in the middle of Grant Park. The Chicago landmark was built in 1927 and is one of the largest fountains in the world, with a baroque-style design modeled after a fountain at the Palace of Versailles. The fountain contains about 1.5 million gallons (5.7 million liters) of water. At the top of each hour (Apr.-Oct.), there's a 20-minute choreographed water show; after dusk, the water dances to music and 820 lights.

Field Museum of Natural History

The **Field Museum of Natural History** (1400 S. Lake Shore Dr., 312/922-9410, www.fieldmuseum.org, 9am-5pm daily, $40 adults, $29 children) may be one of the few attractions known as much for what's not on display as for what is. The museum's library holds 250,000 volumes on the history of the earth and upward of 20 million curios from around the world, each catalogued and set aside for study when not out for all to see.

Like that of many Chicago museums and landmarks, the Field Museum's inception coincided with the 1893 World's Columbian Exposition. In 2000, the museum garnered international attention when it debuted Sue, the largest, most complete, and best-preserved *Tyrannosaurus rex* fossil ever discovered. Several other permanent exhibits exploring Africa and Asia trace the culture and environment of those continents with life-size dioramas. The museum regularly unveils new items and collections, and special events bring regular visitors back for another helping.

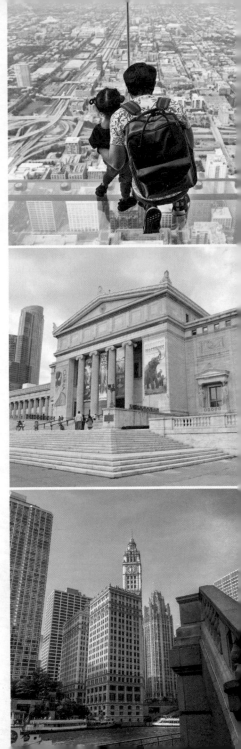

Top to bottom: view from Willis Tower; Field Museum of Natural History; Chicago skyline.

Shedd Aquarium

Perched on the edge of Lake Michigan, the **Shedd Aquarium** (1200 S. Lake Shore Dr., 312/939-2438, www.sheddaquarium. org, 9am-6pm daily June-Aug., 9am-5pm Mon.-Fri., 9am-6pm Sat.-Sun. Sept.-May, $40 adults, $30 children) just happens to be the world's largest indoor aquarium. It offers a wondrous escape from terrestrial life, submerging visitors in aquatic environments stocked with exotic fish and animals.

Built using a $3 million bequest from the second president of Marshall Field and Company, John G. Shedd, the aquarium opened its doors just two months after the 1929 stock market crash. At the opening, some of the exhibits still lacked their aquatic residents, but the Shedd has been steadily improving its offerings ever since.

The aquarium's most striking attribute might be its dolphin and beluga whale exhibits, in the Oceanarium downstairs. A wide, curving window that looks out over the lake borders a simulated Pacific Coast environment with a large open tank. When the weather cooperates, the lake makes the tank look like it extends out for miles, an inspiring illusion, especially as a backdrop to the regular gravity-defying dolphin shows.

Museum of Science and Industry

The **Museum of Science and Industry** (5700 S. Lake Shore Dr., 773/684-1414, www.msichicago.org, 9:30am-4pm Wed.-Sun., $22 adults, $13 children) has long been one of Chicago's most popular destinations, drawing some two million visitors annually. A veritable playground of science-based fun for both adults and children, the museum is packed with interactive exhibits, from flight simulators and tornado experiences to a wild maze that teaches you about the mathematics of nature.

The museum opened in 1933 with the goal of exploring the connection between science and society. Permanent

Museum of Science and Industry

Chicago Athletic Association

Within a historic Venetian Gothic–style building near Millennium Park, you'll find seven impressive restaurants at the **Chicago Athletic Association** (12 S. Michigan Ave., 312/427-3170, www.chicagoathletichotel.com, hours and prices vary by restaurant), the former club for the elite. Established in 1890, the club was the sport home of the rich and famous, with billiard tables, swimming pools, poker rooms, and more. Now restored and open to all, the Chicago Athletic Association serves as a hotel, culinary hub, and social gathering spot.

Dine at **Cindy's,** the rooftop bar and restaurant that features fresh drinks, seasonal fare, and views of Millennium Park or the intimate, eight-seat **Milk Bar. Cherry Circle Room** boasts a swank, mid-century style and throwback cocktails. **The Drawing Room** is a relaxed yet refined spot for breakfast, lunch, dinner, and late-night bites. The **Game Room** is where pub grub meets bocce ball. There's also a coffee shop called **Fairgrounds.** The burger joint **Shake Shack** has a location on the first floor.

and rotating displays include 500 timepieces from the collection of Seth G. Atwood (founder of the Time Museum in Rockford, Illinois); a 110-million-year-old crocodile skeleton; and a collection of historic and antique bikes side-by-side with the cutting-edge cycles of today.

Chicago History Museum

This place is pretty much exactly what it sounds like. Founded in 1856, the **Chicago History Museum** (1601 N. Clark St., 312/642-4600, www.chicagohistory.org, 9:30am-4:30pm Mon.-Sat., noon-5pm Sun., $19 adults, free for children) has been collecting thousands of manuscripts, paintings, costumes, and artifacts, such as the bed on which Abraham Lincoln died, along with exhibits on labor, culture, fashion, and photography. The permanent exhibit, *Chicago: Crossroads of America,* has several galleries that highlight Chicago's retail scene, manufacturing, architecture, social activism, diverse communities, and jazz history. Before hitting Route 66, you've got to stop here. What you glean will bring meaning to all that you see and experience on your road trip.

Museum of Contemporary Art

Boundary-pushing works of art fill the airy space at the **Museum of Contemporary Art** (220 E. Chicago Ave., 312/280-2660, http://mcachicago.org, 10am-9pm Tues. and Fri., 10am-5pm Wed.-Thurs. and Sat.-Sun., $15 adults, free for children). The innovative offerings—which span all mediums and feature cutting-edge artists—aim to show the provocative side of art and culture. Explore the exhibitions, which span the multilevel museum designed by German architect Josef Paul Kleihues; watch live performances; or attend a lecture. No matter how you choose to take in the progressive works of art, you'll leave this museum invigorated and inspired.

Entertainment

The Green Mill (4802 N. Broadway, 773/878-5552, www.greenmilljazz.com, 4pm-midnight daily, cover $10-15) has been hosting jazz greats since 1907. In the 1920s, the venue was a mob hangout—Al Capone had a booth—and the tunnels underneath the building came in handy when the cops raided the joint during prohibition. Today, The Green Mill has a sophisticated speakeasy vibe with art deco decor and one of the longest-running poetry slams in the country. Located in Chicago's Uptown neighborhood, about 20 minutes from Route 66, it's worth the detour.

When the owners of The Green Door Tavern (not to be confused with The Green Mill) bought the building in the 1980s, they broke through a wall in the basement and discovered a 1920s time capsule: a secret speakeasy stocked with early-20th-century bottles, a circus tapestry, and the original cash register. The space is now a separate bar called **The Drifter** (676 N. Orleans St., 312/631-3887, www.thedrifterchicago.com, 5pm-midnight Tues., 5pm-2am Wed.-Fri., 5pm-3am Sat., cover $4-6), a hidden alcove that seats 40 people and serves clandestine libations described on Tarot cards. Knock on the door to get in.

Thalia Hall (1807 S. Allport St., 312/526-3851, http://thaliahallchicago. com, shows at 8pm daily) was founded at the turn of the 20th century as a neighborhood spot with retail storefronts and a public hall for the community. After closing in the 1960s, it sat empty until 2013, when it was beautifully restored. Today, it is home to a beer-focused restaurant concept, an inspired cocktail bar, and one of the coolest music venues in Chicago.

Thalia Hall is located near public transit, five blocks east of the 18th Street Pink Line L stop. The number 18 bus stops at the corner of 18th Street and Racine Avenue; Thalia Hall is half a block away.

Watershed Bar (601 N. State St., 312/266-7677, http://watershedbar.com, 7pm-11pm Thurs.-Sat.) is an inviting parlor designed to look like a relaxed mid-century living room. It even has the same laid-back vibe you'd get if you were having drinks in a friend's well-designed home: comfy couches, good lighting, and feel-good tunes playing softly in the background. Watershed serves up an excellent selection of beers and wines from the Great Lakes region, plus expertly made cocktails with local spirits.

A "temple of satire," **The Second City** (1616 N. Wells St., 312/337-3992, www. secondcity.com) is an improvisational comedy group that is probably best known for sparking the careers of many successful stars, such as Bill Murray, Tina Fey, Amy Poehler, Steve Carrell, Stephen Colbert, Aidy Bryant, and others. The Second City offers nightly shows, so check the online calendar to see what you're in the mood for. It's a good idea to buy tickets in advance.

Food
Breakfast

Though it's only open for breakfast and lunch, ★ **Lou Mitchell's** (565 W. Jackson Blvd., 312/939-3111, www. loumitchellsrestaurant.com, 6am-2pm Wed.-Fri., 7am-2pm Sat.-Sun., $4-16) has been a Chicago institution since the 1920s. Everyone's a fan of the generous portions, friendly service, and always-good food. Stop in for fresh-squeezed orange juice, fluffy pancakes, and thinly sliced fried potatoes that somehow manage to be both crunchy and creamy. Don't let the line for a table thwart you—they hand out sugar-dusted doughnut holes while you wait.

At **Wildberry Pancakes & Café** (130 E. Randolph St., 312/938-9777, www.

wildberrycafe.com, 7am-2pm daily, $8-15), you'll enjoy delicious food made with ingredients from local farms. Quality is the name of the game here. Egg dishes use farm-raised eggs, and coffee is brewed with Intelligentsia beans. Wildberry has even won awards for the best pancakes in Chicago. They also serve eight types of Belgian waffles and eight kinds of French toast. The wait for a table at this modern spot is long, but worth it. There's another location at 196 East Pearson Street (312/470-0590) with the same hours.

Lunch and Dinner

In operation since 1921, ★ **The Green Door Tavern** (678 N. Orleans St., 312/664-5496, www.greendoorchicago.com, 4pm-11pm Tues.-Wed., 3pm-11pm Thurs.-Sat., $8-15) is Chicago's oldest tavern. Its building was constructed in 1872, one year after the Great Chicago Fire. The front door (warped after so many years of use) was painted green during Prohibition—code for a speakeasy. Enter the dark interior and as soon as your eyes adjust, you'll be greeted with a cozy, lived-in space with memorabilia-covered walls, a good beer selection, and a menu of satisfying pub grub. Opt for the corned beef with gooey swiss cheese and sauerkraut or share a bowl of Saratoga thick chips with malt vinegar and whiskey ketchup.

The classic neon sign at **The Berghoff** (17 W. Adams St., 312/427-3170, www.theberghoff.com, 11am-9pm Mon.-Fri., 11:30am-9pm Sat., $13-33) is great, and the history of the place is fascinating. Owner Herman Berghoff arrived in the United States from Germany in 1870. He launched a brewery in Indiana, and during the World's Columbian Exposition in Chicago in 1893, Berghoff sold his beer on the midway. The success of this venture led to the opening of The Berghoff restaurant in 1898, where diners received a free sandwich with their nickel beer. During Prohibition, Herman brewed near-beer and soda pop, which helped keep the restaurant popular. Today, the restaurant serves German-inspired fare such as spaetzle dumplings, bratwurst, knockwurst, smoked Thüringer, and schnitzel.

Since 1964, the staff at the **Billy Goat Tavern** (430 N. Michigan Ave., 312/222-1525, www.billygoattavern.com, 6am-1am Mon.-Thurs., 6am-2am Fri., 6am-3am Sat., 9am-2am Sun., $4-10) has entertained customers by yelling out, "Try the double cheese! It's the best!" In 1978, *Saturday Night Live* made the Billy Goat Tavern's burgers famous with the "Cheezeborger! Cheezeborger!" skit that starred John Belushi, Dan Aykroyd, Bill Murray, and Laraine Newman. If you don't order the cheezeborger (you have to say it like that), they also have breakfast specials and other sandwiches. There are several locations throughout the city, but this one, near the Wrigley Building, is the original.

Formento's (925 W. Randolph St., 312/690-7295, www.formentos.com, 4:30pm-10pm Mon.-Thurs., 4:30pm-11pm Fri.-Sat., $15-66) is a classy throwback supper club with red leather booths, crisp white tablecloths, and bright and flavorful Italian-American cuisine. The dining experience offers a contemporary take on the classics—roasted heirloom beet salad with blood oranges, ricotta, and pistachios, for example, or ravioli stuffed with smoked bacon and shiitake mushrooms.

In Chicago, there's one question to answer: thin crust or deep dish? Sure, **Giordano's** (130 E. Randolph St., 312/616-1200, www.giordanos.com, 11am-10pm Sun.-Thurs., 11am-11pm Fri.-Sat., $15-20) gets big press for stuffed deep-dish pies, but buck the trend—order extra-crispy thin crust and go light on the toppings. (This way you can savor the tangy tomato sauce and cracker crust without a stack of pepperoni in the way.) Giordano's opened its first Chicago pizzeria in 1974 (so it's new by Route 66 standards), and since then dozens of locations have opened throughout the city. This particular spot

Chicago to Springfield

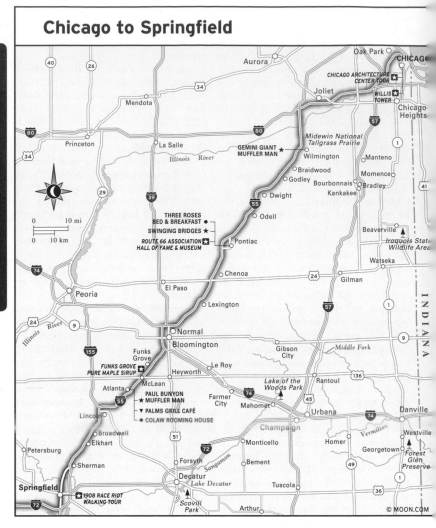

sits near Millennium Park and offers excellent people-watching from window-facing counter seats.

Road Snacks

No road trip is complete without on-the-go food, so stop at **Garrett's Popcorn** (27 W. Jackson Blvd., 312/360-1108, www.garrettpopcorn.com, 10am-8pm Mon.-Sat., 11am-7pm Sun., $5-15). They've been popping creative sweet and salty mash-ups since 1949. The "Garrett Mix" is the perfect marriage of sugary caramel and cheesy goodness. It's an Oprah fave, so give yourself extra time in case there's a line, and grab a few hand wipes on your way out. It's messy, but worth it.

Accommodations

The ★ **Kinzie Hotel** (20 W. Kinzie St., 312/395-9000, www.kinziehotel.com, $190-400) was inspired by John Kinzie, a silversmith, Indian trader, and business-man from the 1700s. The modern guest rooms clock in at more than 300 square feet (28 sq m) and boast big windows with city views. Beds are plush, the furnishings are contemporary, and the staff treats you like a VIP. Also, the Kinzie is probably the most dog-friendly hotel in Chicago. Pups enjoy a gourmet in-room doggie dining menu, pillow-top dog beds, bowls, spa amenities, dog concierge services, access to nearby dog parks, and the best souvenir ever—an "I Explored Chicago" doggie bandana.

For a stay that defies convention, check in to the ★ **Acme Hotel Company** (15 E. Ohio St., 312/894-0800, www.acmehotelcompany.com, $175-350), a fun and trendy boutique hotel in a historic building. Character oozes from every corner, with elevators covered in vinyl records and red lip-print lights on the bathroom mirrors. Rooms feature king, queen, or two double beds, and have flat-screen TVs with Apple plug-and-play and free Wi-Fi; the size can be a little tight, but the quirky decor and quality service more than make up for it.

Experience how the 1 percent live at **The Langham Hotel** (330 N. Wabash Ave., 312/923-9988, www.langhamhotels.com, $425-725). It's a five-star property that sits right on the Chicago River. They have 316 impeccably appointed rooms with staff members ready to provide the ultimate in personalized service. The glass wall between the bathroom and the living area has an automatic privacy feature that frosts at the touch of a button. If you pay an additional fee and join the Langham Club, you receive personalized butler service, valet assistance to pack and unpack your bags and iron clothing, complimentary in town car service within 2 miles (3.2 km) of the hotel, and free access to the 4,000-square-foot (372-sq-m) club lounge, with city views, champagne, and a gourmet buffet station.

For a historic hotel with a modern feel, plus all the amenities you could ask for, the **Stay Pineapple Chicago** (1 W. Washington St., 312/940-7997, www.staypineapple.com, $152-232) is a slam-dunk. In-room streaming services, dog-friendly policies, afternoon coffee and snacks, beach cruisers, unlimited bottled water, and a fitness room round out the offerings. Even better? The hotel's location: It sits mere steps from Millennium Park and the Art Institute of Chicago.

If you're looking for a neighborhood feel, try **Hotel Lincoln** (1816 N. Clark St., 312/254-4700, www.jdvhotels.com, $165-380). The hotel welcomes guests with a lobby full of eclectic furnishings and a cool mosaic of dresser drawers that runs along the front of the check-in counter. The rooms are stylish but unpretentious, with bedside tables that look like 19th-century trunks trimmed in rivets. Chairs come upholstered in old advertising, original works from local artists hang on the walls, and rooms have views of Lake Michigan and Lincoln Park.

The **Talbott Hotel** (20 E. Delaware Pl., 800/825-2688, www.talbotthotel.com, $350-525) exudes the charm of a bygone era with dark wood walls, warm lighting, shiny marble floors, and tufted velvet furnishings in the lobby. Spacious guest rooms offer pillow-top bedding, luxurious linens, individual temperature controls, and smart televisions with streaming capabilities. Need more reasons to book here? You can look forward to exclusive discounts at neighborhood boutiques, spas, and fitness studios, plus you get digital access to *The New York Times*.

Not only is the ★ **Palmer House** (17 E. Monroe St., 312/726-7500, www.palmerhousehiltonhotel.com, $169-575) an exquisite example of opulence—with 24-karat-gold Tiffany chandeliers, gilded sculptures, and a frescoed ceiling in the lobby—but it's also historic. Charles Dickens, Oscar Wilde, Mark Twain, Frank Sinatra, and Liberace all frequented Palmer House. A pastry chef who worked here invented the brownie. And the Palmer was one of the first properties to use the Edison light bulb and the telephone. The hotel also offered the city's first elevators, which were advertised as "a perpendicular railroad that connects floor to floor, rendering passage by the stairs unnecessary." In 2014, the Palmer House, open since 1873, underwent a renovation to incorporate historic elegance with modern comfort. Even if you don't stay here, stop by just to see the lobby—this is one of the grandest hotels in America.

Information and Services

Pick up free brochures and multilingual maps, plus receive complimentary concierge service, at the Choose Chicago visitor information center at **Macy's** (111 N. State St., main floor, www.choosechicago.com). The staff can plan customized itineraries and help you make the most of your time in the Windy City.

To see Chicago through the eyes of a local, contact **Chicago InstaGreeter** (http://chicagogreeter.com/instagreeter) for a free one-hour walk through Chicago's downtown.

◈ Getting on Route 66

As you leave Chicago, you'll need to take the 1955 alignment from West Adams Street and Michigan Avenue. Drive west for about 2 miles (3.2 km), then take a left (southwest) on Ogden Avenue. In 5 miles (8 km), you'll reach Cicero.

Palmer House

Cicero

According to sociologist James Loewen's *Sundown Towns,* there were more than 450 "sundown" towns, neighborhoods, and counties in Illinois. Sundown towns were all-white communities with posted signs warning Black people to leave before sundown. Cicero was one of those sundown towns. In 1951, during the height of Route 66's popularity, 3,500 white people rioted when a Black man tried to rent an apartment in town. Four hundred and fifty National Guard troops and 200 Cook County police officers were called in to mitigate the violence.

Al Capone came to Chicago in 1921 to manage the Four Deuces club, casino, and bordello. Soon after, Chicago voters elected reformer William Dever to clean up the city. Powerful gangster and bootlegger Johnny Torrio worried that his illegal operations might be threatened, so he picked Cicero for a second operational base. He chose Capone as the man to lead the charge.

During the elections of 1924, Capone turned Cicero into a war zone: He bullied voters, kidnapped pollsters, and threatened news reporters, intimidating locals into voting for the people who supported his criminal behavior. It's hard to believe that Al Capone spent less than 10 years ripping and running through Chicago and the surrounding area. His ruthless and violent behavior left such an indelible mark that many people believe his era lasted longer than it did.

Sights
Castle Car Wash
See Al Capone's secret hideout. The 1925 castle-shaped **Castle Car Wash** (3801 W. Ogden Ave. at S. Hamlin Ave.) was built by Louis Ehrenberer. Even though it's been home to several businesses over the years, it's most known for doubling as Capone's hideaway.

It's rumored that Capone lobbied to pave Route 66 for the faster transport of his bootlegged liquor. To confuse cops, Capone painted his bulletproof 1928 Cadillac V-8 the same green-and-black pattern of the police cars at the time and even installed a siren and searchlight on the vehicle. He added holes to the bottom of the windows for rifles to slip through in order to shoot from the sides of the car.

Hawthorne Works Factory
The cops opened fire on Capone and his crew right across the street from the **Hawthorne Works Factory** (southeast corner of Cermack Ave. and Cicero Ave.). From 1905 to 1983, this 200-acre complex manufactured 14,000 consumer projects—everything from telephone equipment to refrigerators and film projectors. Hawthorne was one of the largest manufacturing sites in the country; it employed 45,000 people and had its own hospital, fire department, sports team, and rail yard. Hawthorne Works conducted trailblazing studies on worker motivation

Local Eats

The **Chicago-style hot dog** was born at the 1893 World's Columbian Exposition. It's a steamed (never grilled!) all-beef frankfurter with diced onion, tomato wedges, relish, mustard, pickled serrano peppers, a dill pickle spear, and a dash of celery salt, all crammed into a poppy-seed bun. With all those layers of flavors and textures, there's no need for ketchup; in fact, according to Chicagoans, putting ketchup on a hot dog is the ultimate sin. A good spot to get a classic Chicago dog is the 1950s-era **Henry's Drive-In** (6031 W. Ogden Ave., Cicero, 708/656-9344, 10:30am-9pm Mon.-Sat., 11am-8pm Sun., $7-10).

In Springfield, it's all about the **horseshoe sandwich.** Originated in 1928, this platter-size open-faced sandwich is two thick slices of bread, meat, a pile of french fries, and Welsh rarebit cheese sauce smothering the entire plate. In the original sandwich, the ham was made into the shape of a horseshoe, and the potato wedges on top resembled nails.

Let's not forget about **Chicago deep-dish pizza.** Have a knife and fork handy for this Windy City staple. A buttery crust borders the inch-thick pie. Ingredients include heaping mounds of mozzarella, flavorful sausage, green peppers, and onions, topped off with tomato sauce. When it arrives at your table, all you'll see is the sauce—that's because the toppings are layered from bottom to top, instead of top to bottom like on a traditional pizza.

---

and efficiency, offering loyal lifelong employees (many of whom were immigrants from central Europe) pensions, paid vacations, disability pay, and home loans.

The complex has since been replaced by a shopping mall, but the original water tower remains. To learn more about the factory, tours are available at **The Hawthorne Works Museum and Archives** (3801 S. Central Ave., 708/656-8000, ext. 2321, call ahead for a tour of the archives, free).

To get there: From West Ogden Avenue, head west. Past South Hamlin Avenue, take a right onto West Cermak Road. Cross the railroad tracks; the next block is Cicero Avenue (SR-50). Turn left into the shopping mall and look for the tower looming behind Foot Locker.

To reach The Hawthorne Works Museum and Archives from the Hawthorne Factory site: Exit the shopping mall parking lot and turn left (south) onto Cicero Avenue (SR-50). Take a right (southwest) onto West Ogden Avenue, then take a left (south) onto South Central Avenue.

◈ Back on 66
Keep heading west on Ogden Avenue for a couple of miles to the neighboring suburb of Berwyn.

Berwyn

Sights
Ogden Top and Trim
During Route 66's heyday, Ogden Avenue, from the west side of Chicago to the town of Berwyn, was known as "Automobile Row," with 14 gas stations and numerous garages and car dealerships. The **Ogden Top and Trim** (6609 W. Ogden Ave., 708/484-5422, www. ogdentopandtrim.com) is the only remaining auto business from that time still in operation. The three-generation family-owned shop started in 1919; today, it specializes in innovative restorations and custom interiors for everything from classic Packards to street rods and muscle cars. There's nothing to see on-site, but the website includes photos of the shop's impressive restoration work.

⬥ Back on 66

Oak Park is 4.5 miles (7.2 km) north of Route 66. Drive west on Ogden Avenue (Route 66) and turn right (north) on South Oak Park Avenue.

⬥ Side Trip: Oak Park

Sights
Ernest Hemingway Birthplace and Museum

About 5 miles (8 km) north of Route 66, visit the **Ernest Hemingway Birthplace and Museum** (339 N. Oak Park Ave., 708/445-3071, www.ehfop.org, 1pm-5pm Wed.-Fri. and Sun., 10am-5pm Sat., $15-35). On July 21, 1899, literary history was made when baby Ernest was born, delivered into this world by his father, Dr. Ed Hemingway, upstairs in his mother's bedroom. Hemingway lived in the home until he was six years old. Tour the Queen Anne house for a peek into early 1900s Victorian life, as well as into the early years of the Pulitzer Prize-winning author.

Frank Lloyd Wright Home and Studio

Oak Park has the world's largest collection of Wright-designed buildings, set in a designated Historic District. Just a few blocks from Ernest Hemingway's birthplace is the **Frank Lloyd Wright Home and Studio** (951 Chicago Ave., 312/994-4000, http://flwright.org, 10am-4pm daily). Take a guided 60-minute tour ($20) from trained interpreters who can offer insight into Wright's career and family life, or sign up for the 40-minute neighborhood walking tour ($15). Tip: Purchase tickets in advance on the website.

⬥ Back on 66

To return to Route 66, head south on South Oak Park Avenue for 4.5 miles (7.2 km) and turn right (west) on Ogden Avenue. To continue on to Riverside, drive west on West Ogden Avenue,

passing SR-43, and make a right (north) on Lionel Road, which curves into Riverside Road.

Riverside

As Route 66 passes through the suburb of Berwyn, there's not much to see other than aging strip malls. However, in Riverside, just west of Berwyn, there's a hidden gem for architecture buffs (or for people who love to binge-watch *House Hunters*).

Sights
Riverside Architectural District

The historic **Riverside Architectural District** (bounded by Ogden Ave., 26th St., and Harlem Ave./SR-43) features one of the first planned communities in the United States. Frederick Law Olmsted, who designed Central Park in New York City, ignored the grid layout and developed this tranquil neighborhood with curved roads, parkland, and gas street lighting. The neighborhood also features many homes designed by Frank Lloyd Wright.

To learn more about the village of Riverside, which is a National Historic Landmark, visit the **Riverside Museum** (10 Pine Ave., 708/447-2542, www.riversidemuseum.net, 10am-2pm Sat., free). Since it is only open on Saturday, use the website for information on self-guided driving tours.

⬥ Back on 66: Riverside to Joliet

The 1926 Route 66 alignment went through Joliet. In 1940, Route 66 moved west to go through Plainfield, Shorewood, and Channahon before rejoining the route at Braidwood. To drive to Joliet, return to Ogden Avenue, heading west. Turn left (south) on Lawndale Avenue in Lyons, then turn right (southwest) onto Joliet Road. Joliet Road curves west to turn into West 55th Street. Take a left (south) on East Avenue, then pick up Joliet Road again by turning right (southwest) after about 0.5 miles (0.8 km). Joliet Road travels through Countryside to merge onto I-55 south.

Willowbrook

Food
Dell Rhea's Chicken Basket
One of the best places to eat on Route 66—in the 1930s and 1940s and today—is ★ **Dell Rhea's Chicken Basket** (645 Joliet Rd., www.chickenbasket.com, 630/325-0780, 11am-9pm Sun.-Thurs., 11am-10pm Fri.-Sat., $8-20). The neon sign is legendary, and the fried chicken is out of this world. But the Chicken Basket didn't always serve chicken. Initially, it operated as a simple lunch counter. In the late 1930s, two farm women offered to sell the owner their farm's eggs, including their recipe for fried chicken. Locals and travelers have been worshiping the succulent crispy fried chicken and fried mac-and-cheese balls (make sure to get extra cheese sauce on the side) ever since.

To get here from I-55: Take Exit 274 onto Kingery Highway (SR-83) north. Drive 0.3 miles (0.5 km), then take a right (east) onto Midway Drive, which dead-ends at South Quincy Street. Take a right (south) and drive to North Frontage Road. Dell Rhea's will be on the left (southeast) side of the street.

◆ Back on 66: Willowbrook to Joliet
To rejoin I-55, turn left (southwest) out of the parking lot and take the first right (west) on 79th Street, which will turn into Frontage Road. At the dead-end, take a left (west) on Midway Drive and then the next left on Kingery Highway south (SR-83). Follow signs for I-55 west.

Heading west on I-55, about 6 miles (9.7 km) from Kingery Highway (SR-83), you'll pass through Darien, Woodridge, and Bolingbrook. After the I-355

Frank Lloyd Wright Home and Studio

interchange, Route 66 splits off into pre- and post-1940s alignments. The post-1940s alignment bypassed Joliet and went through Plainfield. But you should take the **pre-1940s alignment** through Joliet. From I-55 near Bolingbrook, take Exit 267 and turn left (south) onto SR-53. When the road comes to a T-junction at Joliet Road, turn right (southwest) and continue south for 8 miles (12.9 km) on SR-53 into Joliet.

Joliet

Joliet became an official part of Route 66 in November 1926, and the Mother Road ran through the town for years before it was rerouted through Plainfield in 1940.

In the 1870s, southeastern Europeans and Irish immigrants arrived in Joliet to work at the Elgin, Joliet, and Eastern Railway and the second-largest steel mill in the country. By 1960, more than one-third of the population of Joliet was employed in the manufacturing sector. With such a large labor force, Joliet became a mecca for manufacturing companies and foundries that produced stoves, beer, horseshoes, windmills, and pianos. Even inmates from the penitentiary here mined the bluish-white limestone from the local quarry, giving Joliet the nickname "City of Stone."

The town appeared unbreakable, but with major changes in the manufacturing industry in the 1970s, Joliet started to decline and the unemployment rate rose to 26 percent. By 1983, Joliet had the highest unemployment rate in the nation. Since the 1980s, the town has diversified its employment base, and the economy has revitalized with retail trade, casinos, and NASCAR.

◆ Route 66 Through Joliet

As you head toward downtown, turn left (east) after Granite Street to follow SR-53. Make an immediate right (south) after crossing the Des Plaines River.

Sights
Route 66 Park

If you want to stretch your legs, as you enter Joliet on SR-53 (Broadway St.), stop for an ice-cream cone at the sweet lil' stand **Rich & Creamy** (920 N. Broadway St., 815/740-2899, 11am-9pm Mon.-Fri., noon-10pm Sun.) and then stroll next door to the **Route 66 Park** (920 N. Broadway St., 217/525-9308, 24 hours daily). The park isn't big, but it's adorned with public art displays, Blues Brothers tributes, and informational kiosks about Route 66.

Joliet Area Historical Museum

You'll get a nice overview of the area, plus good nuggets of information about Route 66, at the **Joliet Area Historical Museum** (204 N. Ottawa St., 815/723-5201, www.jolietmuseum.org, 10am-5pm Mon.-Sat., noon-5pm Sun., $8), 0.5 mile (0.8 km) south of Route 66 Park on SR-53. Exhibits include a 500-square-foot (46.5-sq-m) moon-landing simulator and a museum

gift shop that sells history books and Route 66 gifts and collectibles.

Rialto Square Theater

Meet the "Jewel of Joliet:" The historic **Rialto Square Theater** (102 N. Chicago St., 815-726-6600, www.rialtosquare. com, call for exact dates on year-round tours, $5) is often considered one of the most beautiful theaters in the nation. It opened in 1926—the year Route 66 began—as a vaudeville movie palace. In its time, the remarkable neo-baroque and Byzantine architecture rivaled the motion picture palaces of Chicago and New York. The lobby was inspired by the Hall of Mirrors in the Palace of Versailles; the rotunda featured 18 Corinthian-style columns and a crystal chandelier with 250 lights. The Rialto closed as a movie theater in the 1970s but was saved from demolition in 1980. Today, the theater hosts a range of performances, from live music and comedy to shows to film screenings of cult classics.

Note that North Chicago Street dead-ends one block past the Rialto Square Theater.

Joliet Slammers Baseball

Does it get any more American than baseball? Here, the professional baseball team, the **Joliet Slammers** (815-722-2287, www.jolietslammers.com, tickets $15), play home games at the **DuPage Medical Group Field,** formerly known as the classic **Joliet Route 66 Stadium** (1 Mayor Art Schultz Dr.). The stadium boasts a facade that showcases the area's automobile history and pivotal role in the history of Route 66. The Joliet Slammers are part of the independent Frontier League. To watch them play, get tickets for stadium seats or bring a blanket and stretch out on the general admission lawn.

Joliet Iron Works Historic Site

The second-largest steel mill in the country once stood at the **Joliet Iron Works Historic Site** (Columbia Street,

Rialto Square Theater

815/727-8700, 8am-sunset daily, free). The factory was dismantled in the 1930s, and although the buildings are gone, the remnants of the foundation are still here. What's left today are the abandoned ruins of the stock house, casting beds, gas washers, engine houses, blast stoves, and furnaces.

To get here from downtown Joliet (2 miles/3 km): Take Route 30 east to I-53. Turn left (north) and follow I-53 to Columbia Street. Turn right and drive 0.3 mile (0.5 km) down Columbia Street; the site will be on the left.

Old Joliet Prison

Check out the **Old Joliet Prison** (1125 Collins St., www.jolietprison.org, $20-50), which housed inmates from 1858 to 2002, including the infamous Leopold and Loeb, two wealthy University of Chicago students who kidnapped and murdered a 14-year-old boy. The murder inspired the classic Alfred Hitchcock film *Rope*. Leopold and Loeb were initially held at the Joliet Prison, but then transferred to Statesville Penitentiary. Joliet was also the prison where Jake was released at the beginning of the film *The Blues Brothers*.

You can explore the grounds on one of several tours, including a self-guided tour (9am-5pm daily Mar.-Oct., $20), a guided history tour (11am and 1pm Mon., Thurs., Sat., and Sun., $30), guard tours led by former prison employees (9am Sat.-Sun., $40), haunted history tours (6pm and 8pm Fri., $30), and four-hour photography tours (every other Sunday, $50). Tours are 90 minutes long, except for the photography tour; all tickets must be purchased in advance.

The parking lot on the south side of the prison walls has been transformed into the **Old Joliet Prison Park** (1125 Collins St., www.cityofjoliet.info, dawn-dusk daily, free), where you can peruse eight kiosks with information on the inmates and history of the facility.

Route 66 Raceway

The **Route 66 Raceway** (500 Speedway Blvd., 855/794-7223, www.route66raceway.com, $5-25) hosts racing events and pays homage to drag racing and hot rod culture. At the Route 66 Classic ($20), held in August, you can see custom dragsters pop wheelies and burn rubber. The rest of the year, the raceway features concerts, motorsports, demolition derbies, drag racing, and a swap meet for racers, restorers, and collectors.

The raceway is located south of downtown Joliet, about 2.5 miles (4 km) south of I-80. From downtown Joliet, drive south on SR-53 and turn left (east) on East Laraway Road. The raceway is less than 1 mile (1.6 km) on the right (south).

Food

Savor a taste of Americana at **Joliet Route 66 Diner** (22 W. Clinton St., 815/723-3865, 6am-2pm daily, $2-14). The price is right and the menu features dishes like grilled cheese sammies, meatloaf and

mashed potatoes, and fish and chips. The diner sports wood-paneled tables and the original counter—it looks like the place hasn't changed in decades. It's one block south of U.S. 30 and two blocks south of the Joliet Area Historical Museum.

✦ Back on 66

As you leave Joliet, North Chicago Street dead-ends one block past the Rialto Square Theater. From the intersection of West Clinton Street and SR-53, head south through downtown. Keep following signs for SR-53 until you pass I-80. Continue south on SR-53 for 12 miles (19.3 km) to Midewin National Tallgrass Prairie Preserve.

Midewin National Tallgrass Prairie Preserve

As you continue south on Route 66 (SR-53), the road opens up to 19,000 acres (7,689 hectares) of prairie farmland, and the landscape looks much like it did in the 1800s. Once serving as the Joliet Army Ammunition Plant, the **Midewin National Tallgrass Prairie Preserve** (30239 SR-53, 815/423-6370, www. fs.usda.gov/main/midewin, trails 4am-10pm daily, free) is now returning back to nature. In 2015, Midewin welcomed wild bison. Bringing the bison back to this area, where they once roamed free, is part of a plan to restore the prairie ecosystem. Midewin is the largest tallgrass prairie restoration project in the United States—and a quintessential snapshot of the heartland of America.

First, stop by the **Welcome Center** (8am-4:30pm Mon.-Fri.) for trail maps, exhibits, and information about the cultural and natural history of the area. Picnic tables and portable toilets are available at all trailheads. With the exception of the Welcome Center, there are no sources of drinking water available in the preserve.

The **River Road Seedbed** walk features Midewin's largest native seed production area. You will see rows of native plants in bloom from spring to fall. To access the trailhead from the Welcome Center, turn left on SR-53 and drive 1 mile (1.6 km) to River Road. Turn right and continue for 2.2 miles (3.5 km) to Boathouse Road; turn right again onto gravel Boathouse Road.

The **Explosives Road Trail** is a 1.5-mile (2.4-km) loop hike with access to about 20 bunkers. To reach the trailhead from the Welcome Center, turn right onto SR-53 and after 1.7 miles (2.7 km), turn left onto Explosives Road. Follow the signs to the trailhead and parking area.

✦ Back on 66

Continue south on Route 66 (SR-53) for 2.5 miles (4 km) to the town of Wilmington.

Wilmington

As you approach Wilmington, SR-53 curves to the right (southwest) and turns into East Baltimore Street.

Look for the **Gemini Giant Muffler Man** (810 E. Baltimore St.) on the right (northwest) side of East Baltimore Street. Fiberglass roadside statues like this one were popular in the 1960s as part of a nationwide advertising campaign. Standing more than 20 feet (6 m) tall, each statue has its own special theme—Wilmington's celebrates our love affair with space travel.

This muffler man was named after the Gemini space program. He holds in his hands a silver rocket with the American flag on the tail, a reference to the adjacent restaurant, **The Launching Pad Drive-In** (810 E. Baltimore St., 815/476-6535, https://geminigiant.com, 11am-8pm daily, $8-15). The restaurant opened in the 1950s as a hotdog and ice cream stand. New owners bought it in 1960, and by 1965, it was a full-fledged

Burma Shave

Heading west on SR-53 toward Godley, look for the famous Burma Shave signs. Burma Shave was a brand of shaving cream with a clever advertising campaign from the 1920s to the 1960s. Ads were divided among six evenly spaced signs posted along the edge of the highway. This sign near **Godley** was posted in 1930.

DOES YOUR HUSBAND
MISBEHAVE
GRUNT AND GRUMBLE
RANT AND RAVE
Burma Shave

restaurant. Today, it operates as a Route 66 Welcome Center, fun gift shop, and an eatery offering hot dogs, pizza, salads, and milkshakes.

As you continue west through downtown Wilmington, look for the **Sinclair Dinosaur** (Main St. and E. Baltimore St.), a cute, small, green dinosaur located on top of an auto body shop, with a Route 66 sign immediately below.

✪ Back on 66

Keep cruising southwest on Route 66 via SR-53, and you'll come to the town of Braidwood in about 4.5 miles (7.2 km).

Braidwood and Godley

Soon after its inception in 1873, Braidwood had a population of about 2,000 people, consisting mostly of European immigrants and transients with a slew of political, cultural, and religious differences. Fights were common, and riots broke out during elections.

Braidwood had a coal-mining boom when farmer Thomas Byron struck "black diamonds" in 1864. In 1877, after several pay cuts and years of mistreatment, the miners went on strike. The coal mining companies brought in Black miners, called "black legs," from the Chicago, Wilmington, and Vermilion mines, and the strikebreakers formed groups with plans to kill them. The Governor called

in 1,300 militiamen to restore the peace, but the "black legs" didn't feel safe. Most were eventually run out of town.

By 1890, the United Mine Workers union was formed to demand fair pay and better working conditions. Mining was dangerous work—a snowmelt in February 1883 flooded the mine, killing 74 men and boys. The Braidwood mines were closed in 1900; strip-mining began in 1927, one year after Route 66 began, and lasted until 1974.

Sights
Polk-a-Dot Drive In
Even though it has been around since 1962 and is therefore technically an authentic mid-century eatery, the **Polk-a-Dot Drive In** (222 N. Front St., Braidwood, 815/458-3377, 11am-8pm daily, $7-13) has been re-created as a slick version of a 1950s diner—with jukeboxes at the tables and sculptures of Marilyn Monroe, Elvis Presley, and Betty Boop sitting nearby. This place serves the usual diner fare of burgers and fries, but the ice-cream milk shakes and floats are the highlights.

Route 66 Red Carpet Corridor Festival
Do you love muscle cars, lowriders, and motorcycles? Well, if you happen to be in Godley in early May, take part in the annual **Route 66 Red Carpet Corridor Festival** (Godley, 815/458-2222, www. ilroute66redcarpetcorridor.com, free).

The two-day family event celebrates the people and cars that cruise the Mother Road with food, music, a raffle, a craft fair, and a flea market.

◆ Back on 66
Drive southwest on SR-53 for 2.5 miles (4 km) to Godley, and then continue on SR-53 for 5 miles (8 km) to Gardner.

Gardner

As you approach the town of Gardner along SR-53, turn right (west) onto East Washington Street. After a few blocks, turn left (south) onto North Center Street and look for the **Streetcar Diner** (246-290 N. Center St.). This streetcar was moved to Gardner as a diner in 1932. In 1937, the diner became a playhouse and cottage. After the diner closed in 1939, it became an unofficial Greyhound Bus stop.

The **Route 66 Association of Illinois** (www.il66assoc.org) restored the diner and dedicated the building to the late Bob and Peggy Craft. The Crafts owned the Riviera Roadhouse in Gardner, a popular supper club and speakeasy frequented by Al Capone in the 1920s. After a suspicious fire destroyed the Riviera in 2010, the Streetcar Diner (housed on the premises of the Riviera) was moved to this location. The diner was inducted into the Route 66 Hall of Fame in 2001. You can't go inside, but you can peer through the windows and see the wooden benches and stools that line the chrome counter.

Next to the diner is the **Gardner Jail,** which was built in 1906 and operated through the 1950s. With only two jail cells, however, it was really more of a drunk tank than anything else.

◆ Back on 66
Follow SR-53 through Gardner. SR-53 makes a sharp right (west) after East Odell Street as you head out of town. Turn left (southwest) onto Route 66. This stretch of Route 66 runs south through 7 miles (11.3 km) of green pastures alongside I-55 before it branches off into the town of Dwight.

Dwight

◆ Route 66 Through Dwight
There are two Route 66 alignments that go through Dwight.

1926 Route 66 Alignment
As you approach Dwight on Historic U.S. 66, a left (southeast) turn onto South Brewster Road (aka Dwight Rd.) is the 1926 alignment and will take you through downtown Dwight.

Post-1940s Alignment
If you're short on time, the post-1940s alignment continues straight on U.S. 66 and bypasses downtown.

Sights
Ambler's Texaco Gas Station and Dwight Welcome Center
Dwight has one of the longest-operating gas stations on Route 66. Basil "Tubby" Ambler ran **Ambler's Texaco Gas Station** (417 W. Waupansie St.) from 1938 to 1966. It was built in 1933 in the cottage style to look more residential and thus fit in with the nearby neighborhoods. Over the years, the large, wide-legged brick columns and tall Texaco gas pumps were replaced with straight columns and shorter, squatter Sky Chief gas pumps. It operated as a gas station for 66 years (good number!), and then from 1999 to 2002, it was an auto repair shop. The National Park Service Route 66 Corridor program provided matching funds to restore the station and painted it to match the 1940s color scheme.

Today, it's the **Dwight Welcome Center** (815/584-3077, 10am-4pm daily May-Oct., free), with an outdoor display of a map of the town, a replica of the station inside, and maps and tourist information about local and statewide attractions.

There are also oddities like old fan belts and a collection of vintage S&H green stamps from the 1960s.

Keeley Institute

From 1879 to 1965, the famous—and controversial—**Keeley Institute** (134 W. Main St.) was one of the leading drug and alcohol rehab facilities in the country. Dr. Leslie Keeley claimed a 95 percent cure rate for those suffering from addiction. Patients received four daily injections of a cocktail of chemicals dissolved in red, white, and blue solutions. While Keeley's medical industry peers considered these concoctions mysterious, miraculous, and even pure quackery, the more than 200 centers had a 50 percent success rate and became wildly popular.

The Keeley Institute attracted more than 800 addicts each week and treated more than 400,000 patients. To keep up with the steady stream of new arrivals, roads were paved, electric lights replaced gas lamps, and sewage systems were updated. The Keeley Institute put Dwight on the map, and the town became known as the most famous village of its size in America.

Today the Keeley Institute is housed in the William W. Fox Developmental Center, which serves people with developmental disabilities.

Railroad Depot

Dwight's **Railroad Depot** (119 W. Main St., 815/584-3077) is a Gothic-Romanesque stone structure that dates from 1891. It was designed by Chicago architect Henry Ives Cobb, who also designed the buildings at the University of Chicago. This former Amtrak station is one of the few along Route 66 that feature the original architecture from the late 1800s.

To get here from Route 66, take SR-17 east to South Prairie Avenue and turn right (south). After three blocks, take a left onto West Main Street.

First National Bank

Famed architect Frank Lloyd Wright designed the 1906 **First National Bank** (122 W. Main St., 815/584-1212), across the street from the railroad depot. The building is an early example of Wright's Prairie style, with limestone blocks and deeply recessed horizontal windows. One of the most distinctive architectural features is the interior fireplace, which was uncommon in an office building. It's now owned and operated by Peoples National Bank of Kewanee.

Food

The **Old Route 66 Family Restaurant** (105 S. Old Route 66, 815/584-2920, www. route66restaurant.com, 5am-9pm Sun.-Thurs., 5am-10pm Fri.-Sat., $7-25) is located across the street from Ambler's Texaco Gas Station, right on the corner of SR-17 and Route 66. The restaurant serves a hearty breakfast and their famous "broasted" chicken by the bucket. If you've never heard of broasted chicken, you're not alone. After the chicken slowly marinates, it is lightly breaded and then broasted—a special high-pressure cooking fryer seals in the natural juices while blocking the cooking oil. So you get the taste and texture of fried chicken without all the grease.

Craft cocktails and a fire station theme make **Station 343** (140 E. Main St., 815/584-9343, www.st343.com, 5pm-8:30pm Wed.-Thurs., 5pm-9pm Fri., 11am-2pm and 5pm-9pm Sat., 11am-5pm Sun., $8-29) a unique spot to raise a glass and indulge in good food. Housed in an 1881 building that's been home to a men's clothing shop and a dime store (among other businesses), Station 343 retains the original brick walls and wood floors. Lobster mac and cheese, slow-simmered chili, and pizzas and pastas make up the eclectic menu. While you wait for a table, snap photos of the vintage 1917 Seagrave fire truck, once used by the Pontiac, Illinois, fire department.

❖ Back on 66

As you head south out of Dwight, Historic U.S. 66 parallels I-55 for about 7 miles (11.3 km). As I-55 veers right (west), stay on Route 66 south. In 1 mile (1.6 km), turn left onto Odell Road to follow the 1926 alignment to the town of Odell.

Odell

Upon entering Odell, the road branches off into the post-1940s route and bypasses the town. If time allows, take the pre-1940s alignment. Turn left (southeast) onto Odell Road. In less than 1 mile (1.6 km), Odell Road becomes Prairie Street. In two blocks, take a left (southwest) on North West Street.

Odell was once a railroad town and a major center for grain collection. In the 1870s, more than 1.5 million bushels of grain were shipped out of Odell.

Keep an eye out for an **old Mobil station** (102 S. West St.) on the right (west) side of the road, with a classic logo of the red-winged mustang on the front of the garage. It has long been closed and now is a roadside relic that has stood the test of time.

The road through Odell was paved in 1922, just four years before Route 66 was born. By 1933, locals were so frustrated with Route 66 traffic that they built a **Pedestrian Tunnel** beneath Route 66 in order to cross it. The tunnel is closed now, but you can see the entryway across the street from St. Paul's Church at the corner of South West Street (Route 66) and West Hamilton Street.

As you head south (west) on Route 66, the road curves left, and on the west side is the perfectly restored **Standard Oil Gas Station** (400 S. West St.). This 1932 refurbished classic looks frozen in time. The station was in service through the mid-1960s and operated as a body shop until 1975. The Illinois Route 66 Association spearheaded a grassroots effort to raise the necessary funds to restore it to its former glory; it won the National Historic Route 66 Cyrus Avery Award for its meticulous preservation. Today, the property is a **Welcome Center** (815/998-2133, 11am-3pm daily) and souvenir shop.

❖ Back on 66

As you head south out of Odell, South West Street rejoins Route 66. I-55 parallels Route 66 for about 3 miles (4.8 km) until Route 66 veers south of I-55 near the town of Cayuga. From Cayuga, it is 6 miles (9.7 km) south to Pontiac.

The original 1920s pavement was 18 feet (5.5 m) wide and 6 inches (15 cm) deep. In the 1940s, the 18-mile (29-km) segment that started in Cayuga and ended in Chenoa could not handle the weight and volume of military traffic during World War II. From 1943 to 1944, the road was modernized into 24-foot-wide (7.3-m), 10-inch-thick (25-cm) concrete with 11-foot (3.4-m) driving lanes, 2 feet (0.6 m) wider than the previous ones. The northbound lanes have been repaved, but the southbound lanes, for the most part, still have the original concrete surface.

Pontiac

Pontiac is what small-town life is all about—weekend events where the mayor mingles with the crowd, neighbors who say hello to one another, sidewalks that lead to the town square. As soon as you set foot in picturesque Pontiac, you'll want to stay awhile.

Pontiac was named after Chief Pontiac (1720-1769) of the Ottawa. He was a fierce warrior who fought the British military occupation that was invading the Great Lakes area. Chief Pontiac unified other nations, such as the Ojibwa and Potawatomi, to fight with him. He realized that not all Europeans were bad, and he joined forces with the French, who appeared to hate the Brits as much as he did. He saw the value in adopting some of their customs but realized it was a detriment because his people would become dependent on them and lose their traditions and independence. Ultimately, Pontiac and his allies lost, and the French eventually turned on them, but legend has it that as a result of Pontiac's strategic efforts, the British decided it would be a mistake to underestimate the intelligence and power of tribal nations.

◈ Route 66 Through Pontiac

To explore Pontiac's tree-lined streets, murals, riverside parks, and 18th-century brick buildings, you have to leave Route 66 temporarily. From Route 66, turn left (south) onto Pontiac Road. At the corner, the road splits. Stay to the right to remain on Pontiac Road. Traveling southwest on Pontiac Road, turn left (south) onto North Main Street and drive less than 1 mile (1.6 km) to SR-116. A right turn will take you to the Illinois Route 66 Hall of Fame and Museum.

Sights

If you happen to visit Pontiac from May through August, don't miss the annual **Pontiac Cruise Night** (815/674-1279, www.pontiaccruisenight.com, 5pm-8pm 3rd Sat. May-Aug.). This major community party is held in downtown Pontiac around the square and features classic cars, music, racing hot wheels, raffles, face painting, free museum tours, food, and just an all-around good time.

For more information about Pontiac, visit the **Pontiac City Hall and Visitors Center** (115 W. Howard St., 815/844-5847, www.visitpontiac.org, 8am-5pm Mon.-Fri.).

Old Log Cabin Restaurant

As you approach Pontiac, you'll see the **Old Log Cabin Restaurant** (18700 Old Rte. 66, 815/842-2908, 5am-8pm Mon.-Sat.,

---

Top to bottom: Route 66 mural in Pontiac; Route 66 Association Hall of Fame & Museum; mural by Bob Waldmire

Burma Shave

Soon after the split in **Pontiac**, keep an eye out for another set of Burma Shave signs. A few are missing, so they don't make sense today, but this is what they said in 1942:

IF HUGGING
ON HIGHWAYS
IS YOUR SPORT
TRADE IN
YOUR CAR
FOR A DAVENPORT
Burma Shave

$8-15) on the south side of the highway, right before the turnoff for Pontiac Road. Not hungry? Stop in anyway. You'll meet the nicest people ever, plus get a glimpse into Pontiac's historic past. The restaurant opened in 1926 as a lunchroom and gas station. Made of cedar telephone poles and knotty pine walls, which are still here today, the restaurant attracted customers with the smoke coming off the barbecue from the small building in the back. After Route 66 became a four-lane highway and moved one block to the west side of the Log Cabin, the owners picked up the building and turned it around to face the new road. Hundreds of people from town came to watch this major event. If you walk behind the restaurant today, you can see the original Route 66 alignment along the railroad tracks.

★ Route 66 Association Hall of Fame & Museum

One of your first stops in Pontiac—and one of the most important stops on Route 66, to be honest—should be the **Route 66 Association Hall of Fame & Museum** (110 W. Howard St., 815/844-4566, www.il66assoc.org, 10am-4pm daily, free). It's one of the best and most comprehensive museums about the Mother Road on the route. Designate at least an hour to pore over the artifacts on display, as well as to see the nearly 25 street murals located around town.

The museum makes its home in a historical firehouse. Painted on the exterior is reportedly the world's largest mural of the Route 66 road sign. Be sure to have someone take your photo in front of it. Inside the firehouse, you'll see thousands—literally—of noteworthy artifacts and pieces of Route 66 memorabilia, including a chunk of the original Route 66 pavement. This museum celebrates the people and business owners who made Route 66 one of the most memorable and important highways in the world. One featured tribute is to the late great Route 66 artist Bob Waldmire. His Volkswagen van, rocking chair, and record and rock collections are on display. Legend has it that Waldmire stashed his marijuana under his van in two boxes, which are still there. When the cops inquired about the contents of the boxes, Waldmire said the nests for his snakes were inside and shouldn't be disturbed. He died in 2009, but his spirit lives on in the whimsical artwork printed on his postcards, sold along Route 66.

Walldog Mural & Sign Art Exhibit

The **Walldog Mural & Sign Art Exhibit** (110 W. Howard St., 815/844-5847, 9am-5pm daily Apr.-Oct., free) exhibits feature "walldogs," or artists who painted murals and advertisements on buildings and barns throughout the United States. It was originally a derogatory name for mural painters who worked "like dogs" in all kinds of weather from the 1890s through the mid-1900s. The aged murals are fading cultural keepsakes of the story of American advertising and a reminder of a time when ads were painted by hand.

Mural Walking Tour

There's plenty of free parking in Pontiac, so if the weather is nice and you want to ditch the car, take a walk to see the town's murals. Across from the Route 66 Museum is the **Bob Waldmire Memorial Mural** (E. Howard St.). Waldmire designed the mural, but he died before finishing it, so 500 of his friends stepped in to complete it. The 66-foot-long (20-m) mural tells the story of Route 66, a stunning testament to Bob's dedication and contribution to the Mother Road.

A block south is the **Chautauqua Movement Mural** (southeast corner of W. Madison St. and Main St.). The Chautauqua Movement was a Christian-based educational movement popular in rural America from the late 1800s to the early 1930s. Musicians, entertainers, speakers, and preachers traveled throughout the country to promote small-town values, an early form of mass entertainment and culture. At its peak in 1924, about 40 million people attended the events. President Theodore Roosevelt called the Chautauqua Movement "one of the most American things in America." Critics, however, such as author Sinclair Lewis, considered the movement provincial and claimed that it didn't accurately reflect the reality of American life.

The **Chief Pontiac Mural** is about one block west on Madison Street, at the corner of North Mill Street. Since there were no drawings or paintings of Chief Pontiac, the image is a composite based on descriptions from Ottawa tribe members.

Pontiac Oakland Automobile Museum

Car lovers will enjoy the **Pontiac Oakland Automobile Museum** (205 N. Mill St., 815/842-2345, www.

pontiacoaklandmuseum.org, 9am-5pm daily Apr.-Oct., 10am-4pm daily Nov.-Mar., free). The museum is home to gorgeous vintage Pontiacs and a comprehensive library of brochures, designs, drawings, maps, and service manuals. It's not the biggest auto museum on Route 66, but it's beautiful (and it's free).

The museum is located one block south of the Chief Pontiac mural on North Mill Street.

Swinging Bridges

Don't miss a chance to explore the historical bridges that cross the Vermilion River. There are three swinging pedestrian bridges, and although the wood has been replaced over time, the iron is original. The oldest bridge is the **1898 Pedestrian Bridge,** which was built by the Joliet Bridge Company to help shoe factory workers get to work on the north side of town. It's 190 feet (58 m) long and 4 feet (1.2 m) wide.

If you walk across the bridge, on the other side of the river is **Play Park.** From here, you can easily access the **1926 Swinging Footbridge** by turning left and walking southeast about 500 feet (152 m) along the riverbank to the footbridge. This bridge was built for the Pontiac Chautauqua Assembly and led folks from Play Park to Chautauqua Park.

The newest pedestrian bridge is about 0.5 miles (0.8 km) west at the **Humiston-Riverside Park** (W. Water St. and Oak St.). This bridge was built in 1978 mainly for aesthetic purposes.

To get here from the auto museum, head south on Mill Street and then east on Washington Street; turn right (south) onto Riverview Drive. Riverview Drive curves east after Timber Street; the 1898 Pedestrian Bridge is straight ahead before the curve.

Food and Accommodations

Pontiac lodging options are limited, with the exception of the usual chain motels. Reserve a room in advance at the Three

Roses B&B. If Three Roses is booked, consider at The Chateau Bloomington in Bloomington, about 30 miles (48 km) away.

You'll make new friends, hear local lore, and enjoy excellent food at the **Old Log Cabin Restaurant** (18700 Old Rte. 66, 815/842-2908, 5am-8pm Mon.-Sat., $8-15). For breakfast, order the Route 66 Skillet (eggs, bacon, ham, sausage, onions, green peppers, mushrooms, cheese, and fries). For lunch, get the prime rib sandwich. And for dinner, go for the pork chops; they're cooked perfectly and oh-so-tender.

From the front, **Edinger's Filling Station** (423 W. Madison St., 815/419-2255, www.edingersfillingstation.com, 5:30am-4pm Mon.-Fri., 5:30am-2pm Sat., $4-10) looks like a retro gas station, but inside this brightly colored joint, you'll discover friendly service, delicious breakfast and lunch options, and homemade pies. French-fry fans will love the Sloppy Fries (they're smothered in cheese, Buffalo sauce, and ranch dressing, then dressed with bacon). The Cuban sandwich and wraps are tasty, too.

Meet the locals at the **Pontiac Family Kitchen** (904 W. Custer Ave., 815/844-3155, 6am-9pm daily, $7-12), where the Friday night fish fry and hot turkey sandwiches with cranberry sauce are comfort food favorites.

The delightful ★ **Three Roses Bed & Breakfast** (209 E. Howard St., 630/999-0420, www.threerosesbedandbreakfast. org, $130-160) sits in a beautiful 1890 Victorian home with a lovely front porch, well-appointed rooms, soft beds, and warm hospitality. Each morning, you'll be greeted with a fresh homemade breakfast, and throughout the day you'll enjoy light refreshments (muffins, cookies, coffee, tea, and lemonade).

⬦ Back on 66

To return to Route 66 from downtown Pontiac, take Howard Street west to South Ladd Street (Old Route 66) and turn left. Turn right (west) onto West Reynolds Street and the next left (south) will put you onto Route 66 for about 9 miles (14.5 km) south to the town of Chenoa.

Chenoa

As you approach Chenoa on Route 66, take a left (south) on North Division Street. Stay to the right and in less than a mile merge onto North Veto Street. The Chenoa Pharmacy, on Green Street, is three blocks south.

Chenoa was born as a railroad town that developed into an agricultural center because it has some of the richest, most fertile soil in the world. Today it's a sleepy town with classic old buildings like the **Chenoa Pharmacy** (209 S. Green St., 815/945-4211, http://chenoapharmacy. com, 9am-6pm Mon.-Fri., 9am-noon Sat.), which has been open since 1889 and is one of the longest-running businesses in the area. The pharmacy's wood floors and antique cabinetry are original.

A few doors down and across the street, look for the **Selz Royal Blue Shoes Mural** (224 S. Green St.), an Instagramworthy re-creation of a vintage advertisement that was discovered when the adjoining building was torn down.

⬦ Back on 66

To rejoin Route 66 from the Selz Royal Blue Shoes Mural, head south on Green Street for two blocks to U.S. 24. Turn right (west) and then left (south) onto Route 66. The next town, Lexington, is about 7 miles (11.3 km) south.

Lexington

Lexington was founded in 1836, and its survival was in question until the railroad came to town in 1854. Once Route 66 was underway, Lexington became a railroad stop between Chicago and St. Louis—a key factor in its success. Once rail traffic declined and was replaced by auto traffic, Lexington became a popular stopping point on Route 66 from the 1950s through 1978, when I-55 became the preferred, faster route.

Lexington has repurposed and preserved an old, 1-mile (1.6-km) section of Route 66 as a walkway and park, aptly named **Memory Lane** (102 Morris Ave.). It's the perfect place to get out, stretch your legs, and admire the 1940s vintage billboards and Burma Shave signs. Memory Lane is located right off Route 66 near West Main Street.

Along Route 66 near Main Street, keep an eye out for a restored 1940s red-and-white **Lexington Neon Sign** with an arrow pointing eastward.

✤ Back on 66

Heading south on Route 66, you'll be in the town of Towanda in about 7 miles (11.3 km).

Towanda

Train travel was essential to the development of Towanda. Most towns in the area, such as Pontiac, Lexington, and Bloomington, were laid out around a town square, but Towanda's Main Street was laid out diagonally and parallel to the railroad tracks. Passenger service stopped in the 1940s; in 1955, Route 66 was widened to four lanes and partially divided with a grass median. The former southbound lanes are no longer used, and the northbound lanes are now the two-lane highway. In 1977, when I-55 was developed, Route 66 traffic was rerouted to the northwest side of Towanda, and a 3.25-mile (5.2-km) section of the southbound lane was closed.

A 2.5-mile (4-km) stretch of this abandoned roadway has been developed into the **Towanda Route 66 Parkway and Restoration Project,** a geographic tour and scenic walkway with murals, flower gardens, shrubs, trees, benches, picnic tables, bridges, and flagpoles. There is a large interactive map with historical plaques about Route 66 that originated as a class project for the Normal Community High School. The students and the town also petitioned to save an old Route 66 bridge that was slated for destruction. The walkway begins near SR-29 and runs south parallel to Route 66.

✤ Back on 66

Heading south on Route 66 toward Normal, the 1926 alignment breaks up as it enters from the northeast. Route 66 used to follow the railroad tracks but was rerouted in 1940.

To follow as much of the early route as possible, stay on Old U.S. Route 66 as it heads south out of Towanda. In about 4 miles (6.4 km), Old U.S. Route 66 runs alongside I-55 (Veterans Pkwy.). Route 66 becomes Shelbourne Drive in Normal. Turn left (south) onto Henry Street and then right (southwest) on Pine Street as it veers right (west).

Normal

Normal was named after what is now Illinois State University, but in the 1850s, "normal" schools were institutions that trained high school graduates to become teachers. Many state universities, including Arizona State University and California's UCLA, were once "normal" schools.

Sights
Sprague's Super Service Station and Café

On the left (south) side of Pine Street is **Sprague's Super Service Station** (305 E. Pine St.), a Tudor Revival-style station that was built in 1931 and is one of the largest two-story gas stations on Route 66. Similar to Ambler's Texaco Station in Dwight, Sprague's was built in a cottage-style design to fit in with its homey surroundings. The gas pumps were removed in the late 1970s, and the building was then used as a storefront for manufacturing companies, Yellow Cab, and Avis Rent-a-Car. It's currently a private residence.

Head west on Pine Street, then turn left (south) on Linden Street. Turn right (west) onto East Willow Street and then follow Business U.S. 51 (Center St.) south.

Normal Theater

The **Normal Theater** (209 W. North St., 309/454-9722, www.normaltheater.com, shows $7-10) dates from 1937 and, thanks to a restoration, is now enjoying a second life as a popular movie house. You'll want to have your camera ready for its Streamline Moderne art deco architecture—it's one of the most photographed buildings on Route 66, especially when the neon lights are on. Fun historical fact: This was the first theater in the region wired for sound for "talkies." For Depression-era moviegoers, this $0.10 theater was a welcome escape from the hardships of the time, a way to get lost in the art of film. The week of its opening, the Normal featured films with Bing Crosby, Jack Benny, and Barbara Stanwyck. Today, the theater still plays "oldies but goodies," as well as more current art, indie, and foreign films.

From Business U.S. 51, turn left (east) on West College Avenue. Take a right (south) on South School Street and then turn left (east) on West North Street. The theater is one block down on the right (south) side.

◆ Back on 66

Heading south on Center Street (Business U.S. 51), you'll approach the town of Bloomington. To stay on Route 66, pass East Locust Street and then merge right to keep following Business U.S. 51, which turns into North Madison Street. A newer alignment runs parallel and carries the eastbound traffic (N. East St.).

Bloomington

From North Madison Street (Business U.S. 51), turn left (east) onto West Washington Street and then make another left (north) onto North Main Street.

Sights
David Davis Mansion

Love Lincoln? Then get ready: You're in the land of Lincoln. Before and during Abraham Lincoln's presidency, Judge David Davis helped the president's political and legal career. At the **David Davis Mansion** (1000 Monroe Dr., 309/828-1084, www.daviddavismansion.org, 9am-3:30pm Wed.-Sat., free, $10 suggested donation), docents share the cultural history of this time period, describing servant, domestic, and family life in a Victorian mansion built in 1872. Wander the gardens that are reminiscent of 17th-century Italian and 18th-century English gardens. They're kept in pristine condition thanks to 89 gardeners who have volunteered over 5,300 hours of labor.

Women of the Mother Road

The story of Route 66 isn't complete without the illustrious women who've contributed greatly to the road's growth, success, and preservation. Here, celebrate the Illinoisian women who made a profound impact on the Mother Road.

♦ **Hazel Funk:** Educated and wealthy socialite Hazel Funk was an enterprising businesswoman ahead of her time. In the early 1920s, she inherited **Funks Grove** (page 58), the family's maple syrup business on Route 66. She ran it with great success during the Mother Road's height of popularity. She insisted that the word *syrup*—as it pertained to the Funks Grove brand—be spelled with an "i" in the classic dictionary spelling of the word. This helped distinguish the family's company from others. She also created a land trust to ensure that future generations would reap the benefits of the family business. It worked. To this day, Funks Grove sells out of their syrup every year.

♦ **Sally Rand:** Although she launched her career by starring in several Hollywood films in the 1920s, it was at the World's Fair in Chicago in 1932 that Sally Rand's notoriety reached epic levels. That's where she performed her now-famous burlesque dance with ostrich feathers and fans, an event that helped her cultivate a fan base all along Route 66. Known as one of the early pioneers of burlesque dancing, Sally drew motorists from across the country for her performances. She was a hard worker and a tireless performer, hosting shows at several iconic places on Route 66, like the **Coleman Theatre** (page 135) in Miami, Oklahoma, and the **KiMo Theatre** (page 226) in Albuquerque, New Mexico, before finally putting away her feathers in her late 70s. She's been quoted as saying, "I haven't been out of work since the day I took my pants off."

McLean County Museum of History

Here are a few things you can learn at the **McLean County Museum of History** (200 N. Main St., 309/827-0428, www.mchistory.org, 9am-5pm Mon. and Wed.-Sat., 9am-9pm Tues., $5 adults, free for children) in Bloomington: how to milk a cow, push a steel plow, and beat a rug. There are seven exhibition galleries at this museum, which is located in the former 1901 courthouse. Browse 19,000 objects, see 11,500 rare books, and view 1,700 feet (518 m) of historical papers. The exhibits examine the ins and outs of prairie life for different cultures, from Irish immigrants to South Asians. Also on-site you'll find **Cruisin' With Lincoln on 66** (10am-2pm Sun. May-Sept. only, 9am-5pm Mon.-Sat., 9am-9pm Tues., free), a Route 66- and Lincoln-themed visitors center and gift shop. It offers an interactive Route 66 map, gifts and souvenirs created by local artists, and fascinating history exhibits. Admission is free on Tuesdays for all visitors.

Food

Sometimes you're in the mood for pizza, and if this mood strikes when you're in Bloomington, head to the **Lucca Grill** (116 E. Market St., 309/828-7521, www.luccagrill.com, 11am-9pm Mon.-Thurs., 11am-10pm Fri.-Sat., 3pm-8pm Sun., $7-25). Route 66 road-trippers have been coming here since 1936, and everyone agrees that Lucca's has the best thin-crust pizza in the area. An antique tin ceiling and vintage bar lend old-school charm and serve as a reminder that this place has been around forever.

From Business U.S. 51 south, turn left (east) on East Market Street and then left (north) onto Business U.S. 51, which carries the eastbound Route 66 traffic. Lucca's is on the left (west) side of the road.

Accommodations

Per the name, **The Chateau Bloomington Hotel and Conference Center** (1621 Jumer Dr., 309/662-2020, www. bloomingtonchateau.com, $65-120) looks like a chateau fit for royalty. The large, smoke-free property offers rooms and suites. Rooms feature tasteful furnishings, free Wi-Fi, and in-room coffee. Take a dip in the heated indoor swimming pool or relax in the sauna and whirlpool spa. Washers and dryers are available on every floor (guest laundry facilities come in handy for long road trips).

◆ Back on 66

U.S. 51 south becomes Center Street as it leaves Bloomington. To stay on Route 66, turn right (west) on I-55/Veterans Parkway. Continue west on South Beich Road, which is the frontage road for I-55 for about 7 miles (11.3 km) to Funks Grove.

Funks Grove

Sights

★ Funks Grove Pure Maple Sirup

Since the late 1800s, three generations of the Funk family have been making Funks Grove Pure Maple Sirup (5257 Old Route 66, 309/874-3360, www. funksmaplesirup.com, 9am-5pm Tues.-Fri., 10am-5pm Sat., 1pm-5pm Sun.). In the 1930s, the family had 600 buckets hanging from the trees, which made up to 240 gallons (908 liters) of "sirup" priced at $7 per gallon; by 2001, there were 6,400 taps producing an average 2,000 gallons (7,571 liters) of sirup each season. Today, Funks Grove Pure Maple Sirup remains a Route 66 landmark. Even

though you can't tour the tree farm, you can browse the on-site gift shop for the family's maple products, such as syrup, candies, and creams. The shop also sells cookbooks, Funks Grove shirts and hats, and Route 66 memorabilia.

Sugar Grove Nature Center

About 1 mile (1.6 km) west of Funks sirup is the **Sugar Grove Nature Center** (4532 N. 725 East Rd., 309/874-2174, www. sugargrovenaturecenter.org, 9am-5pm Tues.-Fri., 10am-3pm Sat., noon-4pm Sun. Apr.-Oct., 10am-3pm Tues.-Sat. Nov.-Mar., trails dawn to dusk daily, free), with more than 1,000 acres (405 hectares) of prairieland and woods for hiking and wildlife viewing. It's located in Funks Grove, with four nature preserves and the largest remaining intact prairie in Illinois.

There are 7 miles (11.3 km) of well-maintained trails. Consider hiking the **Orange Trail,** a 0.5-mile (0.8-km) walk along Timber Creek. At just under 2 miles (3.2 km), the **Blue Trail** starts at the nature center and goes to the Funks Grove Church and the Chapel of Temple Trees, which was built by the Funk family, who started the sirup company. Also on-site are plant, butterfly, and herb gardens.

◆ Back on 66

The next stop on Route 66 is the small railroad town of McLean. From Funks Grove, follow Route 66 for 3 miles (4.8 km) west as it curves left (south) onto Steward Road. Stay on Steward Road south for two blocks and take a right (west) on Carlisle Street. Turn left (south) on Main Street to the junction with U.S. 136 in McLean.

McLean

In the 1920s, businesses sprang up to accommodate Route 66 traffic. The most significant business was **Dixie Truckers Home** (598 Main St.), also known as the oldest truck stop in the country. It started as a mechanic's garage, selling sandwiches at a counter with six stools. By the 1930s, it was a full restaurant open 24 hours a day, 365 days a year; the only day in its history that it was closed was due to a fire in 1965. The Beeler family owned and operated the business from 1928 through 2001, when they declared bankruptcy. Since then, it has changed ownership several times. In 2009, it was completely remodeled and is now a more commercial "Travel Plaza," sadly losing much of its Route 66 roadside character.

❖ Back on 66

As you leave McLean, head west on U.S. 136 and then turn left onto Historic U.S. 66 (before the railroad tracks). In about 5 miles (8 km), you'll approach Atlanta.

Atlanta

As Historic U.S. 66 veers southeast from the railroad tracks, turn right onto Sycamore Street. Sycamore Street becomes Arch Street, which will take you into downtown Atlanta. Atlanta may not be big in size, but it's gigantic in heart. Locals will stop and chat with you, and you might even see the mayor ride through town on his bicycle. You'll meet families that have been here for generations, and you'll encounter other Route 66 travelers stopping by to explore the quaint streets.

Sights

Atlanta was the commercial center and hot spot for central Illinois in the mid-1800s. There were more than 40 wood buildings, but fires destroyed many of them. In 1867, the **Downey Building** (110-112 SW Arch St.) became the first brick building in Atlanta. It's a beautiful two-story structure in a classic Italianate style. Over the years, it has been a bank, law office, grocery, millinery shop, and hardware store.

Paul Bunyan Muffler Man

You can't miss him. **Paul Bunyan Muffler Man** stands—nay, looms—across the street from the Palms Grill Cafe holding a gigantic hot dog in place of an ax. The 19-foot-tall (5.8-m) fiberglass sculpture was moved from Bunyon's Hot Dog stand in Cicero to its current location in Atlanta in 2003, when the town won a bid for this larger-than-life piece of Americana.

Atlanta Museum

At the **Atlanta Museum** (112 SW Arch St., 217/648-2112, www.atlantapld.org, 10am-5pm Mon.-Fri. and 10am-2pm Sat. Apr.-Dec., 10am-4pm Mon.-Fri. Jan.-Mar.), browse the extensive collection of photos, memorabilia, archived documents, and other historical treasures related to the history of Atlanta, Route 66, and Abraham Lincoln. Housed in a restored 1860s-era building, the museum also offers genealogy resources.

Seth Thomas Clock

Walking around downtown Atlanta, you'll pass the 1908 library with the 1901 **Seth Thomas Clock** (100 Race St.). The 40-foot (12-m) tower has an eight-sided clock that is still wound by hand. If you time it just right (no pun intended), you might encounter one of the local volunteers who wind it every day—and they just might offer to give you a behind-the-scenes peek into how it's done, including letting you give it a go.

J. H. Hawes Grain Elevator Museum

Until 1975, the 1903 **J. H. Hawes Grain Elevator Museum** (301 SW 2nd St., 217/648-2056, dawn-dusk daily, tours

1pm-3pm Sun. June-Aug., free) was used to store grain before the railroad shipped it out to nearby states. It's the only restored vertical wooden grain elevator on the National Register of Historic Places in Illinois.

From Arch Street, walk southwest one block to Race Street and turn right (northwest). Head two blocks north to 2nd Street and take a left (southwest).

Food and Accommodations

The ★ **Palms Grill Cafe** (110 SW Arch St., 217/648-2233, 10am-3pm Sun.-Mon. and Wed.-Thurs., 10am-8pm Fri.-Sat., $5-12) opened in 1934, and with the help of a grant from the National Park Service Route 66 Corridor Preservation Program, is still there today. The café has been lovingly restored to its roots—the tables, booths, bar, flooring, even the antique cash register. Waiters wear 1940s uniforms and dish out blue-plate specials, beef noodle soup, and grilled-cheese sandwiches. Breakfast is served all day, and the pies win awards. If you're too full for pie, take a slice for the road.

The ★ **Colaw Rooming House** (204 NW Vine St., 217/671-1219, $150) is set in a 1947 Victorian-style house just two blocks from Route 66. The three-bedroom, two-bath house features rooms with lots of natural light, shiny hardwood floors, and antique queen beds, plus a hand-crank record player.

◆ Back on 66

As you leave Atlanta, head southwest on Arch Street, which will rejoin the post-1940s alignment of Route 66. Take Route 66 west for about 8 miles (12.9 km) toward Lincoln.

Top to bottom: Paul Bunyan Muffler Man in Atlanta, Illinois; J. H. Hawes Grain Elevator Museum; Palms Grill Cafe

Lincoln

◈ Route 66 Through Lincoln

The 1926 Route 66 alignment goes through downtown Lincoln, while the 1940s alignment bypasses most of the town.

1926 Alignment

To drive the 1926 alignment, turn left (southeast) on Kickapoo Street just before reaching Lincoln. Make a quick right (southwest) onto Business I-55 (which is still Kickapoo St.). After about 1 mile (1.6 km), turn right (northwest) onto Keokuk Street.

About 2 miles (3.2 km) after Kickapoo Street, the road makes a sharp turn to the left (south). This was one of the deadliest spots on Route 66—according to locals, there was a car crash every few hours, earning it the name "killer curve."

Post-1930s Alignment

If your time is limited, stay on Route 66 (aka Lincoln Parkway) as you approach Lincoln to follow the newer alignment, a four-lane bypass that was built in 1944.

Sights

Lincoln Heritage Museum

The town of Lincoln was named after Abraham Lincoln before he was president. For fans of Lincoln, American politics, and Civil War history, there's no better place to explore than the **Lincoln Heritage Museum** (1115 Nicholson Rd., 217/735-7399, http://museum.lincolncollege.edu, 9am-4pm Tues.-Fri., 1pm-4pm Sat., $7 adults, $4 children). It features remnants of Lincoln's life and legacy, including exhibits that showcase campaign banners from 1860, Lincoln's desk, furnishings from his home, and even a lock of his hair.

The Mill Museum on 66

At the corner of 2nd and South Washington Streets, you'll see **The Mill Museum on 66** (738 S. Washington St., 217/671-3790, 1pm-4pm Thurs.-Sat., free), a 1929 former Dutch-themed restaurant with a large windmill out front. In the 1940s, a barroom and dance hall were added. The Mill was famous for fried schnitzel until it closed in 1996. The building was slated for demolition in 2005, but a community-wide effort saved the historic structure. It now operates as a museum, featuring businesses that served travelers along Route 66 and displaying exhibits that tell stories from local communities.

World's Largest Covered Wagon

Only on Route 66 do you get the chance to obtain photographic proof of the **World's Largest Covered Wagon** (1750 5th St., 217/732-8687)—and with a giant Abraham Lincoln in the driver's seat, no less. The 25-foot (7.6-m) oak-and-steel covered wagon was created in 2001 by David Bentley as part of the 75th-anniversary celebration of the Mother Road. To get there, drive five blocks north to 5th Street and turn left (west). After crossing Lincoln Parkway, look for the wagon.

◈ Back on 66

Heading out of Lincoln, continue south on Washington Street as it turns into Stringer Avenue and turn left (south) on Lincoln Parkway (BUS-55). Drive 2 miles (3.2 km) and turn left (southeast) on Historic U.S. 66. Within 1 mile (1.6 km), the road parallels I-55. In 2.5 miles (4 km), Route 66 curves left into Logan County 22 (near Exit 119). Drive southwest on Route 66 for 3.5 miles (5.6 km) into Elkhart.

Elkhart

Entering Elkhart on Route 66, turn left onto Governor Oglesby Street and drive east for two blocks to North Bogardus Street.

Elkhart had a thriving downtown in 1938. At the height of her career, the child actress Shirley Temple stopped here to eat lunch at The House by the Side of the Road restaurant on her way to a premiere of her film *Little Miss Broadway* in Springfield. It meant so much to the owner of the restaurant that they roped off the area where she ate and no one ever sat there again. The metal **Shirley Temple Silhouette Statue** (209 Governor Oglesby St.) commemorates her visit with a silhouette depicting Temple drinking a soda and being served by a waitress. The statue is located a couple of blocks east of Route 66.

⊕ Back on 66

As you leave Elkhart on Route 66, it's a straight shot about 5 miles (8 km) south to Williamsville. As the pre-1930s alignment enters **Williamsville** (on Oak St.), turn left (northwest) on SR-123 to join I-55 west. In less than 3 miles (4.8 km), take Exit 105 and turn right (south) on Business I-55/Sherman Boulevard.

Sherman

From Business I-55, turn right onto Cabin Smoke Trail. The 1926 segment is on the left (south) side of the road.

Carpenter Park in Sherman has a short **abandoned segment** of Route 66. The two-lane road was paved in 1922 with a mixture of gravel and cement, with expansion joints placed every 30 yards (27 m). Though this segment has been closed since 1936, you can still see parts of the road with its original gravel shoulders and curbs. The post-1930s four-lane

alignment bypassed this segment a few yards east.

The abandoned segment starts at the **Cabin Smoke Trail** and travels about 0.25 miles (0.4 km) south to the Sangamon River and the site of the former Old Iron Bridge (now only concrete abutments remain). Though you can't drive on this section of the road, you can walk along it, which is actually better. Look down to see nature slowly creeping up through the cracks in the road to reclaim its place.

⊕ Back on 66

As Business I-55 curves west, Sherman Road becomes North Peoria Road. To stay on Business I-55, turn left at the Veteran's Parkway stoplight. In about 3 miles (4.8 km), you'll reach Springfield.

Springfield

Get ready for more Abraham Lincoln. The only home he ever owned is in Springfield, also the state's capital. Abraham Lincoln practiced law here from 1843 to about 1852, and he is buried at the city's Oak Ridge Cemetery.

Sights

Many of the Lincoln sites are within walking distance of each other. If you'd like to do a walking tour, visit the **Springfield Convention and Visitors Bureau** (1 S. Old State Capitol Plaza, 800/545-7300, www.visitspringfieldillinois.com, 9am-5pm Mon.-Fri., free) to pick up a brochure and maps.

Abraham Lincoln Presidential Library and Museum

The **Abraham Lincoln Presidential Library and Museum** (212 N. 6th St., 217/558-8844, www.alplm.org, 9am-5pm daily, $15) is one of the most popular presidential libraries. It's a 200,000-square-foot (18,581-sq-m) complex with 40,000 square feet (3,716 sq m)

Springfield

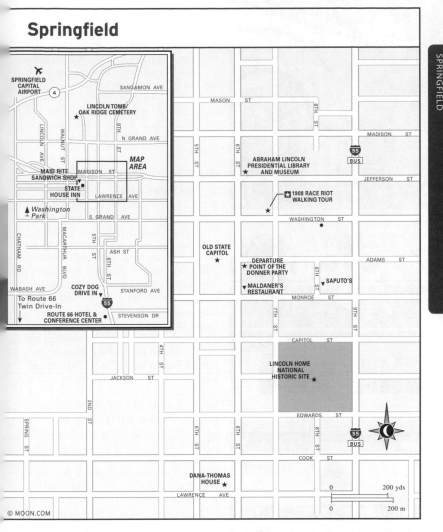

of galleries, theater presentations, historical artifacts, and interactive exhibits.

Lincoln Home National Historic Site
The **Lincoln Home National Historic Site** (426 S. 7th St., 217/492-4241, www.nps.gov/liho, 8:30am-5pm daily, free) is the two-story Greek Revival home that Lincoln lived in from 1844 to 1861. Built in 1839, the property has been restored to look as it did when Lincoln lived here,

and several pieces of furniture on display are originals. Summer is the busy season, so arrive as early as possible.

Lincoln's Tomb State Historic Site
Lincoln's final resting place is north of downtown at the **Oak Ridge Cemetery** (1500 Monument Ave., 217/782-2717, www.lincolntomb.org, 9am-5pm daily), the second-most popular cemetery in America after Arlington National

Cemetery in Washington DC. After Lincoln was assassinated, his body was eventually interred here in 1874. His three youngest sons and Mrs. Lincoln are also buried here. The granite tomb sits on a rectangular base located on a 12.5-acre (5-hectare) plot in a semicircular entranceway with a 117-foot-tall (36-m) obelisk. A bronze reproduction of Lincoln's head sits on a pedestal at the entrance.

Old State Capitol

The **Old State Capitol** (1 Old State Capitol Plaza, 217/785-9363, 9am-5pm daily, free) is where Lincoln's body lay in state after his assassination in 1865. It is also where Lincoln delivered his famous "House Divided" speech. In the speech, Lincoln said he believed "A house divided against itself cannot stand. I believe this government cannot endure, permanently half slave and half free." The speech was a major turning point in Lincoln's career and inspired senatorial debates regarding the moral issue of slavery, whether slavery should be legal in the North, and whether slaves were human beings.

Also at the Old State Capitol, a kiosk in the plaza marks the departure point for the **Donner Party**'s ill-fated trip in April 1846. Look for the kiosk just south of the building between 5th and 6th Streets. Nine covered wagons and 87 emigrants set out on a 2,500-mile (4,023-km) journey to California that was supposed to take four months. After the group tried to take a shortcut, an early snowfall trapped them in the Sierra Nevada Mountains. They ran out of food, and almost half the party died, mostly of starvation; some resorted to cannibalism to stay alive.

★ 1908 Race Riot Walking Tour

Two blocks east of the state capitol

Top to bottom: Dana-Thomas House in Springfield; Cozy Dog Drive In; the Old State Capitol

The Green Book in Springfield

The city of Springfield had more than two dozen listings in the *Negro Motorist Green Book*. Most of these were women-run private residences, or "tourist homes," that provided safe accommodations and meals to Black travelers. Neighbors and sisters **Bessie Mosby** (1614 E. Jackson St.) and **Helen Robbins** (1616 E. Jackson St.) operated two of these; today, only Helen's house still stands. **Dr. Sheppard A. Ware** was a doctor who worked at the state health department and ran a tourist home at 1520 E. Washington St. The building no longer exists, but the tourist home of **Ann Eskridge**, a clerk for the Department of Revenue, still stands at 1501 E. Jackson St. Businesses listed included **Hotel Dudley** (130 S. 11th St.), which also happened to be Springfield's only entry for the 1938 edition of the Green Book; **Hotel Ferguson** (1007 E. Washington St.); **Ideal Drug Store** (801 E. Washington St.); and **Cansler's Lounge** (807 E. Washington St.).

marks a dark chapter in Springfield's history. In 1908, Springfield had a population of 47,000 people; approximately 5.5 percent were Black, the highest percentage of Black residents of any city of comparable size in Illinois. A limited job market heightened racial tensions as industry owners used Black laborers as strikebreakers during labor strikes. Two Black men were accused of rape and assault, which triggered a white lynch mob of about 150 people. The mob lynched Black citizens and looted and destroyed Black-owned businesses and homes. It was a shocking embarrassment that this could happen in Lincoln's hometown. It took about 5,000 National Guard troops to end the two-day riot. The event made national news and led to the founding of the National Association for the Advancement of Colored People (NAACP).

The **1908 Race Riot Walking Tour** is a self-guided eight-marker tour that leads from the county jail where the mob formed to key sites where the riot ensued. The tour begins at the corner of 7th and Jefferson Streets, but your first stop should be the **Springfield Convention and Visitors Bureau** (109 N. 7th St., 800/545-7300, www.visitspringfieldillinois.com, 8:30am-5pm Mon.-Fri., free) to pick up brochures and maps. There are also other historical walking tours at the visitors center.

Dana-Thomas House

There is some impressive architecture in Springfield, including Frank Lloyd Wright's **Dana-Thomas House** (301 E. Lawrence Ave., 217/782-6776, www.dana-thomas.org, 10am-2pm Mon.-Tues., 9am-4pm Wed.-Sun., suggested donation $10). Take a one-hour tour to see one of the best examples of Wright's famed Prairie architecture. The Dana-Thomas House was built in 1902; the home is 12,000 square feet (1,115 sq m) with 35 rooms, 100 pieces of furniture, 250 art-glass windows, 3 main levels, and 16 varying levels.

About four blocks west of the Dana-Thomas House is a **John Kearney sculpture** (425 S. College St.) of a white-tailed deer made from chrome car bumpers. Look for it in front of the Capitol Complex Visitors Center.

Cozy Dog Drive In

The **Cozy Dog Drive In** (2935 S. 6th St., 217/525-1992, www.cozydogdrivein.com, 8am-8pm Mon.-Sat., $2-10) lies south of Springfield, after Route 66 merges with 6th Street. Ed and Virginia Waldmire (parents of Route 66 artist Bob Waldmire, of Pontiac-mural fame) opened the Cozy Dog in 1949. It's still run by the Waldmire family, and the place is packed with souvenirs, Route 66 memorabilia, and throngs of travelers eating cornbread-coated wieners on a stick. The drive-in is

Neon Photo Ops

We live in a digital, high-definition age, which means we don't get to see classic sig-nage illuminated by blinking, flickering neon bulbs anymore. Not so on Route 66. This road trip boasts some of the best retro neon signs, many of them more than half a cen-tury old. This list offers up photo-worthy signs—for motor courts, diners, gas stations, and more—that you'll want to make a part of your trip.

♦ **The Berghoff,** Chicago (page 35)

♦ **Dell Rhea's Chicken Basket,** Willowbrook (page 42)

♦ **Lexington Neon Sign,** Lexington (page 55)

♦ **Cozy Dog Drive In,** Springfield (page 65)

♦ **Luna Café,** Mitchell (page 73)

located on a busy highway, but you can't miss it. Just keep an eye out for a huge yellow sign with two giant hot dogs in a sweet embrace.

Route 66 Twin Drive-In

For a fun night out retro-style, check out the **Route 66 Twin Drive-In** (1700 Recreation Dr., 217/698-0066, www. route66-drivein.com, movies start at dusk Apr.-Oct. daily, $8), a restored drive-in that screens double features.

Food and Accommodations

When in the Midwest, do as the Midwesterners do. That means a visit to **Maid Rite Sandwich Shop** (118 N. Pasfield St., 217/523-0723, www.maid-rite.com, 10am-4pm Mon.-Fri., 11am-2pm Sat., $5-10). This 1926 fast-food franchise sells loose-meat burgers and homemade root beer, and this historic location is one of the few remaining outposts of the popular restaurant. If you've never had a loose-meat burger, it's like a sloppy Joe but without the sauce (and the mess—sort of). Order like a local and ask for extra mustard and onions.

Saputo's (801 E. Monroe St., 217/544-2523, www.saputos.com, 11am-10:30pm Mon.-Fri., 5pm-10:30pm Sat., 5pm-10pm Sun., $8-30) is a family-owned restaurant whose guests have included celebrities, dignitaries, and politicians since 1948. This southern-Italian supper club fea-tures classic dishes like baked lasagna and chicken parmesan. Savor the 1960s-era vibe and old-school decor with a gin martini and a shrimp cocktail.

Get historic at **Maldaner's Restaurant** (222 S. 6th St., 217/522-4313, http:// maldaners.com, 11am-2:30pm Mon.-Fri., 5pm-9pm Tues.-Thurs., 5pm-10pm Fri.-Sat., $8-38). It's been open since 1884 and was a political watering hole back in the day. It's right on Route 66, making it one of the oldest restaurants on the route. When the restaurant tried to take the horseshoe sandwich off the menu, the locals protested until it was added back. This place is all about tradition, as evi-denced by dishes like quail stuffed with sausage, and beef Wellington with truffle sauce.

If you plan to stay the night in Springfield, the **State House Inn** (101 E. Adams St., 217/528-5100, www. statehouseinnspringfield.com, $100-130) is across from the Old State Capitol and Presidential Library. Rooms feature simple yet tasteful furnishings. The pet-friendly property offers a fitness center, free Wi-Fi, and free breakfast.

The **Route 66 Hotel & Conference**

Center (625 E. St. Joseph St., 217/529-6626, www.rt66hotel.com, $55-80) was originally a Holiday Inn; it's been revamped as a Route 66 conference center with a restaurant and comedy club. The rooms are spacious, with basic amenities. The lobby has a 1941 Model T Ford, an old phone booth, and a vintage Shell gas pump.

◆ Back on 66
As you head south out of Springfield, 6th Street turns into I-55 south, and you'll cross **Lake Springfield,** an artificial lake created in the 1930s. When the water level is low, sometimes you can see the submerged 1926 Route 66 alignment.

Post-1930s Alignment
From Springfield to the Illinois-Missouri state line, you have two Route 66 alignments to choose from. The 1926 alignment follows historic Route 4, which predates Route 66 and goes through Chatham, Auburn, Carlinville, Thayer, and Girard. Route 4 has many twists and turns through farmland and old country towns. Since Route 66 only followed this route for four years, there are not many surviving businesses. Take the post-1930 Route 66, which parallels I-55 and travels through the towns of Litchfield and Mount Olive.

Glenarm

Traveling south on I-55, take the first exit south of Lake Springfield (Exit 88, Chatham) and turn right (southwest) on Palm Road, which curves left (south) to parallel I-55. The road becomes Douglas Street and then Frazee Road.

The **Sugar Creek Covered Bridge** (1 Covered Bridge Rd.) looks like it should be on a calendar of picturesque bridges in Vermont. The Sugar Creek Bridge is believed to be one of the oldest surviving covered bridges in Illinois. It's 110 feet (33.5 m) long and was constructed in 1880 using the Burr Arch wooden truss design, a combination of a wooden arch with multiple triangle-shaped supports. To get there, follow signs off Frazee Road.

◆ Back on 66
Continue south on Frazee Road. Take I-55 south for 34 miles (54.7 km) to Exit 52 in **Litchfield.** Turn left (east) onto SR-16 and in less than 1 mile (1.6 km), turn right (south) onto Old Route 66. (Do not follow E. Frontage Road/Historic Route 66, which dead-ends.)

Litchfield

Sights
Litchfield Museum Route 66 Welcome Center
The **Litchfield Museum Route 66 Welcome Center** (334 Old Route 66 N., 217/324-3510, www.litchfieldmuseum.org, 10am-4pm Mon.-Sat. and 1pm-4pm Sun. Apr.-Oct., free) takes a hyper-local approach to its Route 66 displays. You'll see exhibits of local memorabilia and historical information that's specific to exploring the impact the Mother Road had on the small town of Litchfield.

Skyview Drive-In
If you've never seen a movie under the stars, now is your chance. Catch a double feature at the **Skyview Drive-In** (1500 Old Route 66 N., 217/324-4451, www.litchfieldskyview.com, shows start at dusk Apr.-Oct., $7), a few blocks north on Route 66. The venue has been in continuous operation since 1950 (they once had a patio and a dance floor). Today, the drive-in screens current and classic films. Although they don't have the old drive-in speakers that used to hang inside your car door—the sound is tuned via your car radio—they still offer lots of goodies at the snack bar.

Food

The **Ariston Cafe** (413 Old Route 66 N., 217/250-2031, www.ariston-cafe.com, 11am-8pm Tues.-Thurs. and Sun., 11am-9pm Fri.-Sat., $7-24) is legendary. The Adam family ran it from 1924 to 2018, making it one of the longest-operating restaurants on Route 66. The café was originally located on Route 4 in Carlinville two years before Route 66 began. In 1935, the Ariston moved to this spot in Litchfield because this segment of Route 66 was the most heavily traveled road in the state. When it opened, a porterhouse steak cost $0.85 and a BLT was $0.25.

✪ Back on 66

From Litchfield, head south on Old Route 66 for 8 miles (12.9 km); the railroad tracks will be on the east, or left, side of the highway. At the town of Mt. Olive, turn left onto Mt. Olive Road.

Mt. Olive

As you enter Mt. Olive, the post-1940s alignment splits off to the right just after St. John Road. If time is a factor, take this route to continue on Route 66. To enter the town, turn left (south) after St. John Road on Old Route 66 and follow the post-1930s alignment as it curves west into Mt. Olive.

Sights
Union Miners Cemetery and Mother Jones Monument
Mt. Olive is a small mining town that opened its first coal shaft in 1875. The **Union Miners Cemetery** (Mt. Olive Rd. and Old Reservoir Rd., www.motherjonesmuseum.org/motherjonesmonument) is the only union-owned cemetery in the country. In 1898, four miners were killed in the Virden Massacre, a shootout that started when mine operators brought in 180 Black strikebreakers. Labor activist Mary Harris Jones, also known as **Mother Jones,** asked to be buried here next to the coal miners she referred to as "her boys." A granite **monument** memorializes her life and dedication to the cause.

From Old Route 66, turn right (north) on Lake Street. The cemetery is five blocks on the left (west).

Soulsby Shell Service Station
On the west side of Old Route 66, look for the **Soulsby Shell Service Station** (710 W. 1st St., free). Built in 1926—the year Route 66 opened—the station stopped pumping gas in 1991 but continued to serve soda and snacks and check the oil for Route 66 travelers until closing its doors in 1993. The station has been beautifully restored with the help of the Route 66 Corridor Preservation Program. The original gas pumps remain outside, and if the front door is open, you're welcome to pop in and peruse the artifacts (old signs, vintage televisions and radios, antique gas cans) at your leisure.

✪ Back on 66
Route 66 continues south from Mt. Olive, curving left to become East Frontage Road. Continue 3 miles (4.8 km) south toward the town of Staunton.

Staunton

At the intersection of East Frontage Road and Old Route 66, continue south on East Frontage Road for Country Classic Cars, located on the west side of the road.

After looking at so many old-school car props on Route 66, it's refreshing to find that **Country Classic Cars** (2149 E. Frontage Rd., 618/635-7056, http://countryclassiccars.com, 9am-5pm Mon.-Fri., 9am-3pm Sat.) actually has some cars for sale. Browse their inventory of more than 600 classic cars—everything from a 1927 Ford Model T to a 1957 Cadillac and a 1969 Chevy Impala. If you're not in the market to buy, no problem. You're welcome to simply admire the cars housed in several storage sheds, and some older cars rusting away outside. Stop here just to take in the sheer volume and variety of vehicles.

◆ Back on 66

From East Frontage Road, return to the junction with Old Route 66 and head southwest. Cross Staunton Road (Main St.) and follow the signs for Old Route 66 as it heads south. Old Route 66 merges with Bentrup Road, briefly becomes Henry Street, and then dips south onto Historic Old Route 66. Henry's Rabbit Ranch is about 0.5 mile (0.8 km) along on the right (west) south of Henry Street.

Henry's Rabbit Ranch

While many Mother Road attractions feature larger-than-life statues, restored gas stations, or classic cars, **Henry's Rabbit Ranch** (1107 Old Route 66, 618/635-5655, 9am-4pm Mon.-Fri., 9am-1pm Sat., www.henrysroute66.com, free) is probably the only place dedicated to bunnies.

As you check out the Route 66 memorabilia inside an old filling station, owner Rich Henry will bring out a rabbit, set him or her on the counter, and let you pet the furry friend while you chat it up. Rich loves rabbits; he even campaigned for one of them, Montana, to run for president (he has the campaign posters to prove it). Other rabbit-related sights on the ranch include a collection of Volkswagen Rabbits and a giant fiberglass jackrabbit on which you can climb.

◆ Back on 66

Leaving Staunton, head south on Historic Old Route 66. The road will join South Madison Street, which then turns into Sievers Road. Turn right (west) onto Williamson Road (not Williamson Ave.)

Top to bottom: Union Miners Cemetery and Mother Jones Monument in Mt. Olive; artifacts inside the Soulsby Shell Service Station; Route 66 through Mt. Olive

ILLINOIS

Springfield to St. Louis

© MOON.COM

| 0 | 20 km |
| 0 | 20 mi |

136

Nauvoo

Keokuk

61

136

99

Carthage

24

36

63

22

Mexico

Monroe
City

19

Hannibal

Quincy

172

104

24

Rushville

67

Mississippi River

MISSOURI

54

Bowling
Green

Barry

Griggsville

Mt Sterling

Beardstown

Illinois River

19

New
Florence

Warrenton

70

Pittsfield

White
Hall

Meredosia

78

Chandlerville

Jim Edgar Panther Creek
State Fish and Wildlife Area

Missouri River

O'Fallon

Pere Marquette
State Park

79

Kampsville

Hardin

Carrollton

267

Jacksonville

72

SUGAR CREEK
COVERED BRIDGE

ILLINOIS

Springfield

1908 RACE RIOT
WALKING TOUR

44

270

St Louis

270

Grafton

Alton

Jerseyville

67

Carlinville

Glenarm

108

Hartford

CLEVELAND-HEATH

HENRY'S
RABBIT RANCH

Staunton

Farmersville

29

55

Edwardsville

Hamel

55

Mt. Olive

Litchfield

SKYVIEW
DRIVE-IN

3

Collinsville

140

SOULSBY SHELL
SERVICE STATION

UNION MINERS CEMETERY

16

Pana

Belleville

WORLD'S LARGEST
CATSUP BOTTLE

CAHOKIA MOUNDS
STATE HISTORIC SITE

64

50

Vandalia

51

Prairie
du Rocher

Red
Bud

15

Carlyle

*Carlyle
Lake*

4

Ellis
Grove

127

Nashville

70

Chester

and then turn left (south) onto Route 4. Now we're back on the 1926 alignment.

Hamel

As Route 66 (Rte. 4) approaches I-55, turn right (southwest) on Possum Hill Road and take the next left (southeast) onto Old U.S. Route 66 (W. Frontage Rd.) After about 2.5 miles (4 km), the road will veer west from I-55 toward Hamel. Follow Old U.S. Route 66 into Hamel.

Food
Weezy's Route 66 Bar & Grill (108 S. Old Route 66, 618/633-2228, 6am-9pm Mon.-Sat., 7am-9pm Sun., $5-10) is a 1930s roadhouse and regulars' hot spot. Step inside to see the black-and-white checkered floor, red vinyl booths, and chrome tables and chairs. The furniture is actually from Johnny Rockets, the chain restaurant, so it looks a little "processed," but the authenticity comes from the vintage signs, homemade pies, and hearty breakfasts.

◆ Back on 66
From Hamel, continue south on Old U.S. Route 66 (SR-157) for 8 miles (12.9 km) to Edwardsville.

Edwardsville

From Old U.S. Route 66 (SR-157), turn right (west) onto East Vandalia Street (SR-143) and head to the northeast corner of Main Street (SR-159).

Sights
Edwardsville is the third-oldest city in Illinois and has about 40 historic buildings. Built in 1911, the **Bohm Building** (100 N. Main St.) served a steady stream of Route 66 travelers. The first floor contained seven or eight retail outlets, including restaurants, a beauty salon and barbershop, and a pharmacy; the second floor housed 18 office spaces. Over the years, businesses came and went (there are none from that time still operating today), but the character, history, and some recent renovations definitely make it worth a stop. The original front doors, found in the basement, have been restored, and a statue by Frank Lloyd Wright was installed in the alley. The gate door is made from flooring planks that were used in the Bohm barn, while a courtyard wall was designed from barn scrap wood.

Food
It doesn't get much better than the gourmet comfort food served at ★ **Cleveland-Heath** (106 N. Main St., 618/307-4830, www.clevelandheath.com, 11am-9pm Mon.-Thurs., 11am-10pm Fri., 10am-10pm Sat., 10am-9pm Sun., $11-35)—except for maybe the happy hospitality and buzzing energy at this James Beard Award-nominated eatery. Share a plate of deviled eggs (sprinkled with Frank's Hot Sauce, paprika, and parmesan), then tuck into the BLT with oven-cured tomatoes or the pork chop with cheddar-jalapeño bread pudding. The fare at Cleveland-Heath is a much-needed break from standard road-trip eats. Housed in the historic Bohm building, the restaurant includes exposed brick walls and tin ceilings.

◆ Back on 66
Leaving Edwardsville, head west on Old U.S. Route 66 (SR-157). In 5 miles (8 km), continue through the stoplight at South University Drive and follow the curve west onto Chain of Rocks Road.

◆ Side Trip: Collinsville

A post-1940s alignment of Route 66 travels through Collinsville. From Chain of Rocks Road, head south on SR-111 for almost 8 miles (12.9 km). Turn left (east) onto Collinsville Road, and in less than 2 miles (3.2 km) turn right (south) onto Ramey Street.

Sights
World's Largest Catsup Bottle

At the former Brooks Foods plant sits a 170-foot-tall (52-m) replica of a catsup bottle. The **World's Largest Catsup Bottle** (800 S. Morrison Ave., www.catsupbottle. com) was built in 1949 by W. E. Caldwell Company for the G. S. Suppiger catsup bottling plant. The big water tower with an idiosyncratic twist can be seen south of downtown Collinsville on the east side of SR-159.

Cahokia Mounds State Historic Site

Cahokia Mounds State Historic Site (30 Ramey St., 618/346-5160, www. cahokiamounds.org, 9am-5pm Wed.-Sun., suggested donation $7 adults, $2 children) is the largest pre-Columbian settlement north of Mexico. The site was inhabited from about AD 700 to 1400 with a population of up to 20,000 people. Cahokia was one of the most sophisticated prehistoric cities, with more than 120 mounds, plazas, and agricultural fields. It's unknown what actually happened to the Cahokia people and their city, but by 1400 the site had been abandoned. Some believe that climate change and social unrest may have affected crop production and forced the inhabitants to leave. Not much physical evidence remains of their existence except the mounds, which include the 100-foot-tall (30-m) Monks Mound—the largest prehistoric earthwork in North America.

Visit the **Interpretive Center** to pick up a guidebook ($1), which includes several 30- to 45-minute hiking trails. There are also self-guided iPod tours ($3) that take you to the Grand Plaza, Monks Mound, and Woodhenge, the ancient sun calendar. A gift shop sells books, games, and handmade American Indian textiles, ceramics, artwork, and jewelry.

◈ Back on 66

To return to Route 66, drive west on Collinsville Road about one mile to

Cahokia Mounds State Historic Site

SR-111 north (right). Drive 5 miles (8 km) to Chain of Rocks Road and turn left (west) to enter the town of Mitchell.

Mitchell

Chain of Rocks Road is dotted with old motels and retro signs, but none as great as the sign in front of **Luna Café** (201 E. Chain of Rocks Rd., 618/931-3152, 10am-2am daily). It's a huge cocktail glass with a cherry in the bottom. This 1924 roadhouse was popular with Prohibition gangsters like Al Capone—think gambling in the basement and a brothel upstairs—and legend has it that when the red cherry was lit up, the women in the brothel were "working." Today, it's a quiet locals' bar peppered with Prohibition memorabilia inside.

◈ Back on 66

Several Route 66 alignments splinter off into a tangled web of roadways here, so the easiest way to get to St. Louis, Missouri, from Mitchell is to follow I-270 west.

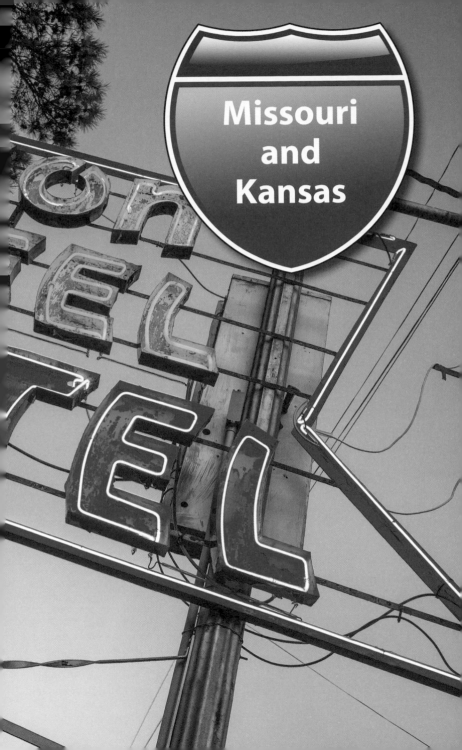

Missouri
and
Kansas

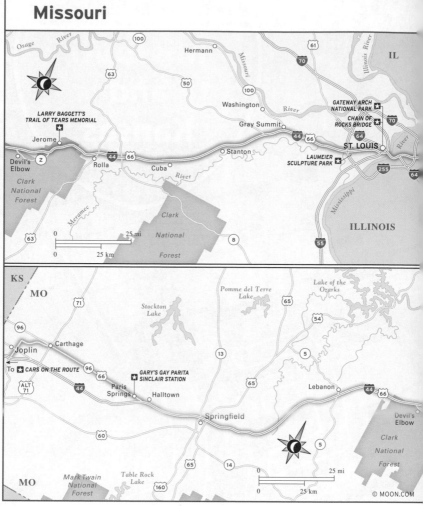

Missouri

A number of important pathways, routes, and trails have roots in Missouri, all of them established long before Route 66 came through. It was these lines—a patchwork of rutted back roads, farm-to-market routes, and Osage migratory paths—that paved the way for the Mother Road.

In 1803, the Louisiana Purchase opened Missouri to western settlement. The Lewis and Clark Expedition, which launched here, symbolized the entrance to the New Frontier. And other seminal trails, such as the Overland, Oregon, and Santa Fe, all originated in Missouri.

In 1858, the U.S. government installed

Highlights

★ **Chain of Rocks Bridge, St. Louis:** Named for the nearby rocky rapids, this bridge crosses the Mississippi River and sports an unusual 30-degree kink in the middle (page 81).

★ **Gateway Arch National Park, St. Louis:** See the breathtaking views from the top of the iconic "Gateway to the West" (page 84).

★ **Laumeier Sculpture Park, Kirkwood:** Dotted with larger-than-life works of modern art, this sprawling, grassy park is free to the public (page 91).

★ **Larry Baggett's Trail of Tears Memorial, Jerome:** Visit this special tribute that honors the lives of American Indians forced to walk across the country to reservations in Oklahoma (page 103).

★ **Gary's Gay Parita Sinclair Station, Paris Springs:** Stop by this 1920s Sinclair station as much for a chance to chat with owners Barb and George as for the Route 66 memorabilia on display (page 116).

★ **Cars on the Route, Galena:** At this vintage service station, take photos of the 1951 boom truck that inspired the character of Tow Mater from Pixar's *Cars* (page 123).

Best Restaurants

★ **Ted Drewes Frozen Custard, St. Louis:** The custard is so thick it's called "concrete" (page 89).

★ **Spencer's Grill, Kirkwood:** This St. Louis landmark has been around since 1947 (page 91).

★ **A Slice of Pie, Rolla:** Pick your pleasure: fruit pies, cream pies, big pies, little pies, even pot pies (page 102).

★ **Cookin' From Scratch, Doolittle:** This country restaurant offers slow-cooked, hearty goodness (page 102).

★ **The Order, Springfield:** This sophisticated eatery is on the ground floor of a historic Masonic building (page 114).

telegraph lines along the Osage trail and called it the "Old Wire Road." This important route was used for communication and the delivery of supplies during the Civil War.

The path was laid, quite literally, but the roads were made of wooden planks that quickly rotted and made travel a miserable experience. The first automobiles appeared in Missouri in 1891, and within 20 years there were more than 16,000 cars on its rickety roads. In 1920, the "Get Missouri Out of the Mud" campaign allocated $60 million to improve the roads. By 1931, the entire Route 66 stretch through Missouri was paved; it was the third state (preceded by Illinois and Kansas) along the Mother Road to turn to smooth asphalt.

During the Depression, federal funds were used to reroute Route 66 along major thruways in an effort to boost tourism and commerce. Even though Route 66 had become one of the busiest highways in the nation, the federal government considered it obsolete because it didn't meet the road-building standards issued under the Federal-Aid Highway Act. Compared to the success of the Pennsylvania and New Jersey Turnpikes, Route 66 fell short. Denser concrete was added to handle the heavy traffic, but once I-44 was under way in 1956, Route 66 quickly became a distant memory. In fact, the original Route 66 signs between St. Louis and Joplin were removed as early as 1977, eight years before the official decommission of the road.

For approximately 300 miles (485 km), large segments of Route 66 remain intact through 11 Missouri counties. This road trip drives over rolling hills and past roadside churches, small towns, and historic landmarks restored with the help of the National Park Service Route 66 Corridor Preservation Program.

Planning Your Time

If you use your time wisely, you can make it across Missouri in **two days**—but there is a lot to do and see. Start the first day in St. Louis and head west about 216 miles (345 km) to spend the night in Springfield, a drive of about 4-5 hours. The second day takes you through three Route 66 states. Exit Missouri through Joplin, zip along the 13-mile (20.9-km) stretch in Kansas, and end in Tulsa, Oklahoma.

Driving Considerations

In Missouri, Route 66 was rerouted more times than in any other state. After the Depression, Springfield, Joplin, and Rolla added alternate routes, but the most

Best Accommodations

★ **Magnolia Hotel, St. Louis:** A favorite of the 1920s Hollywood elite, this hotel maintains all its majestic charm (page 89).

★ **Wagon Wheel Motel, Cuba:** This old-school motor court features cabins with attached garages (page 99).

★ **Munger Moss Motel, Lebanon:** One of the best retro neon signs on all of Route 66 invites motorists to bed down at this vintage motor court (page 106).

★ **Swan Song Inn Bed & Breakfast, Marshfield:** You can call this sprawling estate your home for a night or two (page 109).

★ **Boots Motel, Carthage:** This Streamline Moderne gem has been restored to its retro former glory (page 119).

convoluted changes were in the St. Louis area, where Route 66 branches off into six different roadways west of the Mississippi River.

If you're pressed for time, I-44 offers an alternate option for speedy transport between towns. It's best to drive this portion of Route 66 during **spring** or **fall,** since winter roads can be icy and summers can be hot and muggy. Although you'll be driving through some remote areas of the Ozarks, there are several towns with **gas** stations along the way, so as long as you keep the tank at least half full, you'll be fine.

Getting There

Starting Points
Car

Route 66 has two starting points in Missouri: The **north route** bypasses the city of St. Louis via the McKinley Bridge, while the **post-1930s route** crosses the Mississippi River on the Martin Luther King Bridge.

This road trip starts in St. Louis, then either follows Vandeventer Avenue south or Olive Street and Chouteau Avenue (SR-100), both of which travel west out of downtown. If you're short on time and want to **bypass the city,** enter St.

Louis via the McKinley Bridge, north of downtown.

Car Rental

Enterprise corporate headquarters is in St. Louis. Hit up the airport branch (9636 Natural Bridge Rd., 314/427-2265, www.enterprise.com, 7:30am-6pm Mon.-Fri., 9am-noon Sat.). Also at the airport, you'll find **National Car Rental** (10124 Natural Bridge Rd., 877/222-9058, www.nationalcar.com, 24 hours daily), **Hertz** (10278 Natural Bridge Rd., 800/654-3131, www.hertz.com, 6am-10pm daily), **Avis** (10482 Natural Bridge Rd., 800/831-2847, www.avis.com, 6am-10pm daily), and **Budget** (10482 Natural Bridge Rd., 800/527-0700, www.budget.com, 6am-10pm daily).

Air

St. Louis Lambert International Airport (STL, 10701 Lambert International Blvd., 314/890-1333, www.flystl.com) is the largest airport in the state of Missouri, with nonstop service to nearly 70 U.S. and Canadian airports and five overseas destinations such as Cancun and Jamaica. The airlines include Air Canada, Alaska Airlines, American Airlines, Delta, Frontier, Southwest, and United. The airport is about 12 miles (19.3 km) northwest of downtown St. Louis.

Shifting Landscape

As Route 66 moves west and south through Missouri, it travels through strikingly diverse topography. Leaving St. James, the landscape morphs from **open prairie** to **exposed rock outcroppings.** Then you start to follow the lines of the **Ozark hills.**

As you pass through Pulaski County (Devil's Elbow to Lebanon), you'll find yourself deep in the heart of the Ozarks: dramatic 200-foot (61-m) **rock bluffs,** deep and **verdant valleys,** and rivers snaking through **limestone** rock. The drive from Springfield to Carthage is especially scenic with its hilly contours and **leafy trees.**

The smaller **Springfield-Branson Airport** (SGF, 2300 N. Airport Blvd., 417/868-0500, www.sgf-branson-airport.com) is about 11 miles (17.7 km) northwest of Springfield, in the southwest area of the state. The airport offers service to Atlanta, Charlotte, Chicago, Dallas, Denver, Houston, Los Angeles, Las Vegas, Orlando, Phoenix-Mesa Gateway, and Tampa. Airlines include American, Allegiant, Delta, and United.

Train and Bus

Amtrak (430 S. 15th St., 800/872-7245, www.amtrak.com, 24 hours daily) is located right downtown and is served by three routes: the Texas Eagle, which goes from Chicago through St. Louis, Dallas, San Antonio, and Los Angeles; the Missouri River Runner, which travels daily to Kansas City, Missouri; and the Lincoln Service, which runs between Chicago and St. Louis. Ticket sales end 10 minutes before departure times, and boarding gates close five minutes before the train leaves. At the Amtrak station, you also can catch a **Greyhound Bus** (430 S. 15th St., www.greyhound.com, 314/231-4485, 24 hours daily) with both Network and Express service throughout the United States.

St. Louis

In more ways than one, St. Louis—the largest city on Route 66 besides Chicago and Los Angeles—was critical to shaping U.S. history.

American Indians first settled in the area, building the Cahokia Mounds on the east side of the Mississippi River. The French arrived in the late 1600s, but it wasn't until 1764 that St. Louis was established. Thanks to the mighty Mississipp',

the city became a major fur trading post for beaver and buffalo hides.

In 1803, the French sold the land west of the Mississippi River to the United States as part of the Louisiana Purchase. By the mid-1840s, huge numbers of Irish left their homeland during the Great Potato Famine, landing in St. Louis, and many Germans arrived after the 1848 Revolution.

In addition, Missouri was a border slave state, which made it the hub for filing freedom lawsuits, including the infamous *Dred Scott v. Sanford* case. In the early 1900s, a large number of African Americans migrated from the South to work in the industrial jobs available in St. Louis.

As most beer fans know, St. Louis is home Anheuser-Busch, the first company to bottle and market pasteurized beer, and to transport it in refrigerated railroad cars across the country. St. Louis has had other notable firsts: Most historians agree that the ice-cream cone was invented here at the 1904 World's Fair, when Syrian immigrant Ernest Hamwi ran out of ice-cream dishes and curled a waffle cookie as a makeshift receptacle. On a less sweet note, St. Louis also recorded the first auto theft in 1905.

Sights
★ Chain of Rocks Bridge

Route 66 originally entered Missouri via the McKinley Bridge, but it was rerouted in 1936 to the **Chain of Rocks Bridge** (Chain of Rocks Rd. near Schillinger Rd., 314/416-9930, free). The bridge was built from 1927 to 1929 to bypass downtown and alleviate traffic in the heart of St. Louis; thus, it became the preferred road for Route 66 travelers because it was faster than driving through the city. Nearly 400 elm trees lined the Illinois side, and the Chain of Rocks Amusement Park sat alongside the river.

The steel truss bridge stands 60 feet (18 m) above the Mississippi River. It's named after a 17-mile (27-km) granite

Chain of Rocks Bridge

One Day in St. Louis

Enter St. Louis via the Chain of Rocks Road and stroll over the **Chain of Rocks Bridge.** Head south to the **Mary Meachum Freedom Crossing** and then have a bite to eat at **Bailey's Range.** Take a tram to the top of the **Gateway Arch** and then get exploring—and playing—at the interactive **City Museum.**

At the Riverfront, browse historic buildings along the cobblestone streets of **Laclede's Landing,** stopping for dinner at one of the Landing's restaurants. Then head to **St. Louis Union Station Hotel** to bed down for the night.

The next day, on your way out of town, stop by **Ted Drewes Frozen Custard** and then visit **Laumeier Sculpture Park** and the abandoned town of Times Beach, where the **Route 66 State Park** sits along the Meramec River.

rocky outcrop that formed treacherous rapids in the river and caused huge problems for boaters. The bridge was originally designed to be straight, but boaters protested because the placement of the bridge was going to make river travel even more difficult. The only solution was to incorporate a 30-degree bend in the middle of the bridge. The designer assured officials that the turn wouldn't be a problem, but it caused endless bottlenecks that frustrated Route 66 travelers well into the 1960s. As cars got longer and bigger, and the interstate systems called for wider roads, a new Chain of Rocks Bridge opened less than 2,000 feet (610 m) upstream in 1967.

Fewer people drove the original 1929 bridge, and the city could no longer afford to maintain it, so it closed in 1968 and was slated for demolition in 1975. When the value of steel plummeted in 1976, it became too expensive to tear down, so it sat abandoned until a non-profit organization converted it into a bicycle and pedestrian bridge in 1989. Spared from the wrecking ball, this is one of the best-preserved remnants of large-scale bridge construction from the 1920s.

Getting There

It's best to see the bridge on your way into St. Louis, because there's no safe parking on the west side. To get there from Route 66, head west on Chain of Rocks Road. As it curves south, enter I-270 westbound.

You're taking I-270 just to cross the railroad tracks, so stay in the right-hand lane and immediately exit on Old Alton Road. Turn right (southwest), cross under I-270, and then turn right (northwest) onto West Chain of Rocks Road. Drive west for about 2 miles (3.2 km) to the Chain of Rocks Bridge. Once you arrive, park in the Illinois Parking Area on Chain of Rocks Road. If you don't have time to walk across and just want a great view of the bridge, turn left (south) on West Chain of Rocks Road to the Chouteau Island Fishing Area. If you do park and walk across the bridge, don't leave any valuables visible in the car and bring your wallet and cell phone with you.

◆ Back on 66

To leave Chain of Rocks, drive east on West Chain of Rocks Road to SR-3 (Lewis and Clark Blvd.) and turn right (south). Drive about 7 miles (11.3 km), and when SR-3 splits off onto 4th Street, follow Cedar Street instead, which will take you to the McKinley Bridge heading west across the Mississippi River. Take Exit 34 and turn left (south) on Riverview Drive.

Mary Meachum Freedom Crossing

After crossing the McKinley Bridge, about a mile north along the Mississippi River is the spot where Mary Meachum, wife of John Berry Meachum, helped people cross the Mississippi to escape slavery in May 1855. To see the exact spot, go to

St. Louis

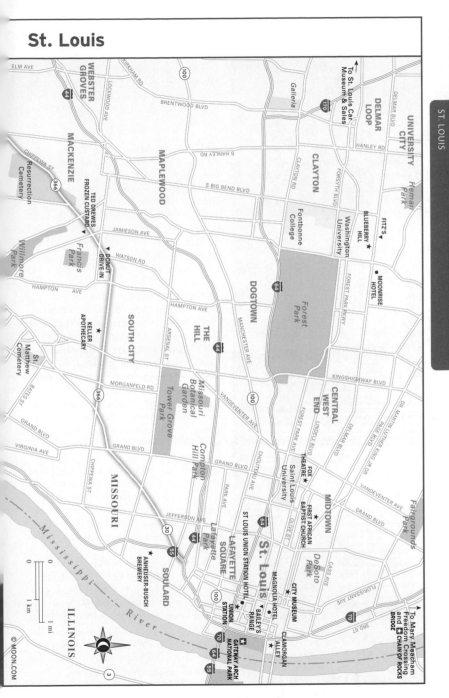

the **Mary Meachum Freedom Crossing** (Prairie Ave. and St. Louis Riverfront Trail, 314/584-6703, dawn-dusk daily, free). A colorful wall mural interprets the historic event. The spot marks the first Missouri site on the National Park Service's National Underground Railroad Network.

⬦ Back on 66
To reach the Mary Meachum Freedom Crossing from the McKinley Bridge, travel west on McKinley Street and turn right (north) onto North Broadway. Drive about 0.75 mile (1.2 km) and turn right (northeast) on East Grand. Take a left on Hall Street (northwest) and then turn right on East Prairie Avenue and continue to the end.

★ Gateway Arch
You've heard about it. You've seen pictures. Now is your chance to experience it up close. The iconic "Gateway to the West" **Gateway Arch National Park** (bordered by I-44 and Sullivan Blvd., 877/982-1410, www.nps.gov/jeff, 8am-10pm daily summer, 9am-6pm daily winter, $14-16 tram to the top) is the tallest constructed monument in the country. Completed in 1965, the 630-foot (192-m) stainless steel monument points westward, symbolizing the path to prosperity, opportunity, and freedom. A pair of elevators takes visitors on a four-minute ride to the top, where you'll find an observation deck and panoramic views—on a clear day you can see 30 miles (48 km) to the east and west. There are no restrooms at the top of the arch.

Near the arch, the **Old Courthouse** (11 N. 4th St.) is the spot where enslaved people Dred and Harriet Scott tried to sue for their freedom in 1847. The case made national news, went to the Supreme Court, and was a catalyst—one of many—of the American Civil War. This was also where

Top to bottom: Union Station fountain; Blueberry Hill; Fox Theatre

Virginia Minor fought for women's right to vote. The exhibits are currently closed to the public as they undergo renovations that include an expansion for new galleries.

Clamorgan Alley

Laclede's Landing (http://lacledeslanding.com, free) is a busy area with cobblestone streets and businesses housed in old warehouses along the riverfront. Once the seat of operations for the steamboat industry and fur trade, these historic warehouses were owned by wealthy residents like **Jacques Clamorgan,** a West Indian fur trader. Clamorgan was unmarried but fathered four children with different women; he signed over his property to his former slave and mistress, Esther. She became one of the earliest female property owners in St. Louis. Clamorgan's **home** was located at 701 North 1st Street. The house is no longer there, but **Clamorgan Alley** has a sidewalk engraving on the ground commemorating his legacy. It's located off Morgan Street between 1st and 2nd Streets.

City Museum

The plain name of this museum belies the fun that waits inside. **City Museum** (750 N. 16th St., 314/231-2489, www.citymuseum.org, 10am-5pm Wed.-Sun., $16 visitors 3 and over, free for children 2 and under) is an innovative, artsy playground made from scrapped pieces of America's infrastructure. The 600,000-square-foot (55,742-sq-m) former International Shoe Company has been transformed into a surreal labyrinth of steel and concrete artworks made from salvaged bridges, construction cranes, chimneys, and abandoned airplanes.

The City Museum is the brainchild of the late sculptor Bob Cassilly, who died in 2011. Cassilly has been quoted as saying, "The point is not to learn every fact, but to say, 'wow, that's wonderful.' And if it's wonderful, it's worth preserving." These powerful words come alive in huge wire-mesh walkways, tile-encrusted floors and columns, a 10-story circular slide, and a human-sized Slinky. An entire wall is made from industrial kitchen food pans.

During spring and summer, a **Ferris wheel** operates on the roof, where there are more tunnels and slides. Also on-site are a **shoelace factory** that shows how bootstraps were made for U.S. soldiers during World War II and a **gift shop** selling one-of-a-kind works by local artists. There are nine **restaurants** on-site, a few of which offer beer, wine, and cocktails.

The City Museum offers "after-hours" on Friday and Saturday nights, when the museum stays open until midnight for adults only. If you'd rather not compete with kids for turf, plan your visit after 5pm on one of these days. The metal objects are large with lots of rough edges, so bring kneepads and a flashlight and wear long pants and closed-toe shoes. There are no lockers—leave your flip-flops, sandals, skirts, and purses in the car. The museum is located about 1 mile (1.6 km) west of the Gateway Arch.

Union Station

The grand **Union Station** (1820 Market St., 314/421-6655, www.stlouisunionstation.com, free) luxuriates on 11 acres (4.5 hectares) in downtown St. Louis. When it opened in 1894, it was reportedly the largest, most beautiful train station in the United States—and today it still maintains its regal elegance. Modeled after a medieval city in southern France, it has sweeping archways, fresco and gold leaf detailing, mosaics, intricate stained-glass windows, and a cavernous vaulted ceiling.

The train shed was one of the largest single platforms ever built—at 140 feet (43 m) tall, 700 feet (213 m) long, and 600 feet (183 m) wide, it spans 42 tracks.

In the 1940s, Union Station served more than 100,000 people, but after World War II, train travel dwindled. In 1976, the station was designated a

ST. LOUIS

National Historic Landmark; two years later, the last train pulled out of the station. It was eventually purchased and given a $150 million restoration, making it the largest adaptive re-use project in America.

The **Whispering Arch** (in the grand entrance on the north side of the building) is an architectural sonic phenomenon. Stand facing the wall at the base of the arch and speak in a normal volume; your voice will be carried along the arch to a person on the other side—they can hear you perfectly. (Make sure to speak directly at the wall, and don't look up at the arch as you talk.)

There are also specialty shops, restaurants, and a hotel within Union Station. Union Station is located about 1 mile (1.6 km) west of the Gateway Arch and less than a mile southwest of the City Museum.

First African Baptist Church

See the oldest continuously operating African American church in Missouri. It all began with unsung American hero John Berry Meachum (husband of Mary Meachum, the woman famous for helping enslaved people cross the Mississippi River), who was born to enslaved parents. Meachum learned carpentry, which earned him enough money to purchase his family's freedom. After he moved to Missouri, he founded **First African Baptist Church** (3100 Bell Ave., 314/533-8003, call ahead, free) in St. Louis and became part of a group of local African American aristocrats.

Meachum owned two Mississippi steamers and a barrel factory; he purchased enslaved people in order to teach them a trade working in his barrel factory until they could make a living on their own. When St. Louis enacted a law banning the education of Black people, Meachum was forced to shut down his school.

In 1847, Meachum circumvented the law by anchoring his steamboat in the middle of the Mississippi River and teaching classes on the boat. Since it was no longer on Missouri land, it was not subject to state law. He called it the Floating Freedom School.

The First African Baptist Church is less than 2 miles (3.2 km) northwest of Union Station. From Market Street near Union Station, turn right (north) on North Jefferson Avenue and then left (west) on Delmar. Drive five blocks and turn right (north) on North Cardinal Avenue. The church is on the left (west) side.

Fox Theatre

When the **Fox Theatre** (527 N. Grand Blvd., 314/534-1678, www.fabulousfox. com, tours 10:30am Tues., Thurs., and Sat. $10; performances $25-70) opened in 1929, it was the second-largest theater in the United States. This opulent performing arts center showcases a style that mixes Byzantine elements and East Indian design; the entrance features

bronze and glass doors with a terra-cotta facade. The Fox was the first theater in the United States to be built with full "talkie" equipment and thus attracted people from all over. For the price of a ticket, folks of modest means could rub elbows with the elite.

The Fox went bankrupt in 1936; one year later, shares were given away as souvenirs because the stockholders believed the Fox had no value. From the late 1930s until 1978, it was leased by Harry Arthur and featured performances by Benny Goodman, Mae West, and Frank Zappa, among others. Today, the Fox hosts a wide range of acts—from Broadway plays to music acts like the Alabama Shakes and Beck.

Fox Theatre is located less than 1 mile (1.6 km) west of First African Baptist Church. From Market Street, head west to turn right (north) on South Jefferson Avenue. Take a left (west) on Olive Street and turn right (north) on North Grand Boulevard.

Forest Park

Stretching 500 green acres (202 hectares) larger than New York's Central Park, **Forest Park** (5595 Grand Dr., 314/367-7275, www.forestparkforever.org, 24 hours daily, free) is one of the largest urban parks in the United States—and one of the prettiest. Running and walking trails circle sparkling ponds, pass under leafy trees, and wind past grassy meadows. At 1,300 acres (526 hectares), the park has plenty of room to house five cultural centers: **St. Louis Art Museum**, **St. Louis Science Center**, **St. Louis Zoo**, **The Muny**, and the **Missouri History Museum**. Fun fact: Forest Park was the site of the 1904 World's Fair.

Whatever you do in Forest Park, don't miss the **Jewel Box** (Wells and McKinley Dr., 314/531-0080, 9am-4pm Mon.-Fri., 9am-11am Sat., 9am-2pm Sun., $1, free Mon. and Tues. 9am-noon). This art deco greenhouse boasts 50-foot (15-m) glass walls and 17 acres (6.9 hectares) of tropical trees, brightly colored flowers,

Forest Park, St. Louis

and exotic plants, plus a fountain and water feature.

Forest Park is located 2 miles (3.2 km) west of the Fox Theatre. From Market Street, head west and turn right (north) on South Jefferson Avenue. Turn left (west) on Olive Street, which turns into Lindell Boulevard. Follow Lindell Boulevard to Kings Highway Boulevard and turn left (south). Turn right (west) on Forest Park Avenue to enter the park.

Blueberry Hill

You'd be remiss to visit St. Louis and not catch live music at one of the city's most established venues. Head to **Blueberry Hill** (6504 Delmar, 314/727-4444, tickets 800/745-3000, www.blueberryhill. com, 11:30am-1:30am Mon.-Sat., 11am-midnight Sun., $5-25), a landmark restaurant and club that's been entertaining the crowds since 1972. Chuck Berry played here weekly for years; current music acts range from indie rock to blues and hip-hop.

If you don't have time for a live show, enjoy the eats at Blueberry Hill's restaurant. It spans the entire block in front of the St. Louis Walk of Fame (where bronze stars and plaques feature St. Louis natives such as Miles Davis, Chuck Berry, Tina Turner, and Josephine Baker) and serves sandwiches, burgers, soups, and salads.

Blueberry Hill also hosts the largest annual dart tournament in the United States, with about 500 participants. Pop-culture memorabilia lines the dart room, which features boards plus video games and pinball machines.

Blueberry Hill is located less than 2 miles (3.2 km) north of Forest Park. From Market Street, head west and turn right (north) on South Jefferson Avenue. Turn left (west) on Olive Street, which turns into Lindell Boulevard. Follow Lindell Boulevard to Kings Highway Boulevard and turn right (north). Take a left (west) onto Delmar Boulevard.

St. Louis Car Museum & Sales

It's not a proper Route 66 road trip without a visit to a car museum. Check out **St. Louis Car Museum & Sales** (1575 Woodson Rd., 800/957-5707, www. stlouiscarmuseum.com, 9am-6pm Mon.-Fri., 10am-2pm Sat., free). You'll see 80,000 square feet (7,432 sq m) filled with classic muscle cars, vintage motorcycles, and airplanes, everything from Bugattis and Bentleys to Caddys from 1914 to the 1970s. And yes, they also sell vintage vehicles.

The car museum is located about 5 miles (8 km) northwest of Forest Park and 13 miles (20.9 km) west of the Gateway Arch. From Market Street, head west to turn right (north) on South Jefferson Avenue. Turn left (west) on Olive Street, which turns into Lindell Boulevard. Follow Lindell Boulevard to Kings Highway Boulevard. Turn right (north) and then left (west) onto Delmar Boulevard. Turn right (north) on North McKnight Road, which turns into Woodson Road.

Anheuser-Busch Brewery

Even though today **Anheuser-Busch Brewery** (12th and Lynch Sts., 314/577-2626, www.budweisertours.com, 9am-5pm Mon.-Thurs., 9am-5:30pm Fri.-Sat., 11am-5pm Sun., June-Aug.; 10am-5pm Mon.-Sat., 11am-5pm Sun., Sept.-May; tour prices vary) is a behemoth corporation (notably as the maker of Budweiser), when it opened in 1852, it was a small-batch brewery. The St. Louis location is the original and also the largest, and as such, offers tours and tastings.

The 45-minute complimentary tour takes visitors to the Clydesdale stables and demonstrates the entire seven-step brewing process. The Day Fresh Tour ($10) shows guests how beer is produced from seed to sip. The 75-minute tour starts at the Clydesdale stables and continues to the beechwood aging cellar, brewhouse, and packaging facility. The History Tour ($25) is held in the

Old Lyon Schoolhouse and showcases 400 items from the Anheuser-Busch archives. The Beermaster Tour ($35) offers guests a behind-the-scenes look at the brewing process, along with a comprehensive two-hour tour of the stables, fermentation cellar, packaging facility, and finishing cellar. Finally, Beer School ($15) is an interactive beer-tasting and food-pairing class that highlights a variety of beers, ingredients, and proper pouring techniques.

Keller Apothecary

If you need to pick up some Advil, or if you're in the mood to step back in time to the 1930s, visit **Keller Apothecary** (5346 Devonshire Ave., 314/352-5201, www. kellerrx.com, 9am-6pm Mon.-Fri., 9am-1pm Sat.). This throwback pharmacy has been serving St. Louis since 1933. Inside you'll find antique mortar and pestles, pillboxes, and beakers on display, plus modern-day pharmacy products. The apothecary is located south of SR-366 near Macklind Avenue.

Food

At **Bailey's Range** (920 Olive St., 314/241-8121, www.baileysrange.com, noon-8pm daily, $4-10) every single burger on the menu (which totals nearly 15 options) is made from grass-fed, Missouri-raised beef, lamb, and chicken. Fancy toppings include arugula pesto, bacon jam, brie, gouda, and Sriracha mayo.

Ever had a craft soda? No? Then try the fizzy goodness on tap at **Fitz's** (6605 Delmar Blvd., 314/726-9555, https:// fitzsrootbeer.com, 11am-8pm daily, $8-15), where more than a dozen flavors range from sassafras root to vanilla bean. For food, go for a classic St. Louis dish— toasted ravioli or a slinger (fries topped with a burger, cheese, chili, and eggs).

For thankfully unpretentious doughnuts, there's **Donut Drive-In** (6525 Chippewa St., 314/645-7714, 5am-10pm Tues.-Thurs., 5am-midnight Fri.-Sat., 5am-2pm Sun.). Get one each of their selection of raised, old-fashioned, jelly, custard, blueberry cake, cinnamon twist, chocolate iced, and buttermilk-glazed doughnuts.

Nearby is ★ **Ted Drewes Frozen Custard** (6726 Chippewa, 314/481-2652, www.teddrewes.com, 11am-11pm daily, Why Donut Drive-In and Ted's are so close in proximity is anyone's guess— how are you supposed to choose between the two? Impossible! You'll just have to try both. Ted's custard is so thick and rich, they refer to it as "concrete" because it doesn't move. In fact, to prove its density, it's served upside down.

Accommodations

The ★ **Magnolia Hotel** (421 N. 8th St., 314/436-9000, www.magnoliahotels. com, $117-345) is an upscale, 18-story landmark west of Laclede's Landing. In the 1920s, the former Mayfair Hotel served movie stars like Cary Grant, John Barrymore, and Douglas Fairbanks, offered a barbershop and beauty parlor, and was the first hotel to put chocolates on guest pillows. (The idea is credited to Cary Grant, who allegedly tried to seduce a female guest by laying a trail of chocolates from the pillow in her bedroom to his penthouse suite.) After the Hollywood glitter faded on the Mayfair, it closed in 2013, reopening as the Magnolia Hotel after a multimillion-dollar renovation. Rooms today blend historic elegance with classically modern decor: tufted headboards, plush bedding, hues of gray and taupe. And yes—a chocolate is included with turndown service. The on-site **Robie's** restaurant pays homage to John Robie, the character played by Cary Grant in *To Catch a Thief.*

Smartly appointed and aptly named, the **St. Louis Union Station Hotel** (1820 Market St. 314/231-1234, http:// curiocollection3.hilton.com, $253-283, parking $35) is located in the middle of iconic Union Station. This pet-friendly hotel offers a refined stay with spacious guest rooms, a pool, fitness center, and several restaurants. Dine amid a bit of history at the on-site **Station Grille** (1820 Market St., 312/802-3460, 6am-10pm daily, $10-36), a former Harvey House, which was a restaurant designed to cater to late-1800s train passengers.

A few blocks east of music venue Blueberry Hill is another pet-friendly lodging option: the **Moonrise Hotel** (6177 Delmar Blvd., 314/721-1111, www. moonrisehotel.com, $130-250, parking $17). The super modern, eco-friendly boutique hotel has custom furnishings and luxury linens in guest rooms, free Wi-Fi, gourmet coffee, and a rooftop bar.

⚑ Back on 66

The 1926-1932 alignment in St. Louis followed Market Street and Manchester Road (SR-100), which traveled from downtown St. Louis to Gray Summit. This road trip takes the **post-1932 alignment** via SR-366 (Chippewa St.). To get to SR-366 from Market Street (near the Gateway Arch), turn left (south) on

Tucker Boulevard. As the road passes under I-44 and over I-55, Route 66 turns into SR-30 (Gravois Ave.). In less than 3 miles (4.8 km), turn right (west) on SR-366 (Chippewa St.). As you drive west on SR-366, Chippewa Street turns into Watson Road through the suburb of Marlborough.

Kirkwood

Sights
Ebsworth Park

There are five Frank Lloyd Wright buildings in Missouri, and one is the house in **Ebsworth Park** (120 N. Ballas Rd., 314/822-8359, www.ebsworthpark. org, tours by appointment, $10), a 1,900-square-foot (177-sq-m) home on 10.5 acres (4.2 hectares) in the Sugar Creek area of Kirkwood. Wright is known for complex geometric designs that extend beyond buildings to furnishings and fabrics, and his talents are on

Ted Drewes Frozen Custard, St. Louis

full display at Ebsworth Park. And everything is original. Tours are 75 minutes long and require reservations. Head north on Kirkwood Road and turn left (west) on West Adams Avenue, which turns into North Ballas Road.

★ Laumeier Sculpture Park

When you need to stretch your road-trip-weary legs, it's **Laumeier Sculpture Park** (12580 Rott Rd., 314/615-5278, www.laumeiersculpturepark.org, 8am-sunset daily, free) all the way. Founded in 1976, Laumeier is one of the largest sculpture parks in the country. In 1968, Matilda Laumeier dedicated 72 acres (29 hectares) to St. Louis County in memory of her husband, Henry. Now the park stretches across 105 acres (42 hectares), throughout which sit nearly 70 large-scale outdoor sculptures. These range from contemporary to abstract, from big to ginormous.

The best way to explore is via one of three walking trails. The paved **Central Pathway** spans a 0.6-mile (1-km) loop;

the 0.8-mile (1.3 km) **Art Hike Trail** follows the park's eastern wooded area; the 0.2-mile (0.3-km) **Western Woodland Trail** takes you by a popular sculpture hidden in the trees. To get to Laumeier from SR-366, turn left (south) onto South Geyer Road and then make another left (east) onto Rott Road. Follow signs for the parking lot.

National Museum of Transportation

The **National Museum of Transportation** (2933 Barrett Station Rd., 314/965-6212, https://tnmot.org, 9am-4pm Mon.-Sat., 11am-4pm Sun., $12) celebrates the thrill of travel. There are more than 200 items on display, as well as a comprehensive history of railroad travel. A car pavilion has a 1963 Chrysler Turbine and the Bobby Darin "Dream Car." There's also a C-47A military transport from World War II and a vintage steam roller.

The crown jewel is a facade from the beloved 1940s **Coral Court Motel**. When located on Watson Road, it was a large complex of 30 buildings. The honey-colored, glazed ceramic tiles and glass blocks curved into a sublime Streamline Moderne style that rivaled any motor court of its day.

The museum is 3.5 miles (5.6 km) north of Route 66. From SR-366, drive north on I-270 to Exit 8 (Dougherty Ferry Rd). Drive left (west) on Dougherty Ferry Road to Barrett Station Road. Turn left (south) on Barrett Station Road and follow the signs to the museum. The entrance is on the right (west) side of the road.

Food

★ **Spencer's Grill** (223 S. Kirkwood Rd., 314/821-2601, 6am-2pm daily, $6-12) is known for their pancakes, a thin yet crispy flapjack with a buttery edge that melts in your mouth. Get yours with fresh blueberries. This diner is small and popular—meaning, you'll likely have to wait for a seat—but it's well worth it.

St. Louis to Springfield

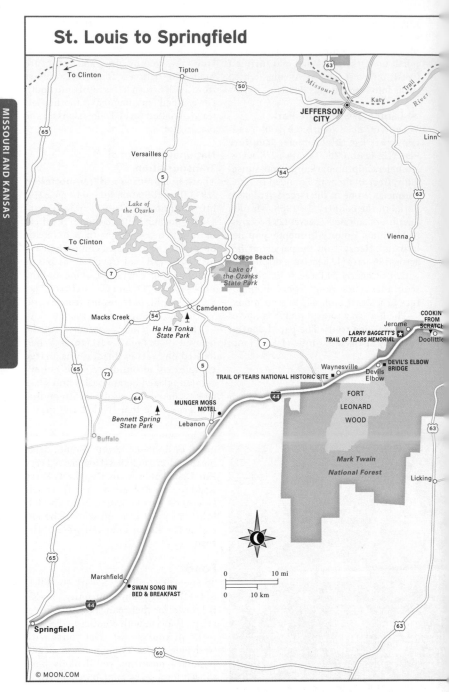

© MOON.COM

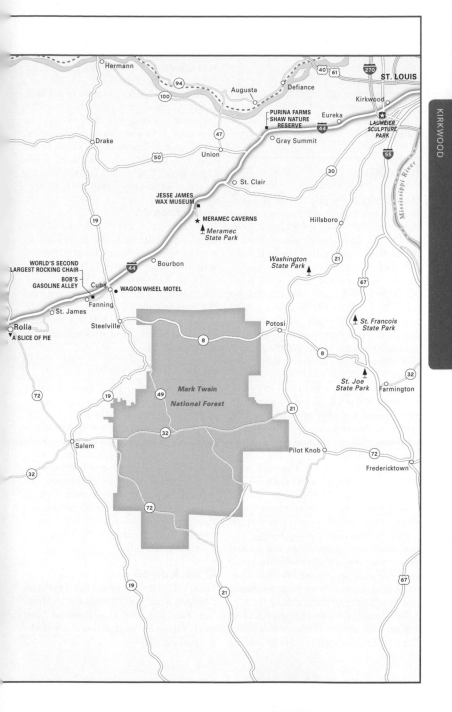

To get there from Watson Road (Route 66), drive 1.5 miles (2.4 km) north on Kirkwood Road.

⬙ Back on 66

Heading west on SR-366 (Watson Road), join I-44 west toward Tulsa to reach Times Beach, near Eureka, in about 10 miles (16.1 km).

Eureka

Near Eureka is the ghost town of Times Beach, once a hopping summer resort community. It all started when, in 1926, land lots in Times Beach were offered to the public—along with a 6-month subscription to the St. Louis newspaper—for $67.50. The community grew. After the Depression hit, the town fell on hard times. By the 1970s, the residents couldn't afford to pave the roads, so they hired a company to come in and "oil" them to control the dust. Little did they know, this oil contained dioxin, a dangerous toxin. By 1985, the entire town of more than 2,000 people was forced to evacuate. In 1997, the federal government purchased and decontaminated the site, removing 265,000 tons (240,404 metric tons) of earth—the cleanup took $33 million and 15 years.

Today, you'll find the 419-acre (170-hectare) **Route 66 State Park** (97 N. Outer Rd., 636/938-7198, http://mostateparks.com, 7am-sunset daily, free), where locals and visitors enjoy the picnic areas and hiking, biking, and horseback riding trails. At the former Bridgehead Inn, a 1935 roadhouse, you'll find the **visitors center** (9am-4:30pm daily, Mar.-Nov.), which displays photos and local Route 66 memorabilia.

To access the visitors center, take Exit 266 off I-44, east of the Meramec River. Turn right (northeast) and then a quick left (west) on North Outer Road. The visitors center is about 0.3 mile (0.5 km) on the left (south) side of the road. Once a bridge crossed the Meramec River, but it is now condemned.

To visit the park, you have to get back onto I-44, head west, cross the river, and get off at the next exit. Follow signs to hop onto I-44 east, then immediately take Exit 265. The road will curve to the right and turn left (southeast) onto South Outer Road. The park is less than a mile on the right (south) side of the highway.

⬙ Back on 66

Drive west on South Outer Road and turn south on Williams Road. In one block, turn right on Augustine Road. Drive 0.5 mile (0.8 km), curving left, then turn right on Autumn Way. Turn right on SR-109, drive under I-44, and then take the first left on 5th Street. Follow 5th Street, which parallels I-44, for less than 3 miles (4.8 km), then turn left (south) on Allenton Road.

Food

'Cue fans should try **Super Smokers** (601 Stockell Dr., 636/938-9742, www.supersmokers.com, 11am-7pm daily, $8-20). This award-winning Missouri-barbecue joint uses an applewood rotisserie to smoke fall-off-the-bone baby back ribs, pulled pork, and beef brisket.

To get here from 5th Street near Exit 264 on I-44, take a right and then an immediate left (west) on 5th Street, and then turn right (north) on North Central Avenue. The restaurant is one block up on the right (east) side.

⬙ Back on 66

From I-44 Exit 261, take a left (south) on Allenton Road and drive under the freeway. Turn right (west) on Business Loop 44 (E. Osage St.) as it passes through the town of Pacific.

Pacific

Here is where Route 66 becomes that picturesque two-lane highway dotted with old motor courts and retro signage that road-trippers crave. The town of Pacific started as a railroad and silica mining center—the fine silica sand in the nearby bluffs was used to make glassware. When Route 66 was realigned through Pacific in 1932, it exposed the mining tunnels, and on the western edge of town, you can see the **sandstone bluffs** and **silica mine caves** along the highway.

✪ Back on 66
Continue heading west on Osage Street. After about 3.5 miles (5.6 km), the road joins the pre-1930s alignment in the town of Gray Summit.

Gray Summit

Sights
Purina Farms
Who knew that the makers of Purina pet food have an animal wonderland open to the public? Stop by **Purina Farms** (500 William Danforth Way, 314/982-3232, www.purinafarms.com, 9:30am-3:30pm Wed.-Sun., free) to experience an animal petting area, wagon rides, animal barn, hayloft, and educational exhibits. The dog arena hosts daily canine performances (10:30am and 1:30pm) by pups who have been adopted from shelters around the country. There are also cow-milking demonstrations (10am and 1pm) at the visitors center. And, of course, pets are welcome.

To get there from Osage Street (Business I-44), turn right (north) on SR-100 (Historic Route 66), go under the freeway, and after about 0.5 mile (0.8 km), turn left (northwest) on Highway MM. The Purina Farms entrance is on the left-hand side of the road.

Shaw Nature Reserve
The natural beauty of the Ozark landscape is best viewed in person, not from the distant remove of a car window. At the **Shaw Nature Reserve** (307 Pinetum Loop Rd., 314/577-9555, www.missouribotanicalgarden.org, 8am-sunset daily, $5), you'll see how the glacial erosion of the Ozark Plateau formed this area on the Meramec River. Explore more than 2,500 acres (1,012 hectares) of tallgrass prairie, woodlands, and wetlands along easy walking paths and challenging self-guided trails. The 17 miles (27.3 km) of hiking trails include the 0.75-mile (1.2-km) **Brush Creek Trail,** which passes 18 types of native trees as it meanders through the **Whitmire Wildflower Garden.** The **Wetland Trail** is a 1-mile (1.6-km) loop with a 300-foot (91-m) boardwalk and observation area.

The **visitors center** (8am-sunset daily) has trail guides and maps, plus information on year-round programs and events.

✪ Back on 66
Leaving Gray Summit, Route 66 (SR-100) dips south and heads west, but to stay on Route 66 continue straight (near I-44 Exit 251). After about 5 miles (8 km), you will cross U.S. 50, and the road joins North Outer Road and parallels I-44. Follow North Outer Road for 5 miles (8 km) to Exit 242; turn left (southeast) to cross under I-44 and turn right (west) onto South Outer Road (North Commercial Ave.) and continue on to St. Clair.

Jesse James and Meramec Caverns

Who knows if it's true or not, but rumors are strong that outlaw baddie Jesse James and his brother (and crime partner) Frank used **Meramec Caverns** as a hideout. Supposedly, the caves were also their means of escape, as the two men discovered that the underground river led them to a secret exit that went undetected by local law enforcement.

Near the caverns, at Exit 230 off I-44, you'll find the **Jesse James Wax Museum** (573/927-5233, www.jessejameswaxmuseum.com, 9am-6pm daily June-Aug., 9am-5pm Sat.-Sun. Apr.-May and Sept.-Oct., $10 adults, $5 children). This oh-so-Route-66 attraction (in that it's odd, kitschy, and based on fictitious lore) posits that James never died in a shoot-out in 1882. Instead, the museum's curators display "evidence" that he survived until 1951, living under a different name, and that when a 100-year-old man turned up in Stanton in 1948, it was, in fact, Jesse James.

St. Clair

In 1849, St. Clair was established as a railroad community, then developed into a zinc and lead mining area.

Food

Dine with the St. Clair locals at **Lewis Café** (145 S. Main St., 636/629-9975, https://lewiscafe.net, 6am-2pm daily, $4-28). The patty melts are excellent (they raise their own beef), and the hand-battered onion rings are crunchy. Save room for a slice of strawberry-rhubarb or apple crumb pie. To get to Lewis Café from Route 66, turn left onto SR-47 (south); it's about 0.5 mile (0.8 km) down the road.

❖ Back on 66

Heading west on Commercial Avenue, turn right (northwest) on SR-30, then take I-44 west. You could drive on the North Service Road, but you'll have to cross over the highway a few times. Also, there's not much to see. To save time, take I-44 for 10 miles (16.1 km) and then Exit 230 into Stanton.

Stanton

Sights
Meramec Caverns

Under the verdant rolling hills of Missouri lie networks of deep caverns. In fact, Missouri is home to more than 6,000 surveyed caves. One of the most popular is **Meramec Caverns** (Exit 230 off I-44, 573/468-2283, www.americascave.com, 9am-7pm daily May-June, 8:30am-7:30pm daily July-early Sept., 9am-6pm daily Sept. and Apr., 9am-5pm daily Oct. and Mar., 9am-4pm daily Nov.-Feb.; $23 adults, $12 children), a 4.6-mile (7.4-km) system of caverns. Discovered in 1720 and developed during the Civil War (when the natural saltpeter was mined for manufacturing gunpowder), the limestone cave drips with stalactites and stalagmites in astonishing natural colors. Though not huge in terms of size, the caves are some of the most sculpturally delicate in the country. Guided 80-minute tours depart every 20-30 minutes and are conducted on well-lit walkways. The interior temperature of Meramec Caverns is a constant chilly 58°F (14°C); bring a jacket and wear sturdy shoes.

From I-44, take Exit 230 in Stanton. Turn left (south) and pass over the railroad tracks. The caverns are about 3 miles (4.8 km) away.

❖ Back on 66

If you're tired of the interstate, you can get off at Exit 230 (Meramec Caverns) and take the pre-1930s alignment instead. After exiting I-44, turn left (east) on Highway W and take your first right (south) onto North Service Road. After about 2.5 miles (4 km), the road becomes East Springfield Road and enters the town of **Sullivan.**

Sullivan was once a mining town rich in lead, iron, zinc, and copper, and it's also the place where media magnate William Randolph Hearst's father was born. Today, there's not much to see here, so keep following Springfield Road until it rejoins the service road alongside I-44. After about 5 miles (8 km), you'll reach the town of Bourbon.

Bourbon

Bourbon got its name from railroad workers who drank whiskey from the general store in the 1850s. They called it the "Bourbon Store," and the name stuck. As you head into town, pull over for a quick selfie at the Bourbon **water tower.**

✪ Back on 66
Old Highway 66 dips south and heads west, rejoining the service road for another 10 miles (16.1 km) into the town of Cuba.

Cuba

Interestingly, there are eight towns in the United States named Cuba. Cuba, Missouri, got its name in sympathy for Cubans fighting for their independence from Spain.

From the late 1800s to the 1930s, Cuba was the state's largest producer and distributor of apples; its barrel-making industry earned it the nickname "The Land of the Big Red Apple." The iron-ore and farming industries employed most residents until the railroad arrived in 1860, after which Cuba became a major shipping center. Shoe manufacturers also set up shop and became a vital part of the economy until they went out of business. By the 1980s, many citizens were living below the poverty level.

Sights
Murals
A **mural project** (http://cubamomurals. com) that attracted Route 66 travelers helped revitalize the town of Cuba. Fourteen outdoor murals line the Mother Road and depict the town's heritage, including Route 66 businesses, a series of Civil War murals, paintings of Amelia Earhart when she landed outside Cuba in 1928, and Bette Davis's 1948 visit to the town in her Packard station wagon. Pick up a brochure and mural map at the **Cuba Visitor Center** (71 Hwy. P, 573/885-2531, www. visitcubamo.com, 8am-5pm Mon.-Fri., 9am-4pm Sat.), located off Exit 208 of I-44.

Carr Service Station
Carr Service Station (102 W. Washington St.) is a 1932 Phillips 66 gas station located at the southwest corner of Route 66 and Highway 19. Over time it has been a Pontiac dealership, a Mobil service station, and a doughnut shop. A fast-food franchise once wanted to buy it, but the owners, Lynn and Bill Wallis, knew it would be torn down so they refused to sell. Thankfully, in 2005 it was restored with a cost-share grant from the National Park Service Route 66 Corridor Preservation Program.

Hayes Family Shoe Store
Shoes—and more importantly, shoe manufacturers—played a big part in Cuba's economic past. The **Hayes Family Shoe Store** (103 S. Smith St., 573/885-7312, 8:30am-5:30pm Mon.-Fri., 8:30am-1pm Sat., free) showcases two shoes that belonged to Robert Wadlow (1918-1940), the tallest man in the world at 8 feet, 11.1 inches (2.7 m) tall. Wadlow traveled the country as a spokesman for a shoe company, and sometimes he would leave a shoe as a novelty item. Two of his shoes, one size 37 and the other size 35, are on display. The store also sells fitness shoes and hunting and work boots, and has an on-site repair shop. The store is located about five blocks west of the Carr Service station.

Women of the Mother Road

The story of Route 66 isn't complete without the illustrious women who've contributed greatly to the road's growth, success, and preservation. Here, celebrate the Missourian and Kansan women who made a profound impact on the Mother Road.

Red's Giant Hamburg

♦ **Julia Chaney:** During World War II, Julia Chaney met and married her husband, Sheldon, who was known as "Red." The two left New York City and settled in Springfield, Missouri. Julia and Red opened a restaurant—**Red's Giant Hamburg** (page 112). Nope, that's not a typo; they left off the "er" because it made the sign too tall. Julia co-owned and operated Red's Giant Hamburg for nearly 40 years.

♦ **Allyne Earls:** A successful businesswoman and the beating heart of Cuba, Missouri, Allyne Earls was the longtime owner of the popular Midway Café (now demolished). She leased the restaurant in the 1930s, eventually buying and expanding it during the '40s. Allyne kept the Midway Café open 24 hours a day, 7 days a week—it's been stated that at one time, the Midway served nearly 600 meals a day to customers. Allyne once said, "When I sold the Midway in 1972, the new owners asked for the keys. What keys? In those 38 years, we never locked the doors."

♦ **Elaine Graham Estes:** At her family's motel and restaurant—the Graham Rib Station—in 1930s and '40s Springfield, Missouri, Elaine Estes worked the cash register, helped with deliveries, and joined her father on quality checks at the meatpacking house. Springfield was then a segregated city, but Elaine's family advertised their business in the *Negro Motorist Green Book,* an annual travel guide that helped Black people safely travel during the Jim Crow era. Elaine says her family's business was to serve, not separate.

♦ **Alberta Ellis:** In Springfield in the early 1950s, Alberta Northcutt Ellis opened a three-story Victorian house as a hotel to provide Black people travelling Route 66 a safe place to stay. Like the Estes family's Graham Rib Station, Alberta's Hotel was listed in the *Negro Motorist Green Book.* The hotel became a welcoming hotspot for Black travelers, including famous athletes and entertainers of the 1950s and 1960s.

♦ **Melba Rigg:** As one of the four women in Galena, Kansas, who saw potential in an abandoned Kan-O-Tex station (now **Cars on the Route,** page 123), Melba Rigg has vision. She also has tenacity. Along with her sister and two other business partners, Melba purchased the station in 2006 and turned it into a must-see destination on Route 66. In the early years, Melba would stand in the street and wave cars down, beckoning them to stop in. But once people crossed the threshold, they hung around, as Melba regaled them with stories of the Mother Road. Melba quickly earned the affectionate nickname "Melba the Mouth" for how fast she could talk. Even though Melba is now retired, the station remains a popular tourist attraction today, drawing visitors from all over.

Food

Have breakfast at **Shelly's Route 66 Café** (402 S. Lawrence St., 573/885-6000, 6am-3pm Tues.-Sat., 7am-2pm Sun., $6-12), located an easy-to-walk 0.25 mile (0.4 km) from the Wagon Wheel Motel. Order homemade biscuits and gravy with crispy hash browns and chat it up with the friendly serving staff. The coffee is hot and good.

At **Missouri Hick Bar-B-Que** (913 E. Washington St., 573/885-6791, http://missourihick.com, 11am-9pm daily, $8-18), owner Dennis Meiser smokes his meat for 12 hours and serves it with five sauces, from smoky to spicy to sweet. Service is attentive and upbeat, and the Memphis-style brisket is not to be missed. Meiser, a master woodworker, built the restaurant's tables, chairs, and even the cedar stairs that lead to an airy balcony.

Accommodations

Lodgings on Route 66 don't get much cuter—or more historic—than the ★ **Wagon Wheel Motel** (901 E. Washington St., 573/885-3411, www.wagonwheel66cuba.com, $62-124). This classic 1930s motor court features cabins built from Ozark stone, which gives a delightful English cottage feel to the entire motel. The arched doorways and pitched roofs only add to the charming vibe. A careful restoration of the motel retained original glass knobs, wood floors, windows, and doors, while also adding modern comforts such as pillow-top mattresses, flat-screen televisions, and free Wi-Fi. Bring your four-legged traveler and enjoy the shaded outdoor patios and decks.

Top to bottom: mural in Missouri from Cuba's mural project; Missouri Hick Bar-B-Que, Cuba; World's Second Largest Rocking Chair, Fanning

🔱 Back on 66

Head west on Route 66 as it dips south, and after a few miles you'll approach two roadside attractions near Fanning.

Fanning

Sights
World's Second Largest Rocking Chair

It might be silly to say "keep an eye out for" the **World's Second Largest Rocking Chair** (5957 Hwy. ZZ, 573/885-1474, 9am-5pm Mon.-Fri., free)—at 42 feet (13 m) tall and 20 feet (6 m) wide, you won't miss it. The gigantic rocker is made of steel pipe, and although it once held the crown of "World's Largest Rocking Chair," in 2015 a 56.5-foot-tall (17.2-m) chair was erected in Illinois. Hence, the Fanning chair's current title. The chair used to rock, but the owner worried that this monstrosity could tip over and kill someone, so now the rockers are welded at the base.

Bob's Gasoline Alley

Why are vintage road signs and advertisements so fascinating? They're retro, they're colorful, and they're a glimpse into bygone eras of road travel. From Route 66, take Beamer Lane north to **Bob's Gasoline Alley** (822 Beamer Ln., 573/885-3637), where you can wander outside among a diverse collection of old advertising signs, highway relics, old gas pumps, die-cast cars, and peddle cars. Much of the rare signage is in perfect condition, and the early 20th-century gas pumps make this a must-stop for car enthusiasts. To get there from Route 66, take a right (north) on Beamer Lane.

🔱 Back on 66

Bob's Gasoline Alley is less than a mile south of I-44; or stay on Highway ZZ (U.S. 66) as it heads west and then north alongside I-44. In about 2 miles (3.2 km), you'll be in the unincorporated town of Rosati.

Rosati

Soon after Rosati was originally settled in 1845, Italian immigrants began to arrive. They built two stores, a saloon, canning plant, church, school, and post office. They also planted Concord grapes to make wine.

🔱 Back on 66

The Mother Road heads west on Highway KK for 6 miles (9.7 km) to the town of St. James. Continue west and turn right (north) onto SR-68. As you cross I-44, take your first left (west) after the freeway entrance onto Parker Lane. Make another quick left onto Historic U.S. 66 (North Outer Rd.).

St. James to Rolla

The Murdon Concrete Company has a huge neon sign of a **dripping faucet** (14241 Old Hwy. 66) on the right (north) side of Route 66, 3 miles (4.8 km) west of St. James. In 3 more miles (4.8 km), turn left (south) to join I-44 west, or stop at the Mule Trading Post before you get on I-44.

In addition to Route 66 maps and books, the newly renovated **Mule Trading Post** (11160 Dillon Outer Rd., Rolla, 573/364-4711, 9am-6pm daily) sells knives, moccasins, pottery, local honey, jams, and jellies, as well as T-shirts, hats, pictures, jewelry, and sculptures. The trading post is on the frontage road south of I-44 near Exit 189.

◆ Back on 66

Head west on I-44 and take Exit 186 into the college town of Rolla.

Rolla

When Route 66 came through Rolla, it was one of the most difficult gravel roads to travel on in Missouri, especially if the weather was bad. The area from Rolla to Lebanon was the last piece of paved road on Route 66 in Missouri; when it was complete, there was a 2-mile (3.2-km) parade with more than 8,000 people out to celebrate.

To follow Route 66 through Rolla, turn left (south) on U.S. 63 (Business I-44) and make another left (south) on North Pine Street. In less than 1 mile (1.6 km), turn right (west) on West 6th Street.

A stubby replica of **Stonehenge** (1400 N. Bishop Ave., 24 hours daily, free) was built in 1984 at the University of Missouri to showcase the stone-carving capabilities of the High Pressure Waterjet Lab at the university's Explosives Research

Bob's Gasoline Alley

Center. This smaller reconstruction was made using 160 tons (145 metric tons) of granite cut by Waterjet equipment. "Stonehenge" is on the east side of Route 66 (Business I-44, N. Bishop Ave.). Turn left at the University of Missouri campus and immediately bear right into the parking lot. Follow the path to Stonehenge.

Food

★ **A Slice of Pie** (634 S. Bishop Ave., 573/364-6203, www.asliceofpie.com, 10am-8pm daily, $6-32) treats the taste buds to more than 25 different award-winning pies, from fruit and cream to silks and custards. But wait, there's more! Cakes, cheesecakes, quiches, pot pies, and homemade breads round out the offerings.

For home-cooked meals, darts, and karaoke, **Rob and Kricket's Tater Patch** (103 Bridge School Rd., 573/368-3111, www.rollataterpatch.com, 11am-10pm Mon.-Tues., 11am-1:30am Wed.-Fri., 8am-1:30am Sat., 8am-10pm Sun., $8-20) brings the fun. An entire page of the menu is devoted to taters: taters loaded with broccoli and melted cheese, cheeseburger taters with ground beef, cheddar, lettuce, tomato, and onion, and Tex-Mex taters with chili and cheese. Entertainment includes poker and pool tournaments, dart leagues, and DJs.

Rob and Kricket's Tater Patch is on Route 66 (Business I-44) on the way out of town, less than 1 mile (1.6 km) west of SR-72. Take a left (south) at County Road 251 (Bridge School Rd.). The restaurant is on the left (east) side of the highway.

⬤ Back on 66

Leaving Rolla, West 6th Street turns into Kings Highway, which then turns into Business I-44. Head west on Business I-44 to get on I-44 west and drive 5 miles (8 km) to Doolittle.

Doolittle

Doolittle sits on the edge of the Fort Leonard Wood military base, which was a training center for infantry troops in 1941. Italian and German POWs were also interned here. The Mother Road experienced a boom during this time because it was the preferred route to shuttle military supplies and transport personnel.

Six cabins, two outhouses, and a broken neon sign are decaying in the forest on a dead-end strip of old Route 66. What remains of **John's Modern Cabins,** once a juke joint in the 1930s called Bill and Bess' Place, has had several owners over the years. During the 1950s-1960s, the owners were John and Lillian Dausch. When improvements were made to Route 66, the Dausches moved their business north of the original location, signing the place John's Modern Cabins. They built three more cabins, a laundry room, and a snack bar where they sold beer on Sunday (which was against the law at the time). The property changed hands two more times, but since the 1970s the cabins have been slowly disintegrating into the earth. Some have fully collapsed, while others retain a few furnishings.

While not for the faint of heart (read: snakes and rusty nails), it's a creepy and cool adventure for those who are up for it. The cabins sit parallel to I-44, southeast of Exit 176. From I-44, take Exit 176, turn left (southeast) onto County Road 7300. In 1.3 miles (2.1 km), turn right (south) onto County Road 7304; the cabins are about 500 feet (152 m) up on the left (east).

Food

★ **Cookin' From Scratch** (90 Truman St., Newburg, 573/762-3111, www. cookinfromscratch.biz, 10:30am-8pm Wed.-Thurs., 7am-8pm Fri.-Sat., 7am-3pm Sun., $8-10) is a family-friendly, down-home diner that serves some good pan-fried chicken—so good because they "do it the hard way." The chicken is partially submerged in oil in a cast-iron skillet and takes 45 minutes to cook. From the hand-patted burgers to the slow-roasted prime rib with homemade mashed potatoes, dishes take time to arrive at your table, but once you bite into the quality food, you'll realize it was well worth the wait.

✪ Back on 66

Follow I-44 west for 6.5 miles (10.5 km) to Exit 172. Turn right (east) onto Highway D (Powellville Outer Rd.) and drive 0.3 mile (0.5 km) east. To continue on Route 66, turn left (west).

Jerome

Sights
★ Larry Baggett's Trail of Tears Memorial

Segments of Route 66 from Rolla to Springfield follow the 1838 Trail of Tears. This was the northern route onto which U.S. troops forced tens of thousands of Cherokee, Creek, Seminole, Chickasaw, and Choctaw to walk 1,200 miles (1,931 km) across the country to reservations in Oklahoma. At least 4,000 died from disease, exposure, and starvation.

Years ago, a past resident of Jerome, Missouri—Larry Baggett—was repeatedly awakened by a loud knocking at his door. But when he answered it, no one was there. Later, an old Cherokee man visited him, saying that Baggett's house was built on the Trail of Tears and that many Cherokee had camped near his home. The knocking was from the spirits who were still trying to walk the trail, but Baggett's house was blocking their path.

Baggett decided to build a set of stairs on a stone wall on his property to help the spirits cross. Suddenly, the knocking ceased. Soon after, he built a stone archway, as well as concrete and stone

sculptures on his property, to memorialize American Indians and honor their struggle.

Baggett died in 2003, and the **Trail of Tears Memorial** (21250 Hwy. D, dawn to dusk, free) is in the process of being restored. Stop by to see this folk-art tribute, including a concrete statue of Baggett out front waving to passersby. There are also statues of an American Indian holding the tail of a buffalo and an elephant emerging from the ground with four trunks.

From I-44, take Exit 172 and turn right (east) at the T intersection onto Highway D toward Jerome. Baggett's memorial is a few hundred yards up on the left.

✪ Back on 66

Drive west on Powellville Outer Road. In less than 4 miles (6.4 km), turn left (southeast) on Highway J. Cross I-44 and then make an immediate right (southwest) on Highway Z (Route 66). In about 2 miles (3.2 km), the road passes through Hooker Cut, once rumored to be the deepest road cut in the United States. To reach Devil's Elbow, turn left on Teardrop Road to take the pre-1930s alignment to Devil's Elbow.

Devil's Elbow

Devil's Elbow got its name from a severe bend in the Big Piney River. A group of lumberjacks lamented over a large boulder and the logjams that occurred in the sharpest part of the bend. It was such a nightmare that they figured it must have been put there by the devil.

The 1923 **Devil's Elbow Bridge** is a steel pony truss bridge that crosses the Big Piney River. The bridge spans 588 feet (179 m) and is almost 20 feet (6 m) wide. This is one of only two bridges in the state with a curved shape. In 1942, the new four-lane road from Fort Leonard Wood accommodated military transport and bypassed the 1926 alignment.

The Devil's Elbow Bridge sat neglected and rusted until it was rehabilitated in 2013. Thankfully, it still retains its historic charm and is one of the best examples of what Route 66 must have looked like in its early days. The bridge is less than 1 mile (1.6 km) after turning left on Teardrop Road.

◈ Back on 66

From Devil's Elbow, follow Teardrop Road west for 1.5 miles (2.4 km) and turn left (southwest) onto Highway Z (Route 66). Highway Z continues west for 6 miles (9.7 km) to St. Robert. Keep heading west as Business I-44 joins Route 66. In another 3 miles (4.8 km), you'll reach the town of Waynesville.

Waynesville

Named after a revolutionary war hero (General "Mad Anthony" Wayne), Waynesville is the oldest town in Pulaski County. During the 1830s, the town operated as a trading post for settlers and trappers while American Indians came through on the infamous Trail of Tears. It was also a major training center for troops during the Civil War.

As you enter Waynesville, about 1 mile (1.6 km) after crossing I-44, keep an eye out for a rock emerging from the hill in the shape of a frog. In 1996, tattoo artist Phil Nelson carved **Frog Rock** out of granite, and it has become a roadside mascot of Route 66 in Missouri.

Sights

Waynesville is a pedestrian-friendly town. To explore it further, take the **Waynesville Downtown Walking Tour** (24 hours, free). The tour starts at Hayes Creamee (Route 66 and Highway 17), continues to the Old Stagecoach Stop (105 N. Lynn St.), which operated as a hospital during the Civil War, and then heads to Laughlin Park and the Trail of Tears encampment. Stops along the way include

Devil's Elbow Bridge, Missouri

a Korean Baptist Church, an early-20th-century courthouse, and a bank. A scenic spot overlooking the valley commemorates the place where Union troops built a fort to protect telegraph wires during the Civil War.

Trail of Tears National Historic Site

During the Trail of Tears, more than 350 Cherokee people camped in the fields along Roubidoux Creek, which is now the **Trail of Tears National Historic Site** (Laughlin Park, Rte. 66 and Olive St., 573/774-6171, www.waynesvillemo. org, dawn-dusk daily, free). A Cherokee named B. B. Canon kept a journal and wrote the following while in Waynesville:

> Dec. 8, 1837- Buried Nancy Bigbears Grand Child, marched at 9 o'c. A.M., halted at Piney a small river, ½ past 3 o'c. P.M., rained all day, encamped and issued corn only, no fodder to be had, 11 miles to day. December 9, 1837 - Marched at 9 o'c. A.M., Mayfields wagon broke down at

about a mile, left him to get it mended and overtake, halted at Waynesville, Mo. 4o'c. P.M., encamped and issued corn & fodder, beef & corn meal, weather extremely cold, 12½ miles to day.

The park has a 1-mile (1.6-km) path that runs along the Roubidoux River. Restrooms, a playground, and a boardwalk that passes over an underwater cave are also on-site.

Food

Hoppers Pub (318 Rte. 66, 573/774-0135, www.hopperspub.com, 4pm-9pm Mon.-Fri., 11:30am-10pm Sat.-Sun., $6-13) is a pub and restaurant in downtown Waynesville that serves burgers, salads, sandwiches, and wraps. In honor of their Mother Road location, they have 66 beers on tap.

A great place for a cold brew is **Piney River Taproom** (326 Rte. 66, 573/433-2739, https://pineyriverbrewing.com, 11am-9pm Mon.-Wed., 11am-10pm Thurs.-Sat., noon-9pm Sun., $6-10). Family-owned, kid-friendly, and pet-welcoming, this taproom offers samples, pints, and growlers of their beer, plus homemade pizzas. You can also bring your own food to enjoy.

◈ Back on 66

Leaving Waynesville, head west on Highway 17 (Route 66) and 5 miles continue to Buckhorn. This area was originally called Pleasant Grove, but was later renamed after the Buckhorn Tavern, a popular stop for stagecoaches on the Wire Road.

Route 66 parallels I-44. At Exit 153, turn left (south) on SR-17 (Red Oak Rd.) and cross the highway to turn right (west) onto Route 66. In about 1.3 miles (2.1 km), turn right (west) onto Highway P and continue to the town of Laquey (pronounced "Lakeway"). Drive 1 mile (1.6 km) and turn left (southwest) onto Highway AA. After about 1.5 miles (2.4 km), turn right (west) on Highway AB.

The road winds to the western edge of Fort Leonard Wood and then runs alongside I-44 to become Heartwood Road for about 6 miles (9.7 km). The road turns becomes Glacier Point Road; at Highway F (near I-44 Exit 135), it turns into Pecos Drive. Head west on Pecos to the laid-back town of Lebanon in 6 miles (9.7 km).

Lebanon

In the late 1880s, Lebanon was a small yet thriving community with an opera house and the historic Gasconade Hotel (destroyed by fire), which accommodated up to 500 guests. But the town really became popular after Route 66 came through in 1926, because Lebanon was one of the largest towns between Rolla and Springfield.

Sights
Route 66 Museum and Research Center

In 1927, a tent camp called Camp Joy opened, charging $0.50 a night. The "Dream Village" had an impressive fountain that tourists lined up for blocks to see. The fountain is no longer around, but a diorama of the "Dream Village" can be seen at the **Route 66 Museum and Research Center** (915 S. Jefferson Ave., 417/532-2148, 8am-8pm Mon.-Thurs., 8am-5pm Fri.-Sat., free), located inside the Lebanon-Laclede County Library. The museum is home to a life-size re-creation of a Phillips 66 gas station with Texaco gas pumps, a tourist cabin, a diner, a collection of salt and pepper shakers from Route 66 restaurants, and blueprints of the construction of Route 66.

To get to the museum from Business I-44, turn left (southeast) onto South Jefferson Avenue. It's located about 0.3 mile (0.5 km) ahead, on the right (southwest) side of the street.

Food and Accommodations
Dowd's Catfish and BBQ (1760 W. Elm St., 417/532-1777, https://dowdscatfishandbbq.com, 11am-8:30pm Sun.-Thurs., 11am-9pm Fri.-Sat., $9-23) serves Mississippi Delta-style fried catfish and shrimp with Southern favorites like okra, corn bread, and peach cobbler.

Now is your chance to stay at one of the most iconic roadside motels on Route 66. The ★ **Munger Moss Motel** (1336 East Rte. 66, 417/532-3111, http://mungermoss.com, $40-65) was originally a sandwich shop on the Big Piney River at Devil's Elbow. After Route 66 was rerouted in 1942, the new owners moved the venue to Lebanon. It reopened in 1946 with 14 cabins and garages next to the rooms. Twenty-six more units were added in 1961. Bob and Ramona Lehman have run the motel for more than 40 years, offering the utmost in hospitality and cleanliness. Today, the well-maintained rooms have a vintage aesthetic with

1970s lampshades, wood-paneled walls, and (depending on which room you get) lots of Route 66 memorabilia. A tribute room to the Coral Court Motel is dressed up in pink. Thanks to the Neon Heritage Preservation Committee, the Route 66 Association of Missouri, and the National Park Service Route 66 Corridor Preservation Program, Munger Moss was able to restore one of the most impressive neon signs on Route 66. As Route 66 enters on Lebanon Pecos Drive, it turns into East Seminole Avenue as the road veers away from I-44. Munger Moss is about 0.5 mile (0.8 km) on the left (southeast) side of the road.

◈ Back on 66

Head southwest on East Seminole Avenue until it dead-ends into Business I-44 (Route 66). Turn right (west) and follow Business I-44 for less than a mile as it curves to the left (southwest) on Business I-44.

◈ Side Trip: Camdenton

Ha Ha Tonka State Park (1491 State Rte. D, Camdenton, 573/346-2986, www.mostateparks.com, 7am-sunset daily Apr.-Oct., 8am-sunset daily Nov.-Mar, free), with breathtaking scenery and the stone ruins of an early-20th-century castle overlooking the Lake of the Ozarks, is worth a trip. Robert Snyder, a prominent businessman, built this estate at the turn of the 20th century. He spared no expense, using only high-quality materials and the best artisans he could find. After Snyder died suddenly in 1906, his brothers finished the job, adding an 80-foot (24-m) water tower, greenhouses, and horse stables. When the family fell on hard times, the property became a hotel, then burned down in 1942.

Start your day at the **visitors center,** which offers self-guided trail brochures

Munger Moss Motel in Lebanon, Missouri

Road Trip Playlist

Curating your road trip playlist is almost as important as mapping the route or booking hotels. Route 66 takes you through vastly different regions of the country, each with its own distinct culture and, yes, music. These song suggestions are tailored to the state you're in.

♦ **"Johnny B. Goode" by Chuck Berry:** St. Louis-born rock and roll pioneer Chuck Berry used to play regularly at Blueberry Hill, a popular stop on Route 66, so it goes without saying that he makes this list. The fun energy and upbeat tempo of "Johnny B. Goode" are just what you need on a long road trip.

♦ **"Moonshiner" by Uncle Tupelo:** This 1990s-era St. Louis band is not only directly related to Wilco (after the band's breakup, most of the members re-formed as Wilco) but is also credited with establishing the genre of alternative country. "Moonshiner" is a sad little ditty that's ideal for a slow drive through the Missouri plains.

♦ **"St. Louis Blues" by W. C. Handy:** The deftly held trumpet notes of this 1920s tune will whisk you back in time. Composer and musician Handy is known as the "Father of the Blues" and is considered one of the most influential songwriters in the country.

and a large relief map of the park carved in stone. The **Castle Trail** is a moderate trek with scenic overlooks of the Lake of the Ozarks and access to the castle ruins. The trailhead is located at two parking areas along Castle Ruins Road; plan 45 minutes for the round-trip trek. Other trails lead to a natural bridge and the Whispering Dell sink basin.

Ha Ha Tonka State Park is near Camdenton, about 25 miles (40 km) north of Lebanon. From Lebanon, turn right (northwest) onto South Jefferson Avenue (SR-32). In 1.5 miles (2.4 km), turn right (northeast) on East 7th Street (SR-5). Follow SR-5 for 19 miles (31 km), turn left (west) on Highway 5-133. After 1.6 miles, turn left (west) to stay on Highway 5-133. Drive 2 miles (3.2 km) and then turn right on Highway D; the park is about 1,200 feet (366 m) ahead on the left.

⊕ Back on 66

Leave Lebanon via Business I-44. Turn right (west) onto Highway W (Route 66) and head south alongside I-44 for about 9 miles (14.5 km). Cross I-44 via Highway C (I-44 Exit 118) in Phillipsburg. Take your first right (west) on Highway CC (Newport Ave.). In 2.6 miles (4.2 km), stay on Newport Avenue, which will veer away from I-44 and head south through the small community of Conway.

Marshfield

As you follow Highway CC into the town of Marshfield, Route 66 turns into West Hubble Drive. Don't let Marshfield's sleepy main street fool you; this small town was the birthplace of Dr. Edwin Hubble, the astronomer who inspired the famous telescope that dramatically changed our fundamental understanding of the universe. See a 1,200-pound, one-quarter-scale **replica of the Hubble Telescope** displayed at the county courthouse (100 S. Clay St., 417/859-3925).

To reach the Hubble Telescope replica from Route 66 (W. Hubble Dr.) turn left (south) on North Marshall Street and then right (west) on West Jefferson Street and then the next left (south) onto Clay Street. The telescope is on the left side of the street.

Accommodations

The ★ **Swan Song Inn Bed & Breakfast** (583 Spring Valley Loop, 417/859-0140, www.swansonginn.com, $129-200) sits a bit off the beaten path, but its picturesque 10-acre lakeside estate offers a peaceful respite from life on the road. Gourmet breakfast greets you each morning and all rooms come with free Wi-Fi and streaming televisions.

From Route 66 (W. Hubble Dr.), turn right (south) on North Elm Street. At Golf Course Road, turn left (east) and take it to Settlers Trail Road. Turn left (north). Drive north to Phoenix Road, then make a right (east) and a quick left (north) to follow Phoenix Road to Spring Valley Loop. Turn right (east) on Spring Valley Loop and drive to the hotel.

◈ Back on 66

Depart Marshfield heading west on West Jackson Street (SR-38) to merge left (southwest) onto West Washington Street. Route 66 (Hwy. 00) travels south alongside I-44 for about 12 miles (19.3 km) into the town of Strafford.

If you skip downtown Marshfield, just continue on West Hubble Drive (Route 66), which turns into West Washington Street (Hwy. 00).

Strafford

Route 66 passed through Strafford, with improvements completed in 1930. SR-14 (which was Pine Street) was Strafford's original commerce center, but with Route 66 just one block away on Main Street, some businesses installed two doors— one on Pine Street, and the other facing Route 66. In 1952, Route 66 was rerouted through the north side of Strafford to divert traffic from downtown, which caused the decline of the town. Historians believe that the **Trail of Tears** also passed through downtown Strafford.

◈ Back on 66

Continue west on Route 66 (Hwy. 00) for 8 miles (12.9 km) into Springfield. You're about to enter the birthplace of the Mother Road.

Springfield

John Woodruff, an entrepreneur from Springfield, teamed up with Cyrus Avery, the chairman of the Oklahoma Department of Highways—also known as the "Father of Route 66"—and together they mapped out the Mother Road's diagonal course. In 1925, Congress enacted a law for national highway construction that made Route 66 possible. On April 30, 1926, a telegram was sent from Springfield's Colonial Hotel (unfortunately, demolished in 1997) proposing that the road from Chicago to Los Angeles be named Route 66. And this is why Springfield is recognized as the birthplace of Route 66.

◈ Route 66 Through Springfield
1926-1935 Alignment

Route 66 had several realignments through Springfield. The 1926-1935 alignment enters Springfield from the northeast to run west along East Kearny Street (SR-744) and cross SR-13. Route 66 continues south along Glenstone and National Avenues to St. Louis Street, which leads downtown to the Public Square.

If you don't have much time but still want to take the 1926-1935 alignment through Springfield, cross I-65 and follow Kearny Street (SR-744) west for 2 miles (3.2 km) and turn left (south) onto Glenstone Avenue (Business I-44). Drive 2 miles (3.2 km) south and turn right (west) on St. Louis Street, which turns into Park Central as it wraps around

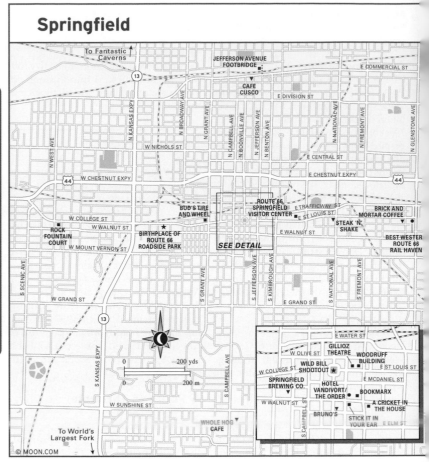

Springfield

To Fantastic Caverns

JEFFERSON AVENUE FOOTBRIDGE

CAFE CUSCO

E COMMERCIAL ST
E DIVISION ST
E CENTRAL ST
E CHESTNUT EXPY

W CHESTNUT EXPY

ROUTE 66 SPRINGFIELD VISITOR CENTER

BUD'S TIRE AND WHEEL

BRICK AND MORTAR COFFEE

E TRAFFICWAY ST
E ST LOUIS ST

STEAK 'N' SHAKE

W COLLEGE ST
ROCK FOUNTAIN COURT
W WALNUT ST

E WALNUT ST

BEST WESTER ROUTE 66 RAIL HAVEN

BIRTHPLACE OF ROUTE 66 ROADSIDE PARK
W MOUNT VERNON ST

SEE DETAIL

W GRAND ST
E GRAND ST

0   200 yds
0   200 m

To World's Largest Fork

WHOLE HOG CAFE

W SUNSHINE ST

© MOON.COM

E WATER ST
GILLIOZ THEATRE
W OLIVE ST
WOODRUFF BUILDING
W COLLEGE ST
WILD BILL SHOOTOUT
E ST LOUIS ST
SPRINGFIELD BREWING CO.
HOTEL VANDIVORT/ THE ORDER
E MCDANIEL ST
BOOKMARX
W WALNUT ST
A CRICKET IN THE HOUSE
BRUNO'S
STICK IT IN YOUR EAR
E ELM ST

the square. West of the square, the road turns into College Street and joins the West Chestnut Expressway (Business I-44). Turn left (west) and keep straight as you leave Springfield. After crossing under I-44, the Chestnut Expressway turns into SR-266.

Post-1936 Alignment
The post-1936 alignment bypasses downtown Springfield via SR-744 west and U.S. 160 south. Unless you have a serious time constraint, stop here: Springfield is too rich in history and too essential to the foundation of Route 66 to be missed.

Sights
Route 66 Springfield Visitor Center
Say hello to the nice and helpful people at the **Route 66 Springfield Visitor Center** (815 E. St. Louis St., 417/881-5300, www. springfieldmo.org, 8am-5pm Mon.-Fri.). They have a wealth of information about the Mother Road, along with souvenirs, brochures, maps of Springfield, and a replica of a 1950s diner, a gas station fuel pump, and a phone booth.

Downtown Springfield is just a few blocks west of the visitors center. There's plenty of free parking, so it's easy to stroll the city, peruse the boutiques, and explore sidewalk cafés, art galleries, restaurants, and theaters.

Woodruff Building

Take a look at the large building on the northwest corner of Park Central East and Jefferson Avenue—this is the **Woodruff Building**, owned by and named after John Woodruff, the man who established the U.S. Highway 66 Association in 1926. The area's first skyscraper, the building received much acclaim when it opened in 1911. Even though it was only 10 stories tall, its height was a big deal at the time, when most buildings stood only four or five stories. Route 66 ran in front of the building, which housed offices, a pool hall, barbershop, and two elevators. The building sold for $700,000 a few years after Route 66 began, and an additional 23,000 square feet (2,137 sq m) were added in 1959.

Gillioz Theatre

Next door to the Woodruff is the **Gillioz Theatre** (325 Park Central East, 417/863-9491, www.gillioz.org), which opened in 1926. An enthusiastic audience cherished the lavish Spanish Colonial Revival architecture, with its terrazzo flooring and a grand Wurlitzer. Maurice Earnest Gillioz financed and built the theater, using primarily steel and concrete; wood was only used for the doors and handrails. An arched stained-glass window, a recessed oculus, decorative urns, plaster friezes, and winged cherubs added to the opulence. As suburban strip malls became more popular in the 1970s, fewer people spent time downtown, and the Gillioz fell into disrepair before closing in 1980. Eventually, a group of locals formed the Springfield Landmarks Preservation Trust and rehabilitated and restored the Gillioz, which reopened in 2006. Today,

Top to bottom: Route 66 Springfield Visitor Center; Gillioz Theatre; Birthplace of Route 66 Roadside Park

the venue hosts acts ranging from indie rock bands to spoken-word artists.

Wild Bill Shootout

It was at 100 Park Central Square that Wild Bill Hickok shot Davis Tutt in the heart over a gambling debt in 1865—the nation's first recorded quick-draw shoot-out. Tutt drew first, but Wild Bill had a better aim; this incident solidified Hickok's reputation as a serious gunfighter. A small plaque in front of the **Park Central Library** (128 Park Central Sq.) commemorates the duel, and there are street markers where Hickok and Tutt stood.

Bud's Tire and Wheel

Bud's Tire and Wheel (701 W. College St., 417/865-5896) opened in 1958 and was one of the first businesses in the area to supply custom wheels. Today, the shop distributes racing tires and high-performance vehicle parts. Colorful murals (north of Route 66 past Grant Ave.) on the side of the building are inspired by the Mother Road and make for a great photo-op.

Birthplace of Route 66 Roadside Park

A drive-through burger joint may not seem revolutionary now, but in 1947 it was. That was the year that Red Chaney thought it would be easier for customers to drive up and order his $0.25 hamburgers through a kitchen window rather than relying on a waitress or carhop. It was this novel idea that made **Red's Giant Hamburg** possibly the first drive-through eatery in America.

The unusual business name was the result of Red's famous sign. The sign was shaped like a cross—the word "Giant" was horizontal, while the word "Hamburger" was vertical (the two words shared an "A" in the middle). However, Chaney had to saw the "er" off of "Hamburger" once he realized the sign was too tall and would touch the power lines. The unusual spelling didn't affect the business. In fact, it made it almost a religious rite of passage for locals and Route 66 travelers.

Unfortunately, Red's closed in 1984. The building was removed, but a replica of the "Giant Hamburg" sign lives on at the **Birthplace of Route 66 Roadside Park** (1200 Block W. College St., 24 hours daily, free).

Rock Fountain Court

Heading west from Park Central Square, keep an eye out on the south (left) side of Route 66 for **Rock Fountain Court** (2400 W. College St.). Though it's no longer operating as a motel, it remains a great example of a well-preserved, 1940s-era motor court. Named for a fountain that once stood in the center, the motor court has nine freestanding cabins arranged in a semicircle, each cabin with a signature Ozark stone facade.

Jefferson Avenue Footbridge

Historians believe the 1902 **Jefferson Avenue Footbridge** (201 E. Commercial, 417/864-7015, 24 hours daily, free) is the first bridge of its kind to be built in the area, and it's one of the longest railroad pedestrian bridges in the country. The completely restored, three-span steel cantilever truss footbridge is 562 feet (171 m) long with 13 train tracks below and 50-foot (15-m) towers. At night, it's beautifully lit and a worthy photo op.

World's Largest Fork

Almost 5 miles (8 km) south of downtown is the **World's Largest Fork** (at the back of the Noble & Associates building, 2215 W. Chesterfield Blvd., 24 hours daily, free). The fork stands 35 feet (11 m) tall and weighs 11 tons (10 metric tons), sticking out of a patch of greenery that makes it look as though it's plunging into a plate of food. Colorado also claims to have the world's largest fork, but regardless, this one is big—take a pic. From downtown, take SR-13 south toward U.S. 60.

Local Eats

To non-Missourians, it's custard. To locals, it's called a **concrete.** Concretes are ice-cream custard treats so thick and dense they have the consistency of concrete. At Ted Drewes in St. Louis, this point is proven by serving them upside down.

Pork steaks, cut from a pig's shoulder, cooked low and slow, and smothered in barbecue sauce, are the perfect backyard barbecue dish.

It seems like every place on Earth has its own take on pizza. Missouri is no different. A traditional **St. Louis-style pizza** boasts an ultra-thin, crispy crust—almost like a cracker—and comes topped with a white processed cheese called Provel (a blend of provolone, swiss, and white cheddar) and a red sauce with a hint of sweetness.

In Springfield, David Leong's **cashew chicken** took the city by storm in the 1970s. It all started when, in 1940, Leong came to the United States from China. He opened Leong's Tea House in 1963 in Springfield, and once he saw how much the locals worshipped fried chicken, he modified the already-established cashew chicken dish from a stir-fried version to a deep-fried remix. He slathered it with oyster sauce and sprinkled it with green onions. It was a hit. You can now find Springfield-style cashew chicken throughout the city.

Fantastic Caverns

What exactly is a drive-through cave? Find out at **Fantastic Caverns** (4872 N. Farm Rd. 125, 417/833-2010, www.fantasticcaverns.com, 8am-dusk daily, $28). Located about 5 miles (8 km) north of Springfield, this attraction offers a jeep-drawn tram that takes visitors on a ride into the cave. You'll see fluted draped stalactites, stalagmites, and flowstones, all deliciously creepy in their otherworldliness. The truly creepy thing about this cave, though, is that the Ku Klux Klan once conducted secret meetings and cross burnings in the cave in the 1920s.

From College Street (Route 66), turn right (north) on SR-13. Turn left (west) on West Farm Road 94 and follow it as it turns south and then west to North Farm Road 125. Turn right (north) and drive about a mile (1.6 km).

Shopping

Take in the carefully curated collection of used books at **BookMarx** (325 E. Walnut St., 417/501-1062, noon-7pm Mon., 10:30am-7pm Tues.-Sat.). Uncover obscure copies of classic literature or snag some reading material for the road, from contemporary fiction and children's books to history titles. The staff is knowledgeable and friendly, but they won't disturb you if you want to sit and read. Be sure to say hello to the bookstore cats.

Continue your analog shopping trip with a visit to **Stick It in Your Ear** (300 E. Walnut St., 417/864-0500, noon-7pm Sun., 10am-10pm Mon.-Thurs., 10am-11pm Fri.-Sat.), a great little record shop in the classic tradition of old-school music stores. This place has one of the best selections of music you'll ever find, from rare and underground stuff to out-of-print albums. They also stock posters, concert T-shirts, and other music paraphernalia.

A Cricket in the House (412 E. Walnut St., 417/865-2758, 11am-6pm Wed.-Fri., 11am-5pm Sat.-Sun.) specializes in a rotating selection of mid-century (and sometimes new) home furnishings, decor, and collectibles. Fun take-home gifts include new and vintage jewelry and clothes, plus cute cards and handmade items.

Food

If you're lucky enough to land a retro room at the Best Western Route 66 Rail Haven, stop at the nearby **Brick and Mortar Coffee** (1666 E. St. Louis St., 417/812-6539, www.brickandmortarcoffee.com, 9am-3pm Mon.-Sat.). They roast and brew artisan, handcrafted, organic coffee from Costa Rica, Kenya, Indonesia, and Papua New Guinea.

Those with a bigger appetite can opt for breakfast at **George's Family Restaurant** (339 S. Glenstone Ave., 417/831-6777, 6am-8pm daily, $6-15), a Springfield favorite. Portions are big, the staff is friendly, and the biscuits and gravy are perfection.

Indulge in dinner and cocktails in a classy setting at ★ **The Order** (305 E. Walnut St., 417/851-5299, 5pm-10pm Mon.-Sat., 5pm-9pm Sun., $12-45), housed in a 1906 former Masonic temple. The Order takes sourcing seriously, and the menu highlights farms, creameries, and ranches that supply ingredients to the restaurant. You'll taste the bounty of the Ozarks in dishes like pork loin with broccolini or gnocchi with local veggies and whipped ricotta.

You haven't been to the Midwest until you've been to Steak 'n Shake. The "steak" in the name refers to the fast-food restaurant's famous steakburgers, a belly-filling burger that fans crave. The 1962 **Steak 'n Shake** (1158 E. St. Louis St., 417/866-6109, www.steaknshake.com, 10am-8pm daily, $5-8) shows off many of the restaurant's original features, such as the porcelain exterior, neon signs, counter, floor tiles, and curb service. The first Route 66 Steak 'n Shake, which opened in 1934, was in Normal, Illinois. But now that it's gone, this location—also listed on the National Register of Historic Places—has gained a following among Route 66-ers. It's west of Glenstone Avenue.

If you want something upscale for lunch, **Bruno's** (416 South St., 417/866-0007, www.dineatbrunos.com, 11am-10pm Mon.-Thurs., 11am-11pm Fri.-Sat., $12-27) serves up Sicilian food in a glorious 1905 building. Choose from beef, chicken, or seafood dishes, a dozen or so pastas, brick-oven pizzas, and desserts baked fresh daily.

Toast with a craft brew at the **Springfield Brewing Company** (305 S. Market Ave., 417/832-8277, www.springfieldbrewingco.com, 11am-8pm Mon.-Fri., 9am-8pm Sat.-Sun, $9-25). The brewery offers a rotating tap selection that ranges from a citrusy saison to a creamy milk stout. The pub menu includes lots of shareable plates, like hummus and nachos, as well as soups, pizzas, sandwiches, tacos, and a weekend brunch.

The **Whole Hog Café** (2731 N. Glenstone Ave., 417/720-4759, http://wholehogsgf.com, 11am-9pm Mon.-Sat. 11am-8pm Sun., $5-16) is one of Springfield's best barbecue spots. The Hog has won awards for their dry-rubbed meat, and they have several house-made sauces. Come hungry, as plates such as pulled pork, burnt ends, and beef brisket come with two hearty sides and a dinner roll.

A warm, colorful interior and Peruvian-inspired food please diners at **Cafe Cusco** (234 E. Commercial St., 417/868-8088, www.cafecusco.com, 11am-9pm daily, $8-21), a couple blocks west of the Jefferson Avenue Footbridge. When Chef Joe Gidman hiked the Inca Trails, he loved the food so much he decided to bring it back to the Midwest. Dishes are savory and sweet, tangy and flavorful, with honey, beet sauce, pineapple, and black olives. There are also many gluten-free, vegetarian, and vegan options.

Accommodations

The **Best Western Route 66 Rail Haven** (203 S. Glenstone Ave., 417/866-1963, www.bwrailhaven.com, $80-180) has been serving Route 66 roadsters since 1938. This pet-friendly hotel offers complimentary breakfast, free Wi-Fi, and a fun 1950s-style lobby. To get there from Kearny Street, head south (left) on North Glenstone Avenue. After 2 miles (3.2 km), turn right (west) on East St. Louis Street (Route 66).

The uber chic **Hotel Vandivort** (305 E. Walnut St., 417/832-1515, www.

Springfield to Galena

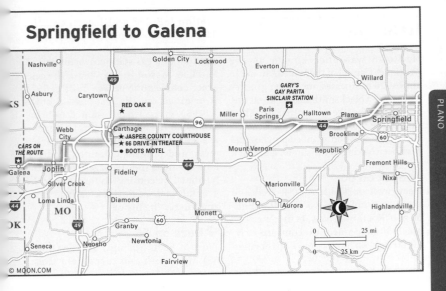

hotelvandivort.com, $182-399) is a boutique hotel in downtown Springfield. Built inside a former Masonic temple, the hotel's contemporary design incorporates many of the original architectural elements. Guest rooms have spacious bathrooms with luxury bath products; optional mobile device control of audio, video, and lighting; and lounge seating. Some rooms even have wet bars.

✦ Back on 66

Depart Springfield via West College Street, heading west. When West College Street joins West Chestnut Expressway (Business I-44), turn left (west) and keep straight until you cross I-44 as the road turns into SR-266.

Plano

About 10 miles (16.1 km) west of Springfield is Plano, a ghost town that was bypassed by Route 66. Look for the abandoned limestone ruin of a **1902 store,** so old that trees grow inside it. This was once a general store that hosted town meetings, dances, and church services.

The ruin is about 1 mile (1.6 km) past Farm Road 55; look for the building at the corner of South Farm Road 45, on the right (north) side of Route 66.

✦ Back on 66

Continue west on SR-266 for 4 miles (6.4 km) to Halltown.

Halltown

Halltown was once known as the "Antiques Capital of the World," home to almost 20 businesses, including grocery stores and a blacksmith shop and garage. Today, it looks like a forgotten stretch of the Mother Road, with old, weathered buildings and wood-planked porches that have been baking in the sun for a century.

◆ Back on 66

Head west on Route 66 (SR-266) and avoid signs to SR-96, a post-1940s alignment of Route 66. You want to stay on the pre-1930s alignment, so continue driving straight on SR-266 into Paris Springs.

Paris Springs

Three miles (4.8 km) west of Halltown, you'll see ★ **Gary's Gay Parita Sinclair Station** (SR-266 and Lawrence 1210, 417/459-0798, https://garysgayparita.com, 8am-6:30pm daily, free), a re-creation of a gas station owned by Fred and Gay Mason in the 1930s. The separate cobblestone garage built in 1926 is original, but the rest burned down in 1955. Gary Turner wanted to bring it back to life and built this homage to roadside travel. Gary has since passed away, and now his daughter, Barbara, and her husband, George, operate the business, welcoming visitors to tour the grounds and sharing fascinating stories and interesting history.

◆ Back on 66

West of Paris Springs, SR-266 (Route 66) dips south and turns right (west) onto South SR-96 (a post-1940s alignment). The next 30 miles (48 km) include a string of sleepy towns with farmhouses dotting the edge of the Ozark Plateau.

Gary's Gay Parita Sinclair Station

Red Oak II

Lowell Davis was so obsessed with the past that he re-created his hometown and moved it 25 miles (40 km) to this spot near Carthage, Missouri. Davis left the "real" Red Oak in Illinois, but when he returned, he found it had become a ghost town. He was heartbroken. So, in 1987, he moved the buildings from Illinois to Missouri to rebuild his hometown, calling it **Red Oak II** (County Loop 122, Kafir Rd., 417/237-0808, www. redoakiimissouri.com, 24 hours daily, free). What remains today is an odd and fascinating staged simulation of a specific time and place, complete with a blacksmith shop, church, general store, Phillips 66 station, feed house, homes, schoolhouse, jail, diner, and a fake cemetery.

The house where Davis lives was the former childhood home of the infamous female outlaw Belle Starr (1848-1889), also known as the "Bandit Queen of the Ozarks." Starr was an expert rider and gunslinger, credited with crimes she probably never committed, but she lived and died like an outlaw.

From Route 66, turn right (north) onto County Road 120. Drive about a mile (1.6 km) to Kafir Road and turn left (west). The entrance is about 1,100 feet (335 m) on the south side.

◈ Back on 66

Heading west, Route 66 (SR-96) dips south and joins East Central Avenue into Carthage.

Carthage

Carthage was established in 1842. About 20 years later, most of the city was burned to the ground by Confederate guerillas during the Civil War. By 1900, there were more than 100 local businesses. When Route 66 came through, the Chamber of Commerce promoted Carthage as "The Open Gate to the Ozarks."

Walking through the town today—with its elegant downtown square and impressive castle-inspired courthouse—there's no hint of its turbulent past.

Sights
Civil War Museum
The notorious 19th-century "Bandit Queen" Belle Starr grew up in Carthage, and her father, Judge John Shirley, operated a hotel on the north side of the courthouse square. After losing everything in the fire, they moved to Texas. The **Civil War Museum** (205 S. Grant St., 417/237-7060, https://carthagemo.gov, 8:30am-5pm Tues.-Sat., 1pm-5pm Sun., donations accepted) exhibits a display on Belle Starr, a mural of the Battle of Carthage, and artifacts about the Civil War in the Ozarks.

Jasper County Courthouse
After the fire in 1861, Carthage was rebuilt in 1866. It claimed to have more

millionaires per capita than any other city in the United States due to its robust lead and zinc mines, marble quarries, and manufacturing businesses. Today, Carthage has four historic districts and more than 550 buildings listed on the National Register of Historic Places, including the 1894 **Jasper County Courthouse** (302 S. Main St., 417/358-0421, www.jaspercounty.org, 8:30am-4:30pm Mon.-Fri., free). Built from native Carthage stone, it's a stunning example of Romanesque Revival architecture with turrets, towers, and arches that lend a decidedly medieval-castle air to the building.

Powers Museum

The **Powers Museum** (1617 W. Oak St., 417/237-0456, www.powersmuseum.com, 10am-2pm Fri.-Sat., noon-4pm Sun., donations accepted) offers rotating exhibits featuring local history, with themes on the Civil War, Route 66, and Ozark culture. A gift shop and research library are also on-site.

66 Drive-In Theater

The **66 Drive-In Theater** (17321 Old 66 Blvd., 417/359-5959, www.66drivein.com, 7:30pm-close Thurs.-Sun. Apr.-Sept., $8) is one of the few drive-ins left on Route 66. It sits on a 9-acre (3.6-hectare) plot in a rural setting, with a 66-foot-high (20-m) screen and art deco ticket booth. The rounded neon sign illuminates the names of the films showing and is a prime photo op. This is big fun on a hot summer night. The drive-in is on the west side of town on the south (left) side of Route 66.

Food

Located in an old bank, **The Carthage Deli** (301 S. Main St., 417/358-8820, www.carthagedeli.com, 7am-7pm Mon.-Fri., 7am-4pm Sat., $4-7) shows off 1950s decor—including a pink Cadillac booth. Depending on where you sit in the

66 Drive-In Theater

Drive-Ins

The prosperous postwar years were a golden age for Route 66, and the Mother Road achieved a new level of popularity inspired by movies, music, and television. Cars were fawned over, and Americans hit the road in record numbers as World War II rations and travel restrictions were lifted. People loved their cars so much they didn't want to leave them—even to eat—thus carhop restaurants became all the rage. And if you're going to eat in your car, you may as well be entertained, too. Although drive-in movie theaters started in the 1930s, they took off in the 1950s as cars became the center of American culture. In 1941, there were 52 drive-in theaters. And by 1956? There were 4,500.

restaurant, you can also enjoy a view of the architecturally splashy courthouse. Perfect meal: French dip sandwich followed by a Turtle Sundae.

Two miles (3.2 km) south of The Carthage Deli is **Iggy's Diner** (2400 Grand Ave., 417/237-0212, https://iggysdiner. com, 8am-8pm Mon.-Sat., $7-13), an 80-seat prefab diner with a chrome Airstream look. You can't go wrong with a burger and crispy onion rings.

Accommodations

The coolest place to stay in Carthage is at the ★ **Boots Motel** (107 S. Garrison Ave., 417/310-2989, www.bootsmotel. homestead.com, $70-75). This Streamline Moderne classic was built in 1939 by Arthur Boots. The motel was designed with black glass, rounded corners, and a smooth stucco facade. With a radio in every room, tile showers, and a furnace with a private thermostat, it was very modern for its time. In 2001, the Boots Motel was threatened with demolition; it was to be replaced by a drugstore, but the deal fell through. New owners bought it in 2011, renovating it with grant money from the National Park Service Route 66 Corridor Preservation Program. This helped to replace the pitched roof with its original, Streamline flat roof. The motel's sign has also been restored, and rooms now feature hardwood floors, built-in vanities, and air-conditioning.

✦ Back on 66

Drive west on East Central Avenue (Route 66) through Carthage. Turn left (south) on Garrison Avenue (SR-571) and after two blocks turn right (west) on Oak Boulevard (Route 66). Follow Oak Boulevard to the right (northwest) and cross SR-171 (I-49). Take the next left (west) onto Old 66 Boulevard. Turn left (south) on North Pine Street and, after about a mile (1.6 km), turn right (west) on East Main Street. Webb City is less than 2 miles (3.2 km) away.

Neon Photo Ops

We live in a digital, high-definition age, which means we don't get to see classic signage illuminated by blinking, flickering neon bulbs anymore. Not so on Route 66. This road trip boasts some of the best retro neon signs, many of them more than half a century old. This list offers up photo-worthy signs—for motor courts, diners, gas stations, and more—that you'll want to make a part of your trip.

♦ **Wagon Wheel Motel,** Cuba (page 99)

♦ **Munger Moss Motel,** Lebanon (page 106)

♦ **Steak 'n Shake,** Springfield (page 114)

♦ **Wilder's Steakhouse,** Joplin (page 122)

Webb City

Webb City is a former mining town that once had one of the richest lead and zinc mines in the world.

The National Park Service has designated downtown Webb City a **Historic District.** There are 49 commercial buildings that date from 1883 and are built in the Italian Renaissance Revival, Romanesque, art deco, and Streamline Moderne styles. Several historic buildings can be seen in the 100 and 200 blocks of North Main Street near Route 66 (Broadway Street). A **mural** (Main and Broadway Sts.) highlighting Route 66 is located at the Bruner Pharmacy. One block west is a small **Route 66 Welcome Center** (Webb and Broadway Sts., 417/673-1154, www.webbcitychamber.com, 9am-4pm Mon.-Fri., free), located in a former gas station.

South of Route 66 at SR-171, **King Jack Park** (555 S. Main St., dawn to dusk daily, free) is home to a 10-foot-tall (3-m) statue of a kneeling miner sculpted by Jack Dawson. Dawson is also the artist of a statue of **praying hands** in the park.

Webb City celebrates Route 66 with a downtown **Route 66 Cruise Night** on the second Saturday of summer months (5pm-8pm Apr.-Sept.). Classic cars compete for trophies as patrons vote for their favorites.

◈ Back on 66

Follow Broadway Street west through Webb City. Turn left (south) on South Madison Street, and after 2.3 miles (3.7 km), turn right (west) on East Zora Street. In less than a mile, turn left (south) on North Florida Avenue. Drive 5 blocks and turn right (west) on Utica Street. Drive two more blocks to turn left (southwest) on Euclid Avenue. Euclid Avenue dead-ends into North St. Louis Avenue. Turn left (south) and, in less than a mile, turn right (west) on Langston Hughes Street. Turn left (south) on Main Street (SR-43) and enter the town of Joplin.

The Green Book in Missouri

Black travelers on Route 66 going through Missouri found plentiful options in the *Negro Motorist Green Book* for hotels, restaurants, barbershops, beauty salons, drugstores, and service stations in big-city St. Louis.

Smaller towns like Joplin and Carthage also had a handful of listings in the Green Book. Nearly all were private residences offering meals and accommodations. For example, in Carthage, the homes of **Alice Peal** (E. Third St.), **Albert Gibson** (Bois De Arc and Fifth St.), and **Melvina Webb** (S. Fulton St.) opened their doors to Black people for food and lodging. In Joplin, more proprietors like **Theo Siebert** (E. Furnace St.) and **Grace Davis** (Virginia Ave.) did the same, as did the **Williams Hotel** (308 Pennsylvania Ave.). Most of these locations have since been demolished.

Around the same time, there existed a Southwest Missouri pamphlet similar to the Green Book. The *Negro City and County Directory* listed businesses, churches, and private homes that welcomed Black people in Missouri towns like Springfield, Joplin, and Carthage. You can see a 1937 edition of the pamphlet on display at the **Joplin History & Mineral Museum** (504 S. Schifferdecker Ave., 417/623-1180, www.joplin-museum.org, 10am-4pm Tues.-Sat., $3).

Joplin

At the turn of the 20th century, Joplin was a boomtown filled with saloons, brothels, and gambling halls. At **City Hall** (602 S. Main St., 417/624-0820, Mon.-Fri. 8am-5pm, free), muralist Thomas Hart Benton's 6- by 14-foot (1.8- by 4.3-m) mural depicts Joplin's lawless past. The mural is on the right (west) side near East 6th Street.

Sights

Lawlessness continued in Joplin well after Route 66 came through town. In 1933, notorious outlaws **Bonnie Parker** and **Clyde Barrow** (aka Bonnie and Clyde) robbed several local businesses. A neighbor tipped off the cops, which led to a shootout at their apartment. Bonnie and Clyde killed two police officers before fleeing Joplin. They left behind a camera.

After the film in the camera was developed, authorities finally knew what the devious duo looked like. The **Joplin History & Mineral Museum** (504 S. Schifferdecker Ave., www. joplin-museum.org, 10am-4pm Tues.-Sat., $3) has some of the photos, along with the outlaws' clothing, jewelry, and other items left in their apartment. To reach the Joplin Museum Complex, drive west on Route 66 (7th St.) and turn right (north) on South Schifferdecker, then quickly turn left (west) into the park. The complex is on the right (east).

The **house** where the shootout took place is 2 miles (3.2 km) south of Route 66 on 34th Street, between Joplin Avenue and Oak Ridge Drive. It's a sand-colored, square building on the north side of 34th Street with two garage doors in front. Bonnie and Clyde lived upstairs. Today, it's a private residence.

While you're at the Joplin Museum Complex, stop into the **National Cookie Cutter Historical Museum** (504 S. Schifferdecker Ave., 417/623-1180, www. joplin-museum.org, 10am-4pm Tues.-Sat., $3), which displays archival cookie cutters. Ask for a free plastic cookie cutter to take home as a souvenir.

Food

Get made-to-order chicken-fried steak for lunch at **Granny Shaffer's Family Restaurant** (2728 N. Rangeline, 417/659-9393, www.grannyshaffers.com, 6am-8:30pm Mon.-Sat., 7am-3pm Sun., $5-12), or go for breakfast and enjoy corned beef hash. Everything is made and served with care; even the coffee is roasted daily in small batches for maximum freshness. Granny Shaffer's is on the newer alignment of Route 66 as you approach East 7th Street.

Wilder's Steakhouse (1216 S. Main St., 417/623-7230, www.wilderssteakhouse. com, 5pm-9:30pm Mon.-Thurs., 5pm-10pm Fri.-Sat., $18-54) offers hand-cut beef, premium seafood, and impeccable service. Order a classic martini at the art deco bar before you settle into a cozy booth for an indulgent steak dinner.

For casual fare, there's **Hackett Hot Wings** (520 S. Main St., 417/625-1333, www.hacketthotwings.com, 11am-9pm Mon.-Thurs., 11am-10pm Fri.-Sun., $10-20). This Memphis-style joint specializes in 13 original flavors of chicken wings. The dry rubs explode with flavor, and the sweet potato puffs help cool down the heat.

◆ Back on 66

As you leave Joplin via Route 66 (W. 7th Ave.) it's only 3 miles (4.8 km) to the Kansas border.

Kansas

Route 66 is a short jaunt through Kansas—you'll be in Oklahoma before you know it—but the 13-mile (20.9-km) journey is loaded with charm and history. Here, Route 66 oozes small-town good vibes. You'll drive over old roadbeds and across marshes. Make time to stop and chat with business owners and locals who've been here for decades.

Kansas was the only state along the Mother Road to be completely bypassed when I-44 replaced Route 66 in the early 1960s. During the heyday of Route 66, Kansas had one of the largest lead mines in the nation; as a result, its roads were finished to facilitate the mining industry. By 1929, Route 66 was paved using waste products from the nearby mines, making

Kansas the second state along the Mother Road to be completely paved.

◆ Route 66 Through Kansas

Leave Missouri on West 7th Street in Joplin and take the two-lane **pre-1940s alignment,** just west after Malang Road. As Route 66 curves south, turn right (northwest) on West Old 66 Boulevard. As you cross the state line in 0.5 mile (0.8 km), West Old 66 Boulevard will turn into Front Street and dip south into the sleepy mining town of Galena.

Galena

The discovery of lead sulfite in 1876 turned Galena into one of the oldest and most prosperous mining towns in Kansas. Within 30 days of finding the lead sulfite, 10,000 miners came to cash in on the boom, and by the turn of the 20th century, there were nearly 30,000 people living here. Galena—named after the ore mined here—was sophisticated for its time, with paved city streets, water, sewers, and electric streetcars that ran from Baxter Springs, Kansas, to Carthage, Missouri. The road that eventually became Route 66 was a critical pathway for the mining industry.

In 1935, a strike occurred at the Eagle Picher lead smelter plant, the leading processor of lead ore in the country. When the miners banded together to protest their working conditions, violence broke out right on Route 66. Hundreds of strikers threw rocks and threatened to shoot any scabs—or strikebreakers—who attempted to enter the plant. Traffic stopped, cars were overturned, and the National Guard had to be called in to help restore peace.

Today, Galena is more or less a collection of run-down historic buildings, a shadow of its former self. There is a charm to the abandoned feel, though, like ghostly memories of what once was. Galena served as the inspiration for the fictional town of Radiator Springs in the Pixar film *Cars*.

◈ Route 66 Through Galena

Route 66 enters Galena via East Front Street. Turn left (south) on Main Street and then right (west) on 7th Street.

Sights

The former site of the **Eagle Picher plant** is on the north side of the road as you enter Kansas. Once one of the largest smelters in the United States, it was in operation from 1878 to 2004. Here, workers processed lead, zinc, and cadmium ores to make zinc oxide, sulfuric acid, manganese dioxide, and other noxious materials. By the early 1970s, the mine was pretty much exhausted. Eagle Picher declared Chapter 11 bankruptcy in 2005 when a series of environmental investigations revealed toxic levels of lead, arsenic, mercury, and zinc in the surrounding soil, sediments, and surface water. The Environmental Protection Agency (EPA) stepped in, and decontamination efforts are under way.

In the late 1930s through the mid-1940s, Works Progress Administration (WPA) writers saw this area covered in man-made mountains of white chert (commonly known as "chat") residue from the mines. They called it a "cinder-covered wasteland." The area has also been called "Hell's half-acre." Today, the contaminated soil has been covered with native grasses. The plant is gone, and the only thing left is a single building at 1203 Clark Street, just north of the railroad tracks about 800 feet (244 m) after Front Street curves south.

As you head south on Main Street, there's a 1952 **Will Rogers Highway plaque** at Howard Litch Memorial Park on the corner of 5th Street.

The **Galena Mining Historical Museum** (319 W. 7th St., 620/783-2192, 10am-4pm Mon., Wed., Fri., free) is located in a railroad depot and offers a modest collection of mining artifacts, equipment, and a model of the Grand Central Mine. There is also a collection of Model Ts and Model As in the back garage.

★ Cars on the Route

Meet the 1951 International boom truck that inspired Tow Mater, the lovable character from Pixar's *Cars*. It sits in front of a historic service station named **Cars on the Route** (119 N. Main St., 620/783-1366, www.kansastravel.org, 10am-4pm Wed.-Sat., 1pm-3pm Sun., free) at the corner of Front and Main Streets. Originally operating as a Kan-O-Tex gasoline station, the building was restored by four Galena women—Betty Courtney, Judy Courtney, Melba Rigg, and Renee Charles—who dubbed it "Four Women on the Route." They operated it as a tourist attraction for years before selling it to the current owners.

In addition to the 1950s boom truck, a replica decorated to look exactly like Tow Mater—with eyes and buckteeth—is parked next to it. For trademark reasons, the replica is named Tow Tater. You'll also see the two red-and-yellow Kan-O-Tex gas pumps and other restored vehicles outside. Inside, Cars on the Route sells snacks and funky souvenirs. Even though the four women no longer own the service station, Melba Rigg can often be found on-site to greet visitors, tell stories, and warmly welcome everyone who stops by.

◈ Back on 66

Head west on East 7th Street for about 3 miles (4.8 km) to Riverton.

Riverton

There's not much in Riverton, but on the right (north) side of the road, stop at the delightful store nestled among the trees: **Nelson's Old Riverton Store** (7109 SR-66, 620/848-3330, www.eislerbros.com, 7.30am-8pm Mon.-Sat., noon-7pm Sun.). It's a small grocery and deli—definitely pick up sandwiches and maybe fresh fruit, veggies, or homemade pie—but it's also the headquarters of the Route 66 Association of Kansas. The store, in continuous operation since 1925, is older than Route 66 itself. If you see locals

sitting at a table out front watching the cars amble by, stop and say hello. These are some of the friendliest folks you'll ever meet.

◆ Back on 66
Follow the **pre-1930s alignment** from Riverton by heading west on Route 66 to SR-400. At the roundabout, continue straight to Beasley Road. In about 1 mile (1.6 km), Beasley Road (Route 66) will curve south; at the turn, take a quick right (northwest) to follow Southeast Beasley Road and then make your first left (southeast) onto Old 66 Highway. In about 900 feet (274 m), you'll cross the Brush Creek Bridge.

Brush Creek Bridge
This is the only remaining example of a "Marsh Arch" bridge on Route 66 in Kansas, named after its designer James Barney Marsh. His signature style featured two arched ribs on either side that look like the top of a wagon wheel. Two other Marsh Arch bridges that crossed Willow Creek and the Spring River on Route 66 were dismantled in the 1990s.

◆ Back on 66
Right after crossing the bridge, turn left (southeast) on Southeast Beasley Road, which dead-ends into 50th Street. Turn right (south), and the road becomes North Willow Avenue as it enters Baxter Springs.

Baxter Springs
Baxter Springs could have been another Dodge City. Named after resident cowboy John Baxter, who died in a gun battle in 1859, the town was known far and wide for its wild ways and population of drifters and gamblers. Today, however, Baxter Springs is a quiet town with old gas stations, historic buildings, and an important Civil War fort.

Top to bottom: Galena Mining Historical Museum; Cars on the Route in Galena; Four Women on the Route service station

Car Culture

The Great Depression heavily impacted the gas industry in Baxter Springs, and oil companies got creative when it came to rebuilding their brands. Many designed gas stations to resemble cottages. Picture this: pitched roofs, shutters on windows, and brick siding. The idea was to call to mind the comforts of home.

One example of this is the **Baxter Springs Independent Oil and Gas Service Station** (940 Military Ave., 620/856-2385, 10am-4pm Tues.-Sat., 1pm-4pm Sun., www.baxterspringsmuseum.org, free). When the station opened in 1930, it was one of the area's finest Tudor cottage-style stations. Less than a year after it opened, it merged with Phillips Petroleum Company, which owned the station until 1958. In 2003, the station was placed on the National Register of Historic Places, and with community support and a grant from the National Park Service Route 66 Corridor Preservation Program, the station has been restored to its 1940s glory. It now operates as the **Route 66 Visitor Center.**

Originally, the area belonged to the Cherokee and was popular for its healing mineral springs, used by the Osage in the 1800s. It was believed the springs could cure illness and rejuvenate the body. The town created a marketing campaign to promote the springs' miraculous healing properties, and people flocked to the area in droves. Many stayed at the Planters, a lavish hotel on the edge of the business district. Eventually renamed the Springs Hotel, it was destroyed by fire in 1913. The springs are also long gone (probably due to the mining industry), but they were located just south of what is now 7th Street, near the Baxter Springs Heritage Center.

◈ Route 66 Through Baxter Springs

Turn left (east) on West 3rd Street and then make a left on SR-69 (Rte. 66/Military Rd.).

Sights
Baxter Springs Heritage Center
Baxter Springs also saw one of the bloodiest battles in the Civil War. In 1863, Confederate guerrillas ambushed and brutally butchered nearly 100 unarmed Union soldiers in 15 minutes. The notorious William Clarke Quantrill led the massacre that targeted the Second Kansas Colored Infantry division, which had recruited free African Americans and formerly enslaved people who had fled to Kansas. Most of the dead are buried in the Baxter Springs cemetery, 2 miles (3.2 km) west of town. The Fort Blair site of the attack is on Route 66 at 6th Street.

The **Baxter Springs Heritage Center & Museum** (740 East Ave., 620/856-2385, www.baxterspringsmuseum.org, 10am-4:30pm Tues.-Sat., 1pm-4pm Sun., free) fills its 20,000 square feet (1,858 m) of space with exhibits featuring the key sites of the Civil War massacre. There are also exhibits on the Buffalo Soldiers, an African American regiment of the United States Army. You can also pick up self-guided driving maps.

To get there, head south on Route 66 (Military Ave.) and turn left (east) on 7th Street. The museum is one block ahead on the right (south) side.

Food
Weston's Café (1737 Military Ave., 620/856-4414, 6am-7pm Mon.-Thurs., 6am-2pm Fri.-Sun., $9-18) is a family-run, no-frills restaurant serving home-style meals and all-day breakfast. Can't beat that.

◈ Back on 66
Head south on Military Avenue. The Oklahoma border is less than 2 miles (3.2 km) away.

Oklahoma

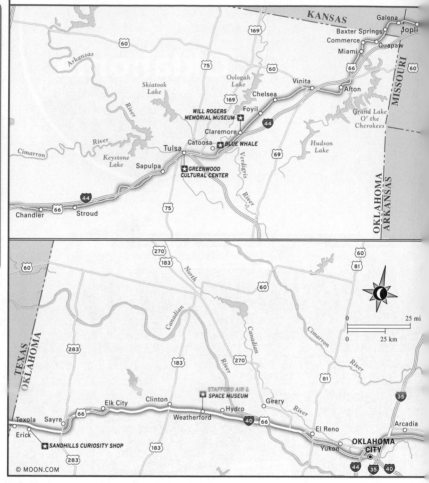

© MOON.COM

Did you know? The idea of the Mother Road was born right here in Oklahoma.

We can thank Tulsa native Cyrus Avery, often called the "Father of Route 66." He was a board member of the Federal Highway System who not only launched the U.S. 66 Highway Association but also coined Route 66 as the "Main Street of America." Many argue that, without Avery's influence, Route 66 might not have become the icon it is today.

Several significant migrations color the history of this state. From 1828 to 1887, the U.S. government began a series of forced migrations that took American Indians off their native land and onto the Trail of Tears to walk to the "Indian Territory"—what eventually became the

Highlights

★ **Will Rogers Memorial Museum, Claremore:** Nearly 20,000 square feet (1,858 sq m) of exhibits memorialize this Route 66 icon (page 142).

★ **Blue Whale, Catoosa:** This is one of the most iconic roadside attractions along Route 66 (page 143).

★ **Greenwood Cultural Center, Tulsa:** This museum and memorial examines one of the worst incidents of racially motivated violence in the 20th century (page 145).

★ **Stafford Air & Space Museum, Weatherford:** Explore the history of space travel at this fascinating museum (page 169).

★ **Sandhills Curiosity Shop, Erick:** You won't forget this strange and wonderful place filled with found treasures and song-and-dance performances by the owner (page 175).

Best Restaurants

★ **Waylan's Ku-Ku, Miami:** This is the last remnant of a 1960s restaurant chain that once had 200 locations throughout the Midwest (page 135).

★ **Clanton's Cafe, Vinita:** You'll find good food at the oldest continually owned family restaurant on Route 66, also featured on *Diners, Drive-Ins and Dives* (page 138).

★ **Molly's Landing, Catoosa:** Here you'll find excellent steak in a rustic log cabin (page 144).

★ **Burn Co. Barbeque, Tulsa:** Get in line early for the best 'cue in Tulsa (page 151).

★ **Rock Cafe, Stroud:** This café opened in 1939 and served as cinematic inspiration for Disney's Pixar animation team (page 155).

state of Oklahoma. These resulted in relocating 67 tribes to Oklahoma; today, about 39 tribes remain. In 1887, the federal government realized the Indian Territory could be farmed, and passed the Dawes Act, opening up nearly 2 million acres (809,370 hectares) of land to white settlement. The historic Land Runs attracted more than 50,000 land-hungry prospectors.

During the Great Depression, overuse of the soil coupled with severe drought eroded the earth. Strong winds blew away the topsoil, forming dark clouds of dust that made working, living, and even breathing nearly impossible. The resulting Dust Bowl saw more than 200,000 survivors use Route 66 to escape poverty. Author John Steinbeck labeled Route 66 as the "path of people in flight" as families headed west. In his song "Dust Bowl Disaster," folk musician Woody Guthrie wrote, "We loaded up our jalopies and piled our families in. We rattled down that highway to never come back again."

Planning Your Time

With selective planning, you can make it across Oklahoma in **two days.** From the state line, this road trip hits Miami, Afton, and Foyil before reaching Tulsa, where you'll spend the night. The next day travels 107 miles (172 km) to Oklahoma City, where you'll spend the second night. Then it's just 115 miles (185 km) to the Texas state line.

Driving Considerations

If you're pressed for time, I-44 from the eastern edge of the state to Oklahoma City will be the alternate option for speedy transport. West of Oklahoma City, I-40 becomes the freeway option.

Route 66 passes through several small towns with gas stations, so there's no need to worry about running out as long as you keep the tank at least half full. To save money, fill up in Tulsa and Oklahoma City, where gas is less expensive. Be forewarned that Oklahoma weather can be

Best Accommodations

★ **The Campbell Hotel, Tulsa:** Built in 1927, this boutique hotel boasts 26 designer-decorated rooms right on Route 66 (page 151).

★ **The Mayo Hotel, Tulsa:** Even if you don't spend the night at this posh hotel, stop in to take a peek at the opulent lobby (page 152).

★ **Skirvin Hilton Hotel, Oklahoma City:** A century of hosting presidents and movie stars gives this hotel a rich history (page 164).

★ **Ambassador Hotel, Oklahoma City:** This spot is a 1920s former medical building turned luxury hotel (page 164).

intense and unpredictable; in November, Oklahoma can be colder and windier than Chicago. Ice storms are also a concern in the winter.

Getting There

Starting Points
Car
The original alignment of Route 66 entered the state at the Kansas border and continued through Quapaw, Commerce, and Miami, a stretch of Route 66 primarily labeled U.S. 69. Once you hit Afton, the road becomes U.S. 60/69 into Vinita, then is mostly labeled Route 66 into Tulsa and Oklahoma City.

Interstate 44 (also called the Will Rogers Turnpike) enters Oklahoma near Afton and is the major east-west artery through the state; I-44 also runs alongside much of Route 66, so it's a good alternate road to use if you're short on time. I-40 enters the state on the east side south of Tulsa and runs directly to Oklahoma City. From Oklahoma City, I-35 is the major north-south route from Dallas, Texas, to Wichita, Kansas.

Car Rental
If you need a car, **Tulsa International Airport** (TUL, 7777 Airport Dr., 918/838-5000, www.tulsaairports.com) serves most national rental-car companies.

Enterprise (7777 E. Apache St., 833/361-2627, www.enterprise.com, 8am-10pm daily) has great customer service. **National Car Rental** (7777 E. Apache St., 855/237-4219, www.nationalcar.com, 8am-10pm daily) tends to be pricier, but they have a good fleet to choose from.

Air
The two major airports closest to Route 66 operate out of Tulsa and Oklahoma City. **Tulsa International Airport** (TUL, 7777 Airport Dr., 918/838-5000, www.tulsaairports.com) is small but offers services on major airlines including United, American, Delta, and Southwest. It's located 5 miles (8 km) northeast of downtown.

The **Will Rogers World Airport** (OKC, 7100 Terminal Dr., 405/316-3200, www.flyokc.com) in Oklahoma City is larger than Tulsa International, with nonstop flights to 28 cities. It's the only airport in the country to use the word "World" in its name and not reference the city in the designation; it also has an art space, outdoor garden, and bronze statue of its namesake. Alaska, Allegiant, American, Delta, Frontier, Southwest, and United fly out of here.

Train and Bus
The *Heartland Flyer* on **Amtrak** (100 South E. K. Gaylord Blvd., 800/872-7245, www.amtrak.com) makes daily trips to

Road Trip Playlist

Curating your road trip playlist is almost as important as mapping the route or booking hotels. Route 66 takes you through vastly different regions of the country, each with its own distinct culture and, yes, music. These song suggestions are tailored to the state you're in.

♦ **"King of the Road" by Roger Miller:** It may be a little *too* on the nose—a tune about road trips penned and performed by an Oklahoma singer-songwriter—but this 1960s classic just never gets old. The Proclaimers' 1988 version is fun, too.

♦ **"Truck Stop Gospel" by Parker Millsap:** You'll hear influences from blues, rock, and country in this wildly propulsive song from Okie boy Parker Millsap.

♦ **"I Ain't in Checotah Anymore" by Carrie Underwood:** Oklahoma native and country crooner Underwood sings about her hometown.

♦ **"This Land Is Your Land" by Woody Guthrie:** It's a tall order to pick just one Guthrie song to play on your drive through Oklahoma. This is one of his most popular tunes, but any of the troubadour's influential songs would provide an appropriate soundtrack.

Oklahoma City from Fort Worth, Texas. The station is in the historic Santa Fe Depot in the Bricktown District.

Greyhound Bus (www.greyhound.com) serves Oklahoma City (1948 E. Reno Ave., 405/606-4382, 9am-1am daily) and Tulsa (317 S. Detroit Ave., 918/584-4428, 1am-5am and 9am-8pm daily).

Quapaw

As you enter Oklahoma on U.S. 69, you'll pass through the quiet mining town of Quapaw. Since 1872, Quapaw has hosted an **Indian powwow,** one of the oldest in the United States at **Beaver Springs Park** (5681 S. 630 Rd.). If you happen to be visiting the first week of July, don't miss it. For more information, contact the Quapaw Tribe (918/542-1853, www.quapawtribe.com).

In downtown Quapaw, **murals** depicting the town's lead and zinc mining history adorn several buildings along Route 66. Look for these as you drive toward the town of Commerce.

✦ Back on 66

Follow Main Street through Quapaw. As the road curves west, it turns into East 50 Road (U.S. 69) and dips south into Commerce. Before you get to Commerce, you might want to take a quick side trip to the ghost town of Picher.

✦ Side Trip: Picher

In the 1920s, Picher was a leading producer of zinc and lead. Then, in 1967, the local Tar Creek turned red from contaminated water that was loaded with toxic heavy metals and had leached into the ground water. The chat piles (mountains of crushed limestone, dolomite, and silica) had risen to more than 300 feet (91 m). Families picnicked, frolicked, played sports, and rode four-wheelers on the poisonous mounds. Even though 34 percent of the children had lead poisoning, authorities didn't declare Picher uninhabitable until 2006, when the Army Corps of Engineers found the town was at risk of collapsing due to the instability of the underground mine shafts.

During its heyday, Picher had a population of nearly 20,000; by 2013, nearly all the residents had accepted federal buyouts and moved away. Picher was mostly demolished and officially dissolved on November 26, 2013. The government has spent more than $300 million trying to clean up the mess, but the waters still run red from heavy metal runoff in Tar Creek.

In 2014, there were 10 citizens left. Gary Linderman, the owner of the Ole Miner Pharmacy, became the "the last man standing." He said, "I'll stay here until I draw my last breath." And he did, at the age of 60 in June of 2015. Today, Picher is an abandoned ghost town and a toxic wasteland.

◈ Back on 66
Picher is only 3 miles (4.8 km) from Route 66. Once the road curves west from Quapaw and turns into East 50 Road, the next major road is U.S. 69. Turn right (north) and drive 3 miles (4.8 km) to Picher. If you're not visiting Picher, then stay west on East 50 Road from Quapaw. Follow U.S. 69 as it heads south into the town of Commerce.

Commerce

Welcome to Commerce, known as Oklahoma's Tornado Alley, the childhood home of baseball great Mickey Mantle, and the site of the brutal murder of Constable William C. Campbell, the 13th and final victim of outlaws Bonnie Parker and Clyde Barrow.

◈ Route 66 Through Commerce
Enter Commerce on Mickey Mantle Boulevard. Soon after the curve, turn right (west) on 4th Street and left (south) on North Main Street.

Top to bottom: Dairy King in Commerce; Waylan's Ku-Ku in Miami; Coleman Theatre

Shifting Landscape

From Commerce, which marks the end of the **Ozark Plateau,** you'll start driving into the **Prairie Plains.** Here, **rolling, tree-studded hills** give way to **wide-open stretches** of land as Route 66 heads into the Texas panhandle.

Sights

Dairy King

Dairy King (100 N. Main St., 918/675-4261, 10am-6pm Mon.-Sat., $5-8) was once a Marathon service station. Today, they sell burgers, ice cream, and Route 66-shaped cookies.

Mickey Mantle Sights

Legendary Hall of Fame baseball switch-hitter Mickey Mantle grew up in Commerce. See his **childhood home** at 319 South Quincy Street, where Mantle lived in the 1930s and 1940s. You can't go inside, but you can walk around the small property; make sure to check out the dents in the side of the tin barn where Mantle spent hours honing his skills to become one of the best baseball players in America. From Main Street, turn left (east) on C Street and then left (north) onto South Quincy Street.

A 9-foot-tall (2.7-m) **statue** of Mantle is on the south side of town, at the entrance of the **Mickey Mantle Field** (400 S. Mickey Mantle Blvd., dawn-dusk daily, free) at Commerce High School.

Conoco Hole in the Wall

The 1929 **Conoco Hole in the Wall** (101 S. Main St., 918/533-2079) is a cottage-style service station built into a brick wall. In the late 1930s, it became a Phillips 66 station and later a beauty shop. Today, it operates as a small souvenir shop, and its red-and-green facade is photo-worthy.

◈ Back on 66

Leave Commerce driving south on Main Street and join U.S. 69 for 3 miles (4.8 km) into the town of Miami.

Miami

The town was named after the Miami (pronounced My-Am-Uh) Indian tribe. In 1891, Dr. W. I. McWilliams was the first white man to receive an official title to own land in the Indian Territory.

Mining played a major part in Miami's growth. Lead and zinc were discovered here in 1905, and just a few years later, by 1909, the town had 9 miles (14.5 km) of sidewalks, three bakeries, three newspapers, 13 churches, two railroads, a public school system, and a three-story hotel. In 1929, mining millionaire George L. Coleman built the Coleman Theatre

with the intention of bringing culture to Miami.

◈ Route 66 Through Miami
Route 66 enters Miami on Main Street (U.S. 69) and continues south for 3.5 miles (5.6 km).

Sights
Coleman Theatre
The **Coleman Theatre** (103 N. Main St., 918/550-2425, www.colemantheatre. org, tours 10am-4pm Tues.-Fri., 10am-2pm Sat., free) is an ornate and beautiful 1,600-seat theater built just before the Great Depression hit; it was considered the most elaborate entertainment venue between Dallas and Kansas City. Will Rogers, The Three Stooges, and vaudeville entertainers all performed here. The stucco facade, arched windows, hand-carved terra-cotta detailing, red-tile roofs, and bell towers make this one of the best surviving examples of a Spanish Colonial Revival building in Oklahoma. Today, the theater hosts tours, films, and performing arts.

Dobson Museum & Memorial Center
The **Dobson Museum & Memorial Center** (110 A St. SW, 918/542-5388, www. dobsonmuseum.com, 1pm-4pm Wed., Fri., Sun., free) houses more than 5,000 historical items, from American Indian artifacts to newspapers and photographs depicting the history of the region's early settlers. One section of the museum is entirely devoted to Route 66 memorabilia. The museum was founded by the Dobson family, who homesteaded here in 1892.

Food
★ **Waylan's Ku-Ku** (915 N. Main St., 918/542-1696, 10am-5pm daily, $6-10) opened up the first drive-through in town. Today, they are loved by, well, everybody and serve 2,000 burgers a week.

Conoco Hole in the Wall in Commerce

Galena to Tulsa

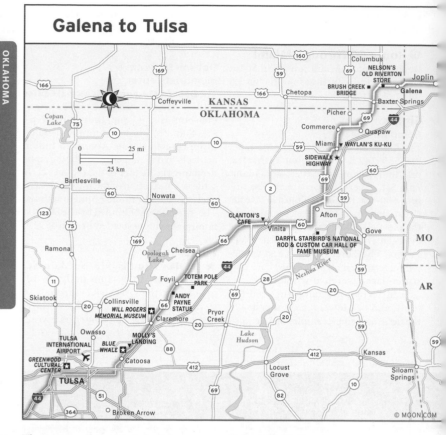

The tasty quarter-pounder burgers are cooked to order, meaning, they take longer, but they're so worth the wait. Also on the menu are deep-fried dill pickles, fried-green tomatoes, and fried squash. The building itself isn't much to look at it, but the greasy goodness is just what you need after hours on the road. Keep your eyes out for the giant green and yellow neon sign with a cuckoo clock.

◆Back on 66

Follow U.S. 69 south from Miami through Narcissa. You'll pass under I-44; soon afterward, the road curves west to reach the mining town of Afton. Or, if you're brave, consider a side trip on the Sidewalk Highway.

Sidewalk Highway

The 1922 **Sidewalk Highway** (also known as Ribbon Road) runs between Miami and Afton and is one of the oldest still-drivable roadbeds on Route 66. Not sure what to expect? It's exactly what it sounds like—a "road" the size of a sidewalk. This 3-mile-long (4.8-km), 9-foot-wide (2.7-m) stretch was built from stone and Topeka asphalt, and laid over a concrete base with 5-foot (1.5-m) gravel shoulders. Today, the rough and narrow patch is covered with dirt and gravel, and the original curbing is still visible in some places.

As you leave Miami, continue south on Main Street (SR-125). (Don't follow U.S. 69, which turns at 3rd Street.) The

Neon Photo Ops

We live in a digital, high-definition age, which means we don't get to see classic signage illuminated by blinking, flickering neon bulbs anymore. Not so on Route 66. This road trip boasts some of the best retro neon signs, many of them more than half a century old. This list offers up photo-worthy signs—for motor courts, diners, gas stations, and more—that you'll want to make a part of your trip.

♦ **Waylan's Ku-Ku,** Miami (page 135)

♦ **Meadow Gold,** Tulsa (page 144)

♦ **Skyliner Motel,** Stroud (page 155)

♦ **Lincoln Motel,** Chandler (page 155)

♦ **Western Motel,** Sayre (page 174)

the Meadow Gold sign in Tulsa

road curves right (southwest) to become East Street SW. Continue heading south. Once you reach East 120 Road (20th Ave. SW), keep going straight for another mile (1.6 km). Turn right (west) onto East 130 Road. Drive 1.5 miles (2.4 km), then turn left (south) onto South 540 Road and make a right (west) on East 140 Road. After 1 mile (1.6 km), turn left (south) on U.S. 69 (SR-66).

Do not drive the Sidewalk Highway when it's wet. And take it slow, especially if you have a low-clearance vehicle.

Afton

Afton is a small town with early 1900s buildings, rusted motel signs, fading auto courts, old gas stations, and two impressive car museums.

✪ Route 66 Through Afton

Route 66 enters Afton on 1st Street (U.S. 60/69) and heads southwest for about 1 mile (1.6 km).

Sights

Darryl Starbird's National Rod & Custom Car Hall of Fame Museum

Darryl Starbird's National Rod & Custom Car Hall of Fame Museum (55251 E. SR-85A, 918/257-3234, www.darrylstarbird. com, 10am-5pm Wed.-Mon. Mar.-Oct., $15) is a 40,000-square-foot (3,716-sq-m) facility with 50 custom-built cars, many of which rival the look and style of spaceships or otherworldly travel craft. This is not your typical antique automobile gallery—these vehicles are true works of art and are unlike anything you've ever seen before. Prepare to be amazed.

From Route 66 (U.S. 69), drive south on U.S. 59 for 5 miles (8 km). Turn right (south) on SR-125 and drive another 5 miles (8 km). Starbird's is on the left (south) side of the road.

✪ Back on 66

Leaving Afton, Route 66 (U.S. 60/69) curves south. After about 4 miles (6.4 km), turn right (west) at East 270 Road to follow U.S. 69. The town of Vinita is less than 10 miles (16.1 km) away.

Vinita

This former railroad town was home to the Will Rogers Memorial Rodeo. Many homes built here in the late 1800s are still standing today; however, the once very popular Harvey House is now gone.

◈ Route 66 Through Vinita

Route 66 enters Vinita on U.S. 60/69 and heads northwest for about 1 mile (1.6 km). Turn left (southwest) to follow U.S. 60/69.

Sights

The Eastern Trails Museum (215 W. Illinois Ave., 918/323-1338, www.easterntrailsmuseum.com, 11am-3pm Mon.-Sat., donations accepted) offers exhibits about the town's railroad, ranching, and military history, plus vintage photographs and artifacts of Route 66. The museum is one block west of U.S. 60.

Food

No matter what you do, don't miss a meal at ★ **Clanton's Cafe** (319 E. Illinois Ave., 918/256-9053, www.clantonscafe.com, 6:30am-8pm Mon.-Fri., 7am-2pm Sat., $5-14). As the oldest continuously family-owned restaurant on Route 66 in Oklahoma, Clanton's has been serving its famous 80-year-old recipe for chicken-fried steak to locals and Route 66 travelers since 1927. Even Guy Fieri of the popular Food Network show *Diners, Drive-Ins and Dives* is a fan—he visited in 2007. The restaurant walls are lined with old photos depicting its longstanding history.

◈ Back on 66

Leave Vinita heading southwest on U.S. 60/69 (Wilson St.). Continue onto U.S. 60/69 as it curves to the right (west). After

---

Top to bottom: an old-school gas station in Afton; Pat's Main Street Diner in Chelsea; Totem Pole Park near Chelsea

Hogue House

Want to see a ready-to-assemble house made from a kit ordered from the Sears catalog? What about the house rumored to be the first Sears "kit home" in Oklahoma?

That's the **Hogue House** (1001 Olive St.) in **Vinita,** considered one of the first—out of more than 70,000 kit homes sold in the United States between 1908 and 1940—to be built west of the Mississippi River. The kit contained all the materials needed to construct the Sears pre-fab house; the 2,400-square-foot (732-sq-m) home cost $1,663 and had a 14-foot (4.2-m) living room, a 12-foot (3.6-m) dining room, a 10-foot (3-m) kitchen, four bedrooms, and a 30-foot (9-m) porch.

The "Sears Saratoga" Hogue House is a classic example of the Sears Modern Home series. The house remained in the same family from 1912 until it was sold for $137,000 in 2014. The house is located one block northwest of Route 66. Turn right (northwest) on East 10th Street, then make another left (southwest) on Olive Street. This is a private residence, so please be respectful and do not disturb the owners.

about 5 miles (8 km), Route 66 curves southwest through the town of White Oak, then heads south for about 10 miles (16.1 km) to Chelsea.

Chelsea

You wouldn't know it by the looks of it, but Chelsea used to be one of the largest towns in Oklahoma. In 1889, it was incorporated under the law of the Cherokee Nation in Indian Territory. That same year, Edward Byrd secured mineral leases from the Cherokee Nation and drilled the first non-commercial oil well in Indian Territory. By the early 1900s, Chelsea became huge for cattle ranching, shipping, and farming oats, corn, pecans, and wheat. Legend has it that Chelsea also had the first state bank in the Indian Territory in 1896.

◈ Route 66 Through Chelsea

Route 66 enters Chelsea on Walnut Street, then curves southwest for about 1 mile (1.6 km).

Sights
Pryor Creek Bridge

The 1926 **Pryor Creek Bridge**, an iron truss bridge spanning 123 feet (37 m) long and 18 feet (5.5 m) wide, dates to the early days of Route 66. The six-panel bridge showcases beams that run diagonally, forming an X. On this "through truss" bridge, the beams cover the top, making it look more like a tunnel. The bridge carried Route 66 traffic until 1932. Although it's rusted, the single-intersection lattice guardrail is intact, and the structure retains its historic significance. It is no longer open to traffic, but you can walk across it. The bridge is on the south side of Route 66 at South 4260 Road, before you reach downtown Chelsea.

Pedestrian Tunnel

As Route 66 became more popular, it became more difficult and dangerous to cross it on foot. As a result, several underground **pedestrian passages** were built throughout the route. You can still see the one in Chelsea (Walnut St. near 6th St.). Other Oklahoma pedestrian tunnels were built in in Tulsa, El Reno, Sayre, and Oklahoma City.

Food and Accommodations

Breakfast is served all day at **Pat's Main Street Diner** (251 W. 6th St., 918/789-2001, 6am-9pm Mon.-Sat., 7am-3pm Sun., $7-10), where the hand-battered onion rings and pies are made from scratch. The waitresses will make you feel right at home with their friendly coffee "warm-ups." (They also warm up your syrup—that doesn't even happen at home.) From Route 66, Pat's is two blocks northwest (turn right) on West 6th Street.

The rooms at the **Chelsea Motor Inn** (325 E. Layton St., 918/789-3437, $60-75) are clean and well-maintained and bring the perfect amount of kitsch and road-trip charm to your Route 66 journey.

Back on 66

Leaving Chelsea, drive southwest for 6 miles (9.7 km) on Route 66 to the town of Bushyhead. Before reaching Foyil, turn east on SR-28 and drive 3.5 miles (5.6 km) to Totem Pole Park. If you don't have time to see Totem Pole Park, keep heading south on Route 66 to the town of Foyil.

Side Trip: Totem Pole Park

A short, 7-mile (11.3-km) round-trip detour takes you to **Totem Pole Park** (21300 E. SR-28A, 918/283-8035, dawn-dusk daily, free), the oldest and largest folk-art monument in Oklahoma, and one of the largest in the country. Built by the late Ed Galloway—a pioneer in the visionary art movement—between 1937 and 1961 as a tribute to the American Indian, the park features four 9-foot-tall (2.7-m) statues, each representing a different group. The largest totem is 90 feet (27 m) tall, with 200 carved images and a turtle at its base. It is estimated to have taken 28 tons (25 metric tons) of cement, 6 tons (5.4 metric tons) of steel, and 100 tons (91 metric tons) of sand and rock to build. Galloway died in 1961, and the Rogers County Historical Society took over the property in 1989, restoring what had fallen into disrepair.

Back on 66

Drive west on SR-28 for 3.5 miles (5.6 km) to return to Route 66. Continue south to Foyil.

Totem Pole Park

Foyil

As you approach Foyil, turn left (south) on Andy Payne Boulevard to take the **1926 alignment.** Andy Payne Boulevard is named after a Cherokee man who won the Transcontinental Foot Race in 1928.

Sights

In the 1920s, Andy Payne loved to run the 5 miles (8 km) from his family farm to school. The year after he graduated, he decided to sign up for what could arguably be considered the first extreme sport in our nation's history: the **Transcontinental Foot Race**, a running race from Los Angeles to New York City. The path the runners were to take between Los Angeles and Chicago was, coincidentally, along Route 66.

The Transcontinental Foot Race (dubbed the "Bunion Derby") was created by Lon Scott and promoted by Charles C. Pyle, known as the P.T. Barnum of

professional sports. Pyle's marketing efforts, product endorsements, and media coverage helped make Route 66 into a household name.

This unique race captured the attention of the public. For one, it was the first footrace across the United States. And for another, it was racially integrated during the height of the Jim Crow era. Five Black people, a Jamaican-born Canadian, American Indians, Pacific Islanders, and many Latinos participated.

On March 3, 1928, Andy Payne (#43) lined up with 275 other runners and set off on a grueling adventure, running through the heat of the Mojave Desert, across freezing mountain passes, and in heavy rains. One runner was hit by a car; another was struck by a motorcycle. By the third day, more than half of the participants had dropped out—but Payne kept running. The race ended 84 days later with 55 people crossing the finish. First across the finish line was Andy Payne, who had run 3,423.5 miles (5,509.5 km) in 573 hours, 4 minutes, and 34 seconds at an average of about 6 miles (9.7 km) an hour. When he won, he set a world record.

Payne won the grand prize of $25,000 (equal to about $350,000 today) and used the money to pay off his family's farm. Then he ran for public office and was elected to serve as a clerk to the Supreme Court in Oklahoma City. A **monument** commemorating Payne and his victory is located on the south end of town.

There's no official address, but the monument can be found in a small park on the south end of Andy Payne Boulevard. It's located on the right (north) side of the street near the highway where Andy Payne Boulevard rejoins Route 66.

◈ Back on 66

Heading southwest through Foyil, Andy Payne Boulevard dead-ends into the newer alignment of Route 66. Turn left (south) and you'll pass through Sequoyah, a town named after the Cherokee chief who created the 86-symbol Cherokee alphabet. In less than 5 miles (8 km), Route 66 becomes Lynn Riggs Boulevard in the town of Claremore.

Claremore

Nestled in the hills of northeastern Oklahoma, Claremore charms with its small-town streets, friendly townsfolk, and array of eateries, antiques shops, and history museums.

◈ Route 66 Through Claremore

The **pre-1958 alignment** runs parallel through Claremore one block north of Lynn Riggs Boulevard. Turn right (west) at J. M. Davis Boulevard (across from Stuart Roosa), and follow the road southwest for about 2 miles (3.2 km).

Sights
★ Will Rogers Memorial Museum

Learn about the life and work of Will Rogers (1879-1935) at the **Will Rogers Memorial Museum** (1720 W. Will Rogers Blvd., 918/341-0719, www.willrogers. com, 10am-5pm daily Mar.-Nov., 10am-5pm Wed.-Sun. Dec.-Feb., $7). Most people know Rogers as a movie star, but he was also a writer, speaker, philosopher, and comedian. His father was a Cherokee senator and judge who helped write the Oklahoma constitution, and his mother descended from a Cherokee chief. This museum delves into his early years and explores his legacy as a newspaper columnist and radio, film, and vaudeville star. Although Rogers is gone, his aphorisms live on. One still rings true for die-hard road-trip fans: "You would be surprised what there is to see in this great country within 200 miles of where any of us live. I don't care what state or what town."

The museum is approximately 1 mile (1.6 km) from Route 66. Turn right (northeast) onto SR-88 (W. Will Rogers Blvd.).

Claremore Museum of History

Even if you haven't seen it, you've likely heard of the musical *Oklahoma!* Here are a few behind-the-scenes facts. Playwright, poet, and author Lynn Riggs was a Claremore native. He wrote *Green Grow the Lilacs,* and the play produced from his book was adapted for the stage by Rodgers and Hammerstein and used as the basis for *Oklahoma!* In fact, several characters were based on Riggs' family and friends. The **Lynn Riggs Memorial** is located in the **Claremore Museum of History** (121 N. Weenonah, 918/923-6490, https://claremoremoh.org, 11am-4pm Tues.-Fri., 11am-3pm Sat., free) and features photos and personal audio recordings of the famed playwright. From Route 66, head east on East Will Rogers Boulevard. After four blocks, turn left (north) on North Weenonah.

Food

The **Hammett House** (1616 W. Will Rogers Blvd., 918/341-7333, www. hammetthouse.com, 11am-8pm Tues.-Sat., 11am-4pm Sun., $10-28) has been serving comfort food classics—fresh-cut steaks, burgers, crisp salads—since 1969. They also serve a little taste of the South, with sweet tea, catfish po'boys, and fried green tomatoes.

The restaurant is less than a mile from Route 66 near the Will Rogers Museum. From Route 66, turn right (northeast) on SR-88 (W. Will Rogers Blvd.).

Ron's Hamburgers and Chili (1220 S. Lynn Riggs Blvd., 918/283-0000, www. ronsburgersandchili.com, 11am-8pm daily, $7-12) is a local chain that dishes out juicy hamburgers with savory onions fried right into the meat. Most burgers come topped with the restaurant's award-winning chili. Portions are large and temptingly tasty—come hungry.

◈ Back on 66

Leaving Claremore, head southwest on J. M. Davis Boulevard until it rejoins Lynn Riggs Boulevard (Route 66). Turn right (south) onto Route 66 and continue for about 12 miles (19.3 km) to Catoosa.

Catoosa

Back in the day, Catoosa was a wild town where cowboys came to play after making money during big cattle drives. Today, Catoosa is better known for its 80-foot-long (24-m), bright-blue sculpture of a smiling sperm whale perched over the surface of a pond.

Sights
★ Blue Whale

It's big. It's blue. It's a giant whale. If ever there was a classic example of a roadside attraction, it would be this, the **Blue Whale** (2680 N. SR-66, 8am-dusk daily, free), built in 1972 by zoologist Hugh S. Davis. Featured on the Food Network, the History Channel's *American Pickers,* and as part of Snapchat's Spectacles marketing campaign, the Blue Whale draws visitors from near and far. Creator Hugh Davis was 60 years old when he decided to use 1,200 feet (366 m) of pipe, 126 sacks of concrete, 20,000 pounds (9,072 kg) of rocks, and 15 tons (13.6 metric tons) of sand to construct an impressive sperm whale, its front resting on the shore of a small pond, its back extending over the water. Davis unveiled the whale as an anniversary gift for his wife, Zelta, who collected whale figurines. It quickly became a local summer hot spot, with townies stopping by from 11am to sunset to swim, fish, play, and picnic in and around the whale. In 1988, the Blue Whale closed as a recreation site, but

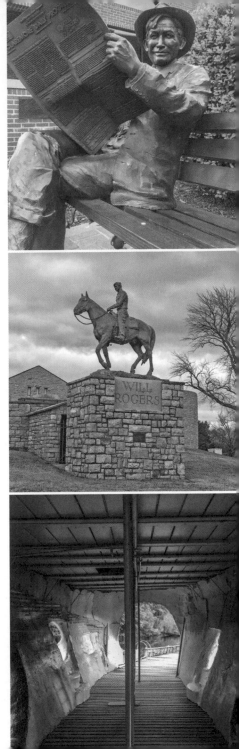

Top to bottom: Will Rogers statue by Sandra Van Zandt in Claremore; Will Rogers Memorial Museum; inside the Blue Whale in Catoosa

visitors still stop by to marvel at its size and hand-built beauty.

Catoosa Historical Society Museum

Located in an old depot, the **Catoosa Historical Society Museum** (207 S. Cherokee St., 918/266-3296, 10am-3pm Tues. and Fri., free) shares information about Catoosa's train history, including a train log from 1897, photographs of early residents, and a mailbox from the days when mail was delivered on horseback.

Food

For a dignified meal in a farm-chic log cabin, try ★ **Molly's Landing** (3700 N. SR-66, 918/266-7853, www. mollyslanding.com, 4pm-10pm Mon.-Sat., $18-40). Order the melt-in-your-mouth filet mignon with peppercorn sauce, or go for fresh crab cakes or grilled quail. An eclectic wine list rounds out the culinary offerings, and lighted bridges lead the way to a memorable dining experience.

From Route 66, cross the Verdigris River and turn right (northwest) onto Old Highway 66. Take the first right, which leads to Molly's Landing in about 700 feet (213 m).

◈ Back on 66

Leaving Catoosa, take Route 66 south for about 1 mile (1.6 km), then turn right (west) on Antry Drive. Take an immediate left (south) on South Cherokee Street. After about 1 mile (1.6 km), turn left (south) on SR-167. Continue under I-44 and then turn right (west) on 11th Street into Tulsa.

Tulsa

History and culture run deep in Tulsa. The city was created as part of the Indian Removal Act (the Trail of Tears), and in the 1830s, Choctaw, Cherokee, Muscogee (Creek), Chickasaw, Cheyenne, Comanche, Apache, Seminole, and other tribes were relocated here after being forced to surrender their land east of the Mississippi River to the federal government. Their new land eventually became the state of Oklahoma.

At the turn of the 20th century, oil was discovered. Tulsa shifted from a small frontier settlement into a boomtown. It soon became the "Oil Capital of the World," and oil barons built towering skyscrapers and architecturally progressive buildings. As a result, Tulsa is now home to one of the largest concentrations of art deco structures in the United States, most of them in pristine condition. The city's preservation efforts extend to its Route 66 signage, including the classic **Meadow Gold neon sign** at 11th Street and Quaker Avenue.

◈ Route 66 Through Tulsa

West of U.S. 169, Route 66 follows 11th Street through downtown Tulsa past several photo-worthy neon Route 66 signs, murals, and old motor courts, including the Desert Hills (near Yale Street). An **older alignment** zigzags less than 1 mile (1.6 km) north of 11th Street on Admiral Place, traveling west to Lewis Avenue, then south to 2nd Street—but the one-way streets make this route tricky to follow.

To take the more direct **post-1932 alignment,** follow 11th Street west all the way to the Arkansas River, where it turns south into Southwest Boulevard. Tulsa is fairly easy to navigate, and most sights are located less than a mile from Route 66.

Sights

Downtown Tulsa is encircled by a loop of freeways and highways—U.S. 244 (north), U.S. 412 (north) and U.S. 75 (east), and SR-51 (west and south). As Route 66 (11th St.) enters downtown, the road crosses U.S. 75; turn north on South Elgin Avenue to begin exploring the downtown area.

Tulsa

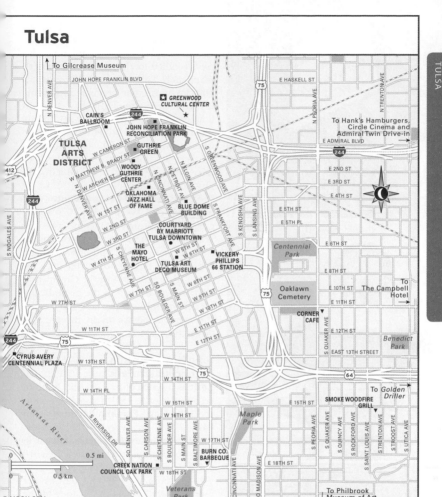

★ Greenwood Cultural Center

Booker T. Washington referred to Tulsa's **Greenwood District** as America's "Black Wall Street." The 35-block area was once a vibrant community with the wealthiest Black neighborhoods in the South. Not only was it a hotbed of jazz and blues in the 1920s, but it also housed more than 300 Black-owned businesses, from theaters and restaurants to hotels and law offices.

Despite the established and prosperous nature of the community—or perhaps because of it—the Greenwood District was thrust in the national spotlight in June 1921, when one of the nation's worst acts of racial violence broke out. The **1921 Tulsa Race Massacre** was instigated by a rumor that a Black man had assaulted a white woman. No one knew what really happened, but most people believe that a 19-year-old Black man tripped while exiting an elevator and grabbed a white woman's arm to steady himself. She screamed,

and he ran. As the story spread through the town, jealousy over Black economic success coupled with inflammatory false reporting led to violence from an angry white mob. The mob set the Greenwood District on fire and prevented firefighters from saving the buildings. After 16 hours of looting and mayhem, hundreds died as Black Wall Street burned to the ground. An estimated 10,000 Black people were left homeless, and nearly all of the wealth and success of the Greenwood District was gone.

The **Greenwood Cultural Center** (322 N. Greenwood Ave., 918/596-1020, www. greenwoodculturalcenter.com, 9am-5pm Mon.-Fri., free) has an important collection of memorabilia and photos of the area before, during, and after the violence. Although most of the Greenwood District was burned to the ground, the Black community persevered and opened thriving businesses, many located just down the street from the cultural center.

John Hope Franklin Reconciliation Park

Built as a space of healing and hope in response to the 1921 Tulsa Race Riot, the **John Hope Franklin Reconciliation Park** (290 N. Elgin Ave., 918/295-5009, www.jhfcenter.org/reconciliation-park, 8am-8pm daily, free) opened in 2010 and gives voice to the role of Black people in Oklahoma. A 25-foot (7.6-m) memorial tower depicts the history of the Black struggle—from Africa to North America—and stands near 16-foot (4.9-m) granite sculptures based on actual pictures from the 1921 riot.

Cain's Ballroom

Since 1924, **Cain's Ballroom** (423 N. Main St., 918/584-2306, www.cainsballroom. com, box office 10am-noon and 1pm-5pm daily, ticket prices vary) has played host to a range of bands, musicians, and

---

Top to bottom: The Campbell Hotel in Tulsa; *Golden Driller*; The Mayo Hotel

Art Deco Architecture

Created in the 1920s, the art deco style is characterized by bold geometric forms, motifs of chevrons (V shapes), and Asian styles from China, Japan, India, and Persia, as well as by expensive materials such as ebony and ivory.

Downtown Tulsa offers up one of the most extensive collections of art deco architecture in the United States. Embark on a self-guided art deco tour of the city—a few places to see include the Philtower and Philcade buildings, Tulsa Club, Atlas Life building, Oklahoma Natural Gas Building, and the Boston Avenue Methodist Church.

For a list of art deco buildings throughout Tulsa, go to the website of the **Tulsa Preservation Commission** (www. tulsapreservationcommission.org) or visit the **Tulsa Historical Society** (2445 S. Peoria Ave., 918/712-9484, www.tulsahistory.org, 11am-3pm Tues.-Sat., $5). Also, **Visit Tulsa** (www.visittulsa.com) provides a downloadable map for a self-guided walking tour of the city's art deco buildings.

Tulsa Art Deco Museum

comedians. Past big names range from Dolly Parton and Hank Williams to Bob Dylan and U2. In 1978, the Sex Pistols even played here (Sid Vicious actually punched a hole in the wall). Today, the shows are as diverse as ever—recent performers include the likes of Chris Stapleton, Gary Clark, Jr., The Decemberists, and comedian Tig Notaro. While the theater is big enough to attract world-famous acts, it's also small enough to offer an intimate experience.

Guthrie Green

Guthrie Green (111 E. Reconciliation Way, www.guthriegreen.com, 6am-10pm daily) is a full square block of urban gardens, a lush park, and an outdoor amphitheater. Visit for yoga on the green, bocce ball classes, storytelling sessions, film screenings, and concerts. If you happen to visit on a Wednesday, **food trucks** line up around lunchtime. Guthrie Green is located in the Tulsa Arts District, between Brady and Cameron Streets, and Boston and Cincinnati Avenues.

Woody Guthrie Center

Woody Guthrie's progressive political views irked Cold War conservatives, but it can't be denied that he composed some of the most significant patriotic songs of America; his anthems about the Dust Bowl gave a voice to so many who had lost so much. The **Woody Guthrie Center** (102 E. Reconciliation Way, 918/574-2710, www.woodyguthriecenter.org, 10am-6pm Tues.-Sun., $8) offers a comprehensive archive of Guthrie's life: 10,000 photos, plus journals, notes, illustrations, and sketches, and lyrics to "This Land Is Your Land" written in Guthrie's own hand. The 12,000-square-foot (1,115-sq-m) facility, on a corner in the Tulsa Arts District, also houses a research facility, educational programs, and songwriting sessions.

Oklahoma Jazz Hall of Fame

The **Oklahoma Jazz Hall of Fame** (5 S. Boston Ave., 918/928-5299, www.okjazz.org, $15-20), once housed in the Greenwood Cultural Center, now lives in the historic art deco Union Depot. It hosts an ongoing concert series, cultural events, and blues, gospel, and jazz performances. An on-site museum displays memorabilia, photographs, and historical information about jazz masters like Chet Baker and Jimmy Rushing.

Tulsa Art Deco Museum

Tulsa Art Deco Museum (511 S. Boston Ave., 918/804-2669, https://decopolis. net, 7am-9pm Mon.-Sat., 8am-1pm Sun.) is a small but informative museum about the design and era of art deco culture. A collection of artifacts such as jewelry, advertising artwork, silverware, and clothing show how pervasive the style was and how it became a part of everyday life. The museum is located in the lobby of the gorgeous Philcade Building; a gift shop and docent-led tours are available upon request.

Underground Pedestrian Tunnels

On the pre-1930s alignment of Route 66 located just northeast of downtown, you'll find a system of **underground pedestrian tunnels** (Admiral Pl. and Harvard Ave.). Originally built to easily transport materials from one building to another, the tunnels soon became safe havens for the wealthy to traverse downtown after a slew of kidnappings of rich businesspeople during the Depression. It was believed that during Prohibition the tunnels were also used to shuttle booze. Look for the entrance on the corner near the Crosstown Church of Christ; it resembles a subway station entrance with a metal cage. The rusted concrete base has exposed rebar, old light fixtures, and art deco accents. The tunnel entrance is usually locked, but it's worth checking out anyway.

Creek Nation Council Oak Park

The birthplace of Tulsa, the **Creek Nation Council Oak Park** (1750 S. Cheyenne Ave., 7am-8pm daily) is located south of the U.S. 64/SR-51/U.S. 75 interchange and

Woody Guthrie Center

Car Culture

Tulsa's 1931 **Vickery Phillips 66 Station** (602 S. Elgin Ave., 918/582-2534), leased to Virgil Vickery in 1946, shows off the signature Cotswold Cottage design employed by the Phillips Petroleum Company. These cottage-style properties looked like adorable little homes, designed that way to be attractive and to better fit with suburban communities. The style featured pitched roofs and a chimney; many were painted dark green with orange and blue trim. By 1930, the Phillips Petroleum Company had installed 6,750 of these gas stations in 12 states, but only a handful remain today, none of which is operational.

near the Arkansas River. A large burr oak tree marks the traditional ceremonial ground chosen by the Lochapoka clan of the Creek tribe. After being forced off their land in 1836 and losing 161 members on the horrific Trail of Tears, 469 tribe members arrived on this hill overlooking the Arkansas River. They named this place Tulasi (Tulsa is derived from the Lochapoka word *tulasi,* which means "old town"). The Tulsa-Lochapoka gathered here for ceremonies until 1896. The park is often referred to as Tulsa's first

City Hall, and commemorative tribal ceremonies are held each year.

Philbrook Museum of Art

The **Philbrook Museum of Art** (2727 S. Rockford Rd., 918/749-7941, www. philbrook.org, 9am-3pm Wed.-Sun., 9am-9pm Fri., $9) was a 72-room mansion built during Tulsa's gilded age, when oil barons had more money than they knew what to do with. Built in 1926, the mansion was designed to look like an Italian villa. Today, the property is surrounded by 23 acres (9.3 hectares) of beautifully manicured gardens and houses collections of art from all over the world. To get there from East 11th Street (Route 66), turn left (south) on South Peoria Avenue and drive 1.5 miles (2.4 km). Turn left (east) on East 27th Place; the Philbrook will be one block straight ahead.

Golden Driller

To see one of the tallest freestanding statues in the country, look no further than the *Golden Driller* (4145 E. 21st St., 918/744-1113, www.exposquare.com, free). Because it's so huge, you won't have to look that hard. Looming over the entrance of Expo Square stands a 76-foot-tall (23-m), 22-ton (20-metric-ton) statue of an oilman resting his giant, golden arm on the top of a (real) oil derrick. The *Golden Driller* was built in 1966 as a monument for petroleum industry workers at a time when Oklahoma was the oil capital of the world. The *Golden Driller*

The Father of Route 66

The origins of Route 66 owe much to **Cyrus Avery** (1871-1963): Even though he was born in Stevensville, Pennsylvania—far from what would become the route of the Mother Road—his family moved to the Indian Territory of the Cherokee Nation in Oklahoma when he was a teenager. In 1924, Avery became the chairman of the State Highway Commission, and in 1925 he was selected by the Department of Agriculture as one of four board members to help number the nation's highways.

A more direct path for the new Route 66 would have passed through the middle of Kansas, but it was Avery's vision and determination to bring business to Oklahoma (he and his wife owned the Old English Inn, a tourist court and restaurant located on what is now the traffic circle at Mingo and Admiral Place) that led state and federal highway officials to build Route 66 right through Avery's home state of Oklahoma.

Avery's convincing argument was that the road followed an important trade route between Chicago and Tulsa. It was originally going to be called Route 60, but the states of Kentucky and Virginia had their hearts set on the number 60, and they won the battle; Avery and his board members settled on 66 because it had not yet been assigned.

can withstand 200-mph (320-kph) tornadoes, and although he has been assaulted by shotgun blasts, the city patches him up and gives him a new paint job every few years.

To get there from East 11th Street (Route 66), turn left (south) on South Sandusky Avenue. In 1 mile (1.6 km), turn right (west) on East 21st Street. Take an immediate right into the Expo Square parking lot. The *Golden Driller* stands by the lot.

Gilcrease Museum

The **Gilcrease Museum** (1400 N. Gilcrease Museum Rd., 888/655-2278, www.gilcrease.utulsa.edu, 11am-4pm Wed. and Fri.-Sun., noon-8pm Thurs., $8) sits on 460 acres (186 hectares) with 23 gardens and features more than 10,000 paintings, prints, drawing, and sculptures by 400 artists from past and present. The museum also has an unparalleled collection of American Indian artifacts, historical manuscripts, and art.

To get there from East 11th Street (Route 66), turn right (north) on South Denver Avenue and drive 1 mile (1.6 km). Turn left (west) on West Edison Street. Drive 1 mile (1.6 km) to North Gilcrease Museum Road and turn right (north). The museum will be on the left.

Cyrus Avery Centennial Plaza

As Southwest Boulevard crosses the Arkansas River leaving downtown, larger-than-life bronze sculptures, flags from the eight Route 66 states, and a large Route 66 sign adorn the Mother Road at **Cyrus Avery Centennial Plaza** (Southwest Blvd. and Riverside Dr., dawn-dusk daily, free). This assemblage pays homage to the man considered to be the "Father of Route 66." A sculpture by Robert Summers depicts Avery climbing out of his Model T to help a farmer in a horse-drawn carriage coming west from Tulsa's oil fields, while Avery's wife, daughter, and cat sit in the car. The sculpture is about 60 feet (18 m) long and 15 feet (4.6 m) high and weighs 20,000 pounds (9,072 kg). Park for free near the pedestrian bridge that crosses 11th Street.

Blue Dome Building

So cool and noteworthy is the **Blue Dome Building** (313 E. 2nd St.) that a hip, burgeoning entertainment district that surrounds it has claimed the name. Originally a 1924 Gulf Oil gas station, the rounded brick building with the sky-blue dome on top has become the beloved landmark of the Blue Dome District, east of downtown Tulsa. In its heyday, the bright blue dome attracted motorists to the 24-hour filling station, where an on-duty attendant lived upstairs. The gas station was also one of the few buildings in the area with hot and cold running water.

Tulsa Arts District

The **Tulsa Arts District** is one of the oldest parts of town, with established red-brick buildings and outdoor green spaces, including Guthrie Green. This walkable neighborhood is a vibrant hot spot for artists, artisans, and musicians, with trendy restaurants, theaters and venues (such as Cain's Ballroom and Brady Theatre), art galleries, and a food truck court. During the **Art Crawl** (www.thetulsaartsdistrict.org, 6pm-9pm, first Fri. of every month), museums, galleries, and studios throw open their doors to let you explore artworks and enjoy live music and performances.

Admiral Twin Drive-In

Live it up old-school style at the **Admiral Twin Drive-in** (7355 E. Easton St., 918/878-8099, www.admiraltwindrivein.com, opens at dusk, $7), situated on the pre-1930s alignment of Route 66. This classic 1950s drive-in shows new movies on two nine-story screens and offers a snack bar with popcorn, candy, soda, burgers, and hot dogs. Your car must have FM radio to hear the movie.

Circle Cinema

It's not often you get to enjoy an art house flick in a nonprofit theater that's also on the National Register of Historic Places. At **Circle Cinema** (10 S. Lewis Ave., 918/592-3456, www.circlecinema.com, $10-35), you can do exactly that. The oldest movie theater in Tulsa (opened in 1928), Circle Cinema now screens indie movies, art films, documentaries, and foreign flicks. Fun fact: When the theater first opened, the price of a ticket was only a dime, and a nickel would buy orange juice and a cup of peanuts.

Food

Hank's Hamburgers (8933 E. Admiral Pl., 918/832-1509, 10am-7pm Tues.-Sat., $4-11) has been frying their legendary hash house burgers since 1949. Hope you're an onion lover—all burgers come with fried and raw onions. The half-pound Hank's Special takes about 15 minutes to cook (be patient; it's worth every juicy bite), while the Big Okie is a four-patty doozy. Split it with your traveling companion or wrap it up and save it for later.

At **Smoke Woodfire Grill** (1542 E. 15th St., 918/949-4440, http://smokewoodfiregrill.com, 11am-9pm Mon.-Thurs., 11am-10pm Fri., 10am-10pm Sat., 10am-9pm Sun., $11-40), nosh on locally sourced American fare cooked over an open flame. The pork tenderloin is sided with pimiento cheese grits and the smoked brisket macaroni and cheese is spiced with Hatch chiles and jalapeños. Savor a break from the road with a fancy craft cocktail.

The best thing about the **Corner Cafe** (731 N. Sheridan Rd., 918/835-3961, www.cornercafetulsa.com, 6am-9pm daily, $7-19) is that it's not pretending to be anything other than what it is: a neighborhood diner serving up a solid breakfast, lunch, and dinner, with regular folk enjoying regular food.

★ **Burn Co. Barbeque** (1738 S. Boston Ave., 918/574-2777, www.burnbbq.com, 10:30am-2:30pm Tues.-Sat., $8-18) has a serious barbecue game. This is, hands down, some of the best 'cue in Tulsa. The locally sourced meat is smoked daily: brisket, pulled pork, Polish sausages, venison, baby back ribs, smoked bologna. Sides range from baked beans and cole slaw to Lay's Classic Potato Chips. Burn Co. closes at 2:30pm, so arrive before noon, when the line can stretch out the door.

Accommodations

Boutique, modern amenities with style await you at the beautifully restored ★ **The Campbell Hotel** (2636 E. 11th St.,

855/744-5500, www.thecampbellhotel. com, $139-209). Built in 1927 and located right on Route 66, this hotel spans an entire block and has 26 impeccably decorated rooms (including one inspired by the Rat Pack), an on-site cocktail lounge, spa services, and envy-inducing interior design.

Courtyard by Marriott Tulsa Downtown (415 S. Boston Ave., 918/508-7400, www.marriott.com, $118-179) makes its home inside the historic Atlas Life Building, complete with an art deco lobby. Book a room on the 7th floor to see the original features from 1922. Rooms are spacious for a historic property, giving you the best of both worlds—creature comforts but with a bit of history.

★ **The Mayo Hotel** (115 W. 5th St., 918/582-6296, www.themayohotel.com, from $170) just might be the most lavish accommodations on Route 66. It features a grand lobby with opulent details and expansive suites that rival one-bedroom apartments in size. The hotel opened in 1925 and played host to many famous guests—including Elvis Presley—and an extensive renovation in 2009 restored the hotel to the former grandeur of its Route 66 vibrancy. Be sure to stop by The Penthouse Bar, a rooftop lounge with great cocktails and 360-degree views of downtown Tulsa.

◈ Back on 66

Leaving Tulsa, Route 66 heads south on Southwest Boulevard. After crossing I-244, continue driving south through Oakhurst, where Route 66 turns into Frankoma Road. After about 4 miles (6.4 km), Route 66 joins SR-66 (Mission St.), heading south into the town of Sapulpa.

Sapulpa

Sapulpa's first permanent settler was Creek Chief Sapulpa in 1850. Later, the town turned into an important site for cattle shipping. Most of the buildings

(90 percent, in fact) in the historic district were built between 1904 and 1952 and designed in the classical and Tudor Revival styles. There used to be a Fred Harvey Restaurant and railroad station, but that was torn down in the early 1960s.

◈ Route 66 Through Sapulpa

In Sapulpa, head south on Mission Street and turn right (west) onto SR-33 (Dewey Ave.) to the west side of town.

Sights
Waite Phillips Filling Station Museum

Stop by to see the impressive restoration of this 1923 **Waite Phillips Filling Station Museum** (26 E. Lee Ave., 918/224-4871, 10am-3pm Tues.-Sat., donations accepted). Not to be confused with the Phillips 66 in Tulsa, this station was run by Frank Phillips' brother Waite. The station is located on the southwest corner about one block south on Route 66.

Sapulpa Historical Society & Museum

Across the street from the Waite Phillips Filling Station is the **Sapulpa Historical Society & Museum** (100 E. Lee Ave., 918/224-4871, www. sapulpahistoricalsociety.com, 10am-3pm Thurs.-Sat., donations accepted), with three floors of exhibits depicting Sapulpa's history. A re-created village brings to life a blacksmith shop, general merchandise store, church, boarding school, and railroad shops, all from the early 1900s.

Heart of Route 66 Auto Museum

Home of the world's tallest gas pump—66 feet tall (20-m)—the **Heart of Route 66 Auto Museum** (13 Sahoma Lake Rd., 918/216-1171, www.heartofroute66.org, 10am-4pm Tues.-Sat., noon-4pm Sun.) offers a memorable experience for auto enthusiasts. While this museum doesn't have the largest or most comprehensive collection, the cars and motorcycles they have on display are immaculately kept. The staff is knowledgeable and friendly, so don't be shy about asking questions. You'll also see vintage auto magazines, mechanic manuals, and car advertisements from the 1960s.

Rock Creek Bridge #18
In the 1920s, crossing **Rock Creek Bridge #18** was a memorable experience for travelers, as it was one of the most dynamic examples of the steel-truss design popular at the time. Truss bridges were developed in the mid-1800s and used everywhere until World War II, when shifting technology allowed for more standardized concrete designs. Rock Creek Bridge may appear quaint now, but in the 1920s and '30s, it was something special. Located on West Ozark Trail, 1.2 miles (1.9 km) west of Main Street (SR-97). Turn right (north) on West Ozark Trail, and the bridge will be after the turn.

Food
Happy Burger (215 N. Mission St., 918/224-7750, 11am-8pm Mon.-Sat., $4-8) lives up to its name. The burgers are delicious, the service is prompt, and the diner atmosphere takes you back to the 1960s. The restaurant was originally built as a Tastee Freeze in 1957, but the owner changed the name to Happy Burger.

◈ Back on 66
Depart Sapulpa via West Dewey Avenue (Route 66) to head west and follow Route 66 south toward Kellyville. After 5 miles (8 km), the road veers west as it crosses under I-44 into the town of Bristow, where Route 66 becomes Main Street.

◈ Detour: Ozark Trail
For a slight, definitely worthwhile detour, take West Dewey Avenue to follow a narrow, rough, bumpy 3.3-mile (5.3-km) section of the 1926 alignment via the Ozark Trail. This is your chance to drive a really old road, which is part of why you're

journeying on Route 66 in the first place, right? You'll see a 120-foot (37-m) concrete and steel truss bridge (now closed) and an old, abandoned drive-in movie theater.

Leaving Sapulpa, head west on West Dewey Avenue (Route 66). Turn right (north) on West Ozark Trail and follow it for 3 miles (4.8 km) until it rejoins the newer alignment. Turn right (southwest) to rejoin Route 66.

Bristow

Bristow was a small trading post in the Creek Indian area at the turn of the 20th century. It quickly became a railroad town when the Oklahoma City Railroad (which later became the San Francisco Railway) extended its line from Sapulpa to Oklahoma City. There were several cotton gins in the area, and oil was discovered around 1915. By the late 1920s, Route 66 brought even more business to town. Many of the garages, auto dealers, and service stations, such as the streamlined, curvilinear **Beard Motor Company** (210 E. 9th St.), accommodated Route 66 travelers. After the turnpike was built in the 1950s, the route bypassed Bristow.

◈ Route 66 Through Bristow
Route 66 enters Bristow on Main Street (SR-48), traveling south for about 0.5 mile (0.8 km) to head west (right) on 4th Avenue for 0.5 mile (0.8 km).

Sights
Railroad enthusiasts will want to explore this 1923 restored depot. The **Bristow Historical Train Museum & Depot** (1 Railroad Pl., 918/367-9335, www.bristowhistory.org, 10am-3pm Mon.-Fri., donations accepted) showcases railroad-related displays and information about Bristow's history from the time of the Indian Territory to the present day.

Tulsa to Oklahoma City

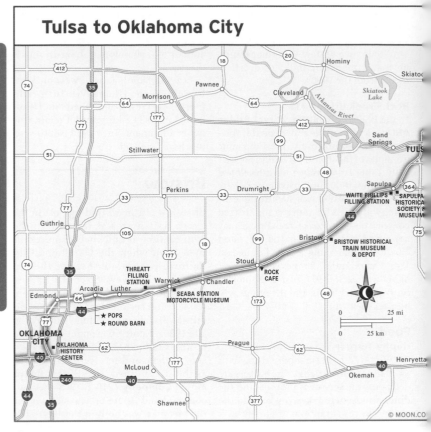

© MOON.CO

⬥ Back on 66

Leaving Bristow, head south on Main Street and then turn right (west) on 4th Avenue. After about four blocks, Route 66 curves south on Roland Street. From this point to the town of Stroud, you're driving over an underground natural gas storage facility built in 1950. Follow Route 66 west for about 7 miles (11.3 km) to Depew.

Depew

You would never know it today, but in the mid-1920s Depew was a busy city with grain mills, three lumberyards, three grocery stores, three service stations, and four hotels, plus a bakery, Chevrolet dealership, drugstore, and dentist. The roads were dirt until Route 66 came through in 1926. However, Depew suffered like so many other towns during the Great Depression. By the late 1930s, there were only two grocery stores, one bank, a hardware store, and a few other businesses. Today, you'll see a historic town lined with empty buildings and long-abandoned businesses.

Route 66 made a loop through downtown Depew for only two years, from 1926 to 1928. To follow the route through town, turn left (south) on Flynn Avenue and then make a right (west) on Main Street. Turn left (north) on Ladd Avenue, which leads back to Route 66.

✦ Back on 66
Complete the Depew Loop, then from Ladd Avenue, turn left onto Route 66 and drive west for 10 miles (16.1 km) to Stroud.

Stroud

In the 1890s, Stroud was a hell-raising party town for cattlemen and cowboys; it was forced "dry" by Oklahoma law in 1907. Today, there are a number of old buildings along Main Street, including the **Skyliner Motel** and its gigantic teal and red sign. Route 66 enters Stroud on Main Street and travels west for about 1.5 miles (2.4 km).

Food
When Route 66 came through Stroud in the 1920s, several businesses popped up, but the only one that remains today is the ★ **Rock Cafe** (114 W. Main St., 918/968-3990, www.rockcafert66.com, 7am-9pm daily, $6-12.50). Owner Dawn Welch likes to keep things simple here, but that doesn't mean your taste buds won't be wowed. You can order fried pickles, a buffalo burger made with farm-raised meat (a dish featured on the Food Network's *Diners, Drive-Ins and Dives*), and an impossibly wonderful fried pork cutlet smothered with mushrooms, grilled onions, green peppers, and cheese.

Rock Cafe opened in 1939 and has been run by women for much of its existence—even the trusty kitchen grill is named Betsy and referred to as "she" and "her." In the 1940s, during World War II, the restaurant doubled as a Greyhound bus stop, and from 1959 to 1983, it was a 24-hour eatery operated by Mamie Mayfield until she retired at age 70. When a tornado almost took out the place in 1999, the National Park Service Route 66 Corridor Preservation Program stepped in to help owner Welch with a cost-share grant. And when a disastrous fire erupted in 2008, funding from the National Park Service and the National Trust for Historic Preservation Southwest Office restored Rock Cafe to its former glory.

✦ Back on 66
Heading west out of Stroud, Route 66 dips south and curves through Davenport. From Davenport, continue another 6 miles (9.7 km) west to Chandler.

Chandler

Chandler was settled during the 1891 Land Rush (the land had previously been occupied by Sac, Fox, and Iowa tribes, but was then opened up for homesteading). A tornado wiped out much of Chandler in 1897. After that, sturdier brick and stone structures were built. Many of these historic brick and sandstone buildings still stand throughout the town. One of the most impressive is the **Chandler Armory,** which houses the Route 66 Interpretive Center. Another photo-worthy structure is the **Lincoln Motel;** swing by to get a picture of its starburst-esque neon sign.

✦ Route 66 Through Chandler
Route 66 enters Chandler on 1st Street and heads south. After passing under the railroad, it then merges with Manvel Avenue, heading south to 15th Street.

Sights
Route 66 Interpretive Center
The **Chandler Armory** was built between 1935 and 1937 for the Oklahoma National Guard as part of the Works Progress Administration (WPA). More than 250 laborers chiseled its sandstone outer walls by hand; 20 inches (51 cm) thick, they were built to withstand tornado winds. As a job site, it offered desperately needed employment during the Great Depression. Once the armory opened, it housed more than 60 men of the 45th Infantry Division. This was also the site where, in 1958, Reverend Burton

Z. "Lee Lee" Lewis, the first Black person ever to serve in the Oklahoma National Guard, was sworn in.

Decades later, the building fell into disrepair. Although it was a mess, the property was listed in the National Register of Historic Places in 1992; it took another 10 years before the armory received a much-needed restoration. In 2007, the stylish **Route 66 Interpretive Center** (400 E. 1st St. 405/258-1300, www.route66interpretivecenter.org, 10am-5pm Mon.-Sat., 1pm-5pm Sun., $7.50) opened with exhibits that tell the stories of the people who lived and breathed Route 66. The vintage billboards are fun to look at, and the interactive video takes you on a "drive" along the 1920s-era Mother Road. Browse the handiwork of local artisans at the center's gift shop.

McJerry's Route 66 Gallery

Artist and painter Jerry McClanahan is a modern-day expert on Route 66. He has been touring, researching, documenting, mapping, and writing about the Mother Road for more than 30 years, so a visit to his gallery is a must. **McJerry's Route 66 Gallery** (306 Manvel Ave., 405/240-7659 www.mcjerry66.com, no set hours, free) houses his paintings, postcards, and prints, which capture special moments from his travels along Route 66. You can even commission him to record your own road-trip experience on canvas. There are no formal hours; call or text ahead of time, or just drop by.

The gallery is located one block north of Route 66 after its merge with Manvel Avenue.

Lincoln County Museum of Pioneer History

The **Lincoln County Museum of Pioneer History** (719 Manvel Ave., 405/258-2425, www.okpioneermuseum.org, 10am-4pm

Top to bottom: Skyliner Motel in Stroud; an old building in Chandler; a cottage-style former gas station in Chandler

Thurs.-Sat., free) fills three buildings more than 100 years old and features children's marionettes and historical paintings of the arrival of the American Indians. The life of early settlers is depicted in exhibits, and there are replicas of an old-fashioned dental office, millinery and seamstress shops, and a general store with items sold during the early 1900s.

◆ Back on 66

Manvel Avenue (Route 66) curves right (west) onto West 15th Street for 7 miles (11.3 km) to Warwick.

Warwick

Even if you're not a motorcycle fan, you've got to see the collection at **Seaba Station Motorcycle Museum** (336992 SR-66, 405/258-9141, www.seabastation.com, 10am-5pm Thurs.-Tues., free). Nearly 70 vintage motorcycles, some dating as far back as 1908, call this restored 1921 brick gas station home. The station was originally owned by John Seaba. He employed 18 people in the late 1930s, worked on Model T Fords, and ran an engine repair shop.

◆ Back on 66

Route 66 heads west from Warwick, and in approximately 10 miles (16.1 km) you'll reach Luther.

Luther

Luther is a small agricultural area that once shipped the largest amount of cotton of any Oklahoma town. In addition to its agri highlights, Luther holds an important spot in Black history. In 1916, the Booker T. Washington High School for African Americans opened, only to be destroyed by a fire in December 1930. The town rebuilt the school in 1931, and many of its graduates (including

Elizabeth Threatt, whose family owned the Threatt Filling Station) went on to colleges throughout the United States. The high school closed in 1957 when the schools integrated.

During the Jim Crow era, Black travelers were often not welcome at restaurants, hotels, and service stations along Route 66, but the **Threatt Filling Station**, at the intersection of Route 66 and Pottawatomi Road, was an exception. A small, unassuming bungalow with a slightly pitched, gabled roof and a wooden door, it served Black people from 1915 to the 1950s. Owner Alan Threatt, Sr., a Black man, had a homestead in the Luther area from which his family quarried native sandstone to build the station. Though it is no longer open to the public, it is still visible from the road.

Food

Go for the moist and buttery fried chicken at the **Chicken Shack** (18725 SR-66, 405/277-5020, 11am-9:30pm Mon.-Thurs., 11am-11:30pm Fri.-Sat., 11am-9pm Sun., $9-22). Here they serve a menu of mostly fried foods, with accompanying sides likes potato wedges, beans, coleslaw, and fried okra. The decor isn't much to write home about, but the food is fresh and near perfect and the service is welcoming. Plus, there's live music.

◆ Back on 66

Leaving Luther, Route 66 turns into to East Danforth Road. Arcadia is about 8 miles (12.9 km) west.

Arcadia

Soon after the Land Rush, Arcadia was established, attracting both white and Black cotton farmers. At the turn of the 20th century, the Deep Fork Township Census reported that the population was 50 percent Black, and it remained that way for decades. When Route 66 arrived, it generated business and more income for locals, but many left to move to larger towns during the Great Depression. The one mainstay that continually brings the crowds to Arcadia—even today—is the Round Barn, built in 1898.

Sights
Round Barn
William H. Odor's neighbors him told it couldn't be done, but he proved them wrong, building what many consider an architectural marvel: an honest-to-goodness round barn. In 1898, Odor soaked lumber and then carefully, painstakingly bent each piece in a rounded shape to construct the 60- by 45-foot (18- by 14-m) **Round Barn** (107 SR-66, 405/396-0824, www.arcadiaroundbarn.org, 10am-5pm daily, free). Instead of simply being used to store hay, the barn hosted all kinds of community gatherings and dances.

Once Route 66 entered Arcadia in 1926, the Round Barn became one of the most-photographed landmarks on the Mother Road. As traffic slowed on Route 66, the barn experienced some neglect, but retired building contractor Luke Robinson saved the barn from total ruin. Today, travelers can walk through the barn, which is lined with photographs and artifacts and has an eclectic gift shop that's more like the best garage sale you've ever been to than a typical touristy shop.

Pops
What do *you* call it—pop? Soda? Coke? All depends on where you're from. But no matter your origin, you'll be impressed by the carbonated sugar drink offerings—more than 600 flavors in all—at this place. **Pops** (660 SR-66, 405/928-7677, www.pops66.com, 6am-10pm daily; restaurant 10:30am-9pm Mon.-Fri., 7am-9pm Sat.-Sun., $8-13) has to be the most unique gas station in America. A colossal 66-foot-tall (20-m), LED-lit sculpture of a bottle emerges over the horizon, inviting travelers to stop at the neo-futuristic

Pops, Arcadia

service station designed by architect Rand Elliott. The 4-ton (3.6-metric-ton) soda bottle reaches skyward over the glass-and-steel station with its massive cantilevered canopy. Inside, the walls shoot overhead at a sharp angle, and colorful bottles of soda line the window in perfect succession.

The diner serves breakfast all day, as well as burgers and shakes. It's usually crowded, so plan to wait about an hour for a table, especially on weekends.

Route 66 has a long tradition of roadside tourist traps that use every clever marketing trick to make you pull off the road and spend your money. In many ways, Pops is no different. It's flashy and gimmicky, but that's half the fun.

◆ Back on 66

As you travel west, Route 66 ends at I-35. Keep heading west and follow U.S. 77 into Edmond. After 3 miles (4.8 km), turn left (south) on Broadway (U.S. 77) and drive 3 more miles (4.8 km) to the Memorial Road/Kelley Avenue exit. Turn left on Kelley Avenue and drive 5 miles (8 km) to join I-44 west. Take the next exit for Lincoln Boulevard (Exit 128A). Turn left and head south on North Lincoln Boulevard into Oklahoma City.

Oklahoma City

Oklahoma City comes with a complicated history that has defined our nation, for better and for worse. Thousands of American Indians were forced off their land in the eastern United States and relocated here in exchange for their original homeland. The government believed this land had no value, but it wasn't long before agricultural and ranching techniques ensured the land could turn a profit. That's when everything changed.

The Dawes Act of 1887 opened up 2 million acres (809,371 hectares) of land to white settlement. Under a cloudless sky at high noon on April 22, 1889, more than 50,000 land-thirsty Americans lined up along the state border. At the crack of a whip, they rushed into Indian Territory on horseback, in wagons, and on foot. By that evening, thousands of plots had been claimed, an event that some considered a display of pioneer spirit. However, the fact of the matter was that the tribes had lost their land again, and their culture, and their way of life. The reservations were dissolved, and the tribes forced to assimilate.

Over the following decade, legal battles filled the courts with people fighting over property ownership. A lottery system was put in place to designate claims, and by 1905, as a result of the Land Rush, Oklahoma City had become one of the biggest boomtowns in the state. Two years later, this area was no longer called Indian Territory: "Oklahoma" became the 46th state of the Union in 1907.

◈ Route 66 Through Oklahoma City

The pre-1930s alignment passed through the northern part of the city. Head south on Lincoln and turn right (west) on 23rd Street. In less than 2 miles (3.2 km), turn right (north) on North Classen Boulevard. After about 1 mile (1.6 km), follow signs marked "OK 66 NW 39th Expy."

Sights

Oklahoma City boasts pedestrian-friendly streets, nice landscaping, public art, bike lanes, and a canal and waterfront area. There's much to see and do here.

Oklahoma History Center

Let the history of Oklahoma unfold before your eyes at this 215,000-square-foot (19,974-sq-m), 18-acre (7.3-hectare) site. A Smithsonian affiliate, the **Oklahoma History Center** (800 Nazih Zuhdi Dr., 405/522-0765, www.okhistory.org/historycenter, 10am-5pm Mon.-Sat., $10) explores everything from aviation, transportation, and commerce to heritage and geology. There are five state-of-the-art permanent galleries, an outdoor oil-field exhibit with drilling derricks, and more than 200 interactive exhibits that not only educate but also entertain.

Once Route 66 arrived in the city, traffic congestion became quite the problem. Picture this: In 1913, there were 3,000 cars. By the 1930s, there were more than 500,000. To handle parking issues, the city attempted to place time limits on parking, but this was difficult to enforce. That is, until Carl C. Magee invented the Park-O-Meter, aka the world's first parking meter. It cost a nickel an hour in 1935 and sparked a huge debate as opponents called it "un-American" to have to pay for parking. However, the effectiveness of the meter caught on quickly. Within

Top to bottom: Lake Overholser; an old school building in Oklahoma City; Gold Dome Building

five years, there were 140,000 parking meters in the United States. Today, you can see **Park-O-Meter No. 1** on display at the Oklahoma History Center.

First Americans Museum

The **First Americans Museum** (659 American Indian Blvd., 405/594-2100, https://famok.org, 10am-5pm Mon.-Fri., 11am-5pm Sat.-Sun., $15), opening September 2021, showcases exhibitions on Oklahoma's 39 American Indian tribes, from arts and culture to history. In addition to the exhibits, the family-friendly discovery center and live education programs offer an immersive, hands-on learning experience. Enjoy lunch at on-site restaurant featuring native cuisine, then browse the gift shop's selection of authentic, handmade items from American Indian artists.

Milk Bottle Grocery

Milk Bottle Grocery (2426 N. Classen Blvd.) was a 350-square-foot (32.5-sq-m) grocery store built in 1930 that, despite its tiny size, maintained a successful business thanks to a strategic location at an old streetcar stop that bisected busy Classen Boulevard. In typical Route 66 fashion, the owners added a supersized sheet-metal sculpture of a milk bottle to the roof in 1948 as a funky advertising gimmick to attract motorists' attention. The bottle, with its long, tapered neck and rounded bottle cap, looks exactly like a 1940s milk container. Even though the store is no longer open, the building—and the infamous bottle—still stand.

Gold Dome Building

The 1958 **Gold Dome Building** (1112 NW 23rd St.) is a geodesic dome based on famous futurist Buckminster Fuller's design. With its bulbous roof made of 625 gold panels, the structure looks like a glowing spacecraft that landed smack in the middle of suburban America. Originally a Citizens State Bank—and considered one of the country's most innovative bank designs at the time of its construction—over the years it's been home to a cultural center, restaurant, and art gallery. Though the building is not currently open to the public, swing by and take some pics.

Oklahoma City National Memorial and Museum

In 1995, a terrorist bombing at Alfred P. Murrah Federal Building by U.S. veteran Timothy McVeigh catapulted Oklahoma City into tragic infamy. About 800 people were maimed, and 149 men and women and 19 children were killed. The **Oklahoma City National Memorial and Museum** (620 N. Harvey Ave., 405/235-3313, https://memorialmuseum.com, 9am-6pm Mon.-Sat., noon-6pm Sun., $15) honors those who lost their lives in the attack. With interactive exhibits and powerful oral histories, videos, and bomb-damaged artifacts, the museum walks you through the day of the attack, and the days, weeks, and years following, to help you understand how this event forever shaped the city. The memorial park contains a survivor tree and a field filled with 168 chairs engraved with the name of each person who died.

Centennial Land Run Monument

The **Centennial Land Run Monument** (200 Centennial Ave., 24 hours daily, free) comprises 45 life-size sculptures that reenact the Land Rush, one of the largest freestanding bronze sculptures in the world. The artwork captures the intense energy of the event in impressive detail, but it should not be overlooked that the moment in history that this monument depicts is one that ripped away land from tribal members, forever changing their lives.

The monument is located in the South End of Bricktown Canal.

Riversport

Do an 80-foot (24-m) free fall off a 700-foot (213-m) zipline across the Oklahoma

River at **Riversport** (800 Riversport Dr., 405/552-4040, www.riversportokc.org, 11am-6pm daily May-mid-Aug., 11am-5pm Sat.-Sun. mid-Aug.-Dec., from $40-80). Or just enjoy a gentle kayak ride. This adventure park offers fun for all thrill levels (and skill levels) and is located right on the water in the Boathouse District. Additional activities include whitewater rafting, tubing, boating, and stand-up paddleboarding. Bonus: Bring your four-legged friend to enjoy the on-site Barks and Brews Dog Park.

City Districts

More than a dozen districts packed with restaurants, nightlife, stores, and art galleries comprise Oklahoma City. You could spend days exploring them all, but there are a few not to miss. **Bricktown,** just east of downtown between the Bricktown Ballpark and the Oklahoma River, is a former warehouse district with great restaurants, breweries, shops,

and hotels. **Automobile Alley,** north of downtown, used to be the city center for car dealerships and now hosts some of Oklahoma's best dining and shopping. The **Paseo Arts District** is home to almost 20 galleries and 80 artists, eateries, coffeehouses, boutiques, and a First Friday gallery walk.

Shopping

At **Plenty Mercantile** (807 N. Broadway Ave., 405/888-7470, www.plentymercantile.com, 10am-6pm Mon.-Sat., noon-4pm Sun.), authenticity, style, and a local sensibility reign. The store features goods and products from all over the country, as long as they're from companies that are socially, ethically, and/or environmentally responsible. The store's cool digs are located inside the former Scott-Chevrolet Dealership in Automobile Alley.

Inter-Tribal Designs (1520 N. Portland Ave., 405/943-7935, www.

Centennial Land Run Monument by Paul Moore

The Green Book in Oklahoma City

More than 100 businesses in Oklahoma appeared in the *Negro Motorist Green Book,* with about 40 of those in Oklahoma City. Many of the businesses that welcomed Black travelers in Oklahoma City were located on the 300 block of 2nd Street. This area was known as the "Deep Deuce" and was the community hub for African Americans during the 1900s-1950s. It was a bustling business, shopping, and nightlife district. Even the weekly newspaper, *The Black Dispatch*, was headquartered in the Deep Deuce.

Unfortunately, many of the Green Book businesses in Oklahoma City have been demolished, but a few structures stand today: **Littlepage Hotel** (219 N. Central St.), where Duke Ellington and Nat King Cole supposedly stayed; **Ruby's Dance Hall and Grill** (322 N.E. 2nd St.); and **Luster's Modern Motel** (3402 N.E. 23rd St.), which is now the Deluxe Motel.

okitd.com, 10am-6pm Mon.-Sat.) is American Indian-owned and -operated. The shop sells authentic clothing, pottery, blankets, *kachinas,* sterling silver and turquoise jewelry, and beading. Built to resemble an old trading post, the store showcases large murals by a Choctaw artist.

Food

Brown's Bakery (1100 N. Walker Ave., 405/232-0363, 5:30am-11am Mon.-Tues., 5:30am-1pm Wed.-Fri., 5:30-noon Sat., $2-8) is one of those family-owned places that have been around forever. Since 1946, Brown's has served up all kinds of baked goodies: cake doughnuts, maple long johns, cinnamon rolls, pies, cheesecake, and thumbprint cookies.

In the 1970s, Vietnamese immigrants flocked to Oklahoma City, and today it has some of the most authentic Asian food you'll ever taste. Most of the restaurants are located around 23rd Street and Classen Boulevard (near the Milk Bottle Grocery). **Lido Restaurant** (2518 N. Military Ave., 405/521-1902, www.lidorestaurantokc.com, 10:30am-9pm Mon.-Thurs., 10:30am-9:30pm Fri., 11am-9:30pm Sat., $7-15) blends Vietnamese and colonial French dishes. Vermicelli bowls come loaded with fresh mint, bean sprouts, and carrots. Don't miss the spring rolls with peanut sauce: yum.

Mad about pho? Go to **Pho Lien Hoa** (901 NW 23rd St., 405/521-8087, 9am-9pm daily, $8-12). This simple, cash-only restaurant sets the benchmark for the best pho in the state with generous portions, perfectly cooked noodles, and a broth that's full of flavor.

Classen Grill (5124 N. Classen Cir., 405/842-0428, www.classengrillokc.com, 7am-2pm Mon.-Wed., 6:30am-2pm Thurs., 6:30am-3pm Fri., 8am-3pm Sat.-Sun., $5-10) is a breakfast joint with funky decor and killer pancakes. Freshly squeezed orange juice, flaky biscuits, and Memphis French toast with peanut butter and bananas ... need I say more?

Cattlemen's Steakhouse (1309 S. Agnew Ave., 405/236-0416, www.cattlemensrestaurant.com, 6am-10pm Sun.-Thurs., 6am-11pm Fri.-Sat., $15-40) is the oldest continuously operating restaurant in Oklahoma City. The restaurant opened in 1910 in Stockyards City and served thousands of people who worked in the stockyards; during Prohibition, this place brewed its own liquid libations. The featured menu item is—you guessed it—steak, from top sirloin and filet mignon to chicken fried steak.

Pinkitzel (150 South E. K. Gaylord Blvd., 405/235-7465, www.pinkitzel.com, 11am-9pm Mon.-Thurs., 11am-11pm Fri.-Sat., 1pm-9pm Sun., $10-35) is a boutique bakery and sweetshop that delights the senses. This sugar-filled wonderland sells cakes, taffy, pralines, truffles, macarons, and cupcakes. Liquid treats show up in the form of pink lemonade and hot cocoa flavored with peppermint or salted caramel.

Accommodations

The sleek **Aloft Oklahoma City Downtown** (209 N. Walnut Ave., 405/605-2100, www.aloftoklahomacitybricktown.com, $160-260) offers accommodations with loft-inspired designs, comfy beds, rainfall showerheads, and plug-and-play connectivity stations for electronics. Splurge on the two-story, 1,900-square-foot (177-sq-m) celebrity suite, which boasts starburst chandeliers and floor-to-ceiling windows. Hotel amenities include an outdoor pool and a rooftop lounge, along with beds, toys, and treats for canine companions.

The historic 1911 ★ **Skirvin Hilton Hotel** (1 Park Ave., 405/272-3040, www.skirvinhilton.com, $189-360) has hosted presidents, actors, politicians, and athletes over its 100-year-plus run. The traditional style of the hotel is a class act. The stately rooms feature solid wood doors, overstuffed chairs with ottomans, and beds with tall, regal headboards. Furry friends are welcome.

For something with understated grandeur, try the ★ **Ambassador Hotel** (1200 N. Walker Ave., 405/600-6200, http://ambassadorokc.com, $183-577). Located in the U-shaped, art deco Osler Building, the structure was built in 1928 as offices for the University of Oklahoma Medical School. It was named after William Osler, the man who established the medical residency program. Today the only hint of the hotel's former life is a medical insignia above the front door. With modern amenities such as iOS docking stations, high-thread-count linens, evening turndown service, and monogrammed robes,

the Ambassador makes sure you're living in the lap of luxury. After you check in, head to the rooftop bar for a cocktail and city views.

◈ Detour: Lake Overholser Bridge

The 1925 **Lake Overholser Bridge** was a critical link for Route 66 drivers until the 1950s. Once the volume of traffic increased and cars got heavier, a newer, wider four-lane highway was built just north of the bridge. Today, the bridge carries local traffic and leads to a leafy lakeside park. Entrance is free and the water vistas bordering the park provide a respite for road-weary eyes.

As you leave Oklahoma City on NW 39th Expressway—and before you cross the North Canadian River, about 0.5 mile (0.8 km) west of North Council Road—keep an eye out for this old bridge south of the highway.

◈ Back on 66

From Oklahoma City, head west on Route 66 (NW 39th St.) for about 10 miles (16.1 km), passing Yukon. After 13 miles (20.9 km), Route 66 curves north and turns into South Rock Island Avenue.

Lake Overholser Bridge

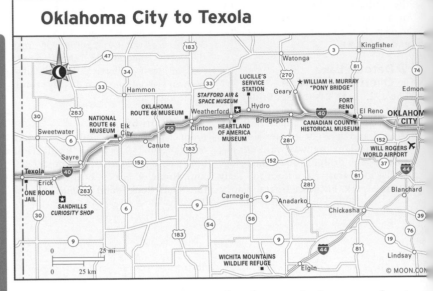

Oklahoma City to Texola

El Reno

Route 66 brought life to El Reno. By the mid-1930s, there were 10 hotels, 24 grocery stores, 27 barbershops, 20 gas stations, and 31 restaurants. When the railroad first popped up in the 1890s, the town became a major crossroads for the north-south and east-west transcontinental lines railway lines. By the 1950s, the railroad industry employed about 1,300 people in El Reno, but the railroad went bankrupt in 1980.

◆ Route 66 Through El Reno

Drive north on South Rock Island Avenue and turn left (west) at East Wade Street. After a few blocks, turn right (north) on U.S. 81 (Choctaw Avenue), then take the next left (west) on Sunset Drive.

Sights

The **Canadian County Historical Museum** (300 S. Grand Ave. 405/262-5121, http://canadiancountymuseum.com, 10am-4pm Wed.-Sat., 1pm-4pm Sun., free) is located on the 98th meridian, the site

where the eastern lands were open for settlement. (The western side of the border was settled by Arapaho and Cheyenne tribes.) Tour a frontier jail, barn, church, one-room schoolhouse, and restored train depot with memorabilia, including a Red Cross canteen from 1918.

Food

For a truly authentic Oklahoma gastronomical experience, try an onion burger. Three restaurants in El Reno specialize in this Depression-era culinary creation, and they're all equally excellent.

Johnnie's Grill (301 S. Rock Island Ave., 405/262-4721, 7am-9pm Mon.-Thurs., 6am-9pm Fri.-Sat., 11am-8pm Sun., $3-7) is the largest of the three restaurants. The no-frills interior resembles a fast-food place.

Robert's Grill (300 S. Bickford Ave., 405/262-1262, 6am-9pm Mon.-Sat., 6am-7pm Sun., $3-6) is a cute spot whose origin dates back to the birth of the Mother Road. There are no tables and only 14 stools, so either get lucky or get your food to go.

Sid's Diner (300 S. Choctaw Ave.,

Local Eats

The **onion burger** was born out of economic necessity during the Great Depression. Since meat was scarce at that time, cooks grilled thin ribbons of onion, then added them to ground beef to bolster the size of the patty. A happy accident occurred: As the onions caramelized, they formed a savory crust on the patty. Thus, the cost-saving measure boosted the flavor and texture of the burger, and now you can enjoy this Okie food item all along Route 66.

It doesn't get any more Oklahoma than a platter of **fresh catfish** deep-fried in cornmeal and served with crispy **tater tots.**

Ranchers were the first to favor the now-ubiquitous **fried fruit pie**, a flaky, chewy pillow of fried dough filled with warm, gooey fruit.

405/262-7757, www.sidsdinerelreno. com, 7am-8pm Mon.-Sat., $5-10) is a bit roomier than Robert's, with red and black booths lining the walls and historic pictures to check out while you wait.

✦ Back on 66

The 18-mile (29-km) segment between El Reno and Hydro is where the road opens up and the vast expanse of the American West begins to emerge. In the 1930s, the standard road width was 20 feet (6 m); in 1935, this segment was straightened and shortened to create a more direct route.

To take the 1926 alignment, leave El Reno driving west on Route 66 (Sunset Drive). As the road begins to curve south, take a right on East 1020 Road, which is the two-lane alignment of Route 66. Fort Reno is a few hundred feet past the turn.

✦ Detour: Fort Reno

The eastern part of El Reno opened up for settlement in the Land Run of 1889; the western section was designated as Cheyenne and Arapaho land. To monitor the region, the Army established **Fort Reno** (7107 W. Cheyenne St., 405/262-3987, www.fortreno.org, 10am-4pm Tues.-Sat., $6) in 1847. The Buffalo Soldiers, an all-Black regiment of the Army, were also stationed here. Later, during World War II, Fort Reno became an internment camp for 1,300 German prisoners of war. Seventy German and

Italian soldiers are buried in the western part of the cemetery.

Fort Reno is located 4 miles (6.4 km) west of El Reno, near I-40 (Exit 119). From the pre-1930s alignment of Route 66, it is just after the turn off Sunset Drive. Note: Entering Fort Reno into GPS may take you to the wrong place, so consult a map.

✦ Back on 66

From Fort Reno, continue west on East 1020 Road. In about 4 miles (6.4 km), turn right (north) on U.S. 270 (N. Calumet Rd.). Drive 4.5 miles (7.2 km), turn left and continue following I-270 for 6 miles (9.7 km) to the town of Geary.

Geary

Geary was Arapaho and Cheyenne country until 1892, when 3.5 million acres (1.4 million hectares) were opened to settlement by the U.S. government. Almost 80 percent of the land wasn't claimed, however, when a terrible drought lasted until 1896. Today, it's a rural farming community with a few old buildings spanning Main Street.

✦ Route 66 Through Geary

Route 66 enters Geary via 150th Street NW and continues 0.5 mile (0.8 km) before heading south (left) on Broadway.

Sights

Upon entering Geary, turn right (north) on Broadway (SR-270) to see the historic **Gillespie Building** (100 E. Main St.). Built in 1903, it later became the American State Bank, which failed during the Great Depression.

Turn right on Main Street and, at the intersection of Canadian Avenue and NE Boulevard, is an old **water trough** that was used by horses and visitors who came through here in the early 1900s.

◈ Back on 66

Drive south on Broadway Avenue, which turns into U.S. 281. In 4 miles (6.4 km), turn left (southwest) to follow SR-8/U.S. 281. Drive 2.5 miles (4 km), and as you approach the Canadian River, you'll see one of the most significant bridges on Route 66.

William H. Murray "Pony Bridge"

The 1933 **William H. Murray Bridge** (locals call it the "Pony Bridge") is the longest truss bridge on Route 66, with a span of nearly 4,000 feet (1,219 m). The bridge got the nickname for its 38 yellow pony trusses, each 100 feet (30 m) long. The camelback design has a curved arch that makes the bridge strong and light—it also makes it appear that it goes on for infinity, a mind-bending optical illusion as you drive it. Head to the west end of the bridge, where a scene from the 1940 film *The Grapes of Wrath* was shot. The bridge is in danger of being torn down and replaced. Cross it now, while you still can.

◈ Back on 66

Head south on U.S. 281. When the road begins to bend right (west), stay straight to continue on Route 66 (don't follow SR-8). The next town is Hydro, about 10 miles (16.1 km) west.

Hydro

Sights
Lucille's Service Station

The two-story **Lucille's Service Station** was built in 1929 and is one of only two stations like it on Route 66 in Oklahoma. Lucille Hamons ran the gas station from 1941 to 2000, when she passed away. Her nickname was "Mother of the Mother Road" thanks to her welcoming spirit to down-on-their-luck Route 66 travelers. Though the station is no longer operating, you can still admire the large, distinctive, tapered piers that support the property, with its porch, exposed rafter tails, and overhanging eaves in the Craftsman style. Vintage gas pumps sit outside, and the owner's living quarters used to be upstairs. Lucille's is located 0.5 mile (0.8 km) west of SR-58 to the right (north) of Route 66.

◈ Back on 66

Drive west on Route 66 (the I-40 frontage road) for 5 miles (8 km) to Weatherford.

Weatherford

Soon after Route 66 came through Main Street in Weatherford, the Works Progress Administration funded the construction of the National Guard Armory. By the 1960s, the company 3M employed many of the folks who lived here. Today, Weatherford has one of the largest wind farms in Oklahoma.

◈ Route 66 Through Weatherford

Route 66 enters Weatherford on Main Street and heads south. Turn left (south) on North Washington Avenue, and then take an immediate right (west) onto Main Street/Business I-40 through downtown.

Sights
★ Stafford Air & Space Museum
The **Stafford Air & Space Museum** (3000 E. Logan Rd., 580/772-5871, www. staffordmuseum.com, 9am-5pm Mon.-Sat., 1pm-5pm Sun., $7) is one of those surprising gems that shouldn't be missed. It's named after astronaut Thomas P. Stafford, a man from Weatherford. Stafford piloted Gemini VI, commanded Apollo 10, and received a Congressional Space Medal of Honor. The museum that bears his name collaborated with the U.S. Air Force Museum, the Smithsonian Institution, and NASA to compile the 3,500 artifacts on display, including rockets (as in, real rockets!), airplanes, and spacecraft, plus other fascinating items such as space food, survival gear, and a Gemini flight suit.

From Route 66 (Main St.), turn right (north on Jim Cobb Dr.). The museum is a few blocks away.

Heartland of America Museum
The **Heartland of America Museum** (1600 S. Frontage Rd., 580/774-2212, www.oklahomaheartlandmuseum.com, 9am-5pm Tues.-Fri., 1pm-5pm Sat., $6) is a local history museum that gives visitors a glimpse into small-town America from the late 1800s through the 1950s. See a collection of classic cars, vintage wedding dresses, a well-stocked general store, a diner where Elvis Presley once ate, a small schoolhouse, and a blacksmith shop.

Weatherford Wind Energy Center
In the midst of oil and gas country, it's refreshing to see a field of wind-loving turbines. These enormous wind turbines generate energy for more than 44,000 homes. Each turbine stands 262 feet (80 m) tall with blades that are 122 feet (37 m) long. To see a turbine blade up close, visit the **Weatherford Wind Energy Center** (522 W. Rainey Ave., http:// cityofweatherford.com/wind-towers) across from City Hall.

Food
If you're over onion burgers, then pay a visit to **Casa Soto** (115 SW Main St., 580/772-0232, 11am-9pm Mon.-Thurs., 11am-10pm Fri.-Sat., $8-15), where the Mexican food is made from family recipes and the tables are populated with loyal locals. You'll enjoy generous portions of authentic food with the nicest customer service imaginable.

◈ Back on 66
Drive west on Main Street leaving Weatherford. Turn left (south) on 4th Street (SR-54); the road goes right and heads west for 6 miles (9.7 km). Turn right (north) at N2330 Road and take the next left (west) at E1030 Road. In 2 miles (3.2 km), turn left (south) on N2310 Road. The Cherokee Trading Post is on the left (east) side of the road before you reach I-40.

Cherokee Trading Post

After gold was discovered in Georgia in 1829, an estimated 16,000 Cherokees were forced at gunpoint to leave their homes and walk to Oklahoma. More than 4,000 died. The Cherokee Nation rebuilt itself in Oklahoma, and you can learn how at the **Cherokee Trading Post** (23107 N. Frontage Rd., 580/275-2476, www.cherokeegifts.com, 8am-10pm daily). The family-owned business offers a wealth of knowledge about Cherokee history, including a list of the Cherokee alphabet with a pronunciation guide, and sells clothing, knives, jewelry, and other accessories.

◈ Back on 66
Drive west on the north I-40 Frontage Road for 3 miles (4.8 km), then join Business I-40 into the town of Clinton.

🔷 Side Trip: Indiahoma

Breathe in the fresh air at **Wichita Mountains Wildlife Refuge** (32 Refuge Headquarters, Indiahoma, 580/429-3222, www.fws.gov/refuge/Wichita_Mountains, dawn-dusk daily, free). Established in 1901 with almost 60,000 acres (24,281 hectares) of wilderness, the refuge is home to more than 250 animal species, including bald eagles, whooping cranes, and black-tail prairie dogs. In 1907, 15 bison were brought here from the New York Bronx Zoo; today, there are 650. There are also about 700 elk and 300 longhorns. You can hike, bike, fish, and camp throughout this wild and rugged landscape.

Exhibits at the **visitors center** (SR-115 and SR-49, 9am-5pm daily) include dioramas, art, sculptures, and taxidermy. Hiking maps, books, and park pamphlets are available in the gift shop. **Doris Campground** (gates open 8am-10pm Sun.-Thurs., 8am-11pm Fri.-Sat. Apr.-Oct.; 8am-8pm Sun.-Thurs., 8am-10pm Fri.-Sat. Nov.-Mar., $12-24), located west of the visitors center, has drinking water, grills, picnic tables, tent sites, a shower/restroom facility, and electric hookups for RVs. Campsites are first-come, first-served, and backcountry camping is by reservation/permit only. Pets are welcome.

The Wichita Mountains Wildlife Refuge is a two-hour drive south of Weatherford. From Route 66 west of Weatherford, take SR-54 south for 15 miles (24 km). Turn right (west) on SR-152 and continue 7 miles (11.3 km). Turn left (south) on SR-54 and drive 38 miles (61 km). Turn left (east) on SR-49 to enter the refuge. Arrive with plenty of gas and observe posted speed limits in order to protect wildlife (and yourself).

Clinton

Cotton was the leading crop in Clinton's early years. About 10 years after Route 66 arrived in Clinton, the Swift meatpacking company (later Bar-S) became the largest employer, with 500 workers. Clinton's claim to fame today is that it's home to a popular Route 66 museum and has one of the oldest trading posts in the state.

🔷 Route 66 Through Clinton

Enter Clinton via Business I-40 and turn left (south) on 4th Street (U.S. 183). Turn right (west) on Opal Avenue, then turn left (south) on 10th Avenue, which turns into Neptune Drive. After about 1 mile (1.6 km), turn right (west) onto Commerce Road.

Sights
Mohawk Lodge Indian Store
The **Mohawk Lodge Indian Store** (22702 Rte. 66 N., 580/323-2360, 9am-5:30pm daily) originally opened in a different location in 1892; it moved to its current location in Clinton in 1940. It was a place where Cheyenne women made and sold handcrafted wares. Historical artifacts and antique photos display its rich history, and tribal treasures are sold across the same counter that was used in 1892. Items include tanned hides, Pendleton blankets, beaded moccasins, handmade pottery, and more.

McLain Rogers Park
The 12-acre (4.8-hectare) **McLain Rogers Park** (10th St. and Bess Rogers Dr., dawn-dusk daily, free) welcomes visitors with a photo-worthy, art deco sign. During the 1930s and '40s, Route 66 road-trippers picnicked here, swam in the Olympic-size swimming pool, and played in the children's park. Today, you'll enjoy all of that and more, including an 18-hole miniature golf course.

Oklahoma Route 66 Museum

Oklahoma Route 66 Museum (2229 W. Gary Blvd., 580/323-7866, www.route66. org, 9am-5pm Tues.-Sat., $7) is a museum entirely dedicated to Route 66. Operated by the Oklahoma Historical Society, it is filled with exhibits, vintage cars, and an indoor "drive-in theatre." Best-selling author and storyteller Michael Wallis narrates the tumultuous history of the fabled road, tracing the major cultural and social changes that have taken place since the 1920s. The museum also does a nice job detailing the impact of the racial and class migrations that occurred along the Mother Road. Outside, check out a restored, prefab, 1940s **Valentine Diner**.

The Route 66 Museum is 1 mile (1.6 km) west of Route 66. From Route 66 (U.S.-183), turn right (west) onto Modelle Avenue and turn left (south) on Business I-40 (W. Gary Blvd). The museum is on the right.

Food

At **White Dog Hill Restaurant** (22901 Old 66 Frontage Rd., 580/323-6922, 5:30pm-9pm Wed.-Sat., $10-30), diners tuck into expertly prepared steaks and seafood. The restaurant lives in the red-stone former Clinton Country Club, with a large deck offering big views of prairie sunsets.

To get to the White Dog, head west on the I-40 Frontage Road about 3 miles (4.8 km) east of Clinton. Turn right (north) on N2290 Road; at the fork immediately after the turn, go right. The restaurant is about 900 feet (274 m) up the road. Note: Do not use GPS to find the White Dog Hill Restaurant.

In the 1970s, Jiggs Botchlett opened **Jiggs Smokehouse** (22203 N. Frontage Rd., 580/323-5641, www. jiggssmokehouse.com, 11am-7pm Tues.-Fri., 11am-5pm Sat., $8-15) as a retail shop for his turkeys and eggs. Today,

Top to bottom: McLain Rogers Park in Clinton; Valentine Diner; Oklahoma Route 66 Museum

the family-run restaurant specializes in sandwiches stacked high with hickory-smoked meats and slathered in barbecue sauce. The Wooly Burger weighs in at 31 ounces (0.8 kg) of smoked ham, summer sausage, relish, and cheddar cheese. This place is truly for carnivores—the only veggies on offer are lettuce, tomatoes, onions, and pickles.

◈ Back on 66

Leaving Clinton, drive west on Commerce Road, which becomes South Frontage Road. In less than 5 miles (8 km), turn right (north) on N2170 Road (Exit 57 near I-40) and cross the freeway. Turn left (west) at North Frontage Road and drive past the town of **Foss** to Exit 50. Turn left to go back across the freeway, then head west (right) on South Frontage Road. Drive 3 miles (4.8 km) west to Canute.

Canute

◈ Route 66 Through Canute

South Frontage Road becomes Old U.S. Highway 66 through Canute. Continue west to the intersection of Main Street.

Sights

As you drive about 10 blocks through the small community of Canute, there are a few roadside sights on the east side of town. Located next to the cemetery as you enter Canute from the east is **Oklahoma's first state park,** built on Route 66 by the Works Progress Administration.

Near Main Street, the mid-century neon signs of the derelict **Cotton Boll Motel** and **Washita Motel** still stand as fading remnants of more vibrant days.

On the northwest corner of Main Street and Route 66 is the 1930s **Canute Service Station,** built in a Pueblo Deco style with a gabled roof and canopy sporting triangular pediments and decorated with red diamonds.

Located in an alley north of Scheidel

Avenue (at Main St.) is an old **jailhouse** that dates to 1918.

On Route 66, about three blocks west of the Canute Station, is the abandoned **Kupka's Service Station** with a canopy whose signature curved corners exemplify the traditional 1930s Streamline Moderne style.

◈ Back on 66

From Canute, head west on Route 66 for 6 miles (9.7 km) to Elk City.

Elk City

Before Elk City was established in 1901, cattle drives from Texas to Kansas came through, making it a popular place to stop. By 1918, Elk City had an ice plant, two flour mills, and two broom factories. By the 1930s, nine cotton gins were in operation and the first cooperative community hospital opened; local farmers could pay $50 for one share of stock, then pay $25 a year for free medical care for their immediate family.

When the U.S. Highway 66 Association held its annual convention in 1931 here, more than 20,000 people came. After Route 66 was rerouted, Elk City didn't suffer like other towns bypassed by the Mother Road; it remained busy thanks to the oil and gas industry. (Elk City's biggest claim to fame is that it was considered the natural gas capital of the world.) Today, the biggest Route 66 attraction is the Old Town Museum complex, which houses the National Route 66 Museum.

◈ Route 66 Through Elk City

Route 66 enters Elk City via North Van Buren Avenue, then dips south before curving west on 3rd Street (Business I-40), the main drag through town.

Sights
National Route 66 Museum

The **National Route 66 Museum** (320

Women of the Mother Road

The story of Route 66 isn't complete without the illustrious women who've contributed greatly to the road's growth, success, and preservation. Here, celebrate the Oklahoman women who made a profound impact on the Mother Road.

♦ **Anita Arnold:** As a high school senior in 1957, Anita made milkshakes at Oklahoma City's Randolph Drug Store, a business listed in the ***Negro Motorist Green Book.*** She met well-known figures as they traveled through, including musicians from the Count Basie Orchestra. As an adult, she discovered that her former high school was lacking the basic funds to prepare students for the future. She joined the Black Liberated Arts Center and worked to bring arts, history, and heritage to a community whose youth had been deprived of a solid educational foundation. She's written books about the history of Black people in Oklahoma City, helped provide professional development training for teachers, and raised money for music instruments. Today, she's the Executive Director of the Black Liberated Arts Center and her old high school is nationally recognized as a model school for arts integration.

♦ **Gladys Cutberth:** Known as "Mrs. Route 66" for her tireless efforts lobbying elected officials in Washington DC to keep the highway's presence in small towns, Gladys also headquartered the National Route 66 Association in her basement for 25 years. For much of that time, she traveled door-to-door along the route to build relationships with the locals and business owners who made their livelihood along the Mother Road. Gladys said that she drove Route 66 so often that she wore out one car per year.

♦ **Lucille Hamons:** One of 10 children, and the only one to graduate from high school, Lucille Hamons was a kind-hearted soul whose generosity earned her the nickname "Mother of the Mother Road." In 1941, Lucille Hamons and her husband, Carl, bought the gas station that would become **Lucille's Service Station** (page 168) in Hydro. They lived in the upstairs apartment with their children, working around the clock to offer service and hospitality to Route 66 travelers. When motorists had no money for gas, much less a roof over their head, Lucille provided food and shelter for whatever they could offer to pay, or sometimes even if they could pay nothing. In 1971, Route 66 moved to I-40, and despite the hardships Lucille faced because of dwindling business and lessening through traffic, she stuck it out, working at the station seven days a week for nearly 60 years until she passed away in 2000.

♦ **Dawn Welch:** As owner of the popular **Rock Cafe** (page 155) for more than 20 years, Dawn Welch has weathered many storms, including a tornado that obliterated the restaurant and a fire that burned it down. She rebuilt the business both times, reinvents the menu to keep things fresh, entertains customers, and works hard to promote other businesses along Route 66, all while raising kids. It's no wonder the character of Sally Carrera in the Pixar film *Cars* is modeled after Dawn.

W. 3rd St., 580/225-3230, www.elkcity.com, 9am-5pm Tues.-Sat., $5) offers travel exhibits of the Mother Road along with re-creations of a chapel, bank, general store, doctor's office, grist mill, and opera house. The museum takes you through the eight states on the Mother Road and gives a glimpse into the lives of early settlers and pioneers who lived and worked on Route 66.

Casa Grande Hotel

The 1928 **Casa Grande Hotel** (103 E. 3rd St.) was the site of one the first meetings of the U.S. Highway 66 Association. At one time, Casa Grande was advertised as the largest and only fireproof hotel between Amarillo and Oklahoma City.

Parker Drilling Rig

Located behind the Casa Grande Hotel is the **Parker Drilling Rig #114**. At 179 feet (55 m)—the approximate height of a 22-story building—this is the world's tallest non-operating oil rig. The Parker Drilling Rig was built in the mid-1960s to drill shafts in order to test-detonate atomic bombs underground; it was later used for oil and gas drilling.

Hedlund Motor Company

The **Hedlund Motor Company** (206 S. Main St.) was established in 1913 and is the second oldest Ford dealership in Oklahoma. The 1918 building, a striking stucco Mission Revival structure with red clay tiles, is on Main Street, about two blocks south of Route 66.

Food

For ladies who lunch (or anyone in the mood for tea and tiny cakes), there's **Country Dove Tea Room** (610 W. 3rd St., 580/225-7028, 11am-6pm Mon.-Sat., $10-12). Step into a renovated 1920s house to sip a cup of tea, nibble on quiche, and dig into a slice of French silk pie.

Family-owned **Lupe's Cocina & Cantina** (905 N. Main St., 580/225-7109, 11am-9pm Mon.-Thurs., 11am-9:30pm Fri.-Sat., 11am-3pm Sun., $10-20) serves cold beer and Tex-Mex dishes like sizzling fajitas and fried avocados. It's located just a few blocks north of Route 66 on Main Street.

◆ Back on 66

Leave Elk City heading west on Business I-40. Soon after passing SR-34 (about 4 mi/6.4 km) from Elk City), take the next right and then a quick left to North Frontage Road. Follow it for about 10 miles (16.1 km) to I-40 (near Exit 25) and turn right (west) on Business I-40, which leads into the town of Sayre.

Sayre

Sayre once served as a major shipping point for wheat, cotton, corn, and livestock; the town promoted itself as the place where the "Spirit of the West is still alive." By the 1930s, there were five oil companies and a gasoline plant keeping people employed. Now a rusted grain elevator by the railroad tracks is the only reminder of Sayre's agricultural past.

◆ Route 66 though Sayre

The Mother Road enters via Business I-40 and turns left (south) on 4th Street (U.S. 283). Route 66 continues through the historic downtown district.

Sights

As you head into town, look for the **Western Motel** (315 NE Rte. 66, 580/928-3353), which sports a vintage yellow-and-blue neon sign with a distinctive font and a neon cactus. There's also a **WPA Pedestrian Tunnel** (4th and Elm Sts.), built to help pedestrians safely cross under the steady stream of traffic on Route 66.

Beckham County Courthouse

The three-story neoclassical brick **Beckham County Courthouse** (302 E. Main St., 580/928-3330, 8am-4pm Mon.-Fri., free) was built in 1911 and is one of the few domed courthouses in Oklahoma.

WPA Land Run Mural

Located inside the post office is a 1940 **WPA Mural** (201 N. 4th St., 8:30am-11am and noon-4:30pm Mon.-Fri., 10am-noon Sat., free) by Vance Kirkland. The mural depicts the Land Run, with whips cracking, horses rearing, and people being trampled when the Cheyenne and Arapaho land was opened up to settlement.

Sayre City Park

Sayre City Park (U.S. 283 S., 580/928-2260, www.sayreok.net, dawn-dusk daily, free) is home to two WPA projects: a 1940 pueblo-style pool house and a red-stone rock wall, both frequented by early Route 66 travelers. It also offers a golf course and miniature golf; tennis, basketball, and volleyball courts; and an RV campground with hookups and a dump station. The park is located 1 mile (1.6 km) south of Sayre off Business I-40.

◈ Back on 66

From Sayre, head south on U.S. 283. In 1 mile (1.6 km), turn right (west) on BK Q, then left (south) on BK 21. Drive south and turn right (west) on North Frontage Road before reaching I-40. Drive west through the town of **Hext**. Route 66 crosses under I-40 and continues south. In less than 2 miles (3.2 km), the road curves west into the town of Erick.

Erick

Erick sits on the edge of the high plains of the Texas Panhandle. Route 66 passed through the north end of Erick, which was once populated with cafés, service stations, and motels. Today, it's a quiet western Oklahoma town of old buildings.

Sights

As you enter Erick on the east side of town, keep an eye out for a graveyard of rusting cars and windmills. (They're located on private property but are visible from the road.)

★ Sandhills Curiosity Shop

Sandhills Curiosity Shop (201 S. Sheb Wooley Ave., 580/729-1747, 9am-8pm daily, free) is odd. And weird. And absolutely terrific. Filled with what some might deem junk and others might deem treasures, the store is stacked—literally—with art, furniture, musical instruments, and more. Pixar producers even visited it while researching the film *Cars*. Owner Annabelle Russell and her husband, Harley, had a wacky musical act called the Mediocre Music Makers. They wrote more than 300 songs and performed them for anyone who stopped by. Annabelle passed away in 2014, but Harley still puts on a good show. Bring cash to leave a small tip; it's the kind thing to do. If you don't have time to stop and stay awhile, at least snap photos of the building's exterior, which is covered with old road signs and vintage advertisements.

The Sandhills Shop is one block south of Route 66 near 3rd Street and Sheb Wooley Avenue.

◈ Back on 66

Leave Erick traveling west on Roger Miller Boulevard and follow Route 66 (Business I-40) for about 7 miles (11.3 km) to the lonely border town of Texola.

Texola

In 1910, the census recorded 361 people living in Texola; now there are scarcely more than 40. As you drive through, it's completely possible that you may not see a single soul.

As Route 66 runs west through town, look for a 1910 **one-room cinderblock jail,** a block north on Main Street. It's a solid, tomb-like building. Legend has it that the walls continue several feet underground so that prisoners couldn't dig their way out. Other abandoned buildings nearby may have been a school, a gas station, and a garage. Who knows? It's all a mystery now.

Despite being a near-ghost town, you'll find signs of life at **Tumbleweeds Grill and Country Store** (Route 66 and Oklahoma Ave., 580/526-3914, www.tumbleweedstexola.com, 9am-5pm daily, $5-10). It's inside the Water Whole #2 building—friendly people serving simple but good food.

Texas

Texas is really big. If you've ever taken I-10 through Texas, you know that you can drive hundreds of miles, and for hours, and still not actually leave the Lone Star State.

Fortunately, Route 66 drivers don't have to endure the road-trip fatigue of Texas. The state actually has the second-shortest Route 66 alignment. (Kansas claims first place with only 13 mi/20.9 km of the Mother Road.) And although Texas is the runner-up, driving through the Panhandle—the rectangular outcrop that sits atop the state—offers many worthy stops punctuated with intriguing must-sees and nice-as-can-be people.

Despite Texas's reputation as a wild and woolly, big and bold state, the Panhandle is an out-of-the-way region with its own pace and attitude. Most Route 66 towns dot a quiet, two-lane highway and hold fewer than 500 residents. Large Texas cities like Dallas or Houston are nowhere near Route 66; Amarillo, the largest city

in the Panhandle, is about one-third of the size of Austin. Overall, this is a low-key and laid-back stretch of Texas.

Route 66 originally spanned 178 miles (290 km) through Texas; today, about 150 miles (24 km) are actually drivable. Most of Route 66 lies under the I-40 Frontage Road. The road trip through Texas will follow I-40 between Jericho and Alanreed as well as the last 18 miles (29 km) as you exit the state from Adrian to Glenrio. But don't fret—even this frontage road brings a rural, middle-of-nowhere feel to your trip.

Planning Your Time

Driving through the Texas Panhandle is a straight shot and can be done in **one day.** Route 66 sights start to appear in Shamrock and McLean, but you can push onward to spend the night in Amarillo. The next day, it's a little more than 100 miles (161 km) for the final stretch to New Mexico.

Driving Considerations

Route 66 runs alongside I-40, so if time is a factor, it's easy to jump on the freeway. Though you'll be passing through several

Highlights

★ **Tower Station and U-Drop Inn Café, Shamrock:** Not only is this former Conoco station a landmark—both architecturally and historically—it's also one of the most interesting stops on Route 66 (page 181).

★ **Devil's Rope Museum and Old Route 66 Museum, McLean:** This museum entirely dedicated to barbed wire has more than 450 types on display. Quirky doesn't even begin to describe this place (page 184).

★ **Palo Duro Canyon State Park, Canyon:** This second-largest canyon in the United States is known as the "Grand Canyon of Texas" (page 187).

★ **Cadillac Ranch, Amarillo:** This surreal public art installation consists of 10 vintage Cadillacs buried upright in a wheat field (page 191).

Best Restaurants

★ **Crush Wine Bar & Restaurant, Amarillo:** Here you'll find expertly made cocktails and locally sourced food (page 190).

★ **Golden Light Café and Cantina, Amarillo:** Established in 1946, this is the oldest restaurant in Amarillo (page 190).

★ **Rooster's, Vega:** A colorful sheet-metal rooster welcomes you to this Tex-Mex restaurant (page 192).

★ **MidPoint Café, Adrian:** Stop for a photo op and a warm slice of pie at the literal midpoint of Route 66 (page 193).

small towns, most of the gas stations on Route 66 are defunct and nonoperational. Plan to **fill up the tank in Shamrock;** the next major gas stop will be **Amarillo**, approximately 90 miles (145 km) west.

Getting There

Starting Points
Car
I-40 enters Texas near the town of Shamrock and is the only major east-west highway through the Panhandle. Leaving Texola, Oklahoma, head northwest on SR-30 and drive until the road turns into the southern frontage road. From this point, it's a straight shot into Shamrock.

I-27 runs south from Amarillo to Lubbock; beyond that, there is no major north-south U.S. interstate nearby.

Car Rental
Avis (10801 Airport Blvd., 806/335-2313, www.avis.com, 8am-10pm daily), **Hertz** (10801 Airport Blvd., 806/335-2331, www.hertz.com, 7am-10pm Sun.-Fri., 9am-5pm Sat.), and **Enterprise** (10801 Airport

Blvd., 806/335-9443, 8am-9:30pm daily) operate out of the **Rick Husband Amarillo International Airport** (AMA, 10801 Airport Blvd., Amarillo, 806/335-1671, http://fly-ama.com/home-rha).

Air
The only major airport in the Texas Panhandle is the **Rick Husband Amarillo International Airport** (AMA, 10801 Airport Blvd., Amarillo, 806/335-1671, http://fly-ama.com/home-rha), named after a NASA astronaut who died on the *Columbia* space shuttle mission. The airport is about 10 miles (16.1 km) east of downtown Amarillo and is served by American Airlines, Southwest, and United, with nonstop service to Dallas-Fort Worth, Denver, Houston, and Las Vegas.

Train and Bus
The Texas Panhandle has no Amtrak service. Amarillo has a **Greyhound bus station** (700 S. Tyler St., 806/374-5371, www.greyhound.com, 24 hours daily), with service throughout the United States.

Road Trip Playlist

Curating your road trip playlist is almost as important as mapping the route or booking hotels. Route 66 takes you through vastly different regions of the country, each with its own distinct culture and, yes, music. These song suggestions are tailored to the state you're in.

♦ **"Amarillo by Morning" by George Strait:** No self-respecting Texas road-trip playlist omits George Strait. Play this twangy tune as you roll into Amarillo.

♦ **"Laredo" by Band of Horses:** Even though Laredo, Texas, is not even close to Route 66 (it's at the southern border of the state), this song has a distinctly open-road feel. The catchy rhythm guitar will carry you into the sunset.

♦ **"Butterflies" by Kacey Musgraves:** Modern-day country crooner from Texas sings a love song.

♦ **"Texas Sun" by Khruangbin and Leon Bridges:** Fort Worth-born Leon Bridges and Houston band Khruangbin come together to perfectly sum up all that is slow and easy and good about Texas.

Shamrock

Shamrock, Texas, was named after an Irish symbol of luck and courage. Before the late 1800s, when Anglos arrived, Comanche and Kiowa herded bison here. Eventually sheep and cattle replaced the bison, and by the time Route 66 arrived in the late 1920s, agriculture and oil had become the two biggest industries. A decade later, Route 66 was paved, and not long after, we got the iconic art deco U-Drop Inn.

Sights

★ Tower Station and U-Drop Inn Café

Tower Station and U-Drop Inn Café (1242 N. Main St., www.shamrocktexas.net, 806/256-2501, free) holds the distinction of being the first commercial business to open when Route 66 came through Shamrock. It was part service station and part café—the only café within 100 miles (161 km), in fact, and the local newspaper called it the "swankiest of swank places to eat." Built in 1936, this art deco marvel sports zigzag motifs, green and orange

neon lights, and a four-sided obelisk. The stucco towers are decked out with gold-glazed terra-cotta tiles. The largest tower rises nearly 100 feet (30 m) above the building, with geometric detailing crowned with a metal "tulip" on top. The entire site is a visual treasure to behold. It's arguably one of the most architecturally significant buildings of its kind and one of the few surviving art deco restaurants like this from the 1930s.

Today, the U-Drop is the city's **Chamber of Commerce** and a splendid **Route 66 Visitor Center** (806/256-2501, 9am-5pm Mon.-Sat.) with a gift shop and friendly staff. Also inside is a re-created café scene, complete with dressed-up mannequins, plus the booth where Elvis Presley once dined. You might recall Tower Station from the animated film *Cars;* it was the inspiration for Ramone's body shop. Bonus points for public restrooms accessible even when the visitors center isn't open. Driving an electric vehicle? There are six recharge stations.

Water Tower Plaza

The tallest tank of its class in Texas, the **Shamrock water tower** stands 176 feet

(54 m) and watches over a small park and plaza, including a delightful mural welcoming travelers to the town. The tower and park are located on the west side of Main Street at 1st Street.

Magnolia Gas Station

Check out the 1930s-era restored **Magnolia Gas Station** (204 N. Madden St. at 2nd St.), with tall gravity-feed gas pumps. Have your phone camera ready for the sweet signage with two flying red Pegasus horses, and be sure to take a peek through the windows for a glimpse at 1930 service station relics.

Pioneer West Museum

Next to the Magnolia Gas Station, the **Pioneer West Museum** (204 N. Madden St., 806/256-3941, 9am-noon and 1pm-5pm Mon.-Fri., free) graces two floors of the 1925 former Reynolds Hotel. Nearly 30 rooms showcase the culture and history of the area, from the Great Plains Indians to pioneers, cowboys, and even astronauts.

As part of the Pioneer West Museum, the 1910 **Zeigler house** shows off the home and office of Bernice Ziegler, a doctor who served the local community during both world wars. You'll see his medical tools, desk, and operating table. To reach the house, head west on Route 66 and turn left (south) on U.S. 83. Continue driving for less than 1 mile (1.6 km) and turn left on 2nd Street. The house is one block down and on the left.

Food

Big Vern's Steakhouse (200 E. 12th St., 806/256-2088, www.bigvernssteakhouse.weebly.com, 11am-10pm daily, $8-30) is a Texas staple. Portions are large (aka, "Texas size"), and the chicken fried steak is delicious. Paired with beer bread and

---

Top to bottom: Tower Station and U-Drop Inn Café, Shamrock; Magnolia Gas Station, Shamrock; 1929 Phillips Petroleum, McLean

Delbert Trew: Barbed Wire Expert

A Panhandle native, Delbert Trew was born in 1933. After a lifetime of ranching and farming, he turned to a career writing for newspapers and magazines. In addition to penning his own columns for local and regional media, Trew was featured in publications around the globe for his "Trew" take on life, as well as his expert knowledge of barbed wire. In 1991, at the request of the Barbed Wire Collectors of America, he opened the **Devil's Rope Museum** in **McLean.** He leased the old bra factory from the city to house the fascinating collection of barbed wire.

So what's the deal with barbed wire? In the late 1800s, before settlers arrived, the West was open range. Millions of bison, cattle, and horses roamed the grasslands eating everything in their path. The animals destroyed crops because regular fencing couldn't corral them. The Land Office at the U.S. Department of Agriculture feared it would be impossible to settle the West because there was no practical solution to controlling the cattle and bison. That was before the invention of barbed wire. Michael Kelly came up with the design, and then Joseph Glidden improved on it by locking the signature sharp metal barbs in place. The invention proved so popular that by 1876, nearly 3 million pounds (1.4 million kg) of barbed wire were sold annually. As Trew once said: "It's a question of whether you fence in or fence out. If you're a rancher, you fence your cattle in, if you're a farmer, you fence cattle away from your crop. In Texas, a barbed wire fence is just as good as the Great Wall of China."

an ice-cold glass of tea, this meal couldn't get any more local.

If you do nothing else while in Shamrock, you must order a cheeseburger at **Rusty's on 66** (207 E. Route 66, 806/243-1616, www.rustyson66.com, 11am-2pm and 5pm-10pm Mon., Tues., and Thurs.-Sat., $8-17). It'll be the best burger you ever had. The restaurant also serves a mean thin-crust pizza, and the staff is a group of the some of the friendliest folks in town.

Tower Plaza Café & Pizzeria (115 N. Main St., 806/256-2323, 10:30am-8:30pm Mon.-Sat., $8-20) serves a little bit of everything: pizzas, burgers, hot sandwiches—all with the hospitality of a small-town joint.

◈ Back on 66

Leaving Shamrock, continue west on the south I-40 Frontage Road. In about 6 miles (9.7 km), you'll pass through the town of Lela. Continue driving about 15 miles (24 km) to Exit 146. Turn right to cross the freeway and then turn left to drive the North Frontage Road. At the "Y," take First Street into the town of McLean.

McLean

In 1901, Alfred Rowe, an English rancher who traveled to and from Europe until his fateful trip on *Titanic,* founded the town of McLean. When Route 66 arrived in McLean in 1927, the 22 auto-related businesses and gas stations drove the local economy. Fun fact: McLean was known as the "Uplift City" after the local bra factory, where women earned $1 for an eight-hour shift.

In the town's heyday, tourist cabins, car dealerships, motels, movie theaters, and restaurants packed the streets of McLean, but unfortunately, now most are gone. As Amarillo became popular, McLean struggled to stay relevant. A drive through this ghost town today will yield little to no sight of inhabitants, but there are a few oddities worth stopping to see. Keep your eyes open for murals painted on the sides of buildings.

Sights

To see the old buildings in the town's center, follow Route 66 (1st St.) through Main, 2nd, and Gray Streets. You'll drive past the **1929 Phillips Petroleum** (219 Gray St.), a Tudor Revival building with a red roof and orange gas pumps that acted as the first Phillips Petroleum filling station in Texas, operating for more than 50 years.

★ Devil's Rope Museum and Old Route 66 Museum

The **Devil's Rope Museum** (100 Kingsley St., 806/779-2225, www. barbwiremuseum.com, 9am-4pm Mon.-Sat., free) has the world's largest collection of published material about barbed wire. What does this mean? You'll see 450 different types and more than 2,000 samples, plus an impressive gallery of artworks made from the "Devil's Rope."

Enclosed in the same space is the **Old Route 66 Museum** (100 Kingsley St., 806/779-2225, 9am-4pm Mon.-Sat., free). Explore a small collection of artifacts donated from Texas Route 66 businesses including road signs, classic advertisements, and a huge tin snake from the famed but now-closed Reptile Ranch. If you're feeling like you need a literal piece of the road to commemorate your trip, the gift shop sells fragments of pavement from the Mother Road.

Food and Accommodations

The hand-cut rib eye at **Red River Steakhouse** (101 W. Rte. 66, 806/779-8940, www.redriversteakhouse.com, 11am-9pm Tues.-Sat., $8-25) is juicy and tender, while the breaded catfish is full of flavor. If you roll in on a Friday night, don't miss the fall-off-the-bone barbecue ribs. Plus: Free cobbler comes with an entrée!

The **Cactus Inn** (101 Pine St., 806/779-2346, $65) is a good value, with basic accommodations and a pleasant staff. Built in 1956, the inn beckons guests with an emerald-green and yellow cactus sign.

◆ Back on 66

Head west from McLean following 1st Street and cross SR-273. After about 1

Devil's Rope Museum and Old Route 66 Museum

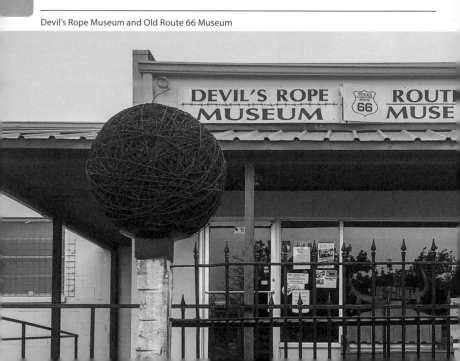

mile (1.6 km), turn left (south) on County Road 26 and follow the road as it curves east (left). Take the next right (south) to cross under I-40 and then curve right (west) to take the South Frontage Road. In 6 miles (9.7 km), you'll reach the town of Alanreed.

Soon after Alanreed, the **pre-1930s alignment** turns into a dirt road that leads to Jericho Gap, an area notorious for stranding motorists in the mud. Back when this dirt road was the only option, people were often forced to stay in private homes, waiting to be towed out.

From Alanreed, you'll follow to the **post-1930s alignment** instead. Turn right (north) on Main Street and take I-40 west to Exit 124. Turn left (south) and drive under the freeway, then take the first right (west) to follow the South Frontage Road for 3.5 miles (5.6 km). At the next I-40 exit (Exit 121), take a quick left to continue following the South Frontage Road for 6 miles (9.7 km) into Groom.

Groom

Groom was named after Colonel B. B. Groom, a cattle breeder from Kentucky who imported Angus cattle from Scotland and bought thousands of feet of barbed wire to manage the livestock.

Sights

As you drive deeper into Texas, the land gets drier, the trees are sparser, and every structure that sits on the flat prairie looms over the horizon. Rambling through this old Texas town with nothing but abandoned service stations and the mint-green **Wheeler-Evans Grain Elevator** serves up an iconic moment—one that will stay in your memory forever—on the Mother Road.

On the north side of I-40 (near Exit 114), you'll find the **Leaning Water Tower,** which, as the name implies, looks like it's going to fall over. Guess what? It's not going anywhere. It was actually built that way. Ralph Britten, a Groom native and Army Air Corps engineer, bought the water tower and moved it here in 1980, tilting it as a marketing ploy to attract passersby. The water tower only leans about 10 degrees, but our eyes trick us into believing it's about to topple over. Squint and you'll notice it has three legs anchored as a sturdy tripod.

In town, drive by **The State National Bank of Groom** (99 Broadway St., 806/248-7531, www.snbgroom.com) to see the life-size horse statue out front. The bank has been in operation since 1904, surviving the Great Depression, the Dust Bowl era, and two world wars.

As you leave Groom, you won't be able to miss the 19-story **Giant Cross** (2880 County Rd., www.crossministries.net) on the north side of Route 66, just west of County Road 295. Erected in 1995, the cross towers over the highway and is one of the largest in the United States; it weighs 2 million pounds (9 million kg) and lights up at night. The grounds are

open 24 hours a day if you want to swing by and snap a pic or simply sit quietly and ruminate.

Food

The Grill (407 Front St., 806/248-0202, 7am-2pm Tues.-Sun., $6-15) gets the job done. Friendly service and home-cooked food in this small restaurant bring all the good feels. Go for the fried biscuits stuffed with cream cheese or the chili burger—it's tasty but messy, so keep a stack of napkins at the ready.

◆ Back on 66

Leave Groom driving west on Route 66/Business I-40 (Front St.) and follow the South Frontage Road for 12 miles (19.3 km). As the road veers away from I-40, turn right at the next road (SR-207) and drive north for 0.5 mile (0.8 km) to Conway.

Conway

When Route 66 came through Conway, the population blossomed from 25 people to 125. Today, the population hovers around 20, and the graceful simplicity of a landscape dotted with dirt roads and windmills makes it look just as it did a century ago.

As a tribute to Cadillac Ranch (outside Amarillo), the **VW Slug Bug Ranch** stuck five graffiti-coated Volkswagen Beetles headfirst in the earth. The windows and wheels are missing, so the shells of the cars are all that remain. The abandoned gas station next to it and wide-open Texas sky beyond make the perfect photo backdrop. The VW Slug Bug Ranch is 0.5 mile (0.8 km) north of Route 66 on SR-207 and the I-40 Frontage Road. It's on the left.

Top to bottom: Leaning Water Tower; The State National Bank of Groom; Wheeler-Evans Grain Elevator, Groom

Local Eats

Do not leave Texas without trying **chicken fried steak.** Beef is pounded into a flat slab, then breaded, pan-fried, and smothered in cream gravy.

Take note: real **Texas chili** contains no beans. Just chiles and beef, often topped with Fritos, grated cheddar, and chopped onions.

Did you know that Texas is one of the top pecan-growing regions in the country? That's why it's a must to get a slice of **pecan pie.**

Some of the tastiest Mexican dishes are actually rooted in **Tex-Mex.** This fusion of American and Mexican cuisines gave the world gooey nachos, hard tacos, and sizzling fajitas, and is notable for its abundance of shredded cheese, flour tortillas, and cumin.

◆ Back on 66

The 7.2-mile (11.6-km) segment between SR-207 and I-40 is among the best-preserved and untouched sections on Route 66 in Texas. This is what is meant by the phrase "the open road." The drive rewards you with miles of expansive prairie land as far as the eye can see. In 1900, this path was a dirt road; after it was paved in the 1940s, it became a major throughway for Route 66 travelers. Today, Texas Farm Road 2161 is listed on the National Register of Historic Places.

From the Bug Ranch, head south on SR-207 (Bus. I-40). After 0.5 mile (0.8 km), turn right (west) on County Road 2161. After County Road L, the road splits; stay right to follow County Road 2161, which heads north to I-40. In less than 2 miles (3.2 km), cross I-40 and turn left (west) to drive on North Frontage Road for about 4 miles (6.4 km). At Exit 85 (Amarillo Blvd.), the road heads left to follow Farm Road 2575 for 4 miles (6.4 km) into Amarillo (do *not* take Business I-40 into Amarillo).

◆ Side Trip: Canyon

★ Palo Duro Canyon State Park

Welcome to the second-largest canyon in the country. (The first is the Grand Canyon, of course.) At 120 miles (193 km) long and 800 feet (244 m) deep, **Palo Duro Canyon State Park** (11450 State Highway Park Rd., Canyon,

806/488-2227, www.tpwd.texas.gov, 7am-7pm daily, $8) is nothing to sneeze at. The 27,173 acres (10,997 hectares) of deep purple and rose-hued spires formed in the Caprock Escarpment during the past 250 million years, etching out rugged cliffs and wind-shorn mesas. Start your exploration at the **Visitor Center** (8am-8pm Sun.-Thurs., 8am-10pm Fri.-Sat. Apr.-May and Sept.-Oct.; 8am-10pm daily June-Aug.; 8am-6pm Sun.-Thurs., 8am-8pm Fri.-Sat. Nov.-Mar.). Here you'll get info on hiking trails and the history of the area, plus you can purchase books, pottery, and jewelry. If you're traveling through in the summer, stay for the live musical *TEXAS* (806/655-2181, www.texas-show.com, 6pm Tues.-Sun. June-Aug, $17-48), performed in the outdoor amphitheater. The show tells the story of Texas's early pioneers. It's been running since the 1960s and draws crowds from around the Panhandle.

The popular **Lighthouse Trail** (2.8 mi/4.5 km one-way) is a moderately difficult trail that leads to the Lighthouse rock formation. The **Rojo Grande Trail** (1.2 mi/1.9 km one-way) travels an easy path through rust-red geological formations at the bottom of the canyon. For those wanting a physical challenge, the **Givens, Spicer, Lowry Trail** (3.1 mi/5 km one-way)—named after the group of runners who helped develop the park's trail systems—presents an exhilarating hike or run with picturesque views.

TEXAS

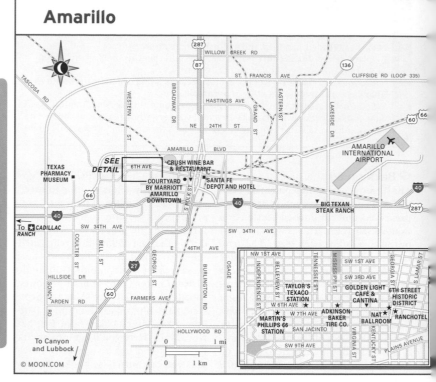

Amarillo

Getting There

Palo Duro is about 30 miles (48 km) south of Route 66 near Amarillo. From I-40 as it enters Amarillo, take I-87 south toward the town of Canyon. After 14 miles (22.5 km), take Exit 110 to follow I-27 south for 3.5 miles (5.6 km). Turn left (east) on SR-217 and drive 13 miles (20.9 km) to the park.

Amarillo

At the turn of the 20th century, the roads in Amarillo were mostly dirt; driving the 110 miles (177 km) from Amarillo to Tucumcari, New Mexico, took an entire day. The 1920s oil boom called for easier and faster transport, and Amarillo secured government funding to build better roads. After the roads were paved

and widened, including the infamous Jericho Gap (the mud trap near the town of Groom), the trip to Tucumcari only took a few hours.

Amarillo was—and still is—the only major city along Route 66 in Texas, and it became a significant cattle feeding and shipping center. The oil industry boosted Amarillo's place as the commercial and corporate center of the Panhandle. Today, you can stay at a chic hotel downtown, dine with the locals, check out a former Harvey House, and meander the historic district to admire the well-preserved art deco architecture.

◆ Route 66 Through Amarillo

Route 66 (Farm Road 2575) turns into Northeast 8th Avenue and then curves north on B Avenue. In about 1.5 miles (2.4 km), turn left (southwest) on

Amarillo Boulevard. Follow Amarillo Boulevard for 4 miles (6.4 km); when the road dips south, it turns into Business I-40 and crosses SR-335. Turn right to follow Indian Hill Road.

Sights

6th Street Historic District

Amarillo's 13-block historic district was added to the National Register of Historic Places in 1994 and offers an insightful look at the town's Route 66 and art deco heritage.

Before hotel chains dominated every commercial corner, there were few overnight options for travelers; it wasn't unusual for people to sleep in their cars or camp beside the road. As Amarillo grew in popularity, it built "tourist camps" and motels on 6th Avenue along Route 66. The adobe **Ranchotel** (2501 W. 6th St.), which eventually became an apartment building, is a prime example of the U-shaped roadside lodging that lined Amarillo streets from 1928 to 1953.

The 1922 Natatorium, called the **"Nat" Ballroom** (2705 SW 6th Ave., 806/367-8908, www.thenatroute66.com, 10am-6pm Mon.-Sat.), shows off Gothic Revival style with a 2-story stucco exterior boasting turrets and deep-set windows and doors. An indoor swimming pool used to live inside the Natatorium (hence the name), but it was converted to a ballroom that hosted musical greats Duke Ellington and Tommy Dorsey. Today, you can shop for eclectic goods from more than 100 antiques dealers who set up shop in the "Nat."

Texas Pharmacy Museum

Opened in 1998 to house the private collection of Billy Walker, a retired drug company representative, the **Texas Pharmacy Museum** (1300 S. Coulter, 806/414-9269, www.ttuhsc.edu/pharmacy/museum,

Top to bottom: Palo Duro Canyon State Park; Cadillac Ranch, Amarillo; Big Texan Steak Ranch, Amarillo

Amarillo's Harvey House

One of the most striking buildings in downtown Amarillo is the **Santa Fe Depot and Hotel** (401 S. Grant St.). It is striking for its height in a city of low-slung structures but also notable for its neon sign atop the roof. Built in 1910 as a Harvey House, the depot covered 6 acres (2.4 hectares) and served passengers until the trains stopped running in 1971.

To get there from Route 66: Travel south on SR-87, then turn left (east) on SE 3rd Avenue and turn right (south) on Grant Street after a few blocks. The station is on the left.

For more information on Harvey Houses, see page 271.

Santa Fe Depot and Hotel

10am-noon and 1:30pm-4pm Tues.-Thurs, free) fills four rooms with pharmacy artifacts, vintage drug advertisements, laboratory glassware, books, mortars and pestles, show globes, and a re-created drugstore from the early 20th century.

Food

Everything at the **Big Texan Steak Ranch** (7701 E. I-40, 806/372-6000, www.bigtexan.com, 10am-10:30pm daily, $15-30) is, well, big. There's a massive sculpture of a steer out front, giant Texas flags lined up outside, and the interior includes a huge two-story dining room with a bar, shooting range, and slot machines. The food is fine, but that's not the main draw. This place is legendary for its free 72-ounce (2-kg) steak dinner. But it's only free if you eat the entire steak—with a baked potato, salad, and shrimp cocktail—in less than an hour.

Dine at Amarillo hot spot ★ **Crush Wine Bar & Restaurant** (627 S. Polk St., 806/418-2011, www.crushamarillo.com, 11am-10pm Mon.-Fri., 1pm-midnight Sat., $12-30). If you get a seat at the bar, you'll rub elbows with chatty business travelers in town for meetings and friendly locals donning cowboy hats and

bolo ties. A bar seat also affords you an up-close show of the mixologists expertly shaking up craft cocktails—not to mention that you won't have to endure the long wait for a table. Order the ribeye with black truffle butter and a side of lemony risotto.

Want to eat at the oldest restaurant in Amarillo? Head to ★ **Golden Light Café and Cantina** (2906 SW 6th Ave., 806/374-9237, https://goldenlightcafe.com, 11am-10pm Mon.-Sat., $5-12), which was established in 1946. The hickory-smoked Gooney's 'shroom burger and the all-natural buffalo burger are delish. The service is good but things do move slowly, so just sit back, relax, and order a local brew.

Accommodations

The **Courtyard by Marriott Amarillo Downtown** (724 S. Polk St., 806/553-4500, www.marriott.com, $92-144) offers the best of both worlds. It's located in the beautiful, historic Fisk Building yet has all the contemporary creature comforts, such as Wi-Fi, spacious rooms, crisp linens, and pillow-top mattresses. Ask for a room with a view of the Santa Fe Building—you'll want a pic of the neon sign lit up at night.

Car Culture

On Route 66, you're never too far from a vintage gas station or a classic-car shop. In Amarillo, stop by the 1939 **Adkinson-Baker Tire Co.** (3200 W. 6th Ave.), which still has its original canopy and remains mostly unchanged from the day it opened for business. The building sports the sleek Streamline Moderne style, a late art deco look known for curved lines and nautical themes. At **Taylor's Texaco Station** (3512 W. 6th St.), admire the white porcelain-enameled wall panels, and at **Martin's Phillips 66 Station** (3821 W. 6th Ave.), behold the oversized triangular canopy and canted plate-glass walls. Of the three stations, Martin's operated until fairly recently, shuttering its doors in the 1990s.

⊕ Back on 66

Driving west on Amarillo Boulevard, Route 66 winds south and turns into Bus-40 as it crosses SR-335. About 1.5 miles (2.4 km) after passing SR-335, turn right and then make a quick left onto Indian Hill Road and drive west for 4.5 miles (7.2 km). Turn left (south) on South Blessen Drive and take the next right (west) on the I-40 North Frontage Road. Drive 20 miles (32 km) through **Bushland** and **Wildorado**, past looming concrete silos, old military bases, and statuesque windmills.

★ Detour: Cadillac Ranch

Great art doesn't have to live in a museum. Sometimes it exists in the middle of nowhere along the interstate. That's **Cadillac Ranch** (I-40 Frontage Rd. near Exit 60, dawn-dusk daily, free), an awe-inspiring public art installation by the Ant Farm art collective. In a Texas wheat field 10 miles (16.1 km) west of Amarillo, you'll find 10 tail-finned, graffiti-soaked Cadillacs, manufactured between 1948 and 1964, each planted nose first in the soil.

This wasn't the original site of the installation. As the suburbs of Amarillo encroached on the area near Cadillac Ranch, the land suddenly became valuable. In 1997, Cadillac Ranch moved 2 miles (3.2 km) west. The new location remains sparse and uncluttered, a Zen backdrop with a horizon line so straight the cars look like they are sprouting from a blank canvas framed by the sky.

As you enter the field off the frontage road, the abstract shapes slowly take form. These aren't Fords, Chevys, or Buicks—these are Cadillacs for a reason. The regal Cadillac was the ultimate symbol of the American Dream. The artwork could be a metaphor for burying commerce and materialism; or it could be viewed as a monument to commercialism and American excess. You decide.

Over the past several decades, the cars have become layered with thick coats of spray paint from visitors who add their own touches of art. Hudson Marquez, one of the Ant Farm artists who designed and built Cadillac Ranch, said he wishes the site was more protected and that people wouldn't litter and spray paint the cars. Though other Route 66 guides may encourage folks to continue this tradition, it's best to leave the spray paint at home.

Getting There

Cadillac Ranch is west of Amarillo near I-40 (Exit 60) on the South Frontage Road. As Amarillo Boulevard (Route 66) curves south, it turns into Business I-40. Turn left (south) on Hope Road, cross I-40, then turn right (west) on the South Frontage Road. Drive east 1 mile (1.6 km) and Cadillac Ranch will be on the right (south) side. Park along the shoulder and enter the pasture through the unlocked gate. Pets are welcome.

The Green Book in Amarillo

Only a handful of Texas businesses appeared in the *Negro Motorist Green Book,* and all of them were located in Amarillo. These included the **Mayfair Hotel** (119 Van Buren St.) and the **Watley Hotel** (112 Van Buren St.), which no longer exist, and the then-popular restaurants **Tom's Place** (322 W. 3rd St.), **New Harlem** (114 Harrison St.), and **Blue Bonnet** (400 W. 3rd St.). Though none are in operation today, the buildings in which Tom's and New Harlem were housed are still standing.

⚐ Back on 66

Leaving Cadillac Ranch, turn left (west) onto the South Frontage Road. Take your next right (north) on Arnot Road. Cross I-40 and turn left (west) on Indian Hill Road.

Vega

Route 66 proudly flaunts its scars amid fragments of broken cement and hollowed-out rubble in the small, wind-whipped town of Vega. At one time, Vega was a sizable community in the Panhandle, with more than 500 people and several gas stations, cafés, and auto courts. But it needed Route 66 to survive, so when the Mother Road was decommissioned, Vega lost its shine. Today, most of the businesses under the weathered wooden awnings are closed.

⚐ Route 66 Through Vega

The oldest alignment of Route 66 went through U.S. 385 (Main St.) and turned on West Main Street. But today this segments dead-ends into a dirt road west of town, so follow the post-1930s alignment instead. As you enter Vega from the North Frontage Road, Business I-40 splits off to the north and turns into Vega Boulevard. Follow Vega Boulevard west through town.

Sights
Dot's Mini-Museum & Boot Tree

Random oddities fill **Dot's Mini-Museum & Boot Tree** (105 N. 12th St., 806/267-2367, dawn-dusk daily, free). Make your way through three buildings with decades worth of collectibles and treasures from the late Dot Levitt. Dot came to Vega in the 1940s with her husband; now her daughter Betty Carpenter runs the place. You'll see Avon perfume bottles, framed photos, antique pistols, and a tree with cowboy boots hanging from the branches, aka the "Boot Tree."

From Business I-40, turn right (north) on U.S. 385 (Main St.). Turn left (west) on West Main Street, then make a right (north) on North 12th Street.

Vega Motel

The 1947, U-shaped **Vega Motel** (1005 Vega Blvd.) was built during the prosperous years of Route 66, with two wings, 12 units, and a small house in the central courtyard. As Route 66 got busier, the exterior was covered with permastone and 8 additional units with garages and kitchenettes were added. By the late 1940s, there were about 30,000 motor courts along the American roadside. The Vega Motel remains a rare example of these classic old-school motor courts.

Food

You might drive right on by Tex-Mex eatery ★ **Rooster's** (1300 Vega Blvd., 806/267-0113, 8am-8pm Mon.-Sat., 10am-2pm Sun., $7-12) without thinking twice. Don't make this mistake. Pull over and head inside for a wonderful meal. This hole-in-the-wall restaurant sits in an old gas station and offers the nicest service ever, plus good eats. Favorites include smothered enchiladas, chicken flautas, stuffed and breaded avocados, and brisket tacos.

Women of the Mother Road

The story of Route 66 isn't complete without the illustrious women who've contributed greatly to the road's growth, success, and preservation. Here, celebrate one of the Texan women who made a profound impact on the Mother Road.

Fran Houser: Here's the woman who inspired the character of Flo of Flo's V-8 Café in the Pixar movie *Cars*. As owner of Adrian's **MidPoint Café** (page 193) from 1990 to 2012, Fran congratulated Route 66 road-trippers for reaching the halfway point of the Mother Road. How? With a warm Texas greeting and a tasty offering of home-baked pies at this little Adrian restaurant. Fran bought the 1920s café after going through a divorce, and like many of the inspiring pioneers you'll find on Route 66, persevered through struggles and setbacks to create one of the best stops on the Mother Road. Though she no longer owns the café, you should still pop in and order a slice of pie.

◆ Back on 66

Leave Vega heading west on Business I-40 until it rejoins the North Frontage Road in 1 mile (1.6 km). Keep an eye out north of the railroad for the old remnants of the unpaved 1926 alignment. From Vega, it's about 11 miles (17.7 km) west to Adrian.

Adrian

Congratulations! You've reached the literal and geographic halfway point of Route 66. The town of Adrian sits 1,139 miles (1,833 km) west of Chicago and 1,139 miles (1,833 km) east of Los Angeles. You'll know you've made it when you see the MidPoint Café—a welcome beacon in the desolate landscape. Across the street from the restaurant, photo-op-worthy signage marks the midway spot.

Adrian was founded in 1909; in 1915, the town had a population of 50 people. When Route 66 came through in 1926, tourism became a steady source of income for the community.

Food

The ★ **MidPoint Café** (305 W. Route 66, 805/536-6379, 8am-5pm Tues.-Sun., $8-14) served hungry travelers 10 years before Route 66 was even paved. This used to be a one-room greasy spoon with a dirt floor called Zella's; after that, it was Jesse's Café. Today, the MidPoint is a bright, cheery restaurant that serves fresh (never frozen) Angus-beef burgers and homemade pies that are utterly delicious. It's impossible to choose just one, but the bourbon pecan pie and Elvis pie won't disappoint. Prepare to hang out awhile to chat with the owners and other 66 road-trippers, plus give yourself time to browse the gift shop.

◆ Back on 66

Leave Adrian in the rearview mirror, heading west on the North Frontage Road for 4.6 miles (7.4 km) to Exit 18 (Gruhlkey Rd.), and jump on I-40 west.

Glenrio

Glenrio sits right on the **Texas-New Mexico border.** For many years, the early Route 66 alignment was just a dirt road; it wasn't paved until the late 1930s. Today, Glenrio is a desolate border town that's fading into the flat Panhandle plains. The tourist courts, cafés, and gas stations are gone, and most of the buildings have fallen down. As we head west in New Mexico, prepare to be wooed by the Land of Enchantment.

New Mexico

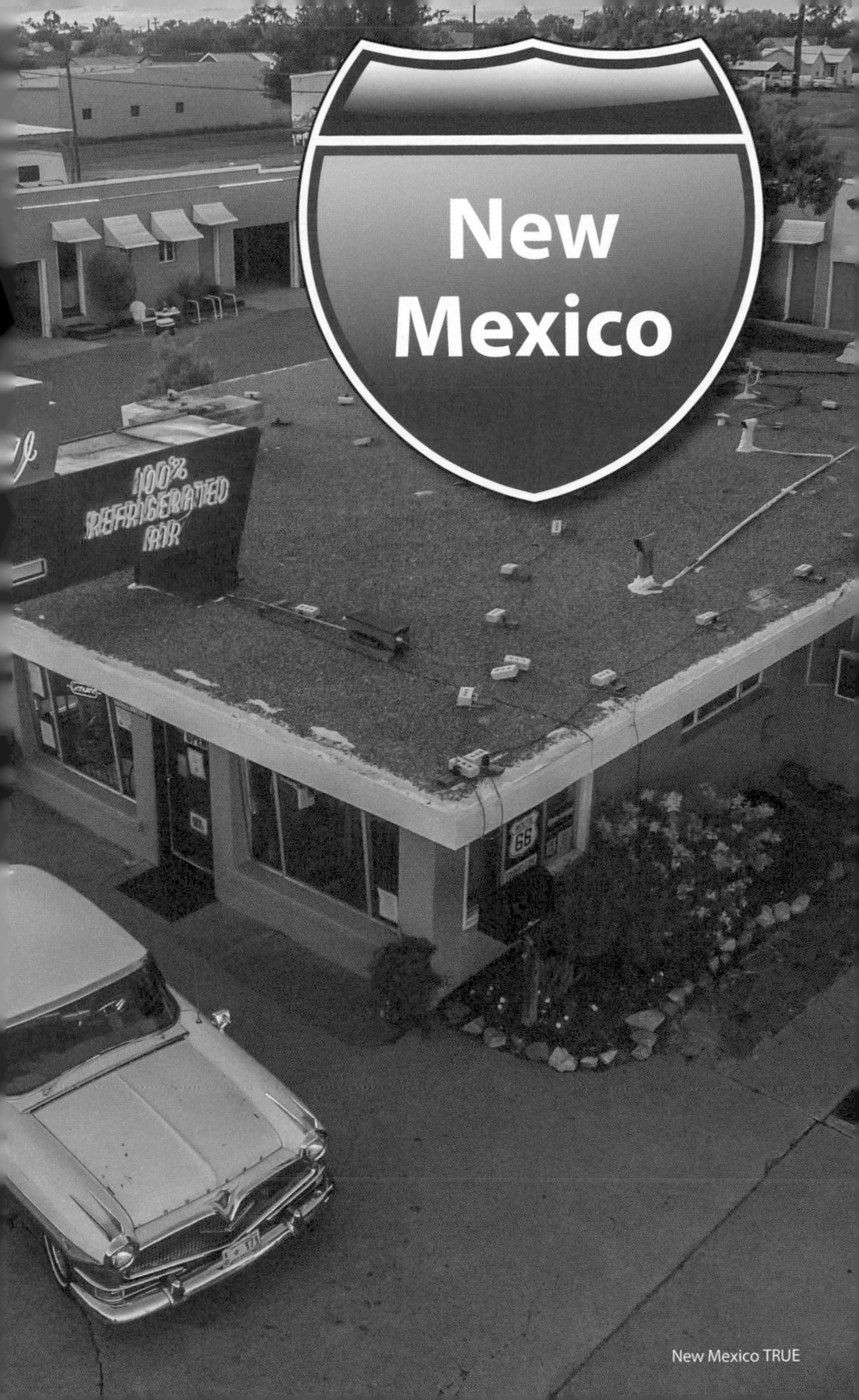

New Mexico TRUE

New Mexico

There isn't another place on Route 66—or on the planet—quite like New Mexico.

On your journey across this mystical land, you'll see the oldest community in the country, one of the oldest churches, and the oldest continuously used public building in the United States. If that's not impressive enough, you'll also bear witness to old-world Spanish villages, color-drenched sunsets, and adobe pueblos set against a blue sky. There's a reason people call New Mexico the "Land of Enchantment."

At one point in time, New Mexico was the wildest part of the West. The state's deep multicultural history encompasses the Spaniards, Mexicans, and American Indians, all of whom fought full-out revolts and bloody battles to claim the territory and retain independence. Once the violence subsided, native communities sat walled off like fortresses. Today, New Mexico is home to 19 pueblos (an American Indian settlement), each of which has its own distinct culture and traditions, as well as two Apache tribes and about 107,000 members of the Navajo Nation.

In 1912, when it became a state, there were only 28 miles (45 km) of paved roads in New Mexico. Between 1933 and 1941, government spending to build roads increased, but the state's diverse topography gave highway engineers quite a challenge. Originally, Route 66 zigzagged northwest along the Santa Fe Trail, from Santa Rosa to Santa Fe, and then dipped south to Albuquerque and Los Lunas before heading west to Gallup. Then in 1937, a major realignment changed Route 66's north-south trajectory into an east-west corridor (and made Albuquerque one of the few Route 66 towns with two alignments that intersect). The new, more direct road shortened the route through the state from 506 to 399 miles (820 to 645 km). After all was said and done, Route 66 became New Mexico's first completely paved highway.

New Mexico TRUE

Highlights

★ **Musical Highway, Tijeras:** Drive over the rumble strips at exactly 45 miles (72 km) per hour to hear the notes of "America the Beautiful" fill your vehicle (page 207).

★ **La Fonda on the Plaza, Santa Fe:** One of the few remaining Harvey Houses is right in the heart of Santa Fe.

Book a room or simply enjoy a rooftop cocktail (page 212).

★ **Earthship Biotecture, Taos:** At this revolutionary and self-sustaining community in the high desert, off-the-grid homes resemble otherworldly sculptures (page 219).

★ **Acoma Pueblo:** Tour this 12th-century Pueblo Indian village, one of the oldest communities in North America (page 231).

★ **Mural Walking Tour, Gallup:** Get out of the car and on to the streets for the powerful visual story these murals tell of Gallup's cultural heritage (page 236).

Best Restaurants

★ **Kix on 66, Tucumcari:** Green chile omelets for breakfast—say no more (page 202).

★ **Comet II Drive-In, Santa Rosa:** This carhop-turned-Mexican-restaurant is not to be missed (page 207).

★ **El Farol, Santa Fe:** Eat *tapas* and watch flamenco dancers at Santa Fe's oldest cantina (page 214).

★ **Sugar Nymphs Bistro, Peñasco:** Here you'll find an ever-changing menu of locally sourced goodies (page 218).

★ **Jerry's Café, Gallup:** It's all about the chiles rellenos at this classic restaurant (page 238).

Planning Your Time

This trip speeds across New Mexico in **2-3 days,** but there's a lot to do. Route 66 enters the state near Glenrio. Spend the night in Tucumcari, just 40 miles (64 km) west. The next day follows the pre-1937 alignment along the backcountry "Santa Fe Loop" (rather than following I-40 between Santa Rosa and Albuquerque), ending in Santa Fe for a second overnight. From Santa Fe, a side trip to Taos will add a day, but it's completely worth it to visit the Earthship Biotecture and other sights. Another overnight—either Taos or Albuquerque—is recommended so you have time to visit the Acoma Pueblo before zipping through Gallup to cross the border into Arizona.

Driving Considerations

There's so much to see and do in New Mexico that you could easily spend two weeks here. Plan ahead in order to experience as much as you can. If time is running out, I-40 and I-25 will quickly get you to the next destination. **Gas** is available in Tucumcari, Santa Rosa, Santa Fe, Albuquerque, Taos, and Gallup.

If you're driving through New Mexico from mid-June through September, it's good to note that this is **monsoon season.**

Nearly every afternoon, the sky opens up to rain—as in, a downpour—for about an hour. Sometimes the showers can be dramatic, punctuated with lightning and thunder. But as soon as the storm passes, the sun pops out, the skies shine, and the air smells fresh and clean.

Getting There

Starting Points

Car

In New Mexico, I-25 joins Route 66 north-south, while I-40 follows it east-west. The recommended **pre-1937 alignment** travels north from I-40 toward Santa Fe via U.S. 84 and I-25. From Santa Fe, I-25 then goes south to Albuquerque before meeting I-40 to head west toward Gallup. If time is an issue, take the **post-1937 alignment,** which follows I-40 east-west from Santa Rosa to Albuquerque.

Car Rental

Albuquerque International Sunport (ABQ, 2200 Sunport Blvd. SE, 505/244-7700, https://abqsunport.com) is the best place to rent a car, thanks to the on-site **Sunport Rental Car Center** (3400 University Blvd., 505/315-7770) with 10 companies, including **Enterprise** (800/736-8222, www.enterprise.com,

Best Accommodations

★ **Blue Swallow Motel, Tucumcari:** Stay at a flawless example of a pre-WWII motor court on Route 66, retro neon sign and all (page 204).

★ **El Rey Court, Santa Fe:** Right on Route 66, this stylish 1930s boutique property offers a 5-acre (2-hectare) oasis (page 216).

★ **Earthship Biotecture, Taos:** Spend the night in a self-sufficient home made of recycled materials (page 220).

★ **Los Poblanos Inn, Albuquerque:** Gardens, lavender fields, and cottonwood trees make this a memorable spot to lay your head (page 229).

★ **El Rancho Hotel, Gallup:** The choice of 1930s A-listers, this historic three-story hotel retains its glitz and glamour (page 238).

6am-midnight daily), **Avis** (800/331-1212, www.avis.com, 6am-11pm daily), and **Budget** (800/527-0700, www.budget.com, 5am-1am daily).

Air

Nearly 5 million people fly in and out of **Albuquerque International Sunport** (ABQ, 2200 Sunport Blvd. SE, 505/244-7700, https://abqsunport.com) every year. This is the largest commercial airport in the state, with nonstop service to 20 cities via Alaska, Allegiant, American, Boutique Air, Delta, Frontier, JetBlue, Southwest, and United. The airport is about 3 miles (4.8 km) southeast of downtown Albuquerque.

Train and Bus

Amtrak's *Southwest Super Chief* (www.amtrak.com, 800/872-7245) passes through astonishing southwestern scenery on its way through stations in Albuquerque (320 1st St. SW) and Gallup (Gallup Cultural Center, 201 E. Rte. 66).

Greyhound (www.greyhound.com) bus service is available at stations in Tucumcari (McDonald's, 2608 S. 1st St., 575/461-1350, 5am-8pm daily), Albuquerque (320 1st St. SW, 505/243-4435, 1am-noon and 2pm-6pm Mon.-Fri.,

1:30am-6pm and 9pm-12:30am Sat.-Sun.), and Gallup (3405 W. Rte. 66, 505/863-9078, 24 hours daily).

⬦ Route 66 Through New Mexico

As you enter New Mexico on I-40, take Exit 369, turn right (north) and then take the first left at Quay Road to follow the North Frontage Road southwest for about 10 miles (16.1 km). As the road bends west, turn left (south) on SR-469, cross I-40 heading south, and then turn right (west) in San Jon to join Route 66 on South Frontage Road. Many small communities that thrived on the Mother Road became ghost towns after I-40 came along. **San Jon** once had a reputation as a rough-and-tumble town in the early 1900s, but it's now all but a memory.

Follow Route 66 west for the next 20 miles (32 km) through the irrigated farmlands and the former Ozark Trail to Tucumcari.

While there is a dirt road option that travels south of I-40 from Glenrio to San Jon, the formerly paved road is not recommended; the road is not maintained and can be dangerous when muddy, especially during monsoon season.

Road Trip Playlist

Curating your road trip playlist is almost as important as mapping the route or booking hotels. Route 66 takes you through vastly different regions of the country, each with its own distinct culture and, yes, music. These song suggestions are tailored to the state you're in.

♦ **"The Dance" by Robert Mirabel:** A Pueblo Indian musician from Taos, Mirabel has won Grammy awards for his powerful Native music. Listen to this song as you drive the High Road to Taos.

♦ **"Stop Moving" by Lindy Vision:** These three Albuquerque sisters make New Wave-inspired synth pop reminiscent of more modern groups like Interpol. The Black Native trio's musical talents are self-taught and their albums are self-written, self-produced, and self-released.

♦ **"New Slang" by The Shins:** Try not to whistle along with the windows down when you hear this 2002 breakout from Albuquerque-based indie darlings The Shins.

♦ **"Far from Any Road" by The Handsome Family:** Despite being from Chicago originally, this alt-country band now calls Albuquerque home. This slow and moody tune (used as the *True Detective* opener) is best played after night falls on the open road.

Tucumcari

During Route 66's heyday, Tucumcari posted billboards along the highway inviting travelers to TUCUMCARI TONITE!, with claims of 2,000 motel rooms. You can still see these signs today, although you won't hit upon nearly as many rooms for lodging. What you will get as you cruise through this dusty town are streets lined with old-school neon signs at legendary motels such as the Blue Swallow, plus dozens of cool murals depicting Route 66 and the region's American Indian history. Stop by famous landmarks—Teepee Curios and La Cita Restaurant—whose kitschy signage just begs to be photographed (a giant rooftop sombrero, for example).

◈ Route 66 Through Tucumcari

From the I-40 South Frontage Road, turn right (north) on Business I-40; the road will cross I-40, curve, and head west for 3.5 miles (5.6 km) along Tucumcari Boulevard. On the west side of town, turn left onto SR-54 and then join I-40 west at Exit 329.

Sights
Mural Tour

Artists Sharon and Doug Quarles painted most of the **40 murals** throughout Tucumcari over a 10-year period in the early 2000s. The Blue Swallow's James Dean mural portrays the Porsche Spyder that cost him his life, while *The Legendary Road* mural outlines the complicated story of America's western migration—it's one of the largest Route 66 murals on the Mother Road, with two beautiful bovine skulls over an image of the open road. Pick up a mural map at the **Chamber of Commerce** (404 W. Rte. 66, 575/461-1694, www.tucumcarinm.com, 8:30am-5pm Mon.-Fri., free).

New Mexico Route 66 Museum

The **New Mexico Route 66 Museum** (1500 W. Rte. 66, 575/461-1641, www.nmrt66museum.org, 9am-5pm Mon.,

Tucumcari to Santa Fe

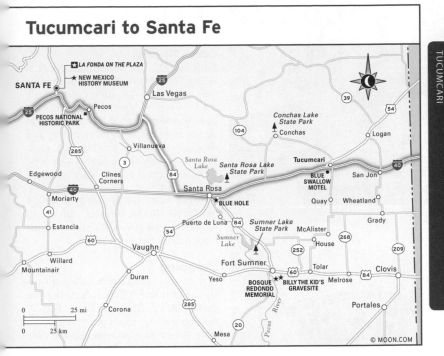

LA FONDA ON THE PLAZA
NEW MEXICO HISTORY MUSEUM
SANTA FE
25
Las Vegas
39
54
Pecos
PECOS NATIONAL HISTORIC PARK
25
Conchas Lake State Park
Conchas
Logan
285
104
Villanueva
Santa Rosa Lake
Santa Rosa Lake State Park
Tucumcari
40
Edgewood
3
84
BLUE SWALLOW MOTEL
San Jon
Clines Corners
Santa Rosa
40
BLUE HOLE
Quay
Wheatland
Moriarty
41
Puerto de Luna
84
Sumner Lake State Park
McAlister
Grady
Estancia
54
268
54
Sumner Lake
House
209
60
Vaughn
252
Willard
Fort Sumner
Tolar
Clovis
Mountainair
Duran
Yeso
BOSQUE REDONDO MEMORIAL
60
Melrose
84
BILLY THE KID'S GRAVESITE
0   25 mi
Corona
285
Portales
0   25 km
20
Mesa
© MOON.COM

Fri., Sat., 9am-1pm Tues.-Thurs., $3) captures key moments along the Mother Road. Peruse photographer Michael Campanelli's photographs, along with vintage cars and historical Tucumcari Route 66 artifacts. The museum is in the back of the Tucumcari Convention Center parking lot. In front of the lot sits artist Tom Coffin's 1997 **sculpture** dedicated to the Mother Road. You can't miss it; it's styled as a massive hood ornament with a chrome "66" and Cadillac tail fins on a sandstone base.

Mesalands Community College Dinosaur Museum

The **Mesalands Community College Dinosaur Museum** (222 E. Laughlin St., 575/461-3466, www.mesalands.edu, 10am-3pm Tues.-Sat. mid-Mar.-mid-Sept., 10am-4pm Tues.-Sat. mid-Sept.-mid-Mar., $8) claims to house the world's largest collection of life-sized bronze skeletons. The collection of original

fossils and replicas from the Mesozoic period fill 10,000 square feet (929 sq m) of exhibition space, and the museum shop sells rocks, minerals, t-shirts, and books.

The museum is located two blocks north of Route 66. Heading west on Route 66, turn right (north) on 1st Street (SR-209). Drive two blocks, then turn right (east) on Laughlin Avenue.

Tucumcari Historical Museum

Learn about the rise and fall of Tucumcari at the **Tucumcari Historical Museum** (416 S. Adams St., 575/461-4201, http://www.cityoftucumcari.com/museum, 9am-3pm Tues.-Sat., $5). Three floors of a 1903 schoolhouse showcase an eclectic range of artifacts, including newspapers, family scrapbooks, and bootleg liquor stills. There's also an original chuck wagon and old firehouse with a 1926 Chevrolet fire truck that still works.

The museum is three blocks north of Route 66. Heading west on Route 66, turn

right (north) on Adams Street. The museum will be on the right.

Odeon Theatre

Built in 1937, the **Odeon Theatre** (123 S. 2nd St., 575/461-0100, call for movie info, $6) may be the oldest continuously used theater in New Mexico. This art deco movie house underwent renovation to restore it to its former glory and now shows first-run movies each week. Even if you don't have time to stay for a flick, the owners will let you pop in and look around.

To get there from Route 66, turn right (north) on SR-104, then turn left (west) on West Center Street. The theater is one block down on the right.

Shopping

In the 1940s, when Route 66 was a two-lane road through Tucumcari, **Tee Pee Curios** (924 E. Rte. 66, 575/461-3773, 8am-6pm daily) was a gas and grocery store. When the road widened, the shop lost its gas pumps, but today the brightly lit neon sign entices travelers to stop in and browse coonskin caps, rubber tomahawks, jewelry, pottery, and Route 66 souvenirs for sale under a concrete tepee.

Food

Del's Restaurant (1202 E. Rte. 66, 575/461-1740, www.delsrestaurant.com, 11am-9pm Mon.-Sat., $10-35) has been serving Route 66 travelers since 1956. The menu goes the distance—from juicy steaks and a fresh salad bar to authentic Mexican fare.

★ **Kix on 66** (1102 E. Rte. 66, 575/461-1966, 6am-2pm daily, $6-12) serves breakfast and lunch in a cheerful coffee shop that calls to mind a classic diner from the 1950s. Breakfast is served all day and you won't want to miss out on the green chile omelet or the grilled and smothered-in-butter cinnamon roll. The

Top to bottom: Odeon Theatre, Tucumcari; La Cita; Tee Pee Curios

Women of the Mother Road

The story of Route 66 isn't complete without the illustrious women who've contributed greatly to the road's growth, success, and preservation. Here, celebrate the New Mexican women who made a profound impact on the Mother Road.

♦ **Mary Colter:** The famed architect for the Fred Harvey Company made her mark on many places along Route 66, but it was New Mexico that she eventually called home. Mary was born in Pennsylvania in 1869, grew up in Minnesota, and soon left home to become a designer and architect. She was one of few women in the profession at the time. For nearly 40 years, Mary served as the chief architect for Fred Harvey, designing such legendary landmarks as El Tovar Hotel, Bright Angel Lodge, and Phantom Ranch at the Grand Canyon; La Fonda in Santa Fe; and La Posada Hotel in Winslow, Arizona. Mary was greatly moved by American Indian cultures, particularly the Sioux in Minnesota, and she pioneered the architectural style we now associate with the Southwest; it's a blend of Spanish Colonial Revival, Mission Revival, and American Indian motifs. Mary Colter retired to Santa Fe in 1948, donating her collection of American Indian pottery and relics to Mesa Verde National Park in Colorado.

♦ **Lillian Redman:** Arriving in New Mexico in a covered wagon in 1915, Lillian homesteaded near Santa Rosa. In 1958, she and her husband purchased the iconic **Blue Swallow Motel** (page 204) in Tucumcari, updating it and adding the now-famous neon sign. The Blue Swallow was as a home away from home for Route 66 travelers, and Lillian was its consummate hostess. She ran the motel for 40 years, welcoming the tired and the weary; if a guest was unable to pay the room fee, Lillian accepted trade as payment or even waived the fee entirely. She also posted a note in every room for guests. An excerpt reads: "May this room … be your second home. May those you love be near you in thoughts and dreams … May the business that brought you this way prosper. May every call you make and every message you receive add to your joy. When you leave, may your journey be safe."

♦ **Fabiola Cabeza de Baca:** This multilingual teacher and activist was born into a ranching family in 1894, but the open road soon called her name. For nearly 30 years, she traveled Route 66 teaching New Mexico's rural population new techniques for agriculture, farming, and homemaking. This enabled people to stay on their own land rather than having to pick up and move to the cities. She taught women the traditional craft of quilting while also introducing them to modern sewing machines. Fabiola spoke English, Spanish, Towa, and Tewa, and was a passionate activist for bilingual education and maintaining Hispanic culture throughout the state. In 1935, she was part of a group of women who founded Sociedad Folklórico de Santa Fe to preserve Spanish language and Hispanic traditions in the state.

♦ **Mary Mochimaru Montoya:** Many women along Route 66 in the 1930s and 40s found work in Harvey Houses, serving train passengers who came through town. Mary, who was born in El Paso, Texas, to a Japanese father and Mexican mother, became employed as a Harvey Girl at the El Navajo Harvey House in Gallup during World War II. She'd grown up in New Mexico, working in local restaurants from the age of 12. To get hired during the war, she dropped her Japanese last name, going by "Mary Montoya" to fly under the radar. After the war, she took her culinary skills to the Route 66 restaurant, Ranch Kitchen, where she became the manager, running it successfully for 30 years.

pet-friendly patio offers a special doggie menu (all items less than $3) for your pooch.

Many folks go to **La Cita** (820 S. 1st St. and Rte. 66, 575/461-7866, 11am-8pm Mon.-Sat., 11am-2pm Sun., $7-12) just so they can walk through a door hatted with a huge sombrero. (A sombrero sculpture sits over the front door—a rare example of quirky western vernacular architecture.) As for the food, well, it's not pretty, but it's tasty. Go for the chicken enchiladas or chile rellenos.

Watson's BBQ (502 S. Lake St., 575/461-9620, https://tucranchsupply.com, 7:30am-5pm Mon.-Fri., 7:30am-4pm Sat., $10-28) is located at Tucumcari Ranch Supply and is decked out in railroad decor, with picnic tables under a large canopy. The smoked brisket, meaty ribs, and juicy fruit cobblers are all outstanding. Watson's is three blocks north of Route 66 on South Lake Street.

Accommodations

The ★ **Blue Swallow Motel** (815 E. Rte. 66, 575/461-9849, www.blueswallowmotel.com, $85-140) opened in 1940 and today stands as a classic example of a pre-WWII tourist court on Route 66. Still in operation today, the motel features an L-shaped layout with 14 restored rooms and attached garages, each covered in a different mural. Rooms are decorated with 1950s furniture from the Franciscan Manufacturing Company and include chenille bedspreads, midcentury accents, and rotary phones. Get a photo of the antique car parked in front of what is arguably one of the best neon signs on Route 66. The Blue Swallow's bird-in-flight symbol harkens back to the classic sailor tattoo: When sailors saw this bird, they knew land—and home—was near.

Open since 1963, the **Historic Route 66 Motel** (1620 E. Rte. 66, 575/461-1212,

---

Top to bottom: Tucumcari's Motel Safari; Blue Swallow Motel; Historic Route 66 Motel

www.rte66motel.com, $50-65) shows off a cool, minimalist Palm Springs style. The mid-century-modern rooms are spacious and clean, and include floor-to-ceiling windows (don't fret; each room is equipped with blackout curtains for those big windows). Bonus points go for being pet-friendly.

The funky and fun **Motel Safari** (722 E. Rte. 66, 575/461-1048, www. themotelsafari.com, $70-115) has been going strong since 1959. You'll enjoy the perfect blend of modern comforts (Wi-Fi, luxury linens, flat-screen HD televisions) with the retro charm of a 1960s motor court (original mid-century furniture, artsy wall murals). Note: All rooms are non-smoking, no pets are allowed, and there are no check-ins after 10pm. Look for the sign with a big camel, which pays homage to Edward Fitzgerald Beale's 1857 expedition, when the U.S. Army used 70 camels to survey the Southwest.

◈ Back on 66

The road west of Tucumcari makes its way along a shallow valley with sandstone mesas in the distance near Montoya and Newkirk. Leaving Tucumcari, join I-40 west at Exit 329 and drive 17 miles (27 km). Take Exit 311 and turn left to cross I-40, then follow the South Frontage Road for 6 miles (9.7 km). Cross I-40 again (no exit) to follow the North Frontage Road for 14 miles (22.5 km) through **Newkirk,** a small ranching community that today is little more than a ghost town.

The next town, **Cuervo,** lies 8.5 miles (13.7 km) from Newkirk. The road between Newkirk and Cuervo can be rough, so take it slow. There are many places where the road dips; if there is deep or running water, do *not* cross it. Turn around and take I-40 instead.

Cuervo was a railroad town and ranching district. Trains stopped here in the early 1900s, and once Route 66 came through, a few gas stations and grocery stores opened. Today, there are remnants of an abandoned stone church, but don't go inside, as the interior is unsafe. In Cuervo, join I-40 west at Exit 291 and drive to Exit 277 at Santa Rosa.

◈ Side Trip: Fort Sumner Historic Site

In the 1860s along the banks of the Pecos River, more than 8,500 Navajo and 500 Mescalero Apache were held captive on the 1-million-acre (404,686-hectare) Bosque Redondo reservation overseen by the troops of **Fort Sumner.** After the U.S. Army forced the Mescalero Apache people to leave their homeland, they brought them to Bosque Redondo in 1863, while the Navajo were forced to walk hundreds of miles here. Upon arrival, they were made to build the fort and dam, dig ditches, and plant cottonwood trees. The plan was to "teach" the Navajo and Mescalero Apache how to be self-sufficient—but they had already been self-sufficient for centuries before the Europeans arrived. No shelter was provided; instead they lived in pits and used tree branches for protection. As the U.S. government severely underestimated the amount of food needed to feed the population at the fort, approximately 20 percent of the American Indians starved to death.

Bosque Redondo Memorial

The site today is the **Bosque Redondo Memorial** (3647 Billy the Kid Rd., 575/355-2573, www.nmmonuments. org/bosque-redondo, 8:30am-4:30pm Wed.-Sun., free). Navajo architect David Sloan designed the Mescalero Apache and Navajo memorial in the shape of an Apache tepee. Take the 0.75-mile (1.2-km) outdoor interpretive trail to see the Indian Commissary where crops were stored; the area where the 1868 Navajo treaty was signed; and the entrance to the Fort Sumner Military Center, with its 30-inch (76-cm) adobe walls, which housed 637 soldiers. There's also a plaque at the site where Billy the Kid was killed by

Sheriff Pat Garrett in 1881. Informational exhibits and a video recap the history of the site. The on-site gift shop sells hand-woven rugs, pottery, books, clothing, and tribal jewelry.

From I-40 in Santa Rosa, take Exit 277 to get on U.S. 84 south. Drive 40 miles (64 km) to the village of Fort Sumner. Turn left (east) on U.S. 60 and continue on U.S. 84. Turn right (south) on Billy the Kid Road. The site is 3.5 miles (5.6 km) on the right (west).

Billy the Kid's Gravesite

Also in Fort Sumner is **Billy the Kid's gravesite;** the famous outlaw was killed here in 1881. There are several signs claiming to have the "real grave of Billy the Kid"; it's still un-clear where he actually is, but his head-stone is in the graveyard behind the Old Fort Sumner Museum. It was sto-len more than once, so now a cage en-closes it. The **Billy the Kid Museum** (1435 E. Sumner Ave., 575/355-2380, www.billythekidmuseumfortsumner. com, 8:30am-5pm daily May 15-Oct. 1, 8:30am-5pm Mon.-Sat. Oct. 1-May 15, $5) has more stories about the infamous teenage outlaw's life.

The gravestone is in the Old Fort Sumner Cemetery in Fort Sumner Park near Billy the Kid Drive and Old Fort Park Road. The museum is on U.S. 60/84 in the east side of the town of Fort Sumner.

Santa Rosa

Santa Rosa was an agrarian community until the railroad came to town in 1901. When Route 66 arrived in 1930, it became an official transportation hub. The origi-nal Route 66 alignment took a sharp turn north here toward Dilia and Romeroville, then headed toward Santa Fe. Santa Rosa remained a part of the east-west align-ment after 1937.

In an otherwise arid land, Santa Rosa stands out for its cool blue lakes. Called the "City of Natural Lakes," this area is also home to the Santa Rosa Sink, sink-holes connected by an underground network of water-filled tunnels. The phe-nomenon formed from millions of years of water erosion, which created a large basin of wetlands. As the geologic strata weakened, collapsed, and dissolved, an artesian well formed. Today it is part of a large system of seven lakes that are con-nected underground.

Santa Rosa is primarily ranch country, with picturesque stone buildings and a quiet downtown. You might recall Santa Rosa's bit part in the film *The Grapes of Wrath*. It was the site where Henry Fonda watches a freight train cross the Pecos River. The bridge in the film is on the right after 1st Street on the west side of town.

Route 66 Through Santa Rosa

From I-40 west, turn right off Exit 277 and follow Business I-40 (Will Rogers Dr.) through downtown. Soon after you cross the Pecos River at the fork, stay right and follow Business I-40 northwest to rejoin I-40 west.

Sights
Blue Hole

Take a refreshing road-trip reprieve with a dip in the **Blue Hole** (1085 Blue Hole Rd., 575/472-3763, www.santarosabluehole. com, 8am-8pm daily with lifeguards on duty, $5). This round, crystal-clear lake is one of the seven Santa Rosa lakes that connect underground. On a hot summer day, cliff dive into the sparkling blue water with its craggy limestone walls, but keep in mind the water is a crisp 62°F (17°C), so prepare for a chilly swim. The 81-foot-deep (25-m) artesian spring-fed lake is known as one of the best natural swimming holes in the state, and it's the scuba diving capital of the Southwest. It attracts visitors from around the world, so it can get busy on weekends.

Car Culture

New Mexico has the perfect weather for preserving classic cars: The dry, temperate climate keeps the rust at bay and the paint job intact. The **Route 66 Auto Museum** (2436 E. Rte. 66, 575/472-1966, www.route66automuseum.net, 7:30am-6pm daily, $5) in Santa Rosa has a small but impressive collection of more than 30 lovingly restored and rebuilt vintage cars—from flame-kissed roadsters to hot rods and trucks.

Heading west on Route 66, turn left (south) on Lake Drive and make another left (east) on Blue Hole Road.

Food

★ **Comet II Drive-In** (1257 E. Rte. 66, 575/472-3663, 11am-9pm Tues.-Sun., $10-15) is a no-frills restaurant serving really good Mexican food. The "drive-in" part of the name comes from the fact that it's housed in a former carhop. The original restaurant opened in 1929 and has been family-run for three generations. This place is serious about green chile—it's a unique strain grown in Puerto de Luna that has been cultivated in New Mexico for more than a century. Maybe that's what brings in the locals and celebrities like Dan Aykroyd and the late, great Johnny Cash. All the food is made from scratch, so no matter what you order, you can't go wrong. A few winners include refried beans and a carnitas burrito with red-chile sauce.

◆ Back on 66

Leaving Santa Rosa, you have a decision to make: Take the longer, more scenic pre-1937 alignment toward **Santa Fe,** or the post-1937 alignment heading west toward **Clines Corners** (much of this route is only accessible via I-40). I recommend the **pre-1937 alignment** that travels north to Santa Fe. Not only is the landscape lovely, but there's so much to see and do in Santa Fe that you'd be remiss to skip it.

If time is a factor, take I-40 west to **Albuquerque** where the two alignments cross. If you take this route, you'll get to experience the ★ **Musical Highway** in Tijeras, just east of Albuquerque. It's a sleepy stretch of road on which the rumble strips have been engineered to sound like they're playing "America the Beautiful" when you drive over them at exactly 45 miles (72 km) per hour. Traveling eastbound on Route 66, you'll hit the Musical Highway near Exit 170 between mile markers 4 and 5.

The Santa Fe Loop

◆ Pre-1937 Alignment to Santa Fe

Leaving Santa Rosa, join I-40 west, and take Exit 256 to follow U.S. 84 north for 41 miles (66 km). Make sure you gas up in Santa Rosa, as you won't encounter any gas stations until you near Santa Fe.

You'll cross the Pecos River right before **Dilia.** There really isn't anything to "do" on this trek to Santa Fe, except enjoy the open road. Take in views of alfalfa pastures, roaming cattle, and craggy mesas. In Dilia, there's an old, buttercream-yellow Catholic church and a bar on the side of the road. Continue on to Santa Fe traveling north on U.S. 84 and cross I-25. Turn left (southwest) on the Frontage Road and in less than 5 miles (8 km), you'll reach **Tecolote** (the Aztec word for "owl"). As you pass over Tecolote Creek on the south end of town, look back to see several concrete bridge supports where the original Route 66 crossed the creek.

Keep heading south on the Frontage Road for another 5 miles (8 km) to the blink-and-you-could-miss-it town of **Bernal.** The next town, **San Jose,** is about 7 miles (11.3 km) west and sits on the south side of the Frontage Road; dirt roads lead off to old sun-soaked adobe homes and a church. On the east side of San Jose, keep an eye out for a rusty truss bridge with weathered wooden planks and no railings.

Leaving San Jose, the Frontage Road crosses to the south side of U.S. 84 and climbs to the top of the **Glorieta Mesa,** with vistas of the valley below. After 13 miles (20.9 km), you'll reach **Rowe;** right after Railroad Way, turn right (northwest) to cross under U.S. 84. Turn left (north) on SR-63, and in less than 3 miles (4.8 km) you'll come to Pecos National Historic Park.

Pecos National Historical Park

Tucked away in the Sangre de Cristo Mountains, **Pecos National Historical Park** (1 Peach Dr., Pecos, SR-63 and Ranger Ln., 505/757-7241, www.nps. gov/peco/index.htm, 8am-6pm daily Memorial Day-Labor Day, 8:30am-4pm daily Labor Day-May 30, free) features the majestic ruins of an ancient pueblo that dates to AD 800. In 1862, Confederate soldiers tried to take Santa Fe; after a three-day battle at Glorieta Pass, it was clear New Mexico would remain a Union state. Look for the 2.3-mile (3.7-km) Civil War Battlefield Trail map at the visitors center, which also offers additional trail maps, information about ranger-led tours, exhibits, and a 10-minute introductory film. Trail ruts, a stage stop from the Santa Fe Trail, and a Civil War battlefield tell the story of the West and its role in shaping and redefining the United States.

◆ Back on 66

Head north for 3 miles (4.8 km) on SR-63 and drive through the town of **Pecos**. Turn left (west) on SR-50 and climb 7,500 feet (2,286 meters) to Glorieta Pass, the highest point on the pre-1937 alignment of Route 66. In 5.5 miles (8.9 km), join I-25 West/U.S. 85 and drive 5 miles (8 km) to Exit 294/Cañoncito. Turn left

(southwest) on Old Las Vegas Highway (SR-300), which parallels I-25. Stay on Old Las Vegas Highway for about 10 miles (16.1 km), then turn right (north) on SR-466/Old Pecos Trail (near Exit 284 on I-25). Drive north about 1 mile (1.6 km) and then bear right to continue following Old Pecos Trail north. In about 1.5 miles (2.4 km), the road merges with Old Santa Fe Trail, which leads into the heart of Santa Fe.

Santa Fe

Santa Fe is the oldest capital city in the United States. Nomadic Paleo-Indians arrived in northern New Mexico around 10,000 BC, and their descendants created the iconic pueblo-style adobe structures that define Santa Fe—and often, the Southwest—today.

From 1926 to 1937, Route 66 came through Santa Fe. Today, the route goes right through downtown, two blocks south of the historic Plaza along tight winding streets lined with old adobe buildings. A distinctive culture and aesthetic—formed by a mix of 17th-century buildings, world-renowned cuisine, southwestern art, and relaxing spas—draw artists, eccentrics, pioneers, rebels, outliers, and everyone in between to Santa Fe. The magic of the city is that everyone feels at home as soon as you set foot here.

◆ Route 66 Through Santa Fe

Entering Santa Fe, head north on Old Santa Fe Trail and turn left (west) on East Alameda Street. Drive two blocks west and then turn left (south) on Galisteo Street. Continue 1 mile (1.6 km) to turn right (west) on Alta Vista Street. At Cerrillos Road (SR-14), turn left (southwest) and drive about 7 miles (11.3 km); pass under I-25 and continue straight for another 2 miles (3.2 km). Turn right (west), then make a quick left (south) to follow the South Frontage Road.

Santa Fe

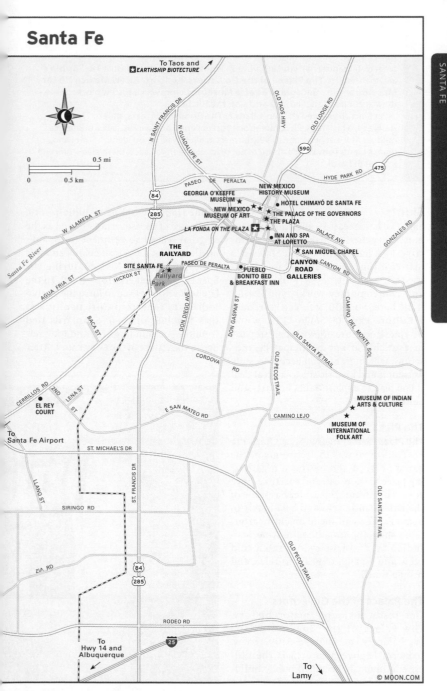

To Taos and
⊡EARTHSHIP BIOTECTURE

N SAINT FRANCIS DR

N GUADALUPE ST

OLD TAOS HWY

OLD LODGE RD

590

HYDE PARK RD

475

0   0.5 mi
0   0.5 km

PASEO DE PERALTA

84

285

W ALAMEDA ST

Santa Fe River

AGUA FRIA ST

HICKOX ST

BACA ST

CERRILLOS RD

2ND ST

LENA ST

To
Santa Fe Airport

LLANO ST

ST. MICHAEL'S DR

ST. FRANCIS DR

SIRINGO RD

ZIA RD

84
285

RODEO RD

To
Hwy 14 and
Albuquerque

25

GEORGIA O'KEEFFE
MUSEUM ★

NEW MEXICO
HISTORY MUSEUM

● HOTEL CHIMAYÓ DE SANTA FE

★ ★ ★
NEW MEXICO
MUSEUM OF ART ★ ★ THE PALACE OF THE GOVERNORS
★ THE PLAZA
LA FONDA ON THE PLAZA ▣ ★
★ INN AND SPA
AT LORETTO

PALACE AVE

GONZALES RD

THE
RAILYARD

SITE SANTA FE ★

PASEO DE PERALTA

Railyard
Park

★ SAN MIGUEL CHAPEL

CANYON
ROAD
GALLERIES CANYON RD

● PUEBLO
BONITO BED
& BREAKFAST INN

DON DIEGO AVE

DON GASPAR ST

CAMINO DEL MONTE SOL

OLD SANTA FE TRAIL

CORDOVA

RD

OLD PECOS TRAIL

● EL REY
COURT

E SAN MATEO RD

CAMINO LEJO

MUSEUM OF INDIAN
ARTS & CULTURE
★

★
MUSEUM OF
INTERNATIONAL
FOLK ART

OLD SANTA FE TRAIL

OLD PECOS TRAIL

To
Lamy

© MOON.COM

One Day in Santa Fe

Honestly, you could spend a week here. And that's just to have time to eat at all the great restaurants! But if you only have 24 hours, start with breakfast at **Tia Sophia's** and then head to **The Palace of the Governors.** Explore the **New Mexico History Museum** and the **Georgia O'Keeffe Museum** before walking a few blocks to see the Mary Colter-designed **La Fonda on the Plaza.**

For lunch, have a red chile enchilada at **The Shed.** From there, walk to **The Railyard,** a hip area with contemporary art galleries, bookstores, cafés, boutiques, outdoor music venues, and a lively farmers market. Walk up Guadalupe Street and, for dinner, hit up **Tomasita's.** If you're not ready for sleep yet, see if there's live entertainment at **El Farol.**

Sights

Santa Fe has at least 15 museums and almost 300 galleries, making it the third-largest art hub in the United States. No matter if you're in the mood for southwestern and cowboy art or modern and contemporary works, you'll find it all here. For $30, you can purchase a **Culture Pass** (505/476-1125, www. newmexicoculture.org/visit/culturepass, or available at any participating museum), which grants you access to state museums and historic sites—a great deal if you plan to explore Santa Fe's arts and culture scene.

The Plaza

The Plaza (San Francisco St. at Old Santa Fe Trail, free) was the terminus of the Santa Fe Trail and has been a gathering place to shop, eat, and socialize since 1610. This cultural epicenter has some of the oldest landmarks and best hotels in Santa Fe. You can spend an entire afternoon shopping for authentic American Indian art and jewelry, or grab a cold brew and a patch of grass to relax and people-watch.

The Palace of the Governors

Get ready for some major history. **The Palace of the Governors** (105 W. Palace Ave., 505/476-5100, www. palaceofthegovernors.org) is the oldest continuously occupied public building in the United States, predating the

White House by 200 years. Built in 1610, the Palace of the Governors served as the original seat of government for Spain's northernmost American colony and was the capitol of New Mexico during the Spanish Colonial era (1610-1680). In the late 1600s, Spain tried to force the Pueblo Indians to convert to Christianity, and they revolted in 1680. Spaniards fled from the surrounding area and took refuge in the Palace of the Governors. After

the Pueblo Indians cut off the Spaniards' water supply, they were able to take back Santa Fe. During this time, about 1,000 Pueblo Indians lived here and added a multistory pueblo-style construction on top of the building that stands today.

When the Spanish returned to New Mexico in 1693, they destroyed the addition. Spanish rule continued until Mexico claimed independence in 1821 and took control of the region. In 1848, the Americans claimed it as a U.S. territory. Today, the building shows remnants of both Spanish and Native constructions, with Territorial elements and Spanish Colonial-Pueblo Revival style. Outside the building, dozens of American Indian artists and tribal members sell authentic handmade crafts and jewelry in the marketplace. The New Mexico History Museum is inside.

New Mexico History Museum

The **New Mexico History Museum** (113 Lincoln Ave., 505/476-5200, www.

nmhistorymuseum.org, 10am-5pm daily May-Oct., 10am-5pm Tues.-Sun. Nov.-Apr., $12) sits adjacent to the Palace of the Governors with an entrance around the corner on Lincoln. Exhibits on four floors explore New Mexican heritage and the history of the Southwest, offering insight into the region's Indigenous people, stories along the Santa Fe Trail, and the role Spanish colonization played in shaping Santa Fe's culture and identity.

Also on-site are New Mexico's first printing press (dating from 1834); a non-circulating library with 40,000 books, 6,000 maps, and more than 750,000 photo archives from as early as 1850; and a beautiful Works Progress Administration wall mural by Olive Rush.

New Mexico Museum of Art

Located across the street from the Palace of the Governors, the **New Mexico Museum of Art** (107 W. Palace Ave., 505/476-5072, www.nmartmuseum.org, 10am-5pm daily May-Oct., 10am-5pm

The Palace of the Governors

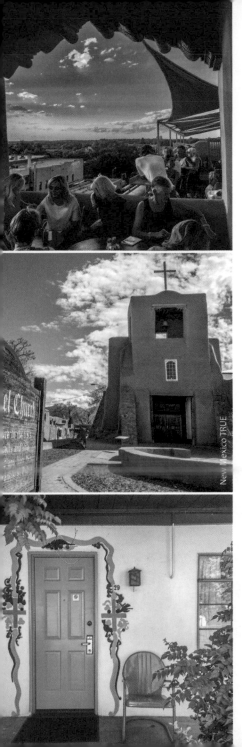

Tues.-Sun. Nov.-Apr., $12) was one of the first spaces to encourage local artists to showcase their work. Today, the museum displays new works from New Mexican and Taos Society artists, as well as Santa Fe art colony members and Hopi pottery makers.

★ La Fonda on the Plaza

La Fonda on the Plaza (100 E. San Francisco St., 505/982-5511, www.lafondasantafe.com, $189-475) is a southwestern luxury hotel in the heart of downtown Santa Fe. Located on the same site as the city's first inn, La Fonda opened in 1922. In 1925, the building changed hands and Fred Harvey leased the property. Brilliant and pioneering architect Mary Colter renovated the interior—adding the San Francisco street entrance and enclosing the front patio—and the site operated as a Harvey House until 1968.

Today, La Fonda is a living and breathing work of art, complete with everything you could want in a hotel. Guest rooms feature original Puebloan artwork and hand-painted furniture, plus plush bathrobes and nightly turndown service. Not overnighting here? No problem. Wander the lobby to soak up the southwestern details (skylights, terra-cotta tiles, hand-stamped chandeliers), then ride the elevator to the rooftop bar. Here, you're afforded the chance to savor a cocktail and a glorious Santa Fe sunset. As soon as the sun sets behind the horizon, the bar takes last call, so be ready to head out after your drink.

At La Fonda's **La Plazuela Restaurant** (505/995-2334, 7am-2pm and 5pm-10pm Mon.-Fri., 7am-3pm and 5pm-10pm Sat.-Sun., $10-40), you can enjoy breakfast, lunch, or dinner in the historic dining room just off the lobby. In between bites of the incredible food, which ranges from

---

Top to bottom: La Fonda on the Plaza in Santa Fe; San Miguel Chapel, Santa Fe; El Rey Court in Santa Fe

American to New Mexican, take in the sights: 460 hand-painted windows and a stunning wrought-iron chandelier. The chargrilled filet mignon is sided with cheesy white corn enchiladas and red and green chiles, and the guacamole is made tableside. Reservations are highly recommended.

San Miguel Chapel

Not only is the **San Miguel Chapel** (401 Old Santa Fe Trail, 505/983-3974, http://sanmiguelchapel.org, 10am-4pm Mon.-Sat., $1) one of the best-preserved examples of adobe architecture in Santa Fe—no small feat, since many of the buildings are well-preserved adobe structures—but it's also the oldest church in the continental United States. Built between 1610 and 1626, and erected by Tlaxcalans under the direction of Franciscan friars, the chapel was partially destroyed in 1640, then again in 1680 during the Pueblo Revolt. The present structure dates to 1710.

As you step inside, you'll see images of Christ on the Cross and Saint John the Baptist painted in the 1630s by the Franciscans. These were used as teaching aids to try to convert the Indigenous peoples to Christianity.

Museum of International Folk Art

The **Museum of International Folk Art** (706 Camino Lejo, 505/476-1200, www.internationalfolkart.org, 10am-5pm daily May-Oct.; 10am-5pm Tues.-Sun. Nov.-Apr., $12) has the world's largest collection of cultural art, with 150,000 artifacts from more than 100 nations. The museum has documented and preserved creative works from folk artists around the world since 1953, championing folk art and its impact on cultural identity before "outsider art" became hip.

Museum of Indian Arts & Culture

The **Museum of Indian Arts & Culture** (710 Camino Lejo, 505/476-1250, www.indianartsandculture.org, 10am-5pm daily May-Oct., 10am-5pm Tues.-Sun. Nov.-Apr., $12) offers an informative introduction to the American Indian communities in northern New Mexico, focusing on the history and contemporary life of the Pueblos, Navajo, and Apache. There's a huge repository of more than 10 million artifacts, with 80,000 archaeological, ethnographic, and fine arts objects.

Georgia O'Keeffe Museum

Georgia O'Keeffe was born in Wisconsin, studied art in Chicago, and lived in New York, but it was New Mexico that changed the course of her life—and her art. O'Keeffe visited Ghost Ranch near Abiquiu in the 1930s and 1940s, and it was here that she painted some of her most famous works. The **Georgia O'Keeffe Museum** (217 Johnson St., 505/946-1000, www.okeeffemuseum.org, 10am-5pm Sat.-Thurs., 10am-7pm Fri., $13) houses the largest collection of her art, with 1,149 paintings, drawings, and sculptures, plus her personal notes, books from her own collection, and other items. Two videos narrated with quotes from O'Keeffe tell the story of her life and work. Serious O'Keeffe fans can sign up for the **Abiquiu Home & Studio Tour** (505/946-1000, by reservation only Mar.-Nov., $45), about one hour north of Santa Fe.

SITE Santa Fe

Santa Fe's thriving art scene extends beyond southwestern art. To check it out, visit **SITE Santa Fe** (1606 Paseo de Peralta, 505/989-1199, http://sitesantafe.org, 11am-5pm Thurs., 11am-7pm Fri., 10am-5pm Sat., noon-4pm Sun., free), a contemporary art space with experimental and innovative exhibits. Keep your mind and eyes open, and expect the unexpected; the forward-thinking curatorial design will keep you engaged and captivated.

Local Eats

New Mexico grows more chile peppers than any other state in the United States. In fact, it takes its chile so seriously that it's even spelled differently. (*Chil* is an Aztec word that means pepper; the Spanish added the "e" at the end.) **New Mexican chiles** have a distinct and delicious flavor thanks to centuries of farmers perfecting the art of growing, drying, and roasting chiles. If you visit in the fall during roasting season, the air is perfumed with their sweet, earthy aroma. With each meal you eat in New Mexico, you'll have a big decision to make: whether to order red or green chile. Green has a tangy flavor, while red has a deep, mellow flavor. If you can't decide, order "Christmas-style" for a bit of both.

Galleries

Choose among three hubs to explore Santa Fe's art galleries: Canyon Road, The Railyard, and downtown. **Canyon Road** (Paseo de Peralta and Canyon Rd., southeast of The Plaza, www.visitcanyonroad. com) is home to more than 80 galleries, and strolling this arts district is a popular pastime for locals and visitors. **The Railyard** (Cerrillos Rd. and Montezuma Ave., and Cerrillos Rd. and Baca St., www.railyardsantafe.com) offers high-end contemporary art galleries, Friday night art walks, and a farmers market that dates to the 1960s and features more than 150 vendors. **Downtown's galleries** focus on southwestern, American Indian, and cowboy art. In total, Santa Fe boasts nearly 300 galleries located throughout the city.

Food

★ **El Farol** (808 Canyon Rd., 505/983-9912, www.elfarolsantafe.com, 3pm-9pm Wed.-Sun., $8-34) is a restaurant, yes. But it's also a hot spot for live entertainment, including a show featuring world-class flamenco dancers and music every Friday and Saturday. This all means you should plan to make an evening of it when you come here. As Santa Fe's oldest cantina, El Farol serves delightful Spanish tapas such as *jamón serrano* (dry-cured ham) with pickled veggies, beef skewers with chimichurri sauce, and flash-fried avocado with lime crema.

The Shed (113½ E. Palace Ave.,

505/982-9030, https://sfshed.com, 11am-2:30pm and 5pm-9pm Mon.-Sat., $12-25) has been a family-owned business since 1953. Famous for spicy red-chile enchiladas and blue-corn dishes, the restaurant calls home a 1692 adobe hacienda. Though the restaurant is popular and thus busy, the charming vibe makes dining here a memorable Santa Fe experience. But do yourself a favor—call ahead and make a reservation.

With a tin ceiling, black-and-white checked floors, and the tantalizing scent of warm *sopaipillas* (pillows of fried dough), the **Plaza Café** (54 Lincoln Ave., 505/982-1664, www.plazacafesantafe. com, 8am-8pm daily, $7-18) puts a New Mexican spin on the traditional American diner. Locals from the nearby courthouse stop by every day to nosh on blue-corn pancakes for breakfast, tortilla soup for lunch, and steak and enchiladas for dinner. It has been family-owned since 1947, and the staff has been working here for decades.

Santa Fe is best experienced on foot, preferably with a to-go latte in hand. Stop by **Collected Works Bookstore & Coffeehouse** (202 Galisteo St., 505/988-4226, www.collectedworksbookstore. com, 8am-6pm daily, $5), an independently owned shop with a terrific coffee bar inside. The lattes are frothy and creamy, the espresso is rich, and the atmosphere is pure '90s-era coffeehouse—in a great way.

You'll find **Café Pasqual's** (121 Don

Gaspar, 505/983-9340, www.pasquals. com, 8am-3pm daily, dinner 5pm-close, $12-40) in a historic pueblo-style adobe building. The festive dining room, decorated with hand-painted Mexican tiles and murals, serves dishes with meticulously selected ingredients, from organic beef, pork, eggs, dairy, and produce to house-made bread, ice cream, and chile sauces. You can't go wrong with the grilled carne asada or the *cochinita pibil* (slow-cooked pork shoulder), but the red quinoa spinach cakes are out of this world.

Tia Sophia's (210 W. San Francisco St., 505/983-9880, http://www.tiasophias. com, 7am-2pm Tues.-Sat., 8am-1pm Sun.-Mon., $6-12) is a true locals' hangout with affordable and yummy eats with fast and friendly service. Go in the morning and order the breakfast burrito topped with chile and cheese. Don't worry if there's a line out front, as it usually moves quickly.

Tomasita's (500 S. Guadalupe St., 505/983-5721, www.tomasitas.com, 11am-8:30pm Sun.-Thurs., 11am-9pm Fri.-Sat., $9-18) specializes in northern New Mexican food and has won awards for their green and red chile sauces. The lengthy menu can seem daunting at first, but usually the daily special is a roundup of several of the most popular items— order that. Wondering what the bottle of honey is doing on your table? That's for the complimentary *sopaipillas* that arrive post-meal. Slather them with butter and drizzle with honey for a sweet-and-savory conclusion to dinner.

The Pantry (1820 Cerrillos Rd., 505/986-0022, www.pantrysantafe. com, 8am-7:30pm daily, $7-20) has been a Santa Fe staple since 1948. Lunch is good, but breakfast is better, especially when you order the "Buenos Días," with potatoes, green chiles, eggs, and cheese.

Top to bottom: Tia Sophia's, Santa Fe; Tomasita's, Santa Fe; Inn and Spa at Loretto, Santa Fe

New Mexico TRUE

Accommodations

Inn and Spa at Loretto (211 Old Santa Fe Trail, 866/582-1646, www.hotelloretto. com, $229-259) sits one block from the Santa Fe Plaza and is walking distance to galleries, museums, restaurants, boutiques, and trails. The impressive hotel offers beautifully appointed guest rooms in an adobe building inspired by the Taos Pueblo. Rooms blend old-world charm and southwestern style, with four-poster beds, fireplaces, and balconies. On-site are four art galleries, a tranquil garden, heated outdoor pool, and full-service spa with a private elevator so you can slip downstairs for a facial or a massage without changing out of your robe.

One block from the Plaza is the **Hotel Chimayó de Santa Fe** (125 Washington Ave., 505/988-4900, www.hotelchimayo. com, $119-369), a beautiful boutique hotel that honors the sacred New Mexico village of Chimayó. The hotel donates a portion of its proceeds to artistic and cultural programs, events, community organizations, nonprofits, and scholarships that preserve and advance New Mexican cultural heritage. Rooms feature original artwork by local artists; many have wood-burning fireplaces with private balconies that overlook a hacienda-style courtyard.

For a cozy B&B experience, there's **Pueblo Bonito Bed & Breakfast Inn** (138 W. Manhattan, 800/461-4599, www. pueblobonitoinn.com, $105-235), a two-story pueblo "estate" tucked away among leafy trees just a short walk from the Plaza. Each room is uniquely designed, many with fireplaces, plus you'll enjoy free Wi-Fi and a homemade breakfast each morning. The owners are happy to share local insights about what to see and do in Santa Fe, so don't be shy about striking up a conversation.

A stylish 1930s property on Route 66, ★ **El Rey Court** (1862 Cerrillos Rd., 505/982-1931, http://elreycourt.com, $116-165) boasts 5 acres (2 hectares) of gardens, patios, fountains, and even a Spanish Colonial courtyard. Each of the 86 rooms has a bright teal door set against cool white adobe (perfect for a classic Santa Fe photo op) and offers a kiva fireplace, kitchenette, original artwork, and signature wood-beamed ceilings. Even though El Rey is not within walking distance of the historic Plaza, it is steps away from one of the best breakfast joints in town: The Pantry.

Back on 66

Exit Santa Fe driving south on Cerrillos Road (SR-14) until you cross U.S. 84/285. At this point, determine whether to take the side trip and head north to **Taos,** follow the post-1937 alignment to **Albuquerque,** or take the detour to **Turquoise Trail.**

If you decide to visit **Taos,** from the south end of Santa Fe, you have two options. Staying on SR-599, which bypasses Santa Fe and rejoins U.S. 84 on the north side of town, is the faster route. Or take Cerrillos Road (SR-14) north through town until it merges with U.S. 84 on the north side of the downtown area.

If you're following the post-1937 alignment, the most direct route to **Albuquerque** is to keep heading south on Cerrillos Road (SR-14) and join I-25 south for 1.7 miles (2.7 km). Turn right (west) onto SR-599 and take the next left to follow the South Frontage Road for I-25. Drive approximately 9 miles (14.5 km) south to Exit 267, where you will join I-25 to follow the post-1937 alignment to Albuquerque.

At the junction of SR-599 and SR-14 and I-25, you can follow the **Turquoise Trail** detour south along SR-14.

Side Trip: Taos

The High Road to Taos

There's a reason photographers love northern New Mexico. Peach trees, apple orchards, and chile farms line the route to Taos, and the mountainous land reaches up to the sky with its strata of

Shifting Landscape

As Route 66 crosses New Mexico, it passes over three distinct topographies with elevations ranging 3,800-7,500 feet (1,158-2,286 m). These include the Pecos and Canadian Valleys of the **Great Plains,** the **Basin and Range Plateau,** and the **Intermountain Plateau.** What you'll see: smooth, flat **plains,** broken **mesas,** rosy **deserts** to the west, brown-and-green **high deserts** to the north, forested wildernesses, and even **snow-capped mountains,** depending on the time of year.

colors—shades of blue during the day, pinks and oranges at sunset.

Follow I-84 north for 20 miles (32 km) to its junction with SR-68 near Española. Turn north (right) onto SR-68, then in 0.5 mile (0.8 km) turn east (another right) onto SR-76. In 7 miles (11.3 km), you'll reach the village of Chimayó.

Chimayó

The village of Chimayó in the Sangre de Cristo foothills was settled around 1740. This region has a long history of fiber arts and talented weavers that spans generations. En route, you'll pass by **El Santuario de Chimayó** (15 Santuario Dr., 505/351-9961, 9am-5pm daily Oct.-Apr., 9am-6pm daily May-Sept., free), a Roman Catholic church built in 1814. Not only is this sanctuary a National Historic Landmark, it's also a shrine to which hundreds of thousands of visitors make a pilgrimage each year. The church is believed to have "holy dirt" that can bestow miraculous healing powers.

Stop for lunch at the James Beard-awarded **Rancho de Chimayó Restaurante** (300 Juan Medina Rd., 505/351-4444, www.ranchodechimayo.com, 11:30am-7:30pm Tues.-Fri., 8:30am-10am and 11:30am-7:30pm Sat.-Sun., $12-27), a New Mexican restaurant and inn. To get here from SR-76, turn right (south) on County Road 98. The restaurant is 0.5 mile (0.8 km) south on the left (east) side of the highway.

Cordova

SR-76 climbs west for 5 miles (8 km) to Cordova, a town known for wood carvings.

Truchas

SR-76 keeps climbing for 4 miles (6.4 km) to Truchas, a Spanish Colonial outpost perched on an 8,000-foot (2.438-m) mesa with spectacular vistas. There are many talented artisans and fascinating art studios and galleries along the road. Download a map of spots to visit through **High Road Artisans** (http://highroadnewmexico.com/map), which also offers a list of workshops, art classes, and info about the art and history of this region.

The **High Road Marketplace** (1642 SR-76, 505/689-2689, 10am-5pm daily) sells artisan-crafted jewelry, art, pottery, quilts, leather goods, soaps, and other gifts. **Cordova's Handweaving Workshop** (32 County Rd. 75, 505/689-2437, by appointment only) makes beautiful blankets and rugs in bold designs, and has been doing so for four generations. **Hand Artes Gallery** (137 County Rd. 75, 505/689-2443, https://handartesgallery.com, by appointment only) features artwork from abstract painters and glass artists, as well as sublime furniture and sculptures.

Las Trampas

Keep driving northeast on SR-76 for 7 miles (11.3 km) to the town of Las Trampas. At one time, a defensive wall surrounded the town to protect inhabitants from Ute, Comanche, and Apache attacks. For centuries, Las Trampas was an isolated and remote village; the community was completely cut off from popular culture. As a result, the Spanish heritage goes back generations and is particular to this region. Today, there are no remains of the defensive wall, but you'll know you are in Las Trampas when you see the ancient church **San José de Gracia** (505/351-4360, 9am-4pm Sat.-Sun., free) on the east (right) side of SR-76. The chapel, built in 1780, stands as one of the best-preserved examples of Spanish Colonial architecture. Note the original wide-plank wooden floors, transverse clerestory window, and ceiling painted with intricate 18th- and 19th-century designs.

Peñasco

SR-76 climbs 6 miles (9.7 km) north through Chamisal to dead-end into SR-75. Turn right (south) onto SR-75 and drive 1.5 miles (2.4 km) east toward Peñasco. Here you should definitely stop at ★ **Sugar Nymphs Bistro** (15046 SR-75, 505/587-0311, www.sugarnymphs.com, 11am-3pm Wed.-Thurs., 11am-7pm Fri.-Sat., 10am-4pm Sun., $10-18) for towering sandwiches made with homemade bread, fresh-as-can-be salads, and homemade desserts like carrot cake and almond-scented butter cake. This place focuses on locally sourced and seasonal ingredients, so the menu is always changing.

From Peñasco, follow SR-75 east for a few miles, then take SR-518 north. Drive 12 miles (19.3 km) through Talpa to SR-68, where you will turn right (northeast).

Taos

Taos is a small high-desert artists' colony hidden in the hills of northern New Mexico. The town was constructed in the Spanish tradition as a fortified plaza surrounded by a defensive wall. Shortly after Spanish occupation, the Pueblo Indians, who were already here, led a revolt against the missionaries in 1680. The Spanish fled, only to return in 1692. These cross-cultural clashes are apparent in the downtown Historic District, where Territorial, Mission Revival, Spanish Colonial, and Pueblo Revival buildings stand side by side.

Artists began arriving in Taos in the late 19th century, and it has since become a spiritual mecca for creatives. A peaceful town with meandering streets and adobe buildings, Taos is the kind of place where you can easily spend a whole weekend.

Sights
Millicent Rogers Museum

The **Millicent Rogers Museum** (1504 Millicent Rogers Rd., 575/758-2462, www.millicentrogers.org, 10am-5pm daily Apr.-Oct., $10) is a must for those interested in pueblo pottery making. The private collection of oil heiress and model Millicent Rogers, the museum holds 20 galleries and exhibition spaces that feature Mexican folk art, modernist and historical jewelry, Navajo weavings, and black-on-black pottery from the San Ildefonso Pueblo.

Heading north on SR-64, turn left (west) on Millicent Rogers Road. The museum is 0.5 mile (0.8 km) south on the right.

Taos Pueblo

The San Geronimo de Taos, commonly known as **Taos Pueblo** (120 Veterans Hwy., 505/758-1028, www.taospueblo.com, 8am-4:30pm Mon.-Sat., 8:30am-4:30pm Sun., $16), has been occupied for more than 1,000 years. This multistory pueblo is the only existing American Indian community designated as both a UNESCO World Heritage Site and a National Historic Landmark. Built between AD 1000 and 1450, the pueblo is currently home to about 150 people, and it is considered one of the oldest continuously inhabited communities in the United States. Tribal members lead walks through the village of adobe dwellings.

To reach the pueblo, follow Paseo del Pueblo Street until the road curves left (northwest) and turn right (east) on Paseo del Pueblo Norte (the highway to the town of Taos). The Taos Pueblo is 2 miles (3.2 km) up the road.

Rio Grande Gorge Bridge

The **Rio Grande Gorge Bridge** is a steel deck arch bridge that overlooks the magnificent Rio Grande. Construction began in 1963, and the bridge opened in 1965 (it was originally called the "bridge to nowhere" because there wasn't enough funding to finish it). Today, it is one of the highest bridges in the United States—a 650-foot (198-m) drop into a 1,300-foot-wide (396-m) gorge. Be careful as the chest-high guardrail will not prevent you from falling over. To find the bridge, take SR-64 north (west) about 10 miles (16.1 km) from Taos.

★ Earthship Biotecture

Earthship Biotecture (2 Earthship Way, 575/613-4409, www.earthshipglobal.com, 9am-5pm daily, $9-15) is a community of off-the-grid homes located in the world's largest self-sufficient residential development. The Earthships are sculptural homes with curved walls and whimsical roofs topped by playful appendages that spin like weather vanes. Walls are made from compacted earth, tires, and cans in order to create "thermal mass," an efficient insulation. Despite the range of temperatures here (from -20°F/-29°C to 100°F/38°C), Earthship homes average a pleasant interior temperature of 70°F (21°C) without benefit of heating or cooling. Power is generated by solar panels and wind-powered devices and then stored in batteries. Water is collected on the roof and used up to four times (sink and shower water becomes gray water, which then feeds the plants; that water is pumped back to the toilets, where it is flushed into a septic tank.) With only 8 inches (20 cm) of water collected per year, this resourceful system ensures there is enough water to run the entire home. The **self-guided tour** ($9) includes a walk through a fully functioning example of an Earthship, plus a 15-minute video, slideshow, and a wall of literature and photos. The **longer, guided tour** ($15) includes visits to several real homes. You can also stay overnight in an Earthship, which is highly recommended.

The Earthship Biotecture is outside Taos on the way back to Santa Fe by the loop route through Tres Piedras. Heading north (west) on SR-64, the Visitor Center is about 2 miles (3.2 km) after crossing the Rio Grande Gorge Bridge; turn right (east) on Lava Lane. The Visitor Center will be the first building on your left.

Food

You'll feel good eating at **The Love Apple** (803 Paseo del Pueblo Norte, 575/751-0050, www.theloveapple.net, 5pm-close Thurs.-Sun., $12-23). That's because they use hormone-free, grass-fed meat, organic dairy products, and produce from local farms. Even the flour is locally milled. All of these carefully gathered meats, cheeses, fruits, and veggies make their way into delicious dishes on a seasonally rotating menu. Reservations are recommended, and the restaurant is cash only.

Look for Love Apple inside a 19th-century chapel, 1 mile (1.6 km) north of Taos Plaza, on the right between Laughing Horse and Lotaburger North.

La Cueva (135 Paseo del Pueblo Sur, 575/758-7001, www.lacuevacafe.com, 10am-9pm Mon.-Sat., $10-15) may be tiny in size, but it's big in flavor. The enchiladas and the chipotle shrimp tacos are great, and the menu includes a strong showing of gluten-free and vegetarian options.

If you need a break from New Mexican cuisine (although why would you?), head to **Sushi a la Hattori** (1405 Paseo del Pueblo Norte, 575/737-5123, 11:30am-2pm and 5pm-8pm Wed.-Fri., 5pm-8pm Sat., $10-30). You'll savor rich and buttery sashimi, sweet and chewy octopus, and ramen full of umami. Despite how authentic this Japanese restaurant is, the breathtaking views of Taos Mountain remind you that you're still in New Mexico.

This restaurant is north of the town of El Prado as you leave Taos on SR-64. It's behind the Overland Sheepskin Company; look for a wooden porch swing and a rusted tractor out front.

Accommodations

El Pueblo Lodge (412 Paseo del Pueblo Norte, 800/433-9612 www.elpueblolodge. com, $135-190) is a chill and affordable hotel with all the right perks: free Wi-Fi, hot breakfast, and a pet-friendly approach. Some rooms include fireplaces, and the location is conveniently within walking distance of the Plaza, shops, and restaurants.

El Monte Sagrado (317 Kit Carson Rd., 855/846-8267, www.elmontesagrado. com, $179-450) offers resort-style luxury that puts sustainability and eco-friendly practices first. Choose from 48 Taos Mountain Rooms, 18 American Indian Suites, 6 Casitas, and 12 Premier Suites. All rooms feature plush bedding, soaking tubs, and fireplaces.

For a once-in-a-lifetime experience, spend the night at ★ **Earthship Biotecture** (2 Earthship Way, 575/613-4409, www. earthshipglobal.com, $140-410). These strange and beautiful, self-sustaining homes are made from recycled materials and are fronted by a two-story, glass-walled greenhouse. Some homes feature fully stocked kitchens, living rooms, handmade bed frames, and bathrooms with recycled-bottle walls that resemble jewels of light.

◈ Back to Santa Fe

To return to Santa Fe, head north on SR-64 out of Taos. Drive 28 miles (45 km) to Tres Piedras and take SR-285 south (left). Follow SR-285 south for 47 miles (76 km) to SR-84. Turn south (left) onto SR-84 and drive 8 miles (12.9 km) through Española. Just north of Santa Fe is the junction with SR-599. Take SR-599 (Veterans Memorial Hwy.) south for 13 miles (20.9 km) to join I-25 south. From I-25, you'll follow the post-1937 alignment south to Albuquerque.

Earthship Biotecture

Post-1937 Alignment to Albuquerque

On I-25 as you approach Exit 264, look west to see **La Bajada Hill,** where Route 66 zigzagged through a steep elevation change from 1926 to 1932. This was treacherous terrain for early horse- and wagon-era travel. Inmates from the nearby penitentiary took sand from the Rio Santa Fe and used a cut-and-fill method to carve 23 hairpin curves. Today, this road is too rough for passenger vehicles, so stay on I-25. In 20 miles (32 km), take Exit 248; turn right (northwest) and then left (southwest) onto SR-313, and in about 6 miles (9.7 km) you'll reach the town of Bernalillo.

Bernalillo

Before the Spanish arrived, Bernalillo had at least two Tiwa-speaking pueblos alongside the river, where there was plenty of water for crop irrigation. Today,

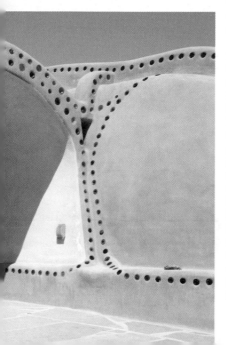

the Santa Ana Pueblo owns the Hyatt Regency.

Silva's Saloon

Back in the early 1930s, Felix Silva was a bootlegger and moonshiner. After Prohibition, he went legit, opening **Silva's Saloon** (955 S. Camino del Pueblo, 505/867-9976, 11am-7pm Mon.-Sat., noon-6:30pm Sun.) on Route 66. When his son took it over, there were still a handful of illicit activities—card games and liquor sales on Sunday—both of which were illegal in New Mexico at the time. Today, the saloon is a local favorite. The hats hanging from the ceiling are from loyal patrons who have passed away, and the bottles dipped in wax that line the wall hail from the 1930s.

Food and Accommodations

The **Range Café** (925 Camino del Pueblo, 505/867-1700, https://rangecafe.com, 8am-9pm daily, $10-18) is a happy place. Warm, friendly service complements regional comfort food (mac and cheese with green chiles, meatloaf) and from-scratch desserts. A bar and live music round out the fun on offer at this eatery.

Set on 550 acres (223 hectares) along the Sandia Mountains and Rio Grande, the **Hyatt Regency Tamaya Resort and Spa** (1300 Tuyuna Trail, 505/867-1234, http://tamaya.regency.hyatt.com, $120-353) in Bernalillo invites you to relax. The 350 pueblo-style guest rooms are decorated with handmade materials by tribal artisans. On-site amenities and activities include five restaurants, three heated outdoor pools, two tennis courts, horseback riding, a yoga and wellness studio, hot-air balloon rides, and a spa and salon. At the hotel's **Corn Maiden Restaurant** (5:30pm-9:30pm Fri.-Sat., $35-50), treat yourself to an elegant dinner that seamlessly blends sophisticated American dishes with flavorful New Mexican cuisine. To get there from SR-313 south, turn right (west) onto SR-550. After about 2 miles (3.2 km), turn right (north) on Tamaya Boulevard and follow the signs to the Hyatt.

⚑ Back on 66

Leaving Bernalillo, drive south on SR-313 for 7 miles (11.3 km). After passing SR-556, the road curves west and dips south onto 4th Street. Continue about 7 miles (11.3 km) into Albuquerque.

⚑ Detour: The Turquoise Trail

The aptly named Turquoise Trail—the nearby mines were filled with the signature stone, thus the name—connects the high country of Santa Fe with Albuquerque. If you'd rather not take I-25 south from Santa Fe to Albuquerque, this 60-mile (97-km) detour, also known as SR-14, offers a pleasant alternative. SR-14 travels south for 42 miles (68 km) through mining towns, to the quirky Tinkertown tourist attraction, and through the arts community of Madrid before reaching I-40 just east of Albuquerque. To access SR-14 from I-25 south, take SR-599 east (left) and turn south (right) onto SR-14 south.

Madrid

Madrid (www.visitmadridnm.com), pronounced MA-drid, is a budding artist colony reminiscent of Santa Fe before it became commercialized. The former mining town has a rich history that dates back to the 1800s. It's unique in that there are only two other mines in the world where both hard and soft coal could be mined from the same shaft. Once coal was no longer a primary commodity, Madrid became a ghost town. But in the early 1970s, artists began moving here, converting many of the old buildings into shops, studios, and galleries. Today, it's a great place to browse for blown glass, clothing, and turquoise jewelry.

Shopping

Seppanen & Daughters Fine Textiles (2879 SR-14, 505/424-7470, www.finetextiles.com) features Tibetan carpets, Navajo and African textiles, and Oaxacan rugs in vibrant colors and artful patterns. Even if you're not in the market for rugs or textiles, stopping by this shop to take in the astonishing selection is worth it.

Weasel & Fitz (2878 SR-14, 505/474-4893, www.weaselandfitz.com) represents work from more than 30 artists. Art materials run the gamut from recycled and found objects to metals and paint. You may see everything from ethnographic and contemporary works to unique nightlights and funky lamps.

Cowgirl Red (2865 SR-14, 505/474-0344, www.cowgirlred.com) sells antiques, jewelry, collectibles, and more than 400 pairs of vintage and new cowboy boots.

Food

The 1920s-era **Jezebel Soda Fountain** (2860 SR-14, 505/471-3915, noon-5pm Mon.-Wed., 10am-5pm Thurs.-Sun.) not only offers up tasty milk shakes, ice-cold sodas, and creamy gelato but also sells jewelry, clothing, furniture, and paintings.

Known locally as "Madrid's living room," **The Mine Shaft Tavern** (2846 SR-14, 505/473-0743, www.themineshafttavern.com, 11:30am-8pm Mon.-Thurs., 11am-11pm Fri.-Sun.) serves roadhouse food (including burgers made from local Wagyu beef) along with 12 beers on tap. There's live music on weekends.

⚑ Back on the Turquoise Trail

Keep heading south on SR-14 for 20 miles (32 km), winding past Placer Mountain and through the towns of Golden and San Antonio. Turn right on SR-536 (west) for 1 mile (1.6 km) to visit Tinkertown.

Outside Albuquerque

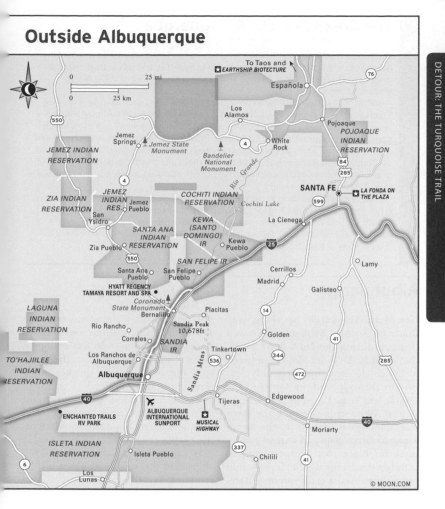

Tinkertown Museum

An Americana wonderland of oddities awaits you in Sandia Park. For more than 40 years, starting in 1962, folk artist Ross Ward collected, carved, and constructed an eclectic assortment of miniature figurines in a 22-room museum. Welcome to **Tinkertown Museum** (121 Sandia Crest Rd., 505/281-5233, www.tinkertown.com, 9am-6pm daily, $3.75), a fascinating collection of myriad miniature scenes that include a 1940s big-top circus, a western town with old-fashioned storefronts, a fortune-teller, and walls made with more than 50,000 glass bottles.

◆ Back on 66

Head south on SR-14 for 5 miles (8 km) to join I-40 west. Follow I-40 west for 7 miles (11.3 km) to Exit 167. Turn right (west) onto Central Avenue (Rte. 66) in Albuquerque.

The Green Book in Albuquerque

When Black travelers came through Albuquerque on Route 66, only 6 percent of the nearly 100 motels along Central Avenue would allow them to stay at their establishments. The **De Anza Motor Lodge** (4301 Central Ave. NE), listed in the *Negro Motorist Green Book,* was one of them.

Built in 1939 and run by Charles G. Wallace, a prominent Zuni trader, De Anza was a gathering spot for artisans, traders, and those who loved southwestern American Indian crafts. Comprising seven buildings in the Spanish Colonial-Pueblo Revival style, it was the largest motel on Central Avenue. The original 30 rooms expanded to 67 and offered "modern" amenities such as private telephones and air-conditioning. The on-site Turquoise Room diner featured a terrazzo floor inlaid with thousands of pieces of turquoise and silver, while seven murals painted by Zuni artist Tony Edaakie depicted a sacred Zuni Shalako ceremony.

Wallace sold the building in 1983, and after several changes in ownership, the property sat empty and crumbling for years. The city of Albuquerque purchased the hotel in 2003, and in 2004, the De Anza was named a city landmark and was listed on the National Register of Historic Places. It even made an appearance in an episode of the television series *Breaking Bad*.

Albuquerque

New Mexico's biggest city has a long, deep Route 66 history. As migrants passed through during the Dust Bowl years, they went to the Jones Motor Company for a vehicle check-up. Black travelers driving through sundown towns in the Ozarks and Texas timed their overnight stay in Albuquerque because the town had hotel options for them; the *Negro Motorist Green Book,* an annual guidebook for Black road-trippers, helped travelers determine which places would serve them. And a cruise along glittering Central Avenue brought the welcome sight of nearly 100 motels, many of them with dazzling neon signs acting as beacons in the night.

Today, fewer than 40 of the motels along Central remain. As Albuquerque spread outward from the city center in the 1960s, people abandoned many areas of downtown, causing the city to raze historic buildings for high-rises and parking lots. Today, some structures are enjoying a much-needed restoration, while others sit crumbling on the roadside.

◈ Route 66 Through Albuquerque

The original 1926 alignment of Route 66 traveled from north to south on 4th Street. In 1937, Route 66 was realigned along Central Avenue. For the post-1937 alignment (and the quickest route traveling west on I-40), take Exit 167 to cross under the freeway, then turn right (west) on Central Avenue. Follow Central Avenue through Albuquerque until it rejoins I-40.

If you opted to take the pre-1937 alignment through Santa Fe, you'll be traveling south on 4th Street as you enter Albuquerque. Turn right (west) on Central Avenue.

Sights

Albuquerque is popular for hosting the **Albuquerque International Balloon Fiesta** (5000 Balloon Fiesta Pkwy. NE, 505/821-1000, www.balloonfiesta.com), the world's largest hot-air balloon event. If you want to see the balloons, plan to arrive the first week in October. Otherwise, it's best to avoid visiting the city in early October, as tourists flood the state.

Albuquerque

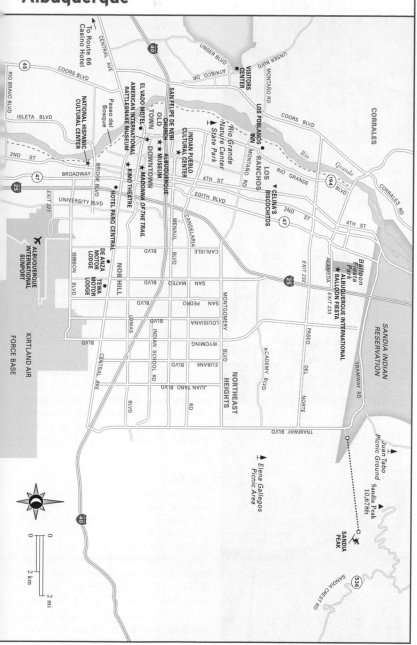

Tewa Motor Lodge

Entering Albuquerque via I-40 and Central Avenue (via the post-1937 alignment), keep an eye out for the 1946 **Tewa Motor Lodge** (5715 Central Ave. NE, 505/255-1632), built in the Pueblo Revival style with projecting *vigas* (wooden roof beams) and rounded parapets. Though the neon sign looks original, unfortunately it isn't. No matter. It's still great for a photo op.

KiMo Theatre

The **KiMo Theatre** (423 Central Ave. NW, 505/768-3522, www.kimotickets.com, 9am-4pm Tues.-Sat.) came to life a year after the birth of Route 66. Opulent film palaces were popular in the 1920s, and the KiMo was one of the most unique. Built to feature stage productions and motion pictures, it was the first theater to fuse art deco with American Indian architectural style. Seven murals flank the interior space, and iconic American Indian motifs include air vents that resemble Navajo rugs, chandeliers shaped like drums, and Navajo symbols placed throughout.

In 1961, a fire destroyed parts of the theater. After falling into disrepair, it eventually closed in 1968, but was saved, restored, and revitalized in the 1990s. Today, the KiMo screens classic movies as well as present-day flicks. Don't have time for a movie? Just stop in to snap pics of the distinctive entryway.

Old Town

Albuquerque began as a farming community and became the sheepherding center of the West. When Spain established a military presence here in 1706, the settlers built a town in the Spanish tradition—a central plaza surrounded by government buildings. Today, this area is Albuquerque's historic **Old Town** (505/221-6490, www.

Top to bottom: Old Town Albuquerque; KiMo Theatre; San Felipe de Neri Church

Madonna of the Trail

An 18-foot-tall (5.5-m) statue, *Madonna of the Trail,* stands as a proud monument of the Mother Road. It was dedicated to pioneer women who traveled the National Old Trails. A total of 12 statues were installed, and this one is identical to the Madonna statue in Upland, California. If you're traveling the pre-1937 alignment through Albuquerque, you'll drive into town along 4th Street; look for the statue at the corner of Marble Avenue.

albuquerqueoldtown.com), with more than 150 shops, galleries, and restaurants in adobe buildings clustered along brick paths. It's a great place to stretch your legs and glimpse a bit of Albuquerque's past. Don't leave without setting foot inside the hushed sanctuary of the 1793 **San Felipe de Neri Church** (2005 N. Plaza St. NW, 505/243-4628, www.sanfelipedeneri.org, free), the oldest chapel in Albuquerque. Five-foot-thick (1.5-m) adobe walls make up the structure, home to current community worship and educational services.

Albuquerque Museum

The **Albuquerque Museum** (2000 Mountain Rd. NW, 505/243-7255, www. albuquerquemuseum.org, 9am-5pm Tues.-Sun., $6), located in the heart of Old Town, showcases and celebrates the diverse arts and culture of the Southwest. Through interactive exhibits, you can discover local legend and lore, explore the area's geography, and soak up its rich history. And while there's a certain throwback joy to sending a handwritten Route 66 postcard to loved ones back home, this museum lets you send an electronic postcard to friends and family.

American International Rattlesnake Museum

In the Southwest, a rattlesnake is something you try to avoid at all costs. But the **American International Rattlesnake Museum** (202 San Felipe St. NW, 505/242-6569, www.rattlesnakes.com, 10am-6pm Mon.-Sat., 1pm-5pm Sun. June-Aug., 11:30am-5:30pm Mon.-Fri., 10am-6pm Sat., 1pm-5pm Sun. Sept.-May, $6) in Old

Town gives you the best—and safest—way to have a positive encounter with a rattler. At this educational center, you'll learn everything you'd ever want to know about snakebites, strike positions, head shapes, fangs, and those signature rattles.

Indian Pueblo Cultural Center

To understand the distinctions between the state's 19 pueblos, visit the **Indian Pueblo Cultural Center** (2401 12th St. NW, 505/843-7270, www.indianpueblo. org, 9am-5pm daily, $8.50). It's a great introduction to the storytelling traditions and evolving histories of the Pueblo people from pre-Columbian to modern times. The retail store at the center sells traditional and contemporary arts and crafts by internationally renowned tribal artists.

From Central Avenue (Route 66), turn right (north) on 12th Street NW and drive 1.5 miles (2.4 km). The Indian Pueblo Cultural Center will be on the left.

National Hispanic Cultural Center

It's easy to spend an entire day at the **National Hispanic Cultural Center** (1701 4th St. SW, 505/246-2261, www.nhccnm. org, 10am-5pm Tues.-Sun., $6), which houses a dynamic collection of multicultural exhibitions; offers live music, dance, and theater performances; and screens films. The permanent collection includes work by contemporary and cutting-edge artists from New Mexico, Latin America, and other regions from the Spanish diaspora. A comprehensive research library includes a genealogy center with more than 12,500 books, magazines, and

Neon Photo Ops

We live in a digital, high-definition age, which means we don't get to see classic signage illuminated by blinking, flickering neon bulbs anymore. Not so on Route 66. This road trip boasts some of the best retro neon signs, many of them more than half a century old. This list offers up photo-worthy signs—for motor courts, diners, gas stations, and more—that you'll want to make a part of your trip.

♦ **Tee Pee Curios,** Tucumcari (page 202)

♦ **Blue Swallow Motel,** Tucumcari (page 204)

♦ **Motel Safari,** Tucumcari (page 205)

♦ **El Vado Motel,** Albuquerque (page 229)

♦ **Rex Museum,** Gallup (page 237)

♦ **Jerry's Café,** Gallup (page 238)

journals on the history and culture of the American Southwest, Central and South America, Spain, and Portugal.

While at the National Hispanic Cultural Center, you must see the **Torréon Fresco** *Mundos de Mestizaje* (noon-5pm Sat.-Sun., free). This 4,000-square-foot (372-sq-m) and 45-foot-tall (14-m) tower houses a mesmerizing mural that depicts 3,000 years of Hispanic history. Muralist Frederico Vigil ground the natural pigments himself, then applied the plaster by hand, painting every inch. It took him 10 years to complete. The result is the largest concave fresco in North America.

From Central Avenue (Route 66), turn left (south) on 8th Street SW and drive 1 mile (1.6 km). Cross Bridge Boulevard and the National Hispanic Cultural Center will be straight ahead.

Mariposa Gallery

Since 1974, **Mariposa Gallery** (3500 Central Ave. SE, 505/268-6828, www. mariposa-gallery.com, 11am-6pm Mon.-Sat, noon-5pm Sun.) has been exhibiting contemporary art, ceramics, jewelry, blown glass, and found-object sculptures. Shop for one-of-a-kind treasures from local artisans.

Food

Named for owner Loyola Baca, **Loyola's Family Restaurant** (4500 Central Ave. SE, 505-268-6478, www. loyolasfamilyrestaurant.com, 6am-2pm Tues.-Sat., $6-10) serves great breakfast burritos with a green-chile sauce hot enough to make you sweat. Loyola opened the restaurant in 1990 and quickly earned a popular following thanks to her warm, outgoing personality and tasty New Mexican dishes. If the dining room looks familiar, that's because commercials and movies, as well as scenes from the TV series *Breaking Bad,* have all been filmed here. Loyola passed away in 2009, and her daughter Sarah took over restaurant operations.

In the 1930s, **Kelly's Brew Pub** (3222 Central Ave. SE, 505/262-2739, https:// kellyspubabq.com, 5pm-9pm Wed.-Mon., $6-14) was the Jones Motor Company, one of the most modern service stations in the West. This was the first station Dust Bowl migrants saw upon arrival in Albuquerque. The original owners built a canopy off the side of the building so the weighted-down jalopies could unload in the shade before being serviced. Today this restored landmark is a restaurant and craft brewery. Get your Instagram snaps by the vintage Fire Chief gas pumps outside.

Pete Powdrell, his wife Catherine, and their 11 children arrived in Albuquerque in the 1960s armed with generations-old recipes for good Louisiana 'cue and not much else. But they worked hard, opening **Powdrell's Barbecue House** (11301 Central Ave. NE, 505/298-6766, www.bbqandsoulfoodabq.com, 11am-7pm Tues.-Sat., $8-30), where they served hickory-smoked pork, beef, and chicken and from-scratch desserts and sides, and Powdrell rose to infamy as the Albuquerque's patron saint of barbecue. The restaurant is still family-owned and -operated today.

For 1950s blue-plate specials and handmade milk shakes, roll up to the **66 Diner** (1405 Central Ave. NE, 505/247-1421, www.66diner.com, 11am-8pm Sun.-Thurs., 11am-9pm Fri.-Sat., $8-14). Burgers, shakes, and killer banana-cream pie are all on the menu.

A refurbished 1938 Texaco station now lives on as the **Standard Diner** (320 Central Ave. SE, 505/243-1440, www.standarddiner.com, 11am-9pm Mon.-Sat., 9am-9pm Sun., $8-16). Forget its name; this place is anything but run-of-the-mill. Comfort food gets an inventive twist on dishes like southern-fried pickles, short-rib sliders, and bacon-wrapped meat loaf.

Does your home state have a signature cookie? New Mexico does. The *biscochito* (also spelled *bizcochito*) is a light and flaky, anise-flavored cookie dusted in cinnamon sugar with a hint of brandy. Locals say **Celina's Biscochitos** (404 Osuna Rd. NW, 505/269-4997, www.celinasbiscochitos.com, 9am-3pm Mon.-Thurs., noon-3pm Fri.) are the best. The recipe is based on that of the owner's grandma, Maggie. From Central Avenue (Rte. 66), turn right (north) on SR- 47 (Broadway Blvd.) and cross I-40. Then turn west (left) on Menaul Boulevard, and after a few blocks, turn north (right)

to continue on SR-47. Drive 3 miles (4.8 km) and turn west (left) on Osuna Road.

The diner in the back of the **Duran Central Pharmacy** (1815 Central Ave. NW, 505/247-4141, http://durancentralpharmacy.com/restaurant, 9am-7pm daily, $10) dishes out red chile that's full of flavor and not too spicy. Huevos rancheros and tortillas are made to order. Check out the fun gifts and locally made items in the pharmacy in the front.

Accommodations

Where to begin with ★ **Los Poblanos Inn** (4803 Rio Grande Blvd., 505/344-9297, www.lospoblanos.com, $256-320)? Stay here for the grand entrance of a long driveway flanked by cottonwood trees. Stay here to stroll the fragrant gardens and 25 acres (10 hectares) of lavender fields, and to see the peacocks that roam the property. Stay here for the understated sophistication of the guest rooms. Stay for the gourmet breakfast of eggs, honey, and fruit straight from the property's farm. Or stay for the free Wi-Fi, complimentary copy of *The New York Times,* use of a cruiser bicycle, or the lavender spa products. I could go on. This is, simply put, one of the best lodging options on Route 66.

An Irishman built the 1937 **El Vado Motel** (2500 Central Ave. SW, 505/361-1667, https://elvadoabq.com, $130-197) in the Pueblo Revival style with exposed wood beams, irregular-shaped windows, buttresses, and a showstopping neon sign. Listed on the National Register of Historic Places in 1993, El Vado was completely restored in 2018 as a full-service motel featuring custom mid-century furnishings, local artwork, and a craft-brew taproom built around the original motel's kiva fireplace.

Here's your chance to sleep in a 1969 Airstream trailer, a 1956 Teardrop, or the luxe 1974 Silver Streak. The well-maintained vintage trailers at **Enchanted Trails RV Park** (14305 Central Ave. NW,

800/326-6317, www.enchantedtrails.com, $56-86) are decked out with retro furnishings, bathrooms, and kitchens. Even if it's just for a night, you'll get to experience the Mother Road as 1940s travelers did when the route's heyday. No smoking, no pets.

When you learn that **Hotel Parq Central** (806 Central Ave. SE, 505/242-0040, www.hotelparqcentral.com, $161) exists in a former 1926 hospital for railroad employees and tuberculosis patients, you might be shocked. A $21 million renovation has transformed the building into a posh hotel. Rooms have high ceilings, tasteful appointments, and luxury linens. The grounds boast landscaped gardens and flower-lined pathways. The hotel's rooftop Apothecary Lounge serves Prohibition-era drinks with a seemingly endless selection of bitters. At Hotel Parq Central, you won't want for anything.

For Route 66 roadsters who like to gamble, there's **Route 66 Casino Hotel** (14500 Central Ave. SW, 505/352-7866, www.rt66casino.com, $99-129). The casino offers 700 slot machines, card tables, a bingo hall, four restaurants, two lounges, and Johnny Rockets, the faux-retro diner chain. The hotel keeps you comfortable with king- or queen-size beds, flat-screen TVs, free Wi-Fi, an indoor pool, and a fitness center.

◆ Back on 66

Leave Albuquerque driving west on Central Avenue and cross the Rio Grande. After about 6 miles (9.7 km), the road runs alongside I-40. Near Exit 149, turn north (right) to cross I-40, then take the North Frontage Road to Exit 140. **Nine Mile Hill** offers stunning views of the Sandia Mountains and beyond. To the west, the valley is framed by mountains that rise more than 10,000 feet (3,048 m)—this is the view early Route 66 travelers wrote about decades ago.

As you continue on the North Frontage Road, look for a Parker-through truss bridge at Exit 140; it's perched over the eroded banks of the Rio Puerco.

Rio Puerco Bridge

The Rio Puerco is a river notorious for flooding. Other bridges that had been built here washed away, so when travelers encountered the area after a storm or during monsoon season, there was no choice but to wait for the water to subside before it was safe to cross. In 1933, the current **Rio Puerco Bridge** was built. At 250 feet (76 m), the bridge was the longest of its kind in New Mexico. The 10 panels set at varying angles made a "camelback" arch, a popular design during the late 1920s and early 1930s. This additional support made the bridge strong enough to handle the Rio Puerco's massive flooding. Today, the bridge is closed to car traffic, but it's open as a pedestrian bridge.

◆ Back on 66

Continue driving west on I-40, following the **post-1937 alignment,** and ignore the Route 66 sign at Exit 126 (this is where the pre-1937 alignment joins the road). At Mesita, take Exit 117, turn right, and follow Old Route 66 Road. This road passes through the rural southwestern countryside of Acoma tribal land and the Rio San Jose Valley, with soothing views of red sandstone cliffs to the north. About 2 miles (3.2 km) from I-40, the road makes a sharp curve to the right; this was called "Dead Man's Curve." The 1926 alignment followed the ancient Native trail and wound its way along the San Jose River toward Laguna.

Laguna

Laguna is a late-17th-century pueblo, the full name of which is San Jose de la Laguna. It's set on a sandstone bluff north of the San Jose River and south of Route 66, one of the few pueblos visible from the highway. Today these are private homes, but the **San Jose Mission Church**

Albuquerque to Gallup

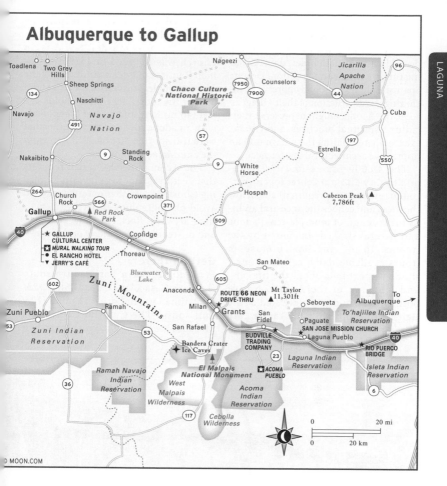

Toadlena
Two Grey Hills
Sheep Springs
134
Naschitti
Navajo
491
Nakaibito
9
Standing Rock
264
Church Rock
566
Crownpoint
371
Gallup
40
Red Rock Park
★ GALLUP CULTURAL CENTER
✚ MURAL WALKING TOUR
● EL RANCHO HOTEL
▼ JERRY'S CAFÉ
Coolidge
Thoreau
602
Zuni Mountains
Bluewater Lake
Zuni Pueblo
Ramah
53
San Rafael
53
Anaconda
Milan
605
ROUTE 66 NEON DRIVE-THRU
Grants
Bandera Crater Ice Caves
Ramah Navajo Indian Reservation
36
West Malpais Wilderness
El Malpais National Monument
117
Cebolla Wilderness

Nageezi
7950
7900
Chaco Culture National Historic Park
57
9
White Horse
Counselors
Jicarilla Apache Nation
96
44
Cuba
197
Estrella
550
Hospah
509
San Mateo
Mt Taylor ▲11,301ft
Seboyeta
To'hajiilee Indian Reservation
Paguate
San Jose Mission Church
Laguna Pueblo
23
Laguna Indian Reservation
✚ ACOMA PUEBLO
Acoma Indian Reservation
Cabezon Peak ▲ 7,786ft
To Albuquerque →
40
RIO PUERCO BRIDGE
Isleta Indian Reservation
6
San Fidel
BUDVILLE TRADING COMPANY

Zuni Indian Reservation

0   20 mi
0   20 km

© MOON.COM

(St. Joseph Blvd., 505/552-9330, 9am-4pm Mon.-Fri., free) is a public place of worship with daily tours. The mission was built in 1701 from fieldstone, mortar, plaster, and adobe. The walls feature original and rare Spanish paintings, murals, and ornately carved wooden doors. A large animal skin covers the altar, and the choir-loft window overlooks the pueblo below.

To get there from Route 66, turn south (left) on Rio San Jose Road. Turn west (right) on Capital Road, then make a left (south) on St. Joseph Boulevard.

⬥ Back on 66

Return to Route 66 and drive 5 miles (8 km) west to **Paraje**, where Route 66 curves back toward I-40 in 2 miles (3.2 km). Continue west to follow Route 66 or consider making a detour south here to visit Acoma Pueblo.

★ Acoma Pueblo

Acoma Pueblo (Pueblo of Acoma, 800/747-0181, www.acomaskycity.org, 9am-5pm daily, $25) is the oldest continuously inhabited settlement in North America. Its village of 250 structures is situated on a 367-foot (112-m) sandstone bluff. The Acoma people have lived here since AD 1150, growing corn, tanning deerskin and buffalo hides, domesticating turkeys, and weaving cotton. Despite Spanish rule and colonial oppression, including the destruction of their village in 1599, the Acoma fought to preserve their culture, spiritual practices, and rituals, eventually rebuilding the village into an impressive architectural masterpiece.

The 40,000-square-foot (3,716-sq-m) **Sky City Cultural Center** (open year-round, guided tour required) sits below the mesa and echoes the ancestral architectural design of mud-plastered adobe and natural stacked stone used by the Acoma. Inside, the **Haak'u Museum** (tours available daily, call for hours) showcases exhibits about the life, art, and language of the Acoma. Native pottery, arts, and crafts are sold at the **Gaits'i** gift shop, while the **Yaak'a Café** (9am-4pm daily) invites guests to dine on traditional Acoma cuisine as prepared by tribal members.

The **San Estevan del Rey Mission Church** was founded in 1629 by Friar Juan Ramirez to force assimilation of the Acoma people. Located on the mesa (and part of the tour), the church stands 150 feet (46 m) long and 40 feet (12 m) wide with an adobe roof and *vigas* beams that were transported 30 miles (48 km) from the San Mateo Mountains.

The Acoma Tribal Council requests that visitors do not wear revealing clothing (short skirts, halter or tank tops) and avoid photographing tribal members or their artwork. Rock climbing, camping, and off-roading are strictly prohibited.

Getting There

From Route 66 in Paraje, turn south (left) on Casa Blanca Road (SR-22/23/Kaatsiima Dr.) and drive 13 miles (20.9 km) south. The Cultural Center and Museum is on the right (north) at Indian

Acoma Pueblo

Service Route 38. Turn left on Indian Service Route 38 to reach the San Estevan del Rey Mission Church, about 0.5 mile (0.8 km) away.

Budville

Back on Route 66 (near I-40 Exit 104) west of Paraje, keep an eye out for Native stone ruins and the 1920s gas station in Budville, on the left (southwest) side of the road.

Budville was named after H. N. "Bud" Rice. In 1928, Rice and his wife, Flossie, operated the **Budville Trading Company,** a car service and trading post. Most of the cars that ended up stranded between Albuquerque and Grants were towed here. The store was held up during a robbery in 1967, and Bud and another employee were murdered. Despite the gruesome crime, his wife continued to operate the business until the late 1970s.

Today the station is closed, but you can still get out of the car to take a few photos of the old-school gas pump.

❖ Back on 66
The pre-1937 alignment climbs 1.5 miles (2.4 km) north toward **Cubero,** then curves west to **San Fidel,** where towering 11,306-foot (3,446-m) Mount Taylor frames the north side of the landscape. Route 66 approaches I-40 again in 3 miles (4.8 km). Cross over I-40 at Exit 96 and follow SR-124 west, which runs alongside the South Frontage Road through McCartys.

McCartys

About 1 mile (1.6 km) after crossing I-40, look for the stone 1933 Spanish Colonial **Church of Santa Maria de Acoma** sitting on a hillside south of Route 66.

In 5 miles (8 km), Route 66 makes a sharp right turn under I-40 to parallel the North Frontage Road. This stretch passes through several miles of lava flow, locally called *malpais.* Much of Route 66 was rerouted around this rugged terrain of ancient magma. To get a closer look, consider a visit to **El Malpais National Monument** (123 E. Roosevelt Ave. NW, 505/876-2783, visitors center 9am-5pm daily, free), accessed via SR-117.

❖ Back on 66
Route 66 continues to parallel I-40 for 3.5 miles (5.6 km). Near Exit 89, the road curves right and climbs 6.5 miles (10.5 km) north. Route 66 then becomes Santa Fe Avenue as it runs through Grants.

Grants

Grants may not be big, but it offers a pleasant park in the middle of town and cool public art, making it a nice place to stop and stretch your legs. This former railroad town grew into a farming community, and in 1950, a Navajo sheepherder discovered uranium on Haystack Mountain. It turned out to be one of the largest uranium reserves in the world. A recession in 1983 eventually forced the uranium mines and mills to close.

Sights

Fire & Ice Park (700 W. Santa Fe Ave., sunrise-sunset daily, free) and **City Hall Park** (600 W. Santa Fe Ave., sunrise-sunset daily, free) sit side by side and offer up more than just a shaded green space. For one, there's the **Route 66 Neon Drive-Thru** (free). Pull your car through the 18-foot-tall (5.5-m) arch shaped like a Route 66 sign—colorful by day and illuminated by night—for a classic photo op. There's also the public art installation **Grants Rocks Kindness Project,** where locals and visitors paint rocks of all sizes and shapes with feel-good designs and messages, then leave them for others to take on their Route 66 journey. Before you leave Fire & Ice Park and City Hall

Park, keep an eye out for the impressive **mural on the water tower** on the north side of town.

Learn about the rich legacy of uranium mining and visit a re-created mine shaft at the **New Mexico Mining Museum** (100 N. Iron Ave., 505/287-4802, www.grants.org, 9am-4pm Mon.-Sat., $3). The self-guided tour offers an educational experience about specialized drilling tools and blasting equipment.

Heading west on Route 66 (Santa Fe Ave.), turn right (north) on Iron Avenue. The museum will be on the right.

Food

You'll get delicious American and Mexican fare at **El Cafecito** (820 E. Santa Fe Ave., 505/285-6229, 7am-8:30pm Mon.-Sat., $3-11). Think tacos, flautas, enchiladas, burgers, hot dogs, and chili dogs. You'll also enjoy quick service from the friendliest staff ever. Breakfast and lunch served.

For dinner, there's **La Ventana Steak**

Grants Rocks Kindness Project

House (110 Geis St., 505/287-9393, 11am-7pm Mon.-Sat., $12-30), which serves up steak, seafood, and Mexican cuisine. From the outside, the restaurant isn't much to look at, but the food is delicious and the service is spot-on. Plus: Great margaritas.

Accommodations

Southwest Motel (1000 E. Santa Fe Ave., 505/287-2935, $39-60) offers clean and comfortable rooms at rock-bottom prices. Look for the fun yellow and orange neon sign of a sun rising over the building.

The **Sands Motel** (112 E. McArthur St., 505/287-2997, $45-55) has a classic 1950 motor court sign and offers basic accommodations with a personable staff. Elvis supposedly stayed in Room 123.

◆ Back on 66

Traveling west on Route 66, **Milan** is only a couple of miles away. There's a Love's Travel Stop if you need to gas up and replenish your snack stash. This pre-1930s alignment was originally the National Old Trails Highway heading to the Continental Divide.

Route 66 (SR-122) heads north for about 14 miles (22.5 km) to **Prewitt**, then goes west for about 10 miles (16.1 km) to Thoreau (pronounced thu-ROO).

Thoreau

Just west of I-40 (Exit 53) sits one of the oldest remaining gas stations on Route 66 in New Mexico. This Standard Oil franchise was originally located 30 miles (48 km) east in Grants. After Route 66 was realigned in 1937, it was moved to Thoreau, becoming the first business on the realigned section of Route 66. Roy Herman bought the station in 1950; by 1963, Herman and his son stopped selling gas and moved the station to the west side of town, where it became a car repair and service station. After all these decades, **Roy Herman's Garage** has retained its historic character.

◆ Back on 66

Keep driving west on SR-122 for 5 miles (8 km) to the Continental Divide, the second-highest point on Route 66 with an elevation of 7,263 feet (2,214 m). Piñon and juniper trees share space with Navajo homesteads and crimson cliffs. Route 66 joins I-40 west at Exit 47. Traveling west on I-40, in 11 miles (17.7 km) take Exit 36 and drive straight to follow Route 66 (SR-118/N. Frontage Rd.) into Gallup.

Gallup

You might be in a hurry to cross the border into Arizona, but set aside time to explore the delightful city of Gallup. This 1880s railroad town offers much in the way of trading posts, museum-quality street murals and public art, retro signs, great food, and townsfolk who smile and say hello when you pass on the street.

Sights

Gallup is one of the most significant trading centers in the Southwest and is known as the "Indian Capital of the World." Navajo Nation land wraps around the northwestern edge of Gallup; the Zuni Reservation sits just to the south. The prices, quality, and authenticity of the Pueblo pottery, handcrafted jewelry, and handloomed Navajo textiles rival that of what you might find in places like Santa Fe.

Gallup Cultural Center

The Southwest Indian Foundation and the city of Gallup formed the **Gallup Cultural Center** (201 E. Rte. 66, 505/863-4131, www.southwestindian.com, 9am-5pm Mon.-Fri. late May-early Sept., 9am-4pm Mon.-Fri. early Sept.-late May, free) to teach visitors about Gallup's rich cultural heritage. The center is located in a former Harvey House Santa Fe Depot designed by Mary Colter. Exhibits cover westward expansion, sand painting, weaving, silversmithing, and Route 66. The gift shop sells tribal clothing, jewelry, pottery, and handbags. If you're there during the summer, stick around for American Indian tribal dances (7pm daily) in the outdoor pavilion.

★ Mural Walking Tour

As you explore Gallup on foot (definitely recommended), you'll see that the cement trash bins located throughout the city are decorated with highly detailed artwork. Even more art awaits with a self-guided **Mural Walking Tour** (http://galluprealtrue.com/the-real-gallup/murals). Download the digital mural map to your phone or pick up a hard copy at the Gallup Chamber of Commerce (106 W. Hwy. 66). Then embark on your tour of 11 commissioned murals that beautifully tell the story of Gallup's past, present, and future. Whatever you do, don't miss the expansive mural depicting the

mural by Be Sargent commemorating the Navajo Code Talkers

1868 return of the Navajo to their home; it's titled *Long Walk Home* and is located on 3rd Street at Hill Avenue.

El Morro Theatre

At the 1928 Spanish Colonial-style **El Morro Theatre** (207 W. Coal Ave., 505/726-2600, www.elmorrotheatre.com, $5), you get the best of both worlds: an atmosphere loaded with history and charm paired with current Hollywood movies.

The theatre is one block south (left) from Route 66. At South 3rd Street, turn left (east) and drive one block to West Coal Street.

Rex Museum

At the **Rex Museum** (300 W. Historic U.S. 66, 505/863-1363, www.gallupnm. gov, 8am-5pm Mon.-Fri., free), you'll see the glorious retro sign first—it juts out cheerfully over the sidewalk. Then step inside this former brothel and grocery store to discover Gallup's colorful mining

and railroad history with exhibits like old hotel registers, books, and newspapers dating from 1886 to 1919.

Shopping

The commercialization of American Indian jewelry started in the late 1800s when Fred Harvey bought rings, bracelets and earrings from the Navajo to sell to tourists at his Harvey Houses. Until then, tribal members made silver for their own use and would occasionally sell it to soldiers stationed on reservations. During the heyday of Route 66, these trading posts became all the rage—there was no shortage of Hopi *kachina* dolls and Navajo Yei deities made into kitschy ashtrays, flowerpots, bookends, spittoons, and jewelry.

Times have changed, and it is now possible to purchase authentic American Indian art and crafts from traders with a connection to the tribal communities. Today, Gallup's shops are filled with sacred objects, symbols, and depictions of rituals that mean something to the people who made them.

Pick up quality western wear at **Zimmerman's** (213 W. Hwy. 66, 505/863-3142, 9am-6pm Mon.-Sat.). **Silver Dust Trading Company** (121 W. Hwy. 66, 505/722-4848, www.silverdusttrading. com, 9am-5pm Tues.-Sat.) has a strong collection of Zuni Pueblo turquoise. **Richardson's Trading Co.** (222 W. Hwy. 66, 505/722-4762, 9am-6pm Mon.-Sat.) sells rare heirlooms including concha belts, Zuni needlepoint, chief blankets, Apache and Navajo baskets, Tohono O'odham trays, and powerful paintings depicting ceremonial dancers.

Food

The Navajo tacos with Indian fry bread, beans, meat, green chile, cheese, and tomatoes are big enough to share at **Earl's Family Restaurant** (1400 E. Hwy. 66, 505/863-4201, 7:30am-8:30pm Mon.-Sat., 7:30am-6pm Sun., $8-14). Or opt for the green chile enchiladas with a slice of

coconut-cream pie for dessert. Earl's has been *the* place in Gallup since 1947. It's also a tourist spot that supports Navajo artisans who sell their handcrafted works tableside.

Tucked away in the old Harvey House train depot (Amtrak still stops here), **Angela's Café** (201 E. Hwy. 66, 505/722-7526, 8:30am-4pm Mon.-Fri., $10-15) serves green salads, excellent sandwiches, and belly-warming homemade soup.

Before you leave the state, eat at ★ **Jerry's Café** (406 W. Coal Ave., 505/722-6775, 8am-9pm Mon.-Sat., $10-16). This locals' fave sports vinyl booths, wood-paneled walls, and a neon sign out front. This is your last chance to indulge in New Mexican cuisine before heading into Arizona; good thing Jerry's serves up the best in the region. Go for the stuffed *sopaipillas* with beef, beans, guacamole, cheese, and your choice of red or green chile. You should be an expert at making that decision by now.

From Route 66, turn left (south) on 4th Street; drive one block and turn left on Coal Avenue.

Accommodations

Film director D. W. Griffith's brother, Joe Massaglia, opened the ★ **El Rancho Hotel** (1000 E. Rte. 66, 505/863-9311, www.elranchohotel.com, $62-143) in the late 1930s. It became a premier hotel and a temporary home for Hollywood's A-list movie stars, such as Katharine Hepburn, Humphrey Bogart, John Wayne, Spencer Tracey, Rita Hayworth, and Mae West. The three-story building with a pitched wood-shake roof, stone chimneys, and balcony is very Old West meets Deep South.

By the mid-1960s, the fascination with the American West began to fade, and the once-glamorous El Rancho appeared dated. After Route 66 was rerouted

Top to bottom: Richardson's Trading Co., Gallup; Jerry's Café, Gallup; El Rancho Hotel, Gallup

through I-40, the property fell into decline. Thankfully, Armond Ortega, a well-known American Indian trader, purchased El Rancho and kept it going. Navajo rugs, dark wood furniture, and an enormous brick and stone fireplace decorate the lobby. A wooden staircase curves up to rooftop patios and showcases photographs of 1950s-era western films. The window-lined Ronald Reagan Suite has a beautiful rock-wall bathroom with cobalt-blue tiles.

An on-site store sells handmade jewelry, rugs, and *kachina* dolls created by Hopi, Navajo, and Zuni artists. Ortega is a fourth-generation trader and knows how to select pieces with excellent craftsmanship and quality.

❖ Back on 66

Leave Gallup, heading west on SR-118 for about 15 miles (24 km) to **Manuelito.** Mustard-yellow and rust-red cliffs line the last 8 miles (12.9 km) on the pre-1930s alignment. Then the road climbs above the railroad as it makes its way around Devil's Cliff mesa. Approaching Arizona, Route 66 passes through a narrow part of the valley alongside deep canyons. Overhead, the sunrays splash a clear blue sky, and the road west stretches out before you.

Arizona

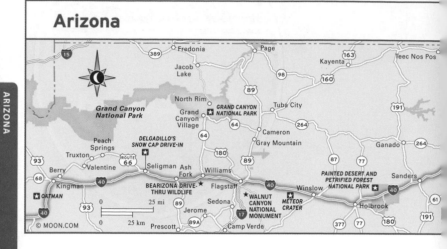

Arizona

A state of blue skies, sunny days, and lunar landscapes. It's no wonder that a diverse mix of people—from American Indians and Spanish explorers to cattle wranglers and outlaws—all fell in love with this place.

Route 66 through Arizona is laid over age-old paths that were developed to facilitate trade between the Great Plains and California. In the late 1850s, Lieutenant Edward Fitzgerald Beale was ordered by the U.S. Department of War to build the Beale Wagon Road across Arizona. It was the shortest route to the West and became a well-traversed immigrant trail that guided thousands of folks in the 1860s and 1870s. The Beale Wagon Road was later followed by the Santa Fe Railway, and then became Route 66. When Route 66 opened in 1926, most of the Arizona portion was unpaved. In 1933, President Roosevelt's National Recovery Administration gave Arizona $5 million to pave the route. The Federal Highway Act of 1956 brought I-40 to the state; the new freeway bypassed several sections of Route 66.

Planning Your Time

Plan at least **two days** for the drive across Arizona. After crossing the state line, spend the first night at La Posada in Winslow (make sure to reserve a room in advance). The next day, stop in Flagstaff, 160 miles (260 km) from the eastern border; this mountain town set in the San Francisco Peaks is packed with breweries, cutting-edge restaurants, and plenty of outdoor activities. It's also a hub for detours to the Grand Canyon and Sedona. Continue east to Williams and Seligman before driving the untouched two-lane stretch of Route 66 through Peach Springs to spend the night in Kingman. From Kingman, you'll leave Arizona via the twisty Oatman Highway.

Driving Considerations

To soak up all of the major attractions along Arizona's portion of Route 66, consider adding two extra days for a side trip to the Grand Canyon or Sedona, or

Highlights

★ **Driving Tour through Painted Desert and Petrified Forest National Park:** See badlands, mesas, ancient petroglyphs, petrified wood, and fossils that date back 200 million years (page 246).

★ **Meteor Crater, near Winslow:** Visit the astonishing site of a giant meteor impact from 50,000 years ago, the best-preserved meteor site on Earth (page 256).

★ **Grand Canyon National Park:** This is just your standard 277-mile-long, 18-mile-wide hole in the ground, and one of the most impressive geological wonders in the world. No big deal (page 266).

★ **Delgadillo's Snow Cap Drive-In, Seligman:** Classic, quirky, and stocked with must-have souvenirs of the Mother Road, this shop is one of the most celebrated stops on Route 66 (page 285).

★ **Oatman:** This mining town from the gold rush days finds new life along the original alignment on Route 66 (page 293).

Best Restaurants

★ **Joe & Aggie's Café, Holbrook:** Established in 1943, Joe & Aggie's is the oldest restaurant in Holbrook (page 251).

★ **E&O Kitchen, Winslow:** Hard to find, yes, but once you're there, you'll savor every bite of some of the best Mexican food in Arizona (page 255).

★ **Turquoise Room Restaurant, Winslow:** Tuck into seasonally focused southwestern fare at this former Harvey House at La Posada (page 255).

★ **Pizzicletta, Flagstaff:** Naturally leavened pizza dough gets the wood-fired treatment at this renowned spot (page 264).

★ **Mr. D'z Route 66 Diner, Kingman:** Vintage Americana meets root beer floats here (page 292).

allocate an extra day to explore the historic districts of Williams and Oatman.

Gas is scarce along Route 66 in the western part of the state, so make sure to gas up in Kingman before heading to Oatman.

Getting There

Starting Points

Car

Route 66 enters Arizona at Lupton, then climbs through the Kaibab Plateau near Flagstaff before dropping in elevation through Ash Fork. On the eastern side of the state, much of the original alignment from Lupton to Flagstaff is not continuous or intact; unfortunately, you will have to take I-40. Once you reach Seligman, 159 miles (260 km) of unspoiled Route 66 await on a two-lane highway. Past Kingman, be sure to take the original alignment via the Oatman Highway, a stunning, winding road through the Black Mountains. Drive this stretch with caution: the Oatman Highway is fraught with hairpin turns, steep grades, and 15-mph (24-kph) switchbacks, earning it the notorious nickname "Bloody Route 66."

Car Rentals

Car rentals are available at both the Flagstaff and Phoenix airports.

Enterprise (2136 E. Rte. 66, Flagstaff, 928/526-1377, www.enterprise.com, 8am-6pm Mon.-Fri., 9am-noon Sat.) has a location right on Route 66.

Air

The two major airports in the region are in Phoenix and Flagstaff. The **Flagstaff Pulliam Airport** (FLG, 6200 S. Pulliam Dr., 928/213-2930, www.flagstaff.az.gov) is served by American Airlines and United with flights to and from Phoenix, Dallas, and Denver. **Phoenix Sky Harbor International Airport** (PHX, 3400 E. Sky Harbor Blvd., 602/273-3300, www.skyharbor.com) is one of the 10 busiest airports in the country and serves about 20 airlines with roughly 1,200 daily flights to more than 100 domestic and international destinations. Phoenix is a 2.5-hour drive from Route 66 in Flagstaff.

Train or Bus

Greyhound (800/231-2222, www.greyhound.com) stops in the towns of Holbrook, Flagstaff, and Kingman.

Since Route 66 was laid out alongside the train tracks, **Amtrak** (www.amtrak.com) offers easy access. The Southwest Chief line stops in Winslow at **La Posada Hotel** (303 E. 2nd St. on Rte. 66), in Flagstaff at the **Station Building** (1 E. Rte. 66), and in Kingman (402 Andy Devine Ave.).

Best Accommodations

★ **Wigwam Motel, Holbrook:** Sleep in a 1930s-era wigwam at this "village," one of seven that were built throughout the country between the 1930s and 1950s (page 251).

★ **La Posada Hotel & Gardens, Winslow:** Spend the night in a historic Harvey House designed by Mary Colter in 1929 (page 255).

★ **Little America Hotel, Flagstaff:** Set in the middle of a ponderosa pine forest, this lodge features 1970s French decor (page 265).

★ **Hotel Monte Vista, Flagstaff:** With a speakeasy and tales of ghostly hauntings, this historic hotel offers more than just a place to bed down for the night (page 265).

★ **Grand Canyon Railway Hotel, Williams:** Well-appointed rooms and an opulent lobby take you back to the bygone era of train travel (page 284).

Lupton and Houck

As you enter Arizona, American Indian trading posts flank both sides of I-40 near the Navajo Reservation, Allentown, Querino, Houck, and Sanders. Little remains of Route 66 today, but the once-vibrant billboards along the frontage road offer a glimpse into the area's bustling past. Much of Route 66 through the eastern section of Arizona sticks to I-40; detours to explore segments of the old alignment at Allentown, Sanders, and Chambers tend to follow gravel roads that are difficult to navigate and not worth the effort.

Part of the 1926-1931 alignment remains along the **Querino Canyon Bridge,** which spans a rocky canyon. This early example of truss design is located along a bumpy but drivable county road. From I-40, take Exit 346 and turn right (north), then take a left (west) at Querino Dirt Road (County Rd. 7250). Proceed with caution and avoid the road when it's wet.

✤ Back on 66

In about 4 miles (6.4 km), Querino Dirt Road (County Rd. 7250) rejoins I-40 via the Frontage Road. Follow I-40 west for 2 miles (3.2 km) to Exit 339. Turn right (north) and then take an immediate left (west) to take the Frontage Road in Sanders.

Sanders

Established in 1881, Sanders was named after C. W. Sanders, an office engineer at the Atchison, Topeka, and Santa Fe Railway. This unincorporated town was an education center for displaced Navajo; the Navajo-Hopi land dispute started in the 1860s and was in the courts for 25 years. Today, little remains of Sanders.

✤ Back on 66

Drive 6 miles (9.7 km) west on the I-40 Frontage Road and turn left (south) on U.S. 191. Join I-40 west and drive 21 miles (34 km) to Exit 311 (Painted Desert/Petrified Forest).

Lupton to Flagstaff

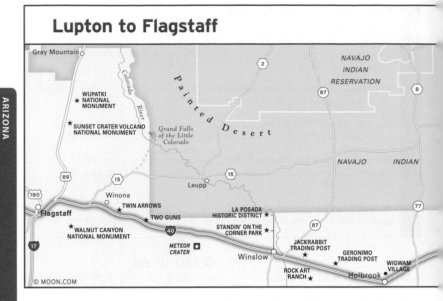

Painted Desert and Petrified Forest National Park

The **Painted Desert and Petrified Forest National Park** (Exit 311 off I-40 in Navajo, 928/524-6228, www.nps.gov/pefo, 8am-5pm daily, hours vary seasonally, $25) has the world's largest and most colorful collection of petrified wood. It is also the only national park in the United States that protects a portion of Route 66. The northern section of the park encompasses the Painted Desert—approximately 146 square miles (378 sq km) of badlands and multihued mesas of stratified layers of mudstone, shale, and siltstone pigmented by iron and magnesium deposits. The southern section of the park contains the Petrified Forest, with historic structures, archaeological sites, and fossils that date back more than 200 million years.

It takes at least 45 minutes to drive the 28-mile (45-km) road through the park, but you'll want to slow down and enjoy the vistas. So allow at least a couple of hours to drive Blue Mesa Road, take a hike, and stop at the photo-worthy viewpoints along the way. Tiponi, Tawa, and Kachina Points feature overlooks with panoramic views, all located less than 2 miles (3.2 km) north of the Painted Desert Visitor Center. There are no camping facilities or overnight parking allowed in the park.

★ Driving Tour
Painted Desert Visitor Center

Less than 0.5 mile (0.8 km) from the I-40 exit is the **Painted Desert Visitor Center** (8am-5pm daily), which houses a bookstore, hands-on petrified wood exhibits, and park information and services. A free film about the park is shown continuously throughout the day. The visitors center is adjacent to a restaurant, gift shop, and gas station; restrooms are available.

Painted Desert Rim Trail

The **Painted Desert Rim Trail** has remarkable views of the Painted Desert. Approximately 1 mile (1.6 km) after the northern park entrance is the pull-off for

Tawa Point, where the Painted Desert Rim Trail begins. The trail travels along the canyon rim and includes informational panels about the wildlife, geology, and ancient people of the region. In 0.5 mile (0.8 km), you'll reach the **Painted Desert Inn** and then **Kachina Point** with its expansive views of the red, orange, pink, and purple rocks. From Kachina Point, the trail enters a 5- to 8-million-year-old volcanic area. Once you reach Kachina Point, turn around and head back to the Tawa Point parking lot.

Painted Desert Inn

The restored 1924 **Painted Desert Inn** (928/524-6228, 9am-5pm daily) is 2 miles (3.2 km) north on the park road. The inn was built with petrified wood and stone in the Pueblo Revival style. Think flagstone terraces and thick, earth-textured walls. In 1940, the Fred Harvey Company managed the inn to serve passengers traveling the Santa Fe Railway before the inn closed in 1942.

In 1947, architect Mary Jane Colter renovated the inn with updated colors and glass windows to showcase the surrounding landscape—a pioneering style of architecture (now popular throughout much of Arizona) that brought the outdoors in. The interior lunchroom, where the Harvey Girls served hungry train passengers, features murals painted by Hopi artist Fred Kabotie. The inn closed again in 1963 and was scheduled for demolition in 1976. The National Park Service saved it by listing it on the National Register of Historic Places. In 1987, the Secretary of the Interior designated the inn a National Historic Landmark.

The Painted Desert Inn reopened in 2006. Though it no longer operates as a hotel and restaurant, the **museum** and **bookstore** feature fascinating architectural and decorative details, such as hammered-tin chandeliers, local pottery, and a vivid mountain lion petroglyph, one of the finest in the region.

Route 66 Studebaker

The park road circles back toward I-40 heading south; however, you cannot access the interstate at this point. Right before you approach I-40, park in a

Road Trip Playlist

Curating your road trip playlist is almost as important as mapping the route or booking hotels. Route 66 takes you through vastly different regions of the country, each with its own distinct culture and, yes, music. These song suggestions are tailored to the state you're in.

♦ **"Arizona" by Kings of Leon:** This dreamy song perfect for the big skies and expansive views of the state is guaranteed to get you in a thoughtful frame of mind.

♦ **"Banditos" by The Refreshments:** The '90s-era song from this high-energy band based in Tempe, Arizona, inspires you to sing along to lyrics that reference the state.

♦ **"Arizona Skies" by Los Lobos:** This Los Angeles band is best known for their Latin-influenced rock music, and this song is a prime example of the musicians' masterful instrumental talents.

♦ **"Take It Easy" by the Eagles:** Easily the most popular song about Winslow, this mellow tune will stick in your head for miles.

pull-out that marks an old Route 66 alignment, complete with big views, historical telephone poles, and a rusted **1932 Studebaker** (Stop Number 4).

Newspaper Rock

Heading south on the park road, you will reach **Newspaper Rock** (Stop Number 6) on the west (right) side of the road. Newspaper Rock contains more than 650 petroglyphs etched into its boulders and offers a glimpse of the people who lived here in the Puerco River Valley close to 2,000 years ago.

Blue Mesa Trail

The **Blue Mesa Trail** (Stop Number 7) is a moderately strenuous paved and gravel 1-mile (1.6-km) hike among blue bentonite clay badlands and petrified wood. The trailhead starts at the Blue Mesa sun shelter just past Newspaper Rock.

Rainbow Forest Museum

At the south end of the park is the **Rainbow Forest Museum** (off U.S. 180, 8am-5pm daily). Museum exhibits include prehistoric animals and petrified wood. Catch a free film about the park,

which is screened continuously throughout the day. A gift shop and snack bar are nearby; restrooms are available.

◈ Back on 66

Drive 28 miles (45 km) south through the park and exit from the south entrance. Take U.S. 180 for 19 miles (31 km) north to rejoin I-40/Route 66 at Holbrook.

Stewart's Petrified Wood Shop

It's a big no-no to take petrified wood from the park. That's why a stop at **Stewart's Petrified Wood Shop** (I-40 Exit 303, Washboard Rd., Holbrook, www.petrifiedwood.com, 800/414-8533, 9am-5pm daily), 13 miles (20.9 km) east of Holbrook, is essential. It's part trading post, part yard sale, part folk art sculpture garden. They sell meteorites, dinosaur bones, tree stumps, bookends, and jewelry made from petrified wood. Meet the ostriches (their eggs are for sale) and see sun-blasted vintage cars and bizarre dinosaur sculptures like a T. rex with a mannequin hanging out of its mouth. Have your camera ready and cash on hand; even if you don't buy something, you'll want to snap a pic of this place.

Women of the Mother Road

The story of Route 66 isn't complete without the illustrious women who've contributed greatly to the road's growth, success, and preservation. Here, celebrate the Arizonan women who made a profound impact on the Mother Road.

♦ **Susie Woo:** Railroad jobs brought the first Chinese immigrants to Winslow, and those who stayed eventually owned and operated grocery stores, restaurants, and laundries. When Wong Suey Ping, or "Susie," immigrated to the United States in the 1930s, she assisted her husband with the family grocery store. She arrived with their five children and no understanding of English. For nearly 15 years, Susie was the only Chinese woman in Winslow. She's quoted in an article in the *Winslow Mail* as saying: "I didn't know if I could make it. I was so lonely." Susie soon learned English, thanks to a woman who taught the language to the Japanese wives of railroad employees. For 43 years, Susie and her husband ran their grocery store before retiring to Phoenix.

♦ **Andrea Arizaga Limon:** Born on Route 66 in Topock to Mexican immigrants, Andrea Arizaga Limon grew up on the Mother Road in the 1930s and '40s. Her father moved the family from Mexico when he got a job on the railroad, and Andrea's young adulthood was spent as a Harvey Girl, meeting and greeting train travelers as they passed through. After Andrea married, she and her husband moved to Cadiz in the Mojave Desert, where she worked as the town's postmaster for nearly 30 years.

♦ **Luz Delgadillo:** Born to Mexican parents, Luz grew up in Seligman. She was the only girl in her family's traveling musical group called the Delgadillo Family Band. It comprised Luz and her six brothers, and they played gigs in Arizona's Route 66 towns, such as Williams, Flagstaff, and Winslow, during the 1940s. Luz's brother, Angel, is known as the "Guardian Angel of Route 66" for his instrumental efforts in preserving the heritage of the route in Arizona.

♦ **Joy Nevin:** Joy was a trained World War II pilot, a self-taught rancher, and an entrepreneur. After recovering from polio in the late 1940s, Joy headed west to Arizona. In Heber, she joined a ranch as a cattle hand before making her way in a truck she retrofitted herself as the traveling sales company Stockmen's Supply Service. From Holbrook to the Grand Canyon, Joy drove Route 66 selling supplies. One of her claims to fame is stopping traffic on Route 66 to assist a pilot needing to make an emergency landing. In her later years, she advocated tirelessly for quality eldercare in Holbrook.

◈ Back on 66

From I-40, take Exit 285 and follow the Route 66 signs. Turn right (west) on Hopi Drive.

Holbrook

Holbrook sits along the banks of the Little Colorado River, with a population of 5,000 people. Founded in 1882, Holbrook has a claim to fame as one of the wildest hell-raising towns in Arizona. Once Route 66 came through in 1926, the town's wild side was tamed as it morphed into a tourist hub for the nearby Petrified Forest.

Sights
Navajo County Historic Court House

You might think a road-trip stop at a courthouse is a snooze, but **Navajo County Historic Court House** (100 E.

Arizona St., 928/524-6558, 8am-5pm daily, later hours in summer, free) is anything but. Here's why: Navajo County was founded in 1881 as a farming, railroading, lumber, and ranching community. Its hub of Holbrook was a lawless Wild West town, and the locals brought in a new sheriff, Commodore Perry Owens, to deal with the criminals. By 1896, Frank Wattron had taken over as sheriff, and in 1898 the county built the courthouse and jail. It was here where the notorious prisoners were caged. The first man to be hanged in the county was George Smiley, on January 8, 1900, and it was such a major event that an invitation was printed on gilt-bordered paper and wired to the Associated Press. It is believed that Smiley's ghost still paces the halls, wanders the stairs, closes doors, and moves objects.

The Navajo County Historic Court House offers a museum that details the history, shows off the original jail cells from more than 100 years ago, and displays prisoners' artwork. Today the historic building is home to the **Navajo County Historical Museum,** the Holbrook Chamber of Commerce, and a visitors center.

The courthouse is a couple of blocks north of West Hopi Drive. From I-40, take Exit 286 and go left (south) on SR-77 to Arizona Street.

Rainbow Rock Shop

For posterity—and social media envy—get a picture of the huge dinosaur statues made from chicken wire and concrete at the **Rainbow Rock Shop** (101 Navajo Blvd., Holbrook, 928/524-2384, 10am-4pm Mon.-Sat.). It took the owner nearly 20 years to build the dinosaurs, and a snap of one will run you $0.25. While there, browse the shop's selection of specialty rocks and petrified wood.

It's located a couple of blocks south of West Hopi Drive. Heading north on U.S.

Painted Desert

180 from the Petrified Forest, it's right on the highway on the left (west) side of the road.

Food and Accommodations

On the main drag through Holbrook is ★ **Joe & Aggie's Café** (120 W. Hopi Dr., 928/524-6540, 7am-8pm Mon.-Sat., $5-15), a Route 66 staple famous for authentic green- and red-chile dishes, Navajo tacos, cheese crisps, and an excellent collection of bumper stickers, magnets, and other kitschy memorabilia for sale. Established in 1943, this is the oldest restaurant in town, serving truly some of the best Mexican food in the state. The original owners (Joe and Aggie) operated the restaurant during the heyday of Route 66.

If you like a big cut of steak with a loaded baked potato, try **Butterfield Stage Co. Steakhouse** (609 W. Hopi Dr., 928/524-3447, 4pm-9pm daily, $11-30). Tables sit snugly in tall-backed wooden booths and the sound system plays Johnny Cash and Hank Williams. While you're waiting for the piping-hot complimentary dinner rolls to arrive, read the funny sayings carved into the walls of each booth.

The tepee-shaped ★ **Wigwam Motel** (811 W. Hopi Dr., 928/524-3048, www.sleepinawigwam.com, $79-86) was part of a chain built in the 1930s through the 1950s. (Frank Redford created the first one in 1937; he disliked the word "tepee," so he called them wigwams.) There were seven Wigwam Villages in Alabama, Florida, Kentucky, Louisiana, Arizona, and California. Only three Wigwam Villages survive today, and two of them are on Route 66 (the other one is in San Bernardino, California). Wigwam Village #6 in Holbrook offers 15 wigwams, each 14 feet (4.3 m) wide at the base and 32 feet (10 m) high with a private bathroom, shower, TV, air-conditioner, and Wi-Fi (yes, Wi-Fi in a tepee!). A vintage teal Studebaker sits out front along with a museum of American Indian artifacts and Route 66 collectibles.

You'll have to walk through a gift shop to get to **El Rancho Restaurant & Motel** (867 Navajo Blvd., 928/524-3332, 11am-9pm daily, $8-15), and there might be a wait for a table, but once you're seated comfortably, you'll enjoy green chile cheese crisps, chicken enchiladas, and fresh, spicy salsa. The motel part of El Rancho is currently undergoing renovations, so for now this is just a place to eat, not stay the night.

⚑ Back on 66

Join I-40 westbound at Exit 289 and take Exit 280 to the Geronimo Trading Post.

Joseph City

Sights
Geronimo Trading Post
Take a break from the road to see the world's largest petrified tree. Seems a good reason to stretch the legs, no? West of Holbrook in Joseph City, off Exit 280, the **Geronimo Trading Post** (5372 Geronimo Rd., 928/288-3241, 8am-5pm daily) offers this 80-ton (73-metric-ton) sight, as well as shelves stocked with Route 66 memorabilia for sale, plus arts, crafts, and handmade jewelry.

Jackrabbit Trading Post
What more reason do you need to visit **Jackrabbit Trading Post** (3386 Rte. 66, 928/288-3230, www.jackrabbittradingpost.com, 9am-5pm Mon.-Sat., 10am-5pm Sun.) than a giant fiberglass jackrabbit you can sit on? Then there's the famous HERE IT IS sign with its graphic of a jackrabbit silhouette, featured in the film *Cars* (albeit in the movie, the silhouette was of a Ford Model T). Both are worthy of a peek. The story of the trading post goes like this—a man named James Taylor (not the singer) built the Jackrabbit Trading Post and painted 30 jackrabbits along the roof. The nearby Geronimo Trading Post had large decorated tepees that attracted visitors, so Taylor amped up his marketing. He plastered billboards of hopping rabbits for more than 1,000 miles (1,610 km) from here to Springfield, Missouri, making this jackrabbit a running mascot of Route 66.

Rock Art Ranch
Rock Art Ranch (tours by reservation, 928/288-3260, May-Oct., $35) is a private cattle ranch on land that was inhabited by Puebloan, Mogollon, and

Top to bottom: Rainbow Rock Shop in Holbrook; Wigwam Motel; Jackrabbit Trading Post in Joseph City

The Green Book in Arizona

The Fred Harvey Company established Harvey Houses—a chain of restaurants and hotels that catered to rail passengers—alongside railroads throughout the western United States. Because Route 66 paralleled much of the railroad, many Harvey Houses were located on the Mother Road. Not only did Harvey Houses offer economic opportunities for women, as young girls left home to work at them, Harvey Houses were also not segregated. This meant they welcomed Black travelers, and thus, were listed in the *Negro Motorist Green Book.* In Arizona, this included **La Posada Hotel & Gardens** in Winslow (architect Mary Colter's masterpiece, still open today), **Escalante Hotel** in Ash Fork (gone), **Havasu Santa Fe Hotel** in Seligman (gone), and **Santa Fe Eating House** in Kingman (also gone).

In addition to La Posada, two other Arizona businesses in the Green Book are still in operation today. Though the accommodations at **El Rancho Restaurant & Motel** in Holbrook are closed for renovations, you can dine at the restaurant, which serves excellent Mexican food. In Flagstaff, you can stay the night at **Motel DuBeau.** It originally opened as Du Beau's Motel Inn—that's how it was listed in the Green Book—and was owned and operated by Albert Eugene Du Beau, a French-Canadian hotelier. He wished to welcome all travelers regardless of race or class. When he listed his property in the Green book, he included the tagline: "Vacation & Recreation Without Humiliation."

Sinaguan cultures. Its claim to fame? It's home to some of the best-preserved ancient petroglyphs and ruins in the world, dating back to 6000 BC, and the rock art covering the cliffs of Chevelon Canyon has captured attention from researchers at the Smithsonian Institution. Brantley Baird, the ranch's owner and proprietor, has lived there since 1948. For a fee, he invites visitors to tour the petroglyphs; Baird discovered many of the sites himself and loves sharing them with the public. In addition to touring the ruins, visit the small museum on the grounds with its collection of American Indian artifacts, cowboy exhibits, and pioneer items.

The ranch is in a remote area between Winslow and Holbrook about 13 miles (20.9 km) from La Posada. Before the Rock Art Ranch turnoff, a restored 1913 bridge crossing Chevelon Creek is one of Arizona's oldest. Take Exit 257 (E. 3rd St.) off I-40 and head south (left) on SR-87 (N. Williamson Ave.). After about 1.5 miles (2.4 km), turn east (left) onto SR-99. Stay on SR-99 for about 6 miles (9.7 km), then head east (left) on Territorial/McLaws Road. It's 2.2 miles (3.5 km) southwest to the ranch entrance.

⚑ Back on 66

From I-40 in Joseph City, drive 20 miles (32 km) west to Exit 257 for Winslow. Turn left (south) and then right (west) on East 3rd Street (SR-87). Turn left again (south) on North Williamson Avenue (SR-99), then make another quick left (east) onto 2nd Street. Look for the La Posada entrance on your right.

Winslow

Winslow was founded in 1882 and operated primarily as a railroad hub. After World War II, the automobile overtook rail travel, spurring Winslow's economic decline. These days, the town has reinvented itself with an underground art and music scene just waiting to be discovered, and a few great restaurants and coffee shops to go along with it. One highlight of this burgeoning artists' colony is the hip Station-to-Station Art on Rails project featuring Cat Power, Jackson Browne, and artist Ed Ruscha.

Sights
La Posada Historic District

There is much to see, explore, and love at **La Posada Hotel & Gardens** (303 E. 2nd St., 928/289-4366, www.laposada. org, open to the public 7am-9pm daily, free). The hotel itself is an awe-inspiring Harvey House designed by Mary Colter, an architect for Fred Harvey, in 1929. Not only was Colter the lead architect for Harvey, she was also one of the most important—and one of the only—female architects of the early 20th century. This 11-acre (4.5-hectare) Spanish Colonial property was said to be Colter's favorite project. Most Americans at the time valued European culture and design, but Colter, ever the pioneer, loved the Spanish and Mexican haciendas of the Southwest. She believed that influences of American Indian, Spanish, and Mexican styles were often undervalued, and so it was a mélange of these styles that inspired her design of La Posada.

La Posada opened during the Depression, which is mainly why it never prospered. The hotel and restaurant closed in 1957, and the Santa Fe Railway used it for office space until 1994. Soon

Top to bottom: La Posada Hotel & Gardens, Winslow; Snowdrift Art Space, Winslow; Old Trails Museum, Winslow

after, it was slotted for demolition, but Allan Affeldt purchased the property and took on a $12 million renovation to transform it into one of the crown jewels of Route 66.

Hotel reservations are hard to come by (you'll need to book months in advance), so if you can't stay the night, get the walking tour map, then meander the grounds, stopping by the art gallery and flowering gardens; thumb through the old books and magazines in the piano room; and walk the hall lined with handcrafted mirrors. At the gift shop, browse Fred Harvey jewelry, *kachinas,* textiles, tinwork, and pottery.

Old Trails Museum

Take a deep dive into Winslow's railroad history at the **Old Trails Museum** (212 Kinsley Ave., 928/289-5861, www. oldtrailsmuseum.org, 10am-3pm Tues.- Sat., free, donations accepted), a few blocks east of La Posada. Talk about "local first"—the extensive collections of photographs, textiles, and oral histories were donated by townspeople.

Standin' on the Corner Park

Some songs never go out of style. The Eagles' song "Take It Easy" is one of them, as evidenced by musicians such as Kings of Leon, Keith Urban, and Bruce Springsteen all covering the tune. In Winslow, Ron Adamson's bronze statue **Standin' on the Corner in Winslow, Arizona** (Kinsley and 2nd Ave., http:// standinonthecorner.com) pays homage to the popular song. Backed by a two-story mural by John Pugh (of store windows reflecting a girl driving by in a flatbed Ford), the statue displays a life-size man standing with guitar in hand. Songwriter Jackson Browne was actually traveling Route 66 and standing on a corner in Flagstaff, Arizona, but the word "Winslow" was easier on the ears.

Snowdrift Art Space

A block west of Standing on the Corner Park is the uber-cool **Snowdrift Art Space** (120 W. 2nd St., 928/289-8201, www. snowdriftart.com, call for an appointment, free). The 22,000-square-foot (2,044-sq-m) multipurpose community art space is run by sculptor Daniel Lutzick and his wife, Ann Mary. A 7,000-square-foot (650-sq-m) gallery features Lutzick's large-scale sculptures, which use corrugated tin, plywood, roofing tar, and rebar.

Food and Accommodations

Hidden behind the Winslow Airport, the ★ **E&O Kitchen** (703 Airport Rd., 928/289-5352, 11am-6:30pm Mon.- Thurs., 11am-7pm Fri., 11am-5pm Sat., $4-11) boasts friendly service and bold, zesty Mexican food, arguably some of the best in Arizona. Tacos, enchiladas, *sopaipillas*—all are great. The salsa bar makes for a nice touch, if you're the type who likes at least three variations on your salsa. It takes a little effort to find, but it's worth it. From downtown Winslow, take SR-99 (N. Williamson Ave.) south and then turn right (west) onto Airport Road. Follow Airport Road all the way to the end and turn left behind the airplane hangar. If you can't find the restaurant, call.

If you choose to stay overnight (which is highly recommended), every room at ★ **La Posada Hotel & Gardens** (303 E. 2nd St., 928/289-4366, www.laposada. org, $129-169) offers a distinct experience. Many feature handmade furniture, Mexican tin-and-tile mirrors, six-foot (1.8-m) cast-iron tubs, hand-painted murals, whirlpool tubs, hand-woven Zapotec rugs, and antique finishes. With most of the rooms under $150, it's a four-star experience for the price of a Holiday Inn. On-site at La Posada is the award-winning ★ **Turquoise Room Restaurant** (305 E. 2nd St., 928/289-2888, www.theturquoiseroom.net, 7am-9pm daily, $12-42), serving an inventive take on southwestern cuisine. For breakfast, don't miss the eggs chilaquiles, and

for dinner, it's all about the churro lamb in a red-corn posole. The restored dining room is in the former Harvey House lunchroom. Note the turquoise-colored beams and backlit, transparent paintings by resident artist Tina Mion. La Posada and the Turquoise Room Restaurant make for two of the most wondrous and delightful places on Route 66—don't miss them.

◆ Back on 66
From I-40, drive 16 miles (26 km) west to Exit 233 and drive 6 miles (9.7 km) south on Meteor Crater Road.

★ Meteor Crater

Picture this: 50,000 years ago, a meteor weighing several hundred thousand tons traveled through space for 500 million years before crashing into Earth at 26,000 miles per hour (41,840 kph). Hard to believe? See for yourself the 550-foot-deep (168-m) hole it left at **Meteor Crater** (I-40 Exit 233, Meteor Crater Rd., 800/289-5898, www.meteorcrater.com, 8am-5pm daily year-round, $22). It's the best-preserved meteorite impact site on the planet, and you can walk the paved trail around part of the crater's rim to experience the enormity of this celestial event. The on-site museum has interactive exhibits, a fascinating history of meteorite activity on Earth, and a film theater.

◆ Back on 66
Back on I-40, go 14 miles (22.5 km) and take Exit 219 to Twin Arrows. Traveling westbound, take the overpass to the South Frontage Road, then head west. A concrete barrier blocks direct access to the town ruins, but you can park a little farther east.

Top to bottom: Meteor Crater; abandoned pool, Two Guns; ruins of the zoo, Two Guns

Two Guns and Twin Arrows

On a sleepy stretch of Route 66, all that remains of the Wild West theme park and tourist town of **Two Guns** are crumbling ruins. The roadside **zoo** with a large sign featuring "Mountain Lions" is on the southern frontage road of I-40 but is difficult to access. The KOA and Shell station are closed, and their dilapidated structures sit on private property.

The **Twin Arrows Trading Post,** built in 1937, was originally called Padre Canyon Trading Post. In 1955, the Troxell family transformed it into a Route 66 icon by planting two feather-tipped telephone poles made to look like twin arrows plunging into the ground; Route 66 enthusiasts and Hopi tribe members restored the arrows with a fresh paint job. The curio shop, Valentine Diner, and gas station sit abandoned.

✚ Back on 66

From Twin Arrows, return to I-40 heading west for 10 miles (16.1 km) to get to Winona.

Winona

The old-school classic Route 66 theme song sings "...don't forget Winona." It's a great line, but sadly it seems as though that's exactly what happened.

✚ Route 66 Through Winona

Pre-1947 Alignment

If you have time—and a good Spotify playlist going—drive a pre-1947 alignment of Route 66. From I-40, take Exit 211. Turn right (north) and follow Townsend Winona Road (County Road 394) for about 10 miles (16.1 km). Townsend Winona Road leads to the **Walnut Canyon Bridge,** which is listed on the National Register of Historic Places. The bridge features a Parker truss with

an upper polygonal chord, concrete abutments, wing walls, and steel lattice guardrails. Why does this matter? This style of bridge construction was common for the time but is now rarely found on Route 66. The bridge is on a short stretch of abandoned roadbed and is closed to traffic.

Keep heading west for 10 miles (16.1 km) on Townsend Winona Road and turn left (south) onto U.S. 89 west into Flagstaff.

1947-1968 Alignment

From I-40, take Exit 204 to follow a 1947-1968 alignment via Santa Fe Avenue (U.S. 180 and U.S. 66). This road can be rough, but it passes the eastern edge of the largest **ponderosa pine forest** in the world. The road dead-ends in 4.5 miles (7.2 km) at U.S. 89. Turn left (southwest) onto U.S. 89 to reach Flagstaff in 4 miles (6.4 km) or turn right (north) to visit Sunset Crater in 15 miles (24 km).

Taking Exit 204 also provides an opportunity to visit Walnut Canyon Monument before exploring the 1947-1968 alignment. From Exit 204, head south (left) for 3 miles (4.8 km) on Walnut Canyon Road.

Walnut Canyon National Monument

Geological cliff formations, limestone ledges, curved buff sandstone walls, and ancient ruins are the impressive features at **Walnut Canyon National Monument** (3 Walnut Canyon Rd., 928/526-3367, www.nps.gov/waca, 9am-4:30pm daily, $15). Archaeologists labeled Indigenous people who lived in the area as "Sinagua," a term from the old Spanish name for the area, Sierra de Sin Agua ("mountains without water"). In the 1880s, the canyon was looted by "pot hunters," which led to establishing a national monument as protection in 1915.

The **Island Trail** (1 mi/1.6 km round-trip) leads directly to the dwellings with access to 25 rooms; however, the climb back is 240 steps at 6,690 feet (2,039 m) in elevation, so it's a workout. It also gets windy, so bring a jacket. Note that pets are not allowed on any park trails or in buildings.

◈ Side Trip: North on U.S. 89

From I-40, take Exit 201 and turn right (northwest) on U.S. 180 toward U.S. 89 north. Turn right and follow signs for the Loop Road (County Road 395). The **Loop Road** takes about an hour to drive—from the juniper grasslands, ponderosa pine forests, and open meadows to Sunset Crater and the red rocks of Wupatki National Monument.

Avoid using GPS, as it may direct you to the monument's administrative offices or on a dirt road through the forest.

Sunset Crater Volcano National Monument

About 900 years ago, a volcano erupted north of Flagstaff and reshaped the entire surrounding landscape. The 34-mile (55-km) scenic loop through **Sunset Crater Volcano National Monument** (6082 Sunset Crater Rd., www.nps.gov/sucr, 9am-5pm daily Nov.-May, 8am-5pm daily June-Oct., $25 per vehicle for access to both Sunset Crater Volcano and Wupatki National Monuments) passes the scene of the eruption and offers views of an enormous volcanic cinder cone.

The **Sunset Crater Volcano National Monument Visitor Center** (6082 Fire Rd. 5454, 928/526-0502, 9am-5pm daily) offers impressive natural history and seismograph exhibits that outline the powerful forces behind earthquakes and volcanoes. Enjoy free admission on Martin Luther King Day in January;

the first day of National Park Week in April; National Public Lands Day in September; and Veterans Day in November.

Allow at least an hour to hike the **Lava Flow Trail** (1 mi/1.6 km round-trip). The lava is sharp and brittle, so be cautious. The trailhead is 1.5 miles (2.4 km) west of the visitor center. For a more challenging hike, take the **Lenox Crater Trail**, found 1 mile (1.6 km) east of the visitor center. The steep 1-mile (1.6-km) loop provides close-up views of the lava flow and basalt formations.

Wupatki National Monument

Located on the loop road through the Sunset Crater Monument, **Wupatki National Monument** (6400 N. U.S. 89, 928/679-2365, www.nps.gov/wupa, visitors center 9am-5pm daily, dwellings dawn-dusk daily, $25 per vehicle for access to both Sunset Crater Volcano and Wupatki National Monuments) is one of the driest and hottest spots on the Colorado Plateau. The monument's 35,422 acres (14,335 hectares) include dramatic vistas, geological volcanic formations, desert wildlife, 900-year-old artifacts, and pueblos from ancient southwestern cultures. The Wupatki ruins lay scattered throughout the park and give a glimpse into the lives of the Cohonina, Sinagua, and Kayenta cultures from the 1100s. The freestanding three-story **Wupatki Pueblo** was one of the most significant pueblos in the area, home to 85-100 people. In the early 13th century, all the settlements were abandoned.

◈ Back on 66

The Loop Road (County Road 395) returns to U.S. 89, exiting Wupatki National Monument. Drive south on U.S. 89 for 25 miles (40 km) into Flagstaff.

Shifting Landscape

The **Colorado Plateau** dominates most of northern Arizona and features a fascinating and diverse landscape. From the New Mexico border to Winslow, you can see for miles in any direction, a stark stretch that leads to the Painted Desert and Petrified Forest. As you near Winona, Route 66 glides over **gentle hills,** and the state's largest mountain range, the **San Francisco Peaks,** rises before you. Elevation gains bring trees, namely **ponderosa pines** and **aspens,** as you enter Flagstaff.

From here to Williams, the landscape is **leafy, mountainous,** and filled with wildlife. It's hard to imagine that just north of this region sits the giant, gaping hole of the **Grand Canyon.** As you descend into Kingman and Oatman, you enter the **high desert,** which is **rugged, rocky,** and dotted with hardy plants. Kingman sits on the edge of the **Mojave Desert,** but its high elevation keeps temperatures cool.

Flagstaff

Flagstaff is a bustling hub with access to seven national parks and monuments, including the Grand Canyon 80 miles (129 km) northwest. Rather than a desert or red-rock landscape, as is typically seen in southern and central Arizona, Flagstaff sits smack in the middle of the world's largest ponderosa pine forest. While the rest of Arizona may experience sunny 60°F (16°C) days October through April, Flagstaff's nearly 7,000-foot (2,134-m) elevation means an average snowfall of about 108 inches (274 cm) annually.

Once you arrive, head to the Historic Downtown Flagstaff & Railroad District to walk the streets lined with shops, historic hotels, restaurants, breweries, and art galleries in beautiful buildings dating back to the early 1900s.

Sights
Lowell Observatory

Flagstaff was named the world's first International Dark Sky Place, receiving the designation in 2001. This means the city implements strategies to keep light pollution low and enforces stargazing-friendly light restrictions. This is good news for **Lowell Observatory** (1400 W. Mars Hill Rd., 928/774-3358, www.lowell. edu, 10am-10pm Mon.-Sat., 10am-5pm Sun., $15), one of the oldest observatories in the United States. Its original 24-inch (61-cm) Alvan Clark telescope lets you stare right into the sun. Lowell gained fame by discovering Pluto in 1930; today, it gives guests a full sky experience with wide-screen multimedia shows, open-deck observatory, hands-on exhibits, and an immersive space theater. Guided tours begin at the **Steele Visitor Center.**

Riordan Mansion State Historic Park

Riordan Mansion State Historic Park (409 W. Riordan Rd., 928/779-4395, http://azstateparks.com/riordan-mansion, 9:30am-5pm daily May-Oct., 10:30am-5pm Thurs.-Mon., Nov.-Apr., $12) is a 1904 Arts and Crafts mansion with log-slab siding and volcanic-stone arches designed by Charles Whittlesey, the creator of the Grand Canyon's El Tovar Hotel. The 13,000-square-foot (1,208-sq-m) manse has 40 rooms that are furnished with original artifacts. Guided tours are available.

Coconino Center for the Arts

The **Coconino Center for the Arts** (2300 N. Fort Valley Rd., 928/779-2300, https://flagartscouncil.org, 11am-5pm Wed.-Sat., fees vary) is the largest exhibit space in northern Arizona, with diverse works from regional artists and a 200-seat indoor amphitheater that hosts films, performances, and concerts year-round.

ARIZONA

Flagstaff

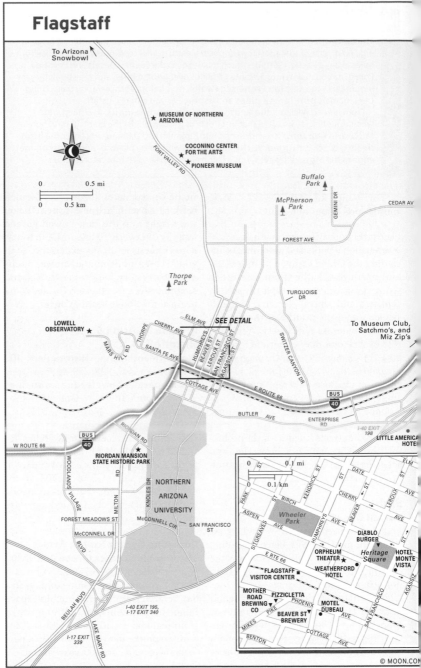

To Arizona Snowbowl

★ MUSEUM OF NORTHERN ARIZONA

★ COCONINO CENTER FOR THE ARTS
★ PIONEER MUSEUM

FORT VALLEY RD

Buffalo Park

McPherson Park

GEMINI DR

CEDAR AV

0   0.5 mi

0   0.5 km

FOREST AVE

Thorpe Park

TURQUOISE DR

LOWELL OBSERVATORY ★

CHERRY AVE
ELM AVE

SEE DETAIL

To Museum Club, Satchmo's, and Miz Zip's

MARS HILL RD
THORPE
SANTA FE AVE

HUMPHREYS
BEAVER ST
LEROUX ST
SAN FRANCISCO ST
AGASSIZ ST

SWITZER CANYON DR

COTTAGE AVE

E ROUTE 66

BUS 40

BUTLER   AVE

ENTERPRISE RD

I-40 EXIT 198

BUS 40

RIORDAN RD

W ROUTE 66

★ RIORDAN MANSION STATE HISTORIC PARK

LITTLE AMERICA HOTEL

WOODLANDS VILLAGE

MILTON RD

KNOLES DR

NORTHERN

ARIZONA

UNIVERSITY

FOREST MEADOWS ST

McCONNELL DR

McCONNELL CIR

SAN FRANCISCO ST

MCCONNELL BLVD

BEULAH BLVD

LAKE MARY RD

I-40 EXIT 195, I-17 EXIT 340

I-17 EXIT 339

Detail

0   0.1 mi

0   0.1 km

PARK ST
BIRCH
KENDRICK ST
DATE ST
CHERRY
LEROUX AVE
ELM ST

ASPEN
STGREAVES AVE
HUMPHREYS ST
BEAVER AVE

Wheeler Park

E RTE 66

DIABLO BURGER

ORPHEUM THEATER ★
Heritage Square
HOTEL MONTE VISTA

★ FLAGSTAFF VISITOR CENTER

WEATHERFORD HOTEL

MOTHER ROAD BREWING CO
PIZZICLETTA
PHOENIX

BEAVER ST BREWERY

MOTEL DUBEAU

SAN FRANCISCO ST

AGASSIZ

MIKES PIKE

BENTON

COTTAGE   AVE

© MOON.COM

Pioneer Museum

Imagine what it was like to live a settler's life at the **Pioneer Museum** (2340 N. Fort Valley Rd., 928/774-6272, www. arizonahistoricalsociety.org, hours vary seasonally, $8). Learn about Flagstaff's history of logging and ranching through the 3-acre (1.2-hectare) museum's outdoor displays of a 1929 Baldwin train locomotive, historic buildings, and a 1950s D-7 bulldozer.

Museum of Northern Arizona

The **Museum of Northern Arizona** (3101 N. Fort Valley Rd., 928/774-5213, www. musnaz.org, 10am-4pm Thurs.-Sun., $12) is a 200-acre (81-hectare) museum that celebrates the rich beauty of the Colorado Plateau with exhibits featuring more than 5 million American Indian artifacts, fine art pieces, and natural science specimens. The museum works directly with American Indians to protect their traditions, culture, and belief systems.

Entertainment

Named for John Steinbeck's signature surname for Route 66, **Mother Road Brewing Company** (7 S. Mikes Pike, 928/774-0492, www.motherroadbeer. com, 2pm-9pm Mon.-Thurs., 2pm-10pm Fri., noon-10pm Sat., noon-9pm Sun.) is on the south side of Flagstaff inside a 1920s building that originally housed a commercial laundry on a now-lost portion of Route 66. During the Depression, a 1930s alignment of Route 66 traveled under the railroad line one block west to handle the heavier Depression-era traffic. Today, the company brews killer IPAs, porters, pale ales, and a Kolsch-style beer with a dry, malty, fruity finish. Also on the menu are seasonal, anniversary, and barrel-aged ales.

The 1926 **Hotel Monte Vista Cocktail Lounge** (100 N. San Francisco St., 928/779-6971, www.hotelmontevista. com, 1pm-2am daily) launched the same year as Route 66. The lounge is on the bottom floor of Hotel Monte Vista.

The lounge existed as a speakeasy during Prohibition and hosted the likes of Humphrey Bogart, John Wayne, and Clark Gable. (Allegedly, Wayne was so drunk he tried to put his horse in the elevator.) You'll find live music Wednesday, Friday, and Saturday, and karaoke on Tuesday and Thursday. The lounge is also rumored to be haunted, with moving bar stools and ghosts busting a move on the dance floor. Good times.

The **Museum Club** (3404 E. Rte. 66, 928/440-5214, www.themuseumclub. com, 11am-2am daily, ticket prices vary by performance) is a legendary honky-tonk filled with history. Tanya Tucker played her first gig here at age 14, and country legends Willie Nelson and Waylon Jennings have graced the stage. It remains an all-American cowboy bar where folks square dance and do the two-step to national and regional acts.

Heritage Square (22 E. Aspen Ave., 928/853-4292, www.heritagesquaretrust. org, free) is an 11,000-square-foot (1,022-sq-m) plaza and Flagstaff's only open-air amphitheater. You'll enjoy artists, performers, events, festivals, movie screenings, and concerts here. Located on Aspen Avenue (between Leroux and San Francisco Sts.) in the heart of the historic downtown, it's a great place to grab a gelato, kick back, and take in the scene like a local.

The **Orpheum Theater** (15 W. Aspen Ave., 928/556-1580, www. orpheumflagstaff.com, ticket prices vary by performance) is a Flagstaff landmark and the city's premier entertainment venue. From artsy film screenings to regional and national music acts—everything from indie rockers to pop chart-toppers—the Orpheum caters to all tastes. Reserve a plush seat on the balcony, then grab a beverage from the full bar before the show.

Shopping

The **Historic Downtown Flagstaff & Railroad District** (1 E. Rte. 66,

928/774-9541, www.flagstaffarizona.org) is a pedestrian-friendly area packed with fashion-forward clothing boutiques, used bookstores, art galleries, restaurants, cafés, outdoor outfitters, and nightlife. The buildings date from the early 1900s, and the surrounding views delight with forested greenery. An **art walk** takes place the first Friday of every month, and there are other annual festivities. Venture south of the railroad tracks near downtown to the **Historic Southside District,** a popular spot with a collection of restaurants, coffee bars, and craft breweries.

Live the analog life at **Bookmans** (1520 S. Riordan Ranch Rd., 928/774-0005, http://bookmans.com, 10am-8pm daily), an extensive used bookstore with music (CDs, records, and the occasional cassette), DVDs, magazines, comic books, collectibles, and board games. Even better: Pets are welcome to shop with you as long as they're on a leash.

Flagstaff is known for outdoor adventures. To gear up, check out **Babbitt's Backcountry Outfitters** (12 E. Aspen Ave., 928/774-4775, www.babbittsbackcountry. com, 8am-8pm Mon.-Sat., 9am-6pm Sun.). It opened in 1888, when David Babbitt turned his lumberyard into a general store. He built the mercantile using locally quarried red sandstone, and that same building is where Babbitt's Backcountry Outfitters is housed today. The Babbitt family still runs the business, where you'll find everything you need for hiking, skiing, camping, climbing, and more. The staff is super knowledgeable, so ask questions.

More outdoors gear is available at **Peace Surplus** (14 W. Rte. 66, 928/779-4521, www.peacesurplus.com, 9am-6pm daily). Located right on Route 66, the store is stocked with a selection of camping, hiking, skiing, and fishing goods.

Winter Sun Trading Company (107 N. San Francisco St., 928/774-2884, www. wintersun.com, 9am-5pm Mon.-Sat., 11am-4pm Sun.) sells American Indian art, jewelry, and carvings from members

historic downtown Flagstaff

of local tribes. It also offers an apothecary with tinctures made from Indigenous, organic herbs.

Earthbound Trading Company (22 N. San Francisco St., 9am-8pm Sun.-Thurs., 9am-9pm Fri.-Sat.) stocks boho-chic apparel, accessories, and gifts, including East Indian and American Indian beaded jewelry, bath products, mosaics, backpacks, purses, and more.

Aspen Place at the Sawmill (Butler Ave. and Lone Tree Rd., www.aspenplace. com) has almost 70,000 square feet (6,503-sq-m) of shops and restaurants—from national brands to locally owned gems.

Recreation

People come from all over to indulge in Flagstaff's outdoor-enthusiasts paradise. From mountain biking and downhill skiing to rock climbing, trail running, and hiking, the surrounding Coconino National Forest beckons adrenaline junkies.

Lava River Cave

Discover the ancient underground **Lava River Cave** (Coconino National Forest, Forest Road 171B, 928/526-0866, www. fs.usda.gov, 24 hours daily, $5), which was formed 700,000 years ago. See the wavelike ripples frozen in the floor from molten rock, and wonder at the stone icicles hanging from the ceiling where volcanic heat partially melted the ceiling, which then dripped and dried. It's pitch-black, so bring several sources of light, and dress warmly! It's about 42°F (6°C) inside, even in summer. Wear sturdy shoes and tread carefully; the rocks are sharp and slippery.

To access the cave, drive 9 miles (14.5 km) north of Flagstaff on U.S. 180 and turn west (left) on FR-245 (at milepost 230). Continue 3 miles (4.8 km) to Forest Road 171 and turn south for 1 mile (1.6 km) to where Forest Road 171B turns left; then it's a short distance to Lava River Cave. The cave is open year-round, but Forest Road 171 and Forest Road 245 may be closed in the winter.

Hiking

Take off on the scenic **Kachina Trail,** a moderate 5-mile (8-km) hike in the Kachina Peaks Wilderness area about 17 miles (27 km) north of Flagstaff. The trail crosses several canyons before descending into a lava cliff with eroded volcanic rocks. It's an especially popular hike in fall due to the brilliant yellow foliage in the aspen groves.

From Flagstaff, drive 7 miles (11.3 km) northwest on U.S. 180. Turn right (north) onto Forest Road 516 (Snowbowl Rd.). Follow this road for about 7 miles (11.3 km) to the Snowbowl Ski Area and park in the first parking lot on the right (south). The trailhead is at the south end of the parking lot.

Biking

The mountain bike trails in the Coconino National Forest range from easy to technical, rocky, single-track downhill routes.

Absolute Bikes (202 E. Rte. 66, 928/779-5969, www.absolutebikes.net, 9am-7pm Mon.-Fri., 9am-6pm Sat., 10am-4pm Sun. Apr.-Dec.; 10am-6pm Mon.-Sat., 10am-4pm Sun. Jan.-Mar.) is a full-service bike shop with mountain, road, cruiser, and tandem bike rentals. The staff works with a local bike advocacy group and the Coconino National Forest to build new routes, and they are the best resource for local info about bike trail rides in the Flagstaff area. Bike rentals ($29-100) include a helmet, pump, repair kit, spare tube, choice of pedals, and personalized fit service. Reservations are necessary.

Arizona Nordic Village

For cross-country skiing, snowshoeing, camping, hiking, biking, and wildlife-watching, the **Arizona Nordic Village** (U.S. 180 at mile marker 232, 928/220-0550, www.arizonanordicvillage.com, 9am-4pm daily) hosts some of the best outdoor recreation activities in the area. There are more than 35 miles (56 km) of ski and snowshoe trails ranging from beginner to expert; many of these trails are also used for hiking and biking in summer, and gear rentals are available on-site (prices vary). Accommodations include cabins and yurts with woodstoves (up to 8 people, $50-90).

Horseback Riding

For a leisurely way to take in the mountain vistas, enjoy a horseback excursion or a horse-drawn wagon ride at the **Hitchin' Post Stables** (4848 Lake Mary Rd., 928/774-1719, www.historichitchinpoststables.com, $55-220), just south of Walnut Canyon. One-, two-, three-, and four-hour trail rides meander through the ancient ruins of cliff- and cave-dwelling American Indian communities. Rides with lunch and dinner included are also available.

Winter Sports

With an average of 260 inches (660 cm) of snow a year in the area, it would be a shame to miss **Arizona Snowbowl** (Snowbowl Rd., off U.S. 180, 928/779-1951 or 928/779-4577 for snow report, www.arizonasnowbowl.com). Ski more than 32 trails with five lifts with a 2,300-foot (701-m) vertical drop. When it's not snowing, ride the Scenic Skyride with fabulous views at 11,000 feet (3,353 m).

Flagstaff Extreme Adventure Course

Just south of Flagstaff, on the west side of I-17, is **Flagstaff Extreme Adventure Course** (Fort Tuthill County Park, 888/259-0125, www.flagstaffextreme.com, 9am-5pm daily, $55), an obstacle course through the towering ponderosa pine trees. The elevated courses vary in difficulty and include suspended bridges, swings, slides, ziplines, nets, and even an aerial surfboard. If you're afraid of heights, this isn't the place for you.

Food

Situated behind a gas station in a shopping center is the family-owned, New Orleans-style **Satchmo's** (2320 N. 4th St., 928/774-7292, www.satchmosaz.com, 11am-8pm Thurs.-Sat., 11am-7pm Sun., $6-12), where you can order fall-off-the-bone barbecue and Cajun and Creole faves like red beans and rice, po'boys, and jambalaya.

For possibly the best wood-fired pizza in Arizona, head to ★ **Pizzicletta** (203 W. Phoenix Ave., 928/774-3242, http://pizzicletta.com, 4pm-9pm daily, $11-30). The dough is naturally leavened, and the organic toppings are sourced from local farms. Start with the burrata (if you're wondering if you should add prosciutto, the answer is yes), then indulge in pizza with gorgonzola and charred kale.

Chow down with the locals right on Route 66 at **Miz Zip's** (2924 E. Rte. 66, 928/526-0104, https://mizzips.com, 7:30am-2pm daily, $6-10, cash only), a no-frills eatery that has been serving ranchers and construction workers since 1952. You'll love the cheeseburgers,

French dip sandwiches, and homemade pies.

Along with their selection of stouts, IPAs, and lagers, the microbrewery **Beaver St. Brewery** (11 S. Beaver St., 928/779-0079, https://beaverstreetbrewery.com, 11:30am-8pm daily, $9-28) serves addictive pesto and cream cheese dip, chicken potpie in a buttery crust, and succulent pork chops.

Every burger at **Diablo Burger** (120 N. Leroux St., 928/774-3274, www.diabloburger.com, 11:30am-8pm daily, $10-30) is made from 100-percent local, open range-raised beef, which is probably why these juicy burgers taste so incredible. Or it could be because of the out-of-the-box toppings such as Hatch chile mayo or an over-easy fried egg.

The delightful Indian food at **Delhi Palace** (2500 S. Woodlands Village Blvd., Ste. 8, 928/556-0019, www.delhipalaceflagstaff.com, 11am-2:45pm and 5pm-9:45pm daily, $9-17) doesn't disappoint. Come hungry for the lamb korma, bold and spicy chicken *vindaloo*, and flaky garlic naan.

Accommodations

★ **Little America Hotel** (2515 E. Butler Ave., 800/352-4386, www.flagstaff.littleamerica.com, $383-393) is a luxe hotel and lodge set on 500 acres (202 hectares) of lush ponderosa pine forest. Thoughtfully detailed rooms are decorated in a retro French-themed decor—classic, traditional, opulent—that lends a warm and cozy vibe to your stay.

Motel DuBeau (19 W. Phoenix Ave., 800/398-7112, www.modubeau.com, $54-85) is a charming historic motel and hostel located on a pre-1934 alignment of Route 66 in downtown Flagstaff. (The route traveled west of the railroad tracks on Beaver Street, then north on Phoenix). Economy rooms feature a double bed, a desk, and a mini-fridge. Deluxe rooms are larger, with one double bed, a flat-screen cable TV, and a lounge chair.

Premium rooms include two double beds and a kitchenette with a microwave.

At the historic ★ **Hotel Monte Vista** (100 N. San Francisco St., 928/779-6971, www.hotelmontevista.com, $85-165), each room is unique, and all come with free Wi-Fi, TVs, and plush bedding. Thanks to its heart-of-downtown location, this might not be the most quiet of accommodations, but a cuppa joe from the amazing coffee bar downstairs more than makes up for it.

Another historic option located just a block from Route 66 is the **Weatherford Hotel** (23 N. Leroux St., 928/779-1919, http://weatherfordhotel.com, $115-205). Opened in 1897 by Texas-born John Weatherford, the hotel offers rooms that sport quaint European décor and claw-foot tubs. The hotel offers three restaurants, including the Zane Grey Bar, a watering hole located on the third floor.

For modern amenities and noteworthy views of the surrounding San Francisco Peaks, book a room at the **Twin Arrows Navajo Casino Resort** (22181 Resort Blvd., 877/630-9530, www.twinarrows.com, $90-180), a full-service gaming hotel with dining and entertainment. Rooms are decorated in southwestern maize, paprika, and turquoise accents, and include state-of-the-art entertainment centers.

Information and Services

The **Flagstaff Convention and Visitors Bureau** (1 E. Rte. 66, 928/213-2951, www.flagstaffarizona.org, 8am-5pm Mon.-Sat., 9am-4pm Sun.) can be found in the historic train station downtown. Come for free maps and brochures, then explore the gift shop with Route 66 and train-themed souvenirs, books, clothing, and memorabilia.

Because Flagstaff is at almost 7,000 feet (2,134 m) in elevation, weather may be a factor for drivers. To ensure you're prepared, contact the following for up-to-date status and conditions.

- National Weather Service (928/556-9161, http://weather.gov/flagstaff)
- Recorded Weather Information (928/774-3301)
- Road Conditions (888/411-7623, www.az511.com)
- Arizona Snowbowl Snow Report (928/779-4577, www.arizonasnowbowl.com)

◈ Back on 66

Before leaving Flagstaff, consider a side trip to the Grand Canyon (1.5 hours away) or Sedona (about 45 minutes away). To continue on Route 66, drive west on Business I-40 (Route 66) for 4.5 miles (7.2 km) to join I-40 west. Continue 14 miles (22.5 km) past Bellemont and take Exit 178 to Parks. Turn right and take the next left on Old Route 66.

☆ ★ Side Trip: Grand Canyon National Park

The **Grand Canyon National Park** (928/638-7888, www.nps.gov/grca, $35) is 277 miles (445 km) long, 18 miles (29 km) wide, and 1 mile (1.6 km) deep. The Grand Canyon is more than a geological nirvana with out-of-this-world vistas and deeply hued buttes—it also has a rich cultural history to rival that of almost any other national park.

In 1540, when Spanish explorer Garcia Lopez de Cardenas gazed at almost 2 billion years of geology from the South Rim of the Grand Canyon, he was not impressed with the view. He considered the area a desert wasteland and was more concerned about finding a way to cross it.

Grand Canyon National Park

Cardenas and his 12 companions spent three days looking for a passage to the Colorado River below with no success. Hopi guides convinced the party to turn around, but some historians believe that the Hopis knew exactly how to access the river and were protecting this sacred area. It would be another 300 years before white explorers attempted to explore the canyon again.

Hotelier and restaurant operator Fred Harvey knew the Grand Canyon would be a world-class tourist destination. In 1901, he convinced the Santa Fe Railway to run a rail line from Williams, Arizona. Although Harvey died the same year, El Tovar Hotel, a Fred Harvey House, opened in 1905 at the South Rim at the end of the Santa Fe Railway line and was operated by his sons and grandsons.

The Grand Canyon was established as a national park in 1919. Today nearly 6 million annual visitors huddle along the South Rim to stare open-mouthed at this wonder of the world.

Getting There

The **South Rim Entrance** (open year-round) is the most convenient access for Route 66 road-trippers. From Flagstaff, take U.S. 180 north for 50 miles (81 km) to SR-64. Turn right (north) onto SR-64 and drive 22 miles (35 km) to the South Entrance. Or, from I-40 in Williams, take SR-64 north for 60 miles (97 km).

It is also possible to access the park via the less-crowded **East Entrance.** From Flagstaff, follow U.S. 89 north for 46 miles (74 km) to Cameron. Turn left (west) and drive 48 miles (77 km) to the east entrance station. It is another mile (1.6 km) west along Desert View Drive to Grand Canyon Village.

If you'd rather not drive, **Groome Transportation** (928/350-8466, https://groometransportation.com, $34 each way) provides round-trip shuttle service (three times daily year-round) from Flagstaff to the Grand Canyon from the Amtrak station (1 E. Rte. 66).

After arriving in the park, leave your car at the visitors center and use one of the park shuttle buses to see the sights.

Sights
Grand Canyon Visitor Center

The **Grand Canyon Visitor Center** (9am-4pm daily year-round) has outdoor and indoor exhibits, including interactive trip planners, a large 3D relief map, videos, and films. A **café** (open year-round) and **bookstore** (9am-7pm daily) are on-site, and bicycle rentals from **Bright Angel Bicycles** (928/679-0992, www.bikegrandcanyon.com, Mar.-Oct., $12.50/hr, $42/day) are available.

Mather Point

Just a short walk past the visitors center on the Rim Trail, **Mather Point** offers the first epic glimpse into the gaping canyon. The promontory, named after Stephen

Grand Canyon Village

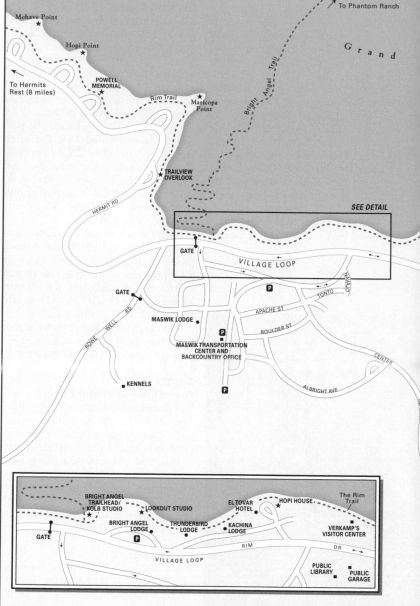

To Phantom Ranch

G r a n d

Mohave Point ★

Hopi Point ★

To Hermits Rest (8 miles)

POWELL MEMORIAL ★

Rim Trail

Maricopa Point ★

Bright Angel Trail

TRAILVIEW OVERLOOK ★

HERMIT RD

SEE DETAIL

GATE ↓

VILLAGE LOOP

NAVAJO

TONTO

GATE

ROWE WELL RD

MASWIK LODGE ■

APACHE ST

BOULDER ST

P

MASWIK TRANSPORTATION CENTER AND BACKCOUNTRY OFFICE

CENTER

KENNELS ■

ALBRIGHT AVE

P

Detail

BRIGHT ANGEL TRAILHEAD/ KOLB STUDIO ★

LOOKOUT STUDIO ★

EL TOVAR HOTEL

HOPI HOUSE ★

The Rim Trail

GATE

BRIGHT ANGEL LODGE ■

P

THUNDERBIRD LODGE ■

KACHINA LODGE ■

VERKAMP'S VISITOR CENTER ■

VILLAGE LOOP

RIM

DR

PUBLIC LIBRARY ■

PUBLIC GARAGE ■

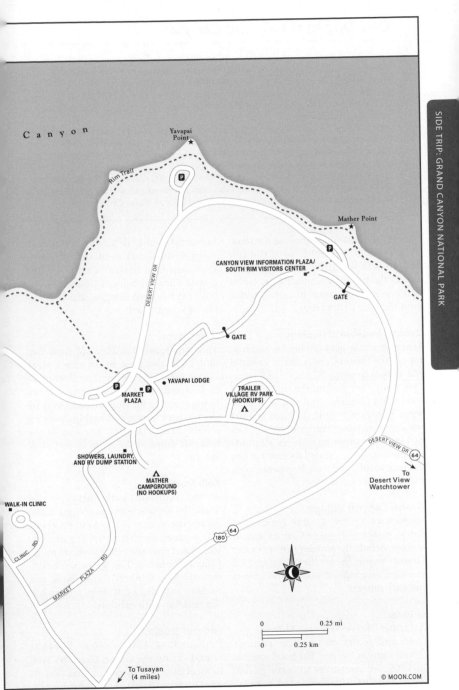

Canyon

Yavapai Point

Rim Trail

Mather Point

CANYON VIEW INFORMATION PLAZA/
SOUTH RIM VISITORS CENTER

GATE

DESERT VIEW DR

GATE

YAVAPAI LODGE

MARKET
PLAZA

TRAILER
VILLAGE RV PARK
(HOOKUPS)

DESERT VIEW DR 64

To
Desert View
Watchtower

SHOWERS, LAUNDRY,
AND RV DUMP STATION

MATHER
CAMPGROUND
(NO HOOKUPS)

WALK-IN CLINIC

CLINIC RD

180 64

MARKET PLAZA RD

0   0.25 mi

0   0.25 km

To Tusayan
(4 miles)

© MOON.COM

One Day in the Grand Canyon

First, ditch the car. Park near the **Grand Canyon Visitor Center** and walk the **Rim Trail** west, stopping at **Mather Point,** the **Yavapai Museum of Geology,** and the **Hopi House** before lunching at **Bright Angel Lodge.** Afterward, explore **Grand Canyon Village,** checking out the Harvey House history exhibit in Bright Angel Lodge, peeking through the lens at the **Kolb Studio,** and soaking in canyon vistas from **Lookout Studio.**

From Grand Canyon Village, hop aboard the **shuttle bus** to **Hermits Rest,** Mary Colter's masterpiece building, with its epic fireplace. At night, have dinner in **El Tovar'**s historic dining room with can't-take-your-eyes-off views over the canyon (make your reservation well in advance).

Drivers who enter the park via the East Entrance (SR-64) can stop at the stunning **Desert View Watchtower** (another Mary Colter masterpiece) and the **Tusayan Ruin and Museum** before parking in the Grand Canyon Visitor Center lots.

Mather (the first director of the National Park Service), juts out beyond the rim and gives first-time visitors a perspective of the canyon's depth. Picnic tables and a small stone amphitheater provide ringside seats to the views.

Yavapai Museum of Geology

Learn about the geology, origin, and history of the Grand Canyon at the **Yavapai Museum of Geology** (928/638-7888, 9am-5pm daily), perched on the south rim of the Grand Canyon—and yes, with even more panoramic views. Located a short walk east of Mather Point along the "Trail of Time," the museum features 3D models; photographs; a scaled diorama of the canyon, fossils, and rock fragments; plus videos of the canyon floor.

Grand Canyon Village

Verkamp's Visitor Center (9am-5pm daily), east of El Tovar in Grand Canyon Village, details the pioneer history of the Grand Canyon. Peruse the bookstore and exhibits, and request information from the park rangers.

El Tovar

A former Harvey House, **El Tovar** sits front and center on the Rim Trail in Grand Canyon Village. The hotel opened in 1905 and continues to serve guests with delightfully appointed rooms,

beautiful lobby, delicious restaurant, and a seasonal deck overlooking the rim. Designed by Charles Whittlesey and constructed with local limestone, the building has been designated a National Historic Landmark.

Hopi House

The **Hopi House** (928/638-7888, 9am-5pm daily) was designed by architect Mary Colter for Fred Harvey. The Puebloan-style sandstone and adobe structure is a living museum for Hopi artisans to share their artistic process of making pottery, jewelry, and blankets. For one of the best gift shops in the park, stop at Hopi House.

Kolb Studio

At the trailhead for the Bright Angel Trail, the **Kolb Studio** (9am-5pm daily) details the history of the Kolb Brothers, two pioneering photographers who explored and promoted the canyon through films and photos. The Victorian building—the Kolb Brothers' former home and studio—includes a gift shop, and an onsite museum with exhibits.

Lookout Studio

Built in 1914, Mary Colter's **Lookout Studio** sits on the Grand Canyon's rim, its local stone and wood construction almost disappearing into the canyon walls.

The Harvey Girls: Pioneers of the West

Starting in the 1880s, young women made an unusual decision—unusual at the time, that is—to leave home and travel the country working as waitresses along the Atchison, Topeka, and Santa Fe Railway. They were employed by the Fred Harvey Company, which opened eateries, known as Harvey Houses, along the rail lines. Ranging in age from 18 to 30, the outgoing Harvey Girls were one of the biggest reasons for the success of Harvey Houses. They also opened the doors of the West, and of the workplace, to women, paving the way for generations of young women to come. A lively fictional take on these pioneering ladies is *The Harvey Girls*, a 1946 film starring Judy Garland. *The Harvey Girls: Opportunity Bound* is a riveting documentary that explores the life of these women, including interviews with those who worked at Harvey Houses in the 1950s and 1960s.

Its terraces offer a perfect opportunity to view the canyon's depths via telescope or spot the skies for California condors in flight. You'll find another gift shop (9am-5pm daily) on-site.

Hermits Rest

Built in 1914 by Mary Colter, **Hermits Rest** nestles into the canyon at the end of the Rim Trail, the chunky stone blocks of the building harmonizing with the environment. More impressive is the massive stone fireplace inside. A snack bar (9am-5pm daily), gift shop (9am-5pm daily), water refill station, and restrooms are also on-site. The start of the Hermit Trail leads steeply into the canyon below.

East Rim

Desert View Drive extends 25 miles (40 km) east from Grand Canyon Village to the East Entrance on U.S. 64. Along the way are six canyon viewpoints, including Grandview Point and Lipan Point, four picnic areas, and a Mary Colter masterpiece.

Tusayan Ruin and Museum

The **Tusayan Ruin and Museum** (9am-5pm daily) contains the remains of a once-thriving, small 800-year-old Puebloan village. The museum showcases handmade crafts from modern local tribes and includes figurines that are up to 4,000 years old. Tusayan is 3 miles (4.8 km) west of Desert View Watchtower

and 22 miles (35 mi) east of the Grand Canyon Village.

Desert View Watchtower

The four-story **Desert View Watchtower** (9am-4:30pm daily) was designed by Mary Colter and modeled after the architecture of ancestral Puebloan people. Inside is the Kiva Room, interior murals painted by artist Fred Kabotie, and a rooftop observation area with 360-degree views of the Colorado River, the Painted Desert, and the San Francisco Peaks. The Watchtower is the tallest structure in the park and located 24 miles (39 km) east of Grand Canyon Village. Nearby you'll find a grocery store, snack bar, gas station, and seasonal campground.

Hiking

It's easy to be seduced by the magnificent views of the Grand Canyon. Although there are several trails from the South Rim, don't think you can hike to the river and back in less than one day; many attempt this, and of these, more than 250 hikers are rescued each year. There are no easy trails into or out of the Grand Canyon. Use common sense, be aware of your limitations, and always stay on the trail. Even the most experienced hikers say trekking through the Grand Canyon was more difficult than they expected due to the high altitude, elevation, and the dry desert climate.

Rim Trail

The **Rim Trail** follows the rim of the Grand Canyon for 13 miles (20.9 km)—one-way—from the South Kaibab trailhead west to Hermits Rest. It's mostly flat, often paved, and offers excellent views of the inner canyon; have your camera ready. Many sections are also suitable for wheelchairs. Popular sections include the 0.7 mile (1.1 km) between Mather Point and Yavapai Museum of Geology; the 1.3 miles (2.1 km) between Yavapai and Verkamp's; and the 0.6 mile (1 km) from Verkamp's to Kolb Studio in Grand Canyon Village.

Bright Angel Trail

The **Bright Angel Trail** descends from Grand Canyon Village to drop 12 steep miles (19.3 km) to the Colorado River. While it is not possible to hike to the river and back in a day, some shorter sections are doable as a day hike. From the trailhead to the Upper Tunnel is 0.4 mile (0.6 km) round-trip; the Lower Tunnel is 1.7 miles (2.7 km) round-trip (1-2 hours). In 3 miles (4.8 km) round-trip (2-4 hours), you'll reach the 1.5-Mile Resthouse, which has restrooms and water (seasonally). Don't push your luck much farther than the 3-Mile Resthouse, which is a brutal 6 miles (9.7 km) round-trip (4-6 hours), with restrooms and water (seasonal). The trailhead is next to Kolb Studio along the Rim Trail and near Bright Angel Lodge.

South Kaibab Trail

The **South Kaibab Trail** offers the best views for a relatively short yet steep hike. Those in good shape should make it to Ooh Ahh Point (1.8 mi/2.9 km round-trip, 1-2 hours), with a 600-foot (183-m) change in elevation. The views change around every bend, making the experience worth the struggle. Extending down into the canyon to Cedar Ridge (3 mi/4.8 km round-trip, 2-4 hours) increases the elevation change to 1,120 feet (341 m). The hike back up to the rim is always

harder; give uphill hikers the right of way. Dress in layers, wear good hiking boots, and bring water and food, as there is no water along this trail.

To reach the trailhead, park at the visitors center and take the free Kaibab/Rim Route shuttle bus to Yaki Point.

Food

The Grand Canyon Visitor Center is home to the **Bright Angel Bicycles and Café** (928/679-0992, www.bikegrandcanyon.com, 6am-7pm daily May 1-Labor Day, 8am-5pm daily Labor Day-Mar. 1, 7am-6pm daily Mar.-Apr.), a coffee bar with prepackaged meals to go.

In El Tovar Hotel, the **El Tovar Dining Room** (Grand Canyon Village, 928/638-2631, www.grandcanyonlodges.com, 7am-10:30am, 11:30am-2pm, and 5pm-9pm daily, $14-48) offers an extravagant foodie experience, all in a rustic-chic setting with native-stone and Oregon pine construction, adorned with Hopi, Apache, Mojave, and Navajo murals. Dishes merge traditional and southwestern influences, such as roasted duck with prickly pear orange glaze. It's the most popular dining spot in the Grand Canyon, so reservations are not only highly recommended, but necessary. Although there is no formal dress code, shorts and flip-flops are discouraged.

For a less formal ambience at the same property, opt for the **El Tovar Lounge** (928/638-2631, 11am-11pm daily), which offers a limited menu and creative cocktails. The outdoor deck is a prime people-watching spot and the perfect place to soak in the legendary scenery of the park.

There are several dining choices at Bright Angel Lodge. **Fred Harvey Burger** (9 Village Loop Dr., 928/638-2631, www.grandcanyonlodges.com, 7am-10:30am, 11am-3:30pm, 4:30pm-9pm daily, no reservations, $8-23) is a casual restaurant serving breakfast, lunch, and dinner. This is American comfort food: biscuits and gravy, burgers, and steak. Slightly more upscale is **Arizona Steakhouse**

(9 Village Loop Dr., 928/638-2631, 11:30am-3pm and 4:30pm-9pm daily, no reservations, $22-38). Sip local beers and wines, then cut into hand-cut aged steaks and dishes featuring Indigenous ingredients. The **Canyon Coffee House** (6am-10am daily, $3) serves coffee and continental breakfast items. In summer, **Bright Angel Fountain** (11am-6pm seasonally) is the place to take the kids for ice cream, soda, and snacks.

Grab a quick bite or sit down for a meal at the **Maswik Food Court** (Maswik Lodge, 928/638-2631, www. grandcanyonlodges.com, 6am-8pm daily, $5-15) at the west end of Grand Canyon Village. Affordable menu options range from home-style dinners to packaged lunches prepared to go. The **Maswik Pizza Pub** (noon-8pm daily, $20) has more of a sports bar setting and serves pizzas, salads, and cold beer.

The Market Plaza has the **Canyon Village Market** (928/638-2262, 6:30am-9pm daily May-Sept., shorter winter hours), which sells clothing and gifts as well as groceries, and a **deli** (6:30am-8pm May-Sept., shorter winter hours) that creates made-to-order sandwiches. At **Yavapai Lodge**, the **Lodge Restaurant** (7:30am-9pm daily May-Sept., shorter winter hours, $15), **Coffee Shop** (5am-10pm daily May-Sept., shorter winter hours), and **Lodge Tavern** (11am-10pm daily July-Feb.) all offer good eats to fulfill any traveler's cravings.

Hermits Rest Snack Bar (8am-8pm daily in summer, 9am-5pm daily in winter) offers an unusual—in a good way—spot for a quick snack. Order sandwiches, ice cream, chips, cookies, or hot chocolate, and savor your treat next to the enormous 1914 stone fireplace designed by Mary Colter.

Near the East Entrance, you can get groceries and souvenirs at the **Desert View Market & Deli** (928/638-2393, 8am-8pm daily in summer, shorter winter hours), as well as chili, Indian tacos, salads, pizza, and chips from the snack bar.

Accommodations

Accommodations tend to be full throughout the year, so it's best to book rooms at least eight months in advance. Most **reservations** (888/297-2757, www. grandcanyonlodges.com) can be made online at the six main lodges up to 13 months in advance.

The **Yavapai Lodge** (Market Plaza, 1 Main St., 877/404-4611, www. visitgrandcanyon.com, $150-200) offers rooms with clean basic necessities; choose from a king bed, two queen beds, and bunk beds that sleep 4-6 people. Internet access is available on-site (but not in the rooms). The prime location is what you're paying for—it's walking distance to the general store, visitors center, and the Rim Trail.

El Tovar Hotel (Grand Canyon Village, Apache St. and Center Rd., 888/297-2757, www.grandcanyonlodges.com, $197-489) is a grand National Historic Landmark built in 1905 by Charles Whittlesey, the chief architect for the Atchison, Topeka, and Santa Fe Railway. The Fred Harvey Company owned El Tovar, and it's one of the few Harvey House facilities still in operation. The rooms include many suites to choose from—no two rooms are alike. Amenities include TVs, Keurig coffeemakers, room service, and air-conditioning. An upscale restaurant is on-site.

Maswik Lodge (Grand Canyon Village, 888/297-2757, www.grandcanyonlodges. com, $107-205) is about 0.25 mile (0.4 km) south of Grand Canyon Village in a ponderosa pine forest. The complex has 250 motel-style rooms, a gift shop, a food court, and a pizza place. Rooms are located in two-story buildings (no elevators), and access is via exterior stairwells and walkways. Amenities include in-room coffeemakers, refrigerators, cable TV, and air-conditioning.

Thunderbird and **Kachina Lodges** (Grand Canyon Village, 888/297-2757, www.grandcanyonlodges.com, $215-265) offer contemporary lodging options close to the rim. Rooms include either one king or two queen beds with full baths; "canyonside" rooms have partial views. Amenities include coffeemakers, fridges, and flat-screen TVs. Each lodge is within walking distance of restaurants, gift shops, Kolb Studio, and the Bright Angel trailhead.

Bright Angel Lodge (Grand Canyon Village, 888/297-2757, www.grandcanyonlodges.com, $105-225) is a rustic landmark built by Mary Colter as a less expensive alternative to the elite El Tovar. Centrally located and mere steps from the rim, the lodge offers 90 lodging options, from units with shared baths to standard lodge rooms and cabins. The on-site Bright Angel History Room features historic postcards, a 100-year-old El Tovar menu, and exhibits about the Harvey Girls. Amenities include two restaurants, a bar, and a coffee nook. The trailhead for the Bright Angel Trail is nearby.

Camping

There are two campgrounds within the park. Reservations for each can be made up to six months in advance and are highly recommended.

Mather Campground (Market Plaza, 877/444-6777, www.recreation.gov, $18, year-round) is the largest campground in the park with 319 sites for tents and RVs. Centrally located south of Market Plaza, it has amenities that include fire rings at each campsite, drinking water, bathrooms with coin-operated showers, and laundry services; leashed pets are permitted. RV sites do not have hookups, but there is a dump station. The campground is serviced by the Village Route shuttle bus. From November through March, sites are available on a first-come, first-served basis; however, water may be turned off.

Desert View Campground (Desert View Dr., $12, first-come, first-served, mid-Apr.-mid-Oct.) is near Desert View Watchtower, 25 miles (40 km) east of Grand Canyon Village. The 50 sites can accommodate tents and small RVs (less than 30 feet/9 m). Amenities include fire grills and picnic tables; drinking water and restrooms are available in the campground. Reservations are not accepted, and sites fill by noon. A grocery store and snack bar are nearby. If entering the park via the East Entrance, this will be the first campground you come to.

If you are traveling with an RV and need hookups, try **Trailer Village RV Park** (877/404-4611, www.visitgrandcanyon.com, from $50, year-round), which is adjacent to Mather Campground near Market Plaza. Reservations are recommended for the 84 pull-through sites (up to 50 feet/15 m) with hookups. Amenities include Wi-Fi, drinking water, and the bathroom and laundry facilities at Mather Campground.

Tours

Air tours originate at the Grand Canyon Airport in Tusayan, Arizona, near

the South Rim of the park. **Westwind Air Service** (480/991-5557, www.westwindairservice.com, $152) offers 45-minute tours into the deepest part of the canyon, with views of the Colorado River, the Painted Desert, and the Desert View Watchtower. **Grand Canyon Airlines** (866/235-9422, www.grandcanyonairlines.com, air tours start at $159) has been in business since 1927 and is one of the world's oldest air tour companies.

Daily **bus tours** (888/297-2757, www.grandcanyonlodges.com) with guides outlining the history and geology of the canyon are also available.

⊕ Side Trip: SR-89A to Sedona

There's nothing like Sedona. You've heard of the area's breathtaking red rocks, but not until you see them for yourself will you understand their strange and magnetic beauty. In fact, these pink and maroon buttes, mesas, and spires are believed to harness mystical energy, and the vortexes scattered throughout the area draw spiritualists from all over the world. But you don't have to be a crystal-loving hippie to "get" Sedona; it's also a hot spot for outdoor enthusiasts with trails for hiking, biking, and off-roading. This doesn't even touch on the town's foodie scene or its luxury resorts and spas. Just 30 miles (48 km) south of Flagstaff via SR-89A, Sedona beckons with its art galleries, boutiques, wineries, restaurants, jeep excursions, vortex tours, aura readings, and more.

Getting There

From Flagstaff and Business I-40, head south on South Milton Road and turn right (west). Take your first left onto SR-89A. Follow SR-89A south for 25 miles (40 km) into Sedona.

Bell Rock, near Sedona

Scenic Drives

Oak Creek Canyon

Oak Creek Canyon Scenic Drive (SR-89A) is a 24-mile (39-km) drive between Flagstaff and Sedona. From Flagstaff, take I-17 South to SR-89A. The breathtaking road descends 4,500 feet (1,372 m) from the top of the Mogollon Rim, winding through sandstone canyons and rock formations around every curve.

Along the way, visit one of the state's most unusual swimming holes. **Slide Rock State Park** (6871 N. SR-89A, 928/282-3034, www.azstateparks.com, hours and rates vary seasonally, $10-30) is a natural water park in Oak Creek Canyon. Huge rock formations surround a cool creek with a red-sandstone "waterslide." Three short hiking trails are available, but there is no camping. The rocks are slippery, so water-resistant shoes are recommended; if you are wearing light-colored clothing, the sediment from the rocks can cause stains.

The best seasons to enjoy this drive are late spring, summer, and early fall; however, the creek water is usually too cold in fall and winter. The park gets extremely busy during the summer months, and there may be a long wait to enter it. If the parking lot is full, enter via the southbound turn lane. If that lane reaches the highway, the park will be inaccessible until the road clears.

State Route 179

In Sedona, SR-89A splits to head west. Stay south on SR-179 to take in the area's spectacular scenery. From Sedona, SR-179 winds 7.5 miles (12 km) south through the Coconino National Forest along some of the most striking red-rock sandstone and geological formations in the country. There are several places to pull off the road to snap pics, or to simply sit and contemplate the wonder of it all.

In about 3 miles (4.8 km), look for **Cathedral Rock,** one of the most-photographed natural landmarks in all of Arizona (besides the Grand Canyon, of course). It's also home to one of the four main energy vortexes in Sedona. Back on SR-179, continue south and in less than 1 mile (1.6 km), turn east (left) onto Chapel Road and drive 1 mile (1.6 km) to view the **Chapel of the Holy Cross** (www.chapeloftheholycross.com). The church, which juts out dramatically from the red rocks and features giant windows overlooking the landscape below, is open to the public.

Return to SR-179 and drive 3 miles (4.8 km) south to the parking lot for **Bell Rock** (6246 SR-179). Not only is this distinctive, bell-shaped monolith another one of Sedona's four vortexes, it's often considered to be the strongest. There are two parking lots; the lot for Courthouse Vista is the closest to the base of the rock.

Sights

As you drive into Sedona, the majority of the restaurants and hotels are either on the route or within 0.25 mile (0.4 km) of the highway. The town of Sedona is divided into four sections: The **Village of Oak Creek** (SR-179) has restaurants and hiking trails; **Uptown** is full of tourist-friendly shops and attractions; **Oak Creek Canyon** has B&Bs and mountain biking trails; and **West Sedona** is more residential.

Sedona is the epicenter for spiritual seekers and for those in need of a little R&R. For a quiet refuge among the juniper trees, visit **Amitabha Stupa and Peace Park** (2650 Pueblo Dr., 877/788-7229, dawn-dusk daily, free). All are welcome to stroll the grounds around the rare 36-foot (11-m) stupa, which is a five-minute walk from Pueblo Drive along a well-marked trail.

Tlaquepaque Arts & Shopping Village (336 SR-179, 928/282-4838, www.tlaq.com, 10am-6pm daily)—pronounced Tla-keh-pah-keh—has been the self-proclaimed "art and soul" of Sedona since the 1970s. This distinctive arts, retail, and culinary center is fashioned after a traditional Mexican village, with cobblestone walkways, vine-covered walls, and arched entryways situated on the banks of Oak Creek. Make time to explore the specialty shops, galleries, and restaurants.

A Spa For You (30 Kayenta Ct., Ste. 1, 928/282-3895, www.aspaforyou.com, 7am-8pm daily, call for appointment, $80-310) offers signature massages, body wraps, and Japanese facial massages that restore the body and rejuvenate the spirit. To get there, drive west on SR-89A and turn right (north) on Navajo Drive. Continue two blocks and turn left (west) on Hopi Drive. Take your first right into the parking lot; the spa is straight ahead on the right.

If you want to really lean in to the Sedona experience, book a session to balance your chakras or participate in a guided meditation. **Sedona Red Rock Tours** (928/282-0993, www.sedonaredrocktours.com, $150-450) offers a full suite of treatments, sessions, and experiences, many of which take place among the magical red rocks.

Hiking

Brins Mesa Trail (5 mi/8 km round-trip) is an easy-to-moderate trek that offers unobstructed views of the red-rock formations. From the trailhead, you'll pass by Devil's Sinkhole, a 100-foot-wide (30-m) and 50-foot-deep (15-m) active sinkhole that formed in the 1880s. The trail winds through canyon arches and up to Soldier Pass.

To access the trailhead from Sedona, go north on SR-89A for 0.2 mile (0.3 km) to Jordan Road. Turn left on Jordan Road and continue 0.7 mile (1.1 km) to Park Ridge Drive. Turn left onto Park Ridge Drive and continue 0.1 mile (0.2 km) to where the pavement ends. From there, continue 0.5 mile (0.8 km) on the dirt road that leads to the trailhead.

The **Palatki Heritage Site** (10290 Forest Road 795, 928/282-3854, www.fs.usda.gov, 9:30am-3pm daily, $5), built by the Sinagua people, showcases the dwellings and rock art of these ancient people. Three trails traverse the site, considered to be among the largest cliff dwellings between AD 1150 and 1350, and each trail is an easy 0.25-mile (0.4-km) hike. Reservations are required.

From Sedona, take SR-89A west for 5 miles (8 km) and turn right onto Forest Road 525. Continue north for 5 miles (8 km), then stay straight to continue north onto Forest Road 795. Drive 2 miles (3.2 km) to the parking lot for the Palatki ruins.

Food

If you want to eat at **Elote Cafe** (350 Jordan Rd., 928/203-0105, www.elotecafe.com, 5pm-9pm Tues.-Sat., $20-30), and you do, it's best to arrive early because the wait will be long. Order a margarita, chat with the locals, and Instagram the sunset until you can dive into the wildly delicious Mexican dishes. Start with the namesake elote appetizer—fire-roasted corn with spicy mayo, lime, and cotija cheese—then share a plate of carne asada with guajillo chile sauce and blue cheese.

Even the kale is massaged at **ChocolaTree Organic Oasis** (1595 W. SR-89A, 928/282-2997, www.chocolatree.com, 11am-4pm daily, $8-12). The vegetarian, organic, locally sourced menu offers flavorful options such as mushrooms sautéed in garlic almond cream sauce or enchiladas stuffed with sweet potato and three-bean chili. The on-site store sells herb tinctures, nut butters, pet products, and healthy snacks to go.

Sip champagne by the creek while you indulge in an exquisite fine-dining experience; wild game, imported truffles, and artisan cheeses are just a few of the culinary treats on the prix fixe menu at **Cress on Oak Creek** (301 L'Auberge Ln., 855/905-5745, www.lauberge.com, 11:30am-8pm daily, $70-85) at L'Auberge de Sedona. Reservations are recommended at least two weeks in advance.

Indian Gardens Café & Market (3951 N. SR-89A, 928/282-7702, http://indiangardens.com, 7:30am-5pm Mon.-Thurs., 7:30am-6pm Fri.-Sun., $8-12) offers a menu of soups, salads, sandwiches, and small plates, plus single-origin coffees from Latin America, Africa, and Indonesia. Grab any of their goodies to go before embarking on a day hike.

Known and beloved for their giant and delicious sandwiches, **Sedona Memories Bakery and Cafe** (321 Jordan Rd., 928/282-0032, 10am-2pm Mon.-Sat., $8-10, cash only) bakes their bread fresh every day. If you call ahead to order your sammie (and you should; the line gets long around lunchtime), they'll give you a free cookie.

Eat breakfast with the locals at the **Coffee Pot** (2050 SR-89A, 928/282-6626, www.coffeepotsedona.com, 6am-2pm daily, $10). This classic diner offers 101 omelet choices, plus chicken-fried steak and eggs, fluffy waffles, and even a kitschy gift store in which to wander while you wait for a table. The coffee is hot and the food is great.

For a steak house experience you can only have in the Southwest, go to the **Silver Saddle at the Cowboy Club** (241 N. SR-89A, 928/282-4200, www.cowboyclub.com, 11am-9pm daily, $15-30). Nosh on cactus fries, buffalo, and rattlesnake under wrought-iron antler chandeliers and gas lanterns.

They take their microbrews seriously at the **Oak Creek Brewing Company** (2050 Yavapai Dr., 928/204-1300, https://oakcreekbrew.com, 2pm-8pm Mon.-Thurs., noon-10pm Fri.-Sat., $6-9). The pub fare goes down easily with their award-winning lagers, porters, seasonal stouts, and pale ales.

Sedona closes down early, but **Sound Bites Grill** (101 N. SR-89A, 928/282-2713, www.soundbitesgrill.com, 11:30am-9pm Mon.-Thurs., 11:30am-10pm Fri.-Sat. $19-56) serves good food with friendly service and evening entertainment. Performers include Grammy-nominated artists, jazz musicians, and retro rock and roll groups.

Accommodations

Adobe Hacienda B&B (10 Rojo Dr., 602/550-0422, www.adobehacienda.com, $219-249) is Sedona's only bed-and-breakfast on a golf course. Decor includes 100-year-old Oaxacan doors; rooms are spacious and have cactus garden and red-rock views, kiva fireplaces, and bathrooms with southwestern features such as hand-painted Mexican sinks and punched-tin mirrors.

Just a few steps from Tlaquepaque shopping area, the **El Portal Sedona Hotel** (95 Portal Ln., 800/313-0017, www.elportalsedona.com, $270-329) is a pet-friendly—nay, pet-*welcoming*—adobe inn with river-rock fireplaces and flagstone floors. Several rooms include outdoor fenced patios. Your four-legged companion will receive a pet basket upon check-in, complete with a blanket and treats.

Hilton Sedona Resort and Spa (90 Ridge Trail Dr., 928/284-4040, www.hiltonsedonaresort.com, $269-374) has views that go on for days and beautifully appointed rooms with fireplaces, private balconies, and luxurious beds with down-filled comforters. There's also an 18-hole golf course on-site.

Las Posadas of Sedona (26 Avenida de Piedras, 928/284-5288, www.lasposadasofsedona.com, $209-279) is a boutique inn with luxe 650-square-foot (60-sq-m) suites, each with a double-sided fireplace, kitchenette, and—for those who don't like to cook—a complimentary gourmet breakfast. It's tucked away in the picturesque Village of Oak Creek (about 8 mi/12.9 km from the center of Sedona). Pets are welcome.

The **Amara Resort & Spa** (100 Amara Ln., 928/282-4828, www.amararesort.com, $179-359) offers modern accommodations in Uptown Sedona, blessedly away from the tourist center. The resort has an infinity-edge saltwater pool, daily yoga classes, and beds with posh pillow-top mattresses and headboards made from locally fallen trees. Pets are welcome.

Junipine Resort (8351 N. SR-89A,

Flagstaff to Needles

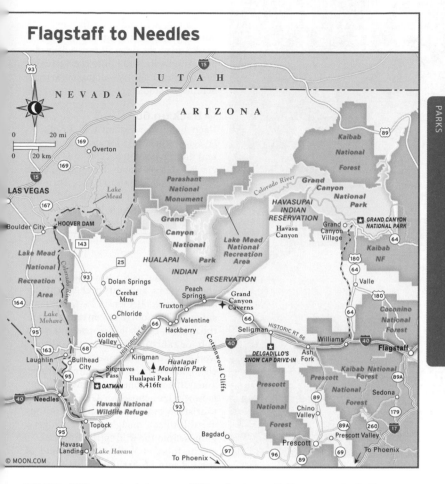

© MOON.COM

928/852-4589, www.junipine.com, $255-442) has well-equipped creek-side condos with spacious accommodations (ranging 900-1,400 square feet/84-130 sq m) that have spiral staircases, balconies, kitchens, redwood decks, free movies, and fireplaces. The resort is nestled in a pine forest about 15 minutes outside Sedona.

Parks

◆ Route 66 Through Parks

To drive the post-1940s alignment, take I-40 west from Flagstaff for 14 miles (22.5

km), past Bellement, and take Exit 178 to Parks. Turn north (right) and take the next left onto Old Route 66.

Sights

Between Flagstaff and Williams sits Parks, a small town that existed as a railroad depot and sawmill in a former life. It's also an example of an interesting facet of the Mother Road: sometimes Route 66 only moved a few feet, so when the new alignment shifted one block, the **Parks in the Pines General Store and Post Office** (12963 Old Rte. 66, 928/635-4741, 8am-7pm Mon.-Sat., 8am-6pm Sun.) changed

its front door from the south side of the building to the north side to face the new road. Today, the general store sells pizza, pastrami melts, and Philly cheesesteaks. The original 1926-1931 alignment is right behind the store.

◆ Back on 66

Keep heading west on Old Route 66 (Wagon Wheel Rd.) for about 5 miles (8 km) and then jump back onto I-40 west via Ponderosa Road (Exit 171). Drive 5.5 miles (8.9 km) to Exit 165. Turn left (south) on SR-64, cross under I-40, and continue on to Historic Route 66.

Williams

This mountainside town is long on charm, views, and craft beer. Originally settled by sheepherders in 1874, Williams sits at a 6,780-foot (2,067-m) elevation in the heart of the Kaibab Forest and was a hub for ranching, lumber, and railroad workers. With them came saloons, brothels, opium dens, and gambling parlors. Today, life is a bit more tame as Williams is now a launchpad for Grand Canyon tourists. Many of the historic buildings are still intact, though, so you can get a glimpse into the wild spirit of its past.

The folks of Williams are proud of their Route 66 heritage. This was the last town on Route 66 to be bypassed by I-40, and the locals fought to keep travelers coming through until the bitter end, October 13, 1984, just nine months before the official decommission of the Mother Road. In the end, the town let go with a bang-up celebration, including a live performance by Bobby Troup singing his signature song, "(Get Your Kicks on) Route 66."

Even though Williams was bypassed more than 30 years ago, it's still a fairly

Top to bottom: bear at Bearizona Wildlife Park; Flintstones Bedrock City and Raptor Ranch; the Williams Depot

busy spot and full of 19th-century character like railway-themed hotels, museums, restaurants, events, and parades. Plan to spend at least an afternoon, and if you have the time, book a room in a historic brothel for the night.

◆ Route 66 Through Williams

The 1926 alignment entered Williams in the north part of the town and made several turns before reaching downtown. We are going to take the **post-1940s alignment** that leads straight into downtown. From I-40, take Exit 165 and turn left. Drive under I-40 and follow Route 66 (Railroad Ave.). Railroad Avenue travels one-way through downtown Williams for six blocks. Once you reach the end of Railroad Avenue (one block after 9th St.), turn left and double back, taking the road that is parallel heading east. From here to 2nd Street is the 1926 alignment.

Sights

Stop by the **Williams Visitor Center** (200 W. Railroad Ave., 928/635-4061, https://experiencewilliams.com, 8am-5pm daily, free) to load up on information and maps and then embark on a 40-minute, self-guided walking tour of the historic district of Williams. The friendly staff at the visitor center can answer any question you have, and the center's website includes a comprehensive list of lodging and dining, things to do, and upcoming events.

Bearizona Wildlife Park

Getting up close and personal with a black bear may or may not be on your bucket list. Regardless, it's an experience everyone should try at least once—and safely. Enter **Bearizona Wildlife Park** (1500 Historic Rte. 66, 928/635-2289, https://bearizona.com, 9am-4pm daily, $25). On a 2.5-mile (4-km) drive in your own vehicle (keep the windows rolled up!) through the 160-acre (65-hectare) park, you'll see black bears, plus other animal species including bison, badgers,

bighorn sheep, burros, and wolves. After the drive, enjoy a nature walk with goats, pigs, and horses. Be sure to time your visit to coincide with one of the daily shows, such as Birds of Prey (11am, 1pm, 3pm), Bobcat Feeding (10:40am), Otter Feeding (11:40am), and a live animal meet-and-greet (1:40pm).

Grand Canyon Railway

You've been driving a lot. This is an epic road trip, after all. So if you want to see the Grand Canyon but would rather not be behind the wheel, experience the romance of train travel on the **Grand Canyon Railway** (200 W. Railroad Ave., 800/843-8724, www.thetrain.com, $67-226). Sit back and enjoy the scenic five-hour round-trip journey to the South Rim of the Grand Canyon on a vintage diesel-powered train. On-board entertainment, cocktails, small bites, and a knowledgeable staff make this a worthwhile excursion. All trains depart from the Williams Depot.

Williams Depot

Even if you're not taking the train, stop by the **Williams Depot** (200 W. Railroad Ave.), a former Harvey House, for a slice of history. You'll see turn-of-the-20th-century locomotives, a coal car, and a 1923 Harriman coach. The depot also houses a **visitors center** (928/635-4061, https://experiencewilliams.com, 8am-5pm), with a gift shop and offbeat exhibits, such as a stuffed version of the local squirrel with huge tufted ears.

Flintstones Bedrock City and Raptor Ranch

Flintstones Bedrock City (101 S. U.S. 180, 928/635-3072, https://raptor-ranch.com, 6am-sunset daily, $5) is a park inspired by everyone's favorite prehistoric family. Recently, new owners converted it into **Raptor Ranch,** a wildlife education facility, bird of prey breeding project, and home of the Northern Arizona Raptor Foundation. Happy news, they kept

Bedrock City intact, so not only can you embark on a self-guided tour of Raptor Ranch's natural history and falconry museum and see live demonstrations with raptors and various species of birds of prey, you can also peek inside the colorful structures modeled after the Hanna-Barbera cartoon, such as the characters' homes, a beauty parlor, post office, and even a jail.

Entertainment

Grand Canyon Brewing & Distillery (301 N. 7th St., 800/513-2072, www.grandcanyonbrewery.com, 2pm-11pm daily) is where you go when you want to taste award-winning craft beer. And who doesn't want that? The Sunset Amber Ale is sweet and malty, while the Black Iron IPA is robust and peppery. You can't go wrong with any of the seasonal beers, either.

Spenser's Pub (235 N. Grand Canyon Blvd., 928/635-4010, www.thetrain.com, 4pm-10pm daily) is a beautiful oak bar that dates to 1887. Tucked inside the historic Grand Canyon Railway Hotel, a former Harvey House, it's the perfect spot to clink your martini glasses in a toast.

The World Famous Sultana Bar (301 W. Rte. 66, 928/635-2021, 10am-2am daily) is a crusty dive bar—in the best way possible—housed in an early 19th-century building teeming with history. The Sultana claims to have the longest-operating liquor license in the state of Arizona; it once operated as a speakeasy during Prohibition. A wooden trapdoor leads to underground tunnels (built by Chinese workers) that housed an opium den and were used by bootleggers and outlaws. The Sultana also premiered the first "talkie" film in the area in 1930.

Another great dive bar is the **Canyon Club** (126 W. Railroad Ave., 928/635-2582, 10am-1am daily), with pool tables, DJs, shuffleboard tournaments, and weekend karaoke. An outside patio is perfect for those warm, slow nights in Williams.

Shopping

Thunder Eagle Native Art (221 W. Rte. 66, 928/635-8889, 9am-10pm daily) has an excellent selection of locally made American Indian jewelry, pottery, and art.

You're in the West, so you might as well pick up some real western wear in a real Old West town. Hit up **Western Outfitters and DeBerge Saddlery** (316 W. Rte. 66, 928/635-4013, https://westernoutfittersaz.com, 8am-8pm daily). They sell hand-tooled holsters, knife sheaths, belts, purses, hats, and Stetson boots.

Shop **Double Eagle Trading Company** (526 U.S. 180, 928/635-5393, 9am-5pm daily) for fun Grand Canyon and Route 66 souvenirs, plus pelts, hides, horns, and handmade American Indian arts and crafts such as rugs, pottery, jewelry, moccasins, and more.

The Gallery in Williams (145 W. Rte. 66, 928/635-3006, www.thegalleryinwilliams.com, 10am-7pm daily) is an artists' cooperative that sells local artists' work including oil, acrylic, and watercolor paintings, woodwork, sculpture, fiber arts, and jewelry.

The Grand Canyon Railway Gift Shop (233 N. Grand Canyon Blvd., 928/635-4010, 6:30am-9pm daily) is within the Grand Canyon Railway and offers clothing, books, toys, and unique train-related gifts.

Recreation

If you've ever wanted to move mountains, dig giant holes, or operate life-size Tonka toys, the **Big Toy Playground** (671 S. Garland Prairie Rd., www.bigtoyplayground.com, 928/606-5711, 10am-4:30pm daily, $200-400) is for you. It's a construction amusement park for adults. Standard sessions are 90 minutes. No experience is required.

The **Elephant Rocks Golf Course** (2200 Country Club Dr., 928/635-4935, www.elephant-rocks.com, 6:30am-6pm daily Apr.-Oct., greens fees $25-64) was designed in the 1920s. Today it's a city-owned, 18-hole championship course named after the massive lava rocks on the property that resemble the shape of elephants.

Route 66 Zipline (200 N. Grand Canyon Blvd., 928/635-5358, http://ziplineroute66.com, 10am-7pm daily in winter, 9am-10pm daily in summer, $12-20) offers a high-flying adventure. Passengers are seated and strapped into a harness that zips across Grand Canyon Boulevard in downtown Williams at 30 miles (48 km) per hour. The zip-line platform is fashioned to resemble a 1950s diner with Route 66 signage and a classic red Chevy. No climbing or hiking is required.

Food

Pine Country Restaurant (107 N. Grand Canyon Blvd., http://pinecountryrestaurant.com, 928/635-9718, 7am-9pm daily, $8-25) serves comfort food for breakfast, lunch, and dinner in a homey setting. From-scratch biscuits start the day off right, while a New York strip steak or a piled-high Navajo taco make for the perfect dinner. Homemade pie for dessert is a must.

Donning cherry-red paint and boasting a large dining patio, the 1950s-themed **Cruiser's Route 66** (233 W. Rte. 66, 928/635-2445, www.cruisers66.com, 11am-9pm daily) serves up cold beer, stacked burgers, and friendly service, replete with endearments like "sweetie" and "hon." Let it be known—the milk shakes are delicious.

Rod's Steak House (301 E. Rte. 66, 928/635-2671, www.rods-steakhouse.com, noon-8pm Mon.-Sat., $26-46) opened in 1946, during the heyday of Route 66. Owner Rod Graves raised Hereford cattle and organized the first rodeo in Williams in 1941, and soon after, he and his wife, Helen, opened the restaurant. The menu is classic 1940s-era steakhouse, and the steer-shaped neon sign is photo-worthy.

Red Raven (135 W. Rte. 66, www.redravenrestaurant.com, 928/635-4980, 11am-2pm and 5pm-9pm Wed.-Sat., $21-39) is intimate, artsy, and cozy. The menu includes local craft beers, a hefty wine list, and steak, seafood, and shared plates.

There's a lot going on at **Grand Canyon Coffee and Cafe** (137 W. Railroad Ave., 928/635-4907, www.grandcanyoncoffeeandcafe.com, 6am-3pm Sun.-Thurs., 6am-7pm Fri.-Sat., $7-10). With a menu featuring dishes influenced by Mexican, American, and Chinese cuisines, this eatery offers something for everyone. Solid picks include huevos rancheros, sweet and sour chicken, and the cheeseburger with green chile.

With so many steakhouses in Williams, **Dara Thai** (145 W. Rte. 66, 928/635-2201, 11am-2pm and 5pm-8pm Mon.-Sat., $8-12) might be the best place for a vegetarian meal. The small dining room is not a good option for groups, but service is fast and friendly so the tables turn quickly.

Goldie's Route 66 Diner (425 E. Rte. 66, 928/635-4466, 7am-9pm daily, $6-20) is a mid-century diner with a cantilevered counter and a dining room with glass walls.

Accommodations

The **Red Garter Inn** (137 Railroad Ave., 800/328-1484, www.redgarter.com, $155-189) is a beautifully restored Victorian saloon and bordello from 1897 that teems with history. The rooms with period furniture, high ceilings, and balconies overlook the Grand Canyon Railway depot and are just steps away from art galleries and restaurants.

For a clean and cozy resting spot, **The Lodge on Route 66** (200 E. Rte. 66, 928/635-4534, www.thelodgeonroute66.com, $160-260) sits right in the heart of Williams within walking distance of the historic district.

Sleep in a 1950 Pullman railway car at **The Canyon Motel & RV Park** (1900

Historic Rte. 66, www.thecanyonmotel. com, 928/635-9371, call for rates), a vintage, escape-from-the-ordinary lodging experience. Bonus features are the indoor pool, horseshoe pit, and laundry facilities, which come in handy on a long road trip.

The ★ **Grand Canyon Railway Hotel** (235 N. Grand Canyon Blvd., 928/635-4010, www.thetrain.com, $169-359) is next door to the Grand Canyon Railway and one block from downtown Williams. Designed to look like an early 20th-century hotel, the Grand Canyon offers an elegant throwback to the days of rail travel. Before bedding down for the night, order a hot chocolate and sit by the fireplace in the grand lobby.

◈ Back on 66

As you leave Williams, head west on Railroad Avenue (Rte. 66) to I-40. Drive about 20 miles (32 km) west on I-40 and take Exit 146 (SR-89 S). Turn right (north) on SR-89 (also called Business I-40) and drive west into Ash Fork. SR-89 (Business I-40) turns into Lewis Street, which is one-way.

Ash Fork

In 1960, the Santa Fe Railway moved the rail line north, and as a result, Ash Fork lost about half its population because the railway employed most residents. Today, Ash Fork has a large number of stone quarries and calls itself "The Flagstone Capital of the World."

Sights

Ash Fork had a large Harvey House called Escalante that was built in 1907 and closed in 1948. A scale model of Escalante can be found in the small, hyper-local **Ash Fork Historical Society's Route 66 Museum** (901 W. Old Route 66, 928/637-0204, 9am-3pm Mon.-Fri., free). To get there from Business I-40/Lewis Ave., turn left at 8th Street; the museum will be on the right.

Your epic Route 66 road trip isn't complete until you get a pic of the now-defunct **DeSoto's Salon** (314 W. Lewis Ave.), a former 1958 Texaco station with a 1960 DeSoto sitting on the roof—with Elvis in the driver's seat.

Food

If you're hungry, **Lulu Belle's BBQ** (33 W. Lewis Ave., www.lulubellesbbq.com, 928/637-9818, 11am-8pm daily, $10-25) serves savory barbecue, tender steaks, and twice-baked potatoes with crispy corn on the cob and decadent cast-iron cobbler. There's also the **Ranch House Cafe** (111 W. Park Ave., 928/637-2710, 6am-8pm daily, $10), with homemade green chile, chicken-fried steak, and patty melts.

◈ Back on 66

As you leave Ash Fork on Business I-40/Lewis Street, rejoin I-40 and drive 5 miles (8 km) west to Exit 139. Turn right onto Crookton Road (Rte. 66), where you can finally ditch I-40 and begin 159 miles (260 km) of pristine Route 66, the longest unbroken stretch of the Mother Road.

The Guardian Angel of Route 66

Born on Route 66 just as the Mother Road was being constructed, **Angel Delgadillo** has seen it all—from the military convoys during World War II that used the route to transport supplies to the postwar motorists who traveled on holiday. As anyone who has met Angel will tell you, he's a warm-hearted, genuine soul with a big smile and a bigger heart.

In 1950, he opened his barbershop in Seligman on Route 66, eventually moving it to a different location in 1972 to take advantage of the traffic. Because of the sheer number of cars rolling through during that time, Angel recalls sometimes having to wait 15 minutes before he could cross the street to walk home. After the road's decommission in 1985, Angel was instrumental in preserving the heritage of the Mother Road in Arizona, and in keeping Seligman alive. He founded the Historic Route 66 Association of Arizona, started selling Route 66 souvenirs in a gift shop/visitors center, and now feeds hungry tourists at Delgadillo's Snow Cap Drive-In. His shop and restaurant are two of the most popular sights on Route 66. Angel has been interviewed 300 times and featured in 70 magazines and television outlets as the unofficial spokesperson and the beloved guardian angel of Route 66.

Seligman

Seligman may be small—it's basically a one-street town—but it's mighty, largely in part to the efforts of resident barber and business owner Angel Delgadillo, who founded the Historic Route 66 Association of Arizona in 1987. He, along with other locals, worked tirelessly to keep the historic segments of their portion of the Mother Road protected, including the iconic vintage **Supai Motel sign.** Today, Seligman is the first stop heading west on the longest uninterrupted stretch of Route 66.

Sights
★ Delgadillo's Snow Cap Drive-In
Route 66, which is also called Chino Street, goes right through the heart of Seligman. Once you arrive, keep an eye out for **Delgadillo's Snow Cap Drive-In** (301 W. Rte. 66, 928/422-3291, 10am-6pm daily spring-fall, $10) on the left. Grab an ice-cream cone at the Snow Cap and then walk down one block west to **Angel & Vilma Delgadillo's Route 66 Gift Shop and Visitor Center** (22265 W. Rte. 66, 928/422-3352, www.route66giftshop. com, daily 9am-5pm). Ask for Angel. He is one of the warmest people you'll ever meet and a great storyteller with extensive knowledge about Route 66. His stories inspired John Lasseter, the producer of the Pixar classic *Cars*.

Food and Accommodations
Westside Lilo's (22855 W. Rte. 66, 928/422-5456, www.westsidelilos.com, 7am-9pm daily, $15) combines happy service, huge portions of home-style American fare, cold beers, and all-day breakfast. It's a road-tripper's dream.

Route 66 Roadrunner (22330 W. Rte. 66, 928/232-2004, www. route66roadrunner.com, 7am-7pm daily, $5-12) is a gift shop, café, and coffee bar located in a vintage building that was formerly a 1936 Chevy garage.

Both locals and tourists love the buffalo burgers at the **Road Kill Café** (22830 W. Rte. 66, 928/422-3554, 7am-9pm daily, $8-20). They also serve hearty breakfasts with crispy hash browns and peanut butter French toast.

The **Canyon Lodge** (22340 W. Rte. 66, 928/422-3255, www.route66canyonlodge. com, $75) has immaculate Route 66, Marilyn Monroe, and Elvis-themed rooms with pictures and memorabilia on the wall.

The **Historic Route 66 Motel** (22750 W. Rte. 66, 928/422-3204, $75) has super clean rooms with free Wi-Fi, free parking, and awesome Route 66 bedspreads. What more could you ask for?

The **Aztec Motel & Gift Shop** (22200 W. Rte. 66, 928/422-3055, $60) is a quirky, family-owned property that is loved by frequent returnees. Enjoy murals painted to look like real life street scenes, clusters of fake-but-adorable forest animals, and old-school motel keys.

A cool neon sign illuminates the way to **Supai Motel** (22450 W. Rte. 66, 928/422-4153, www.supaimotelseligman.com, $62-78), where the accommodations are simple but clean. You'll enjoy free Wi-Fi, free parking, and an easy walk to Seligman's best offerings.

◈ Back on 66

As you leave Seligman, drive west on Route 66 for about 20 miles (32 km) until you reach the Grand Canyon Caverns.

Grand Canyon Caverns

The **Grand Canyon Caverns** (Rte. 66, mile marker 115, Peach Springs, 928/422-3223, www.gccaverns.com, 9am-5pm daily, $22-100) are the largest dry caverns in the United States and range 200-300 feet (61-91 m) deep. The four cave tours vary from 25 minutes to 2.5 hours in length. Also on-site are a classic gas station, a restaurant, and a gift shop.

Accommodations

The **Grand Canyon Caverns** (928/422-3223, www.gccaverns.com/rooms-packages) provides multiple lodging options, including **The Caverns Inn** ($100), a three-bedroom **Bunkhouse** ($230), and **The Cavern Suite** ($800), a motel room located 22 stories underground. There is also an **RV and Campground** (928/422-3223, first-come, first-served, $40) with 48 hookup sites for

Delgadillo's Snow Cap Drive-In

RVs and "open-air rooms" for campers; amenities include flush toilets, showers, and a swimming pool.

◈ Back on 66
Drive 12 miles (19.3 km) west on Historic Route 66 to Peach Springs.

Peach Springs

As you drive west on Route 66, you'll reach Peach Springs, the tribal headquarters for the Hualapai (pronounced "WALL-ah-pie"; the name means "people of the tall-pines") Indian Reservation. In the 1880s, the peach trees in the area led folks to the water source that was eventually used to water steam-engine trains. The **Hualapai Tribal Forestry** (863 Rte. 66) is on the north side of the road in an old stone building erected in 1928. It was formerly operated as the Peach Tree Trading Post, where the Hualapai

swapped craft items for food, clothing, and medicine. It was also a meeting place for people to discuss the local news and gossip. When Route 66 came through, there were several cafés, businesses, motor courts, and a Fred Harvey restaurant that served travelers.

Food
Diamond Creek Restaurant (900 Rte. 66, 928/769-2800, 6:30am-8:30pm daily, $7-18) serves standard fare and American Indian specialties such as fry bread, Hualapai stews, and tacos.

◈ Back on 66
As you leave Peach Springs, head west on Route 66 and pass through the ghost town of Truxton.

Truxton

The now-closed **Frontier Motel** (16118 E. Rte. 66) opened in 1951 with a landmark sign that has been restored with the support of the Historic Route 66 Association of Arizona and the National Park Service's Route 66 Corridor Preservation Program.

◈ Back on 66
Less than 10 miles (16.1 km) west of Truxton is the town of Valentine.

Valentine

Keepers of the Wild Nature Park (13441 E. Rte. 66, www.keepersofthewild.org, 928/769-1800, 9am-5pm Wed.-Mon., $20) is a nonprofit sanctuary for abandoned, neglected, and retired wildlife. Lions, tigers, bears, primates, wolves, and coyotes find a home here. For an additional $10, you can tack on a guided Safari Tour or Feeding Tour.

Just down the road from the wildlife sanctuary is the **Truxton Canyon Training School,** a boarding school that forced

American Indians (mostly Hualapai) to assimilate into mainstream American culture. The school was in operation from 1903 to 1937, when the children were separated from their families and subjected to hard labor.

In the town of Valentine, turn right (northwest) on Music Mountain Circle. The Truxton Canyon Training School building is on the southeast side of the road.

◈ Back on 66

To return to Route 66, continue straight a few hundred feet until Music Mountain Circle dead-ends. Take a left (southeast) and drive 250 feet (76 m) to Route 66 and turn right (west).

Hackberry

Just around the bend from Valentine is the once-thriving mining town of Hackberry, which dates back to 1874. When the railroad came through in 1882, the town "moved" 4 miles (6.4 km) from its original site and became a major loading stop for cattle. A silver mine earned almost $3 million before closing in 1919. Soon after, Hackberry became a ghost town.

When Route 66 came through in 1926, the **Hackberry General Store** (11255 E. Rte. 66, 928/769-2605, 8am-6pm daily) became a major service stop. It helped revive Hackberry until I-40 bypassed the town, and people abandoned it again. According to the *Victoria Advocate,* Bob Waldmire, the late Route 66 artist and the owner of the Hackberry General Store, was believed to be the sole resident of Hackberry from 1992 to 1997. Today, the store is a living museum with vintage gas pumps, old signs, a bright red 1956 Corvette, and lots of souvenirs and Route 66 memorabilia.

Just 6 miles (9.7 km) west of the Hackberry General Store, the kitsch continues with a 14-foot-tall (4.3-m) tiki sculpture, the *Giganticus Headicus,* which looks like a partially buried Easter Island head. It can be found at the corner of Antares Road near the old Kozy Corner Trailer Court.

◈ Back on 66

From Hackberry, Route 66 heads north for 6 miles (9.7 km) and then dips southwest for 20 miles (32 km) into Kingman.

Kingman

Kingman sits in the Hualapai Valley between the Hualapai and Cerbat mountain ranges. Founded in 1882 as a railroad town, Kingman became a major supply center for ranchers and miners. Approaching town on Route 66, the road becomes East Andy Devine Avenue, the name of a character actor often featured as a devoted, comic-relief sidekick in Westerns. (Devine was the wagon driver in John Ford's *Stagecoach.*) Don't miss the hand-painted car names on the **Old Trails Garage building,** or its illuminated retro neon Packard sign.

◈ Pre-1940 Alignment

To drive the scenic, paved pre-1940 alignment from Route 66 (Andy Devine Ave.), turn left (south) on 4th Street. After about 1,000 feet (305 m), follow the main road as it curves to the right (southwest) onto Old Trails Road. Soon after it passes under a railroad trestle, slow down; the road takes a sharp left and then narrows between boulders on a blind curve. Once the road veers away from the railroad tracks, turn around and drive back to the post-1940 alignment via 4th Street and take a left (west) on Andy Devine Avenue.

Sights
Powerhouse Visitor Center
The **Powerhouse Visitor Center** (120 W. Andy Devine Ave., 928/753-9889, 9am-4pm Tues.-Sat., $4) is also the headquarters of the **Route 66 Museum.** The

Neon Photo Ops

Wigwam Motel in Holbrook

We live in a digital, high-definition age, which means we don't get to see classic signage illuminated by blinking, flickering neon bulbs anymore. Not so on Route 66. This road trip boasts some of the best retro neon signs, many of them more than half a century old. This list offers up photo-worthy signs—for motor courts, diners, gas stations, and more—that you'll want to make a part of your trip.

♦ **Wigwam Motel,** Holbrook (page 251)

♦ **Orpheum Theater,** Flagstaff (page 261)

♦ **The World Famous Sultana Bar,** Williams (page 282)

♦ **Supai Motel,** Seligman (page 285)

♦ **Old Trails Garage,** Kingman (page 288)

♦ **El Trovatore Motel,** Kingman (page 292)

museum depicts the historical evolution of Route 66 with vibrant murals, photos, an old Studebaker, life size dioramas of a Dust Bowl family, and wall-size quotes from *The Grapes of Wrath*. The Powerhouse is located in the former Desert Power & Light Company building, which was built in two phases in 1907 and 1911. This light company supplied the power to build Hoover Dam. The center provides info on a walking tour with 27 places to explore in and around downtown Kingman.

The entry fee includes admission to the nearby **Mohave Museum** (400 W. Beale St., 928/753-3195, www.mohavemuseum. org, 9am-4pm Tues.-Fri., $4), which has an extensive Hualapai culture display and a section dedicated to the actor Andy Devine.

Hualapai Mountain Park

If you want to hike, bike, camp, or sleep in the mountains, the **Hualapai Mountain Park** (6250 Hualapai Mountain Rd., https://parks.mohavecounty.us,

Kingman

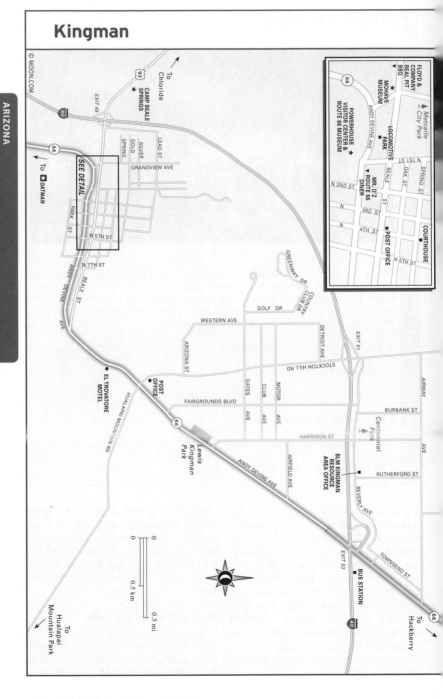

ARIZONA

877/757-0915, $20-100) has tepees and cabins (for up to 12 people) equipped with stoves, heaters, and refrigerators. There are 10 miles (16.1 km) of hiking trails that offer magnificent views of the landscape.

To get there from Route 66, turn left (southeast) onto Hualapai Mountain Rd. (SR-147) and drive about 11 miles (17.7 km) until you reach the ranger station on your right. If you use your GPS, it will take you past the station. If you reach the Hualapai Mountain Resort, you've gone too far; the ranger station is about 1 mile (1.6 km) back.

Camp Beale Springs
Camp Beale Springs (928/757-7919, dawn-dusk daily, free, day pass required) is where the Hualapai were interned in 1871 in barracks until the infamous forced Trail of Tears march. The reservoir built here is still partially standing today, and the area is used for hiking and a picnic site. There is a historical marker at the site to pay homage to the Hualapai who suffered here.

Before heading to Camp Beale Springs, get a day pass (free) from the Powerhouse Visitor Center. Camp Beale Springs is on the northwest edge of Kingman. To get there from Route 66, turn right (north) on 1st Street and a quick left (west) onto West Beale Street. After about 1 mile (1.6 km), take a right (northeast) onto Fort Beal Drive. Camp Beal Springs is less than a mile west of the intersection of Fort Beale Drive and Wagon Trail Road.

Food and Accommodations
Floyd & Company Real Pit BBQ (420 E. Beale St., 928/757-8227, 11am-2pm and 4pm-7pm Tues.-Thurs., 11am-8pm Fri.-Sat., $15-30) smokes its meat with hickory wood and dishes out southern comfort with recipes that have been gathered over six generations from three families.

Top to bottom: Mr. D'z Route 66 Diner; Route 66 signage; murals in Kingman

For pizzas and pastas, try **Vito's Italian Cuisine** (2775 E. Northern Ave., 928/757-7279, 11am-9pm daily, $15-20).

★ **Mr. D'z Route 66 Diner** (105 E. Andy Devine Ave., 928/718-0066, 7am-9pm daily, $12) is known for its Harley Dogs, a quarter-pound hot dog served on a hoagie roll with spicy sauce. The retro diner is decked out in vintage Americana with turquoise and pink booths, a black-and-white checkered floor, and a blue 1954 Chevy parked outside.

El Trovatore Motel (1440 E. Andy Devine Ave., 928/753-6520, www.eltrovatoremotel.com, $60) is one of the few pre-WWII Kingman motels still standing. Built in 1937, it was originally a service station, and the tourist court was added in 1939 with rooms costing a mere $3 per night. El Trovatore holds the honor of being the first air-conditioned motel in the state. Today, it's a refurbished hotel with Hollywood-themed rooms that celebrate former guests Clark Gable, Marilyn Monroe, and James Dean.

◈ Back on 66

Make sure you get fuel in Kingman before you head to Oatman. Leaving Kingman via Route 66 (W. Andy Devine Ave.), follow signs to Oatman. You'll be driving next to I-40; keep an eye out for Exit 44. Turn right (west) on Shinarump Road and cross under I-40. Drive 0.3 mile (0.5 km) and turn left (southwest) on Oatman Road.

If you're making the side trip to Chloride, take U.S. 93 north and then backtrack to Kingman.

◈ Side Trip: U.S. 93 to Chloride

Getting There

From Kingman, take U.S. 93 (W. Beale St.) north for about 18 miles (29 km). Turn right (east) at the Chloride billboard at County Road 125. Chloride is 4 miles (6.4 km) north up the road.

the ghost town of Chloride

You Could Fry an Egg

You've heard the phrase: "It's so hot outside you could fry an egg on the sidewalk." The locals in Oatman test this theory with the annual **Oatman Sidewalk Egg Fry.** The event is just what it sounds like: Every July 4 at noon, when the sun shines directly from above and the temperature crests at about 115°F (46°C), contestants crack eggs on a frying pan set on the pavement—some even cook directly on the road. After 15 minutes, a judge declares a winner: the egg that looks the best.

Sights

Just north of Kingman is the ghost town of Chloride, named after the silver chloride ore discovered here. Chloride was a busy town with more than 70 mines in operation. The **post office,** established in 1862, is the oldest continuously operating post office in the state of Arizona. Chloride also has an old general store with some original items; 30 vintage tractors; gift shops; hiking trails; and what may possibly be the largest collection of homes with junkyard art ever.

Oatman Highway

The Oatman Highway snakes its way through the sharp switchbacks of Sitgreaves Pass and over the Black Mountains, dotted with ramshackle houses and tattered windmills, until reaching Cool Springs. This scenic backcountry highway is highly recommended, but it is very steep—vehicles over 40 feet (12 m) should not attempt it—and drivers must also watch for bighorn sheep and wild burros on the road. It's hard to believe this was a major thoroughfare on Route 66.

Cool Springs

The 1920s gas station in Cool Springs was in ruins before Ned Leuchtner, a real estate agent from Chicago, bought it in 2001 and restored it based on old photographs. After Route 66 bypassed the Oatman Highway in 1953, the station was abandoned within a decade. There used to be a café, bar, and cabins on the property, but today only a gas station remains, with museum-quality tall red Mobil gas pumps (not operational). The spot does offer good cats and cool drinks.

★ Oatman

As you head west on Route 66, tight hairpin curves lead to **Oatman,** a mining town named after Olive Oatman. The legend goes that, at the age of seven, Olive Oatman was kidnapped and enslaved by Apache—but it's more likely she was taken by the Tolkepaya (Western Yavapai) tribe and sold to the Mojave,

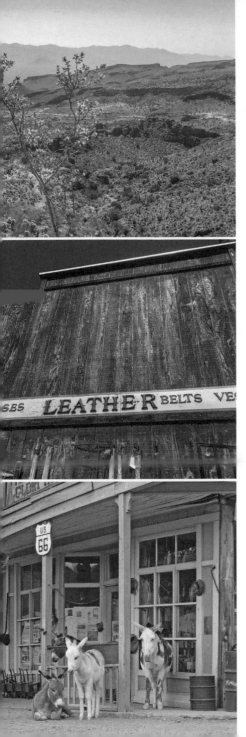

who then tattooed her chin. Some sources report that the chin tattoo was the mark of a slave; others believe that most of the women in this tribe received blue cactus chin tattoos as a way to identify them as Mojave in the afterlife. In 1857, when she was 19, authorities at Fort Yuma rescued Olive, trading her for blankets, beads, and a white horse.

Today, Oatman is a gold rush town with plank sidewalks and wild burros roaming Route 66, blocking traffic and shaking down tourists for treats. The burros are direct descendants of those that the miners brought to the area in the late 1800s. From 1908 to 1915, Oatman was a hopping town with 20 saloons within a three-block radius, more than 10,000 people, and two gold mines worth more than $25 million. By comparison, Kingman at that time had a population of about 300 people. In 1941, the U.S. government halted gold-mining operations, as metals other than gold were needed for the war effort.

With the closing of the mines, Oatman's population dwindled from 10,000 to 200. As the railroad community also began to decline, a spring about 5 miles (8 km) away ceased being used to water the trains. To avoid the tortuous curves along the mountain road, a new alignment of Route 66 was routed via I-40 in 1952. After the gas station shut down, the population dwindled to three people and remained that way for 30 years. It wasn't until the late 1970s, when a Route 66 organization promoted the original Route 66 alignment, that the town came back to life.

General Store

As you approach Oatman, be mindful of the roaming wild burros. They are not shy and will approach the car looking for food. If you want to feed them, visit the **General Store** (180 Main St.,

Top to bottom: Oatman Highway; an old shop in Oatman; Oatman burros

928/768-9448, www.oatmangeneralstore.com, 10:30am-5pm daily), which sells burro pellets and carrots. The **Ghost Rider Gunfighters** (928/234-0344, www.oatmanghostriders.com) stage a gunfight in front of the store at 1:30pm and 3:15pm daily.

Food and Drinks

The walls and ceiling of **The Oatman Hotel & Restaurant** (181 Main St., 928/768-4408, 10am-6pm Mon.-Fri., 8am-6pm Sat.-Sun., $8-15) are covered in dollar bills, a reference to a time when miners started getting paid with paper rather than gold dust and coins. However, the mines were so filthy that any paper money would be destroyed. Miners needed a safe place to keep their money, so they set up a system with their local bartender to put a dollar bill behind the bar with their name on it to cover their drinking tab. (In the early 1900s, a beer was about $0.05 and a shot of whiskey was about $0.10-0.15.) The oldest dollar bill, from 1923, is framed behind the bar. Today, the walls are papered with more than 100,000 notes, and the tradition continues as tourists leave their own signed dollar bills wherever they can find a spot.

Though Carole Lombard and Clark Gable honeymooned upstairs, the hotel itself is no longer in operation. The restaurant, however, serves pulled pork sandwiches, buffalo burgers, and donkey ears (fries).

Judy's Saloon (260 Main St., 928/768-4463, 10am-10pm daily) is the place to shoot pool and catch up on the local gossip.

◆ Back on 66

Head west on Route 66 out of Oatman, following the Oatman-Topock Highway southwest for 3.5 miles (5.6 km). Turn left (southeast) on SR-10 and continue following the Oatman-Topock Highway for 20 miles (32 km) to the Arizona-California border.

◆ Side Trip: London Bridge

In 1968, Robert McCulloch bought **London Bridge** (yes, the famous one in England) for $2.46 million and had it taken apart brick by brick and shipped across the Atlantic Ocean to the desert town of Lake Havasu. Don't be mistaken: This is not London's Tower Bridge, a Victorian Gothic structure that spans 800 feet (244 m) and has 200-foot (61-m) towers. This is an impressive 1830s granite bridge with five semi-elliptical arches that gracefully frame Lake Havasu.

The **Lake Havasu City Visitor Center** (422 English Village, 928/855-5655, www.golakehavasu.com, 9am-5pm daily, $10) has a 90-minute walking tour of the bridge.

Getting There

From Oatman, head west on the Oatman-Topock Highway for 25 miles (40 km) as it dips south toward I-40. Take I-40 east for 9 miles (14.5 km) to SR-95 (right); follow SR-95 south for 19 miles (31 km). Turn right onto Palo Verde Boulevard South and take a quick left onto London Bridge Road.

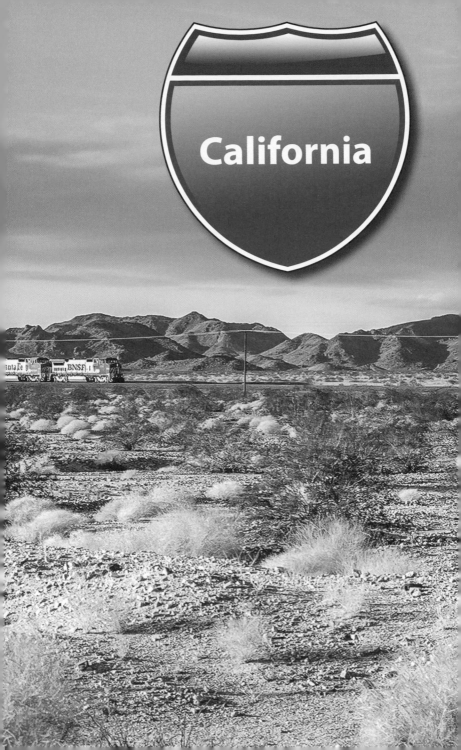

California

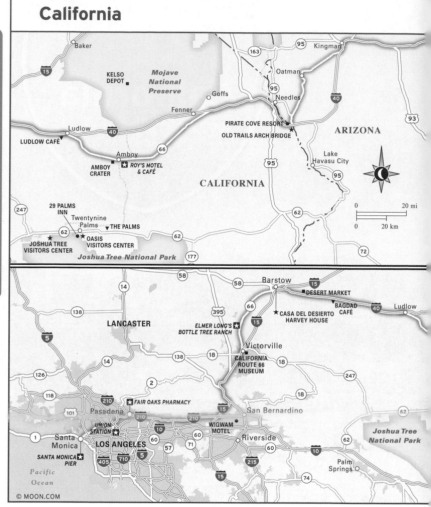

© MOON.COM

As the Mother Road crosses the Colorado River—also the border of Arizona and California—a parched and desolate desert unfolds before you.

This is the same dry and barren landscape that greeted more than 200,000 Dust Bowl survivors in the 1930s. (When the Joad family first set eyes on California in John Steinbeck's *The Grapes of Wrath*, they feared they had traded one barren homeland for another.) As travelers attempted to enter California, many faced armed police officers who turned away "undesirables." About 40 percent of those immigrants who did make it across the state border picked cotton and grapes in the San Joaquin Valley, earning about $1 a day.

Highlights

★ **Roy's Motel & Café, Amboy:** Opened in 1938, Roy's was the only place to find gas, food, and lodging in the middle of the Mojave; today it's home to one of the most famous neon signs on Route 66 (page 312).

★ **Elmer Long's Bottle Tree Ranch, Oro Grande:** Folk artist Elmer Long created a veritable forest of glass and light in his front yard with 200 installations of "trees" made from antique bottles and other found-art objects (page 322).

★ **Fair Oaks Pharmacy, Pasadena:** In operation since 1915, this soda fountain, pharmacy, and restaurant is a neighborhood staple (page 328).

★ **Union Station, Los Angeles:** See the architectural marvel and cultural hub known as the "last of the great train stations" (page 332).

★ **Santa Monica Pier, Santa Monica:** Route 66's journey culminates at this carnival pier stretching over the Pacific Ocean (page 340).

Best Restaurants

★ **Bagdad Café, Newberry Springs:** This desert gem offers hearty burgers (page 318).

★ **Emma Jean's Holland Burger, Victorville:** This classic Route 66 diner has been around since 1947 (page 323).

★ **Mitla Café, San Bernardino:** Four generations of one family have kept this Mexican-food restaurant going for more than 80 years (page 325).

★ **Clifton's, Los Angeles:** Celebrate the end of your Route 66 trip at this legendary spot (page 337).

★ **Musso & Frank Grill, Los Angeles:** Sip a martini Don Draper-style at this iconic Hollywood lounge (page 338).

This eerie, empty introduction to the state is in direct contrast to the sun-splashed beaches of Los Angeles and Santa Monica—also the end of Route 66. Yet the dry, cracked landscape and bizarre Joshua trees hold their own solitary beauty. As you travel west on Route 66, the lonely vistas give way to the green pastures, swaying palms, and fruit trees of the Inland Empire. Upon your arrival in Los Angeles, culture-rich museums, luxe shopping, and buzzing nightlife let you indulge your cosmopolitan side before you slip on the flip-flops and succumb to the laid-back beach vibe of Santa Monica and the Pacific Ocean.

Planning Your Time

With approximately 315 miles (505 km) of Route 66 still intact in California, there is a lot of ground to cover in your final **two days.** Needles marks the California state line, and it's a remote and desolate 140 miles (225 km) to the next service town of Barstow, an overnight option. Los Angeles is about a five-hour drive west of Needles, but if you stay true to Route 66, add at least a few hours to your travel time to account for inland traffic. Those with no time to spare can push on to Los Angeles (traffic willing), but a better option is to skip Barstow and stretch your journey another day with a side trip south to Joshua Tree instead.

Once you arrive in Los Angeles, consider staying one night in downtown LA (the original end of Route 66) and one night in Santa Monica (the post-1930s terminus). After a long drive, this will make life easier when it comes to navigating one of the most gridlocked cities in the country.

Driving Considerations

Crossing the California border, make sure you have a full tank of **gas;** otherwise, gas up in Needles because you'll soon be driving through the Mojave Desert, where fuel is scarce. A worthwhile excursion is to spend a day or two in Joshua Tree, which involves a beautiful three-hour drive through one of the most remote areas in the country. Make sure your car is gassed up and in good working order—there is no cell phone service for most of the drive. Spend the night in Twentynine Palms or head west on SR-62 to the town of Joshua Tree.

Best Accommodations

★ **Wigwam Motel, San Bernardino:** Book a tepee for the night at this iconic Route 66 stop (page 325).

★ **Hotel Figueroa, Los Angeles:** Relish the glamour of 1920s LA at this restored Spanish Colonial boutique hotel (page 339).

★ **The Line, Los Angeles:** Location, location, location. This modern hotel is in the heart of one of LA's most culturally diverse 'hoods (page 339).

★ **Hotel Shangri-La, Santa Monica:** With its ship-inspired architecture and Streamline Moderne decor, this hotel is more than just a place to sleep (page 343).

Getting There

Starting Points

Car

From the California border, Route 66 parallels I-40 east to west into Barstow. In between, an isolated section of the alignment follows the National Trails Highway through Amboy; however, the road is rough and subject to frequent closure during heavy rains and flash floods. From Barstow, Route 66 turns south, still following the National Trails Highway and paralleling I-15 through Victorville into San Bernardino and the Inland Empire. A good stretch of Route 66 through the Inland Empire is along Foothill Boulevard, which at one time was flanked with fruit trees and is now lined with strip malls. From Foothill Boulevard west is where you will begin to encounter LA's infamous traffic, which will not ebb until you reach the shores of the Pacific.

Car Rental

Enterprise (8734 Bellanca Ave., Los Angeles, 310/649-5400, www.enterprise.com, 24 hours daily) at Los Angeles International Airport has affordable prices and a wide selection of cars (from the baggage claim, walk outside to the center island and wait at the Rental Car Shuttles sign). **Budget** (2501 N. Hollywood Way, Burbank, 818/841-0447, www.budget.com, 5:30am-11pm Mon.-Fri., 6am-11pm Sat.-Sun.) offers efficient customer service at Hollywood Burbank Airport. **Hertz** (1426 Santa Monica Blvd., Santa Monica, 310/394-2449, www.hertz.com, 8am-5pm Mon.-Fri., 9am-noon Sat.) is located right on Route 66 in Santa Monica. **Avis** (888 S. Figueroa St., Los Angeles, 213/533-8400, www.avis.com, 8am-4pm Mon.-Fri., 8am-1pm Sat.-Sun.) has a convenient location less than 1 mile (1.6 km) from the original downtown terminus of Route 66.

Air

Route 66 is best driven westward, but if you start the trip in Los Angeles, you have two airports to choose from. **Los Angeles International Airport** (LAX, 1 World Way, Los Angeles, 855/463-5252, www.flylax.com) is the second-busiest airport in the country. Flying into **Hollywood Burbank Airport** (BUR, 2627 N. Hollywood Way, Burbank, 818/840-8840, www.hollywoodburbankairport.com) may be a better option—it's less crowded and easier to get in and out. Avoid flying into Ontario International Airport in the Inland Empire; you will have to backtrack and drive west through LA traffic to begin the Route 66 road trip. For domestic flights, plan to be at the airport two hours before the departure; for international flights, arrive three hours early. The I-405 freeway is the main route to LAX, but if it's backed up, you can get off the freeway and take La Cienega Boulevard instead.

Train and Bus

Six of the seven commuter Metrolink rail lines run through **Union Station** (800 N. Alameda St., 800/371-5465, www.metrolinktrains.com) in downtown Los Angeles. Metrolink connects Los Angeles to San Bernardino, Riverside, Orange, San Diego, and Ventura counties. From Union Station, cabs (or the metro) offer service to downtown car rental companies.

While some Greyhound buses stop at Union Station, the main depot for **Greyhound** (1716 E. 7th St., 213/629-8401, www.greyhound.com) operates in an industrial area just east of downtown Los Angeles. If you're in the middle of downtown, do not walk to the Greyhound station, as you'll pass through some sketchy areas. It's best to take a taxi or the metro.

Park Moabi

As I-40 heads west into California, take the Park Moabi Road exit (Exit 153) and turn right (north). Continue driving north, crossing railroad tracks in about 0.5 mile (0.8 km). Turn right (east) onto National Trails Highway/Route 66. In less than 1 mile (1.6 km), the road curves right to head south. The road then passes under I-40 in 0.2 mile (0.3 km). Continue south on National Trails Highway.

Sights
Old Trails Arch Bridge

In about 200 feet (61 m), look for the **Old Trails Arch Bridge,** an 800-foot (244-m) span that carried cars across the Colorado River from 1916 to 1948; it was part of the original Route 66 alignment when the road opened in 1926. When built, the bridge was the longest and lightest of its kind, an engineering wonder thanks to a unique cantilevered construction system. The bridge was featured in the 1940 film *The Grapes of Wrath* and became listed in the National Register of Historic Places in 1988. Though no longer drivable today, it's a graceful architectural marvel and a link to Route 66's past.

Pirate Cove Resort

At the intersection of Park Moabi Road and the National Trails Highway is **Pirate Cove Resort** (100 Park Moabi Rd., Needles, 866/301-3000, www.piratecoveresort.com), which sits on the banks of the Colorado River nestled among palm trees and white-sand beaches. It's a little slice of paradise in the middle of a stark desert. The riverfront resort offers boat rentals, yacht charters, waterfront cabins, and boat tours through the red rock canyon of Topock Gorge and Havasu National Wildlife Refuge. Dry-land adventures include off-road vehicle rentals.

The resort's **accommodations** ($249-399) include beachfront cabins and marina-adjacent cabins; most have a boat slip. If you'd rather push on to Barstow, at least stop here and enjoy a drink at the beach bar or dine at the pirate-themed **restaurant** (11am-6pm daily, $10-15) while the kids play at the water park.

⬥ Back on 66

Leave Pirate Cove Resort heading south on Park Moabi Road. In 400 feet (122 m), turn right (west) on National Trails Highway (Route 66).

Neon Photo Ops

Santa Monica Pier

We live in a digital, high-definition age, which means we don't get to see classic signage illuminated by blinking, flickering neon bulbs anymore. Not so on Route 66. This road trip boasts some of the best retro neon signs, many of them more than half a century old. This list offers up photo-worthy signs—for motor courts, diners, gas stations, and more—that you'll want to make a part of your trip.

♦ **Welcome to Las Vegas,** Las Vegas (page 307)

♦ **Roy's Motel & Café,** Amboy (page 312)

♦ **Route 66 Motel,** Barstow (page 321)

♦ **Santa Monica Pier,** Santa Monica (page 340)

Needles

The town of Needles, named after a rock formation on the Arizona border, is the gateway to Route 66 in California. Founded in 1883, Needles is one of the oldest towns in San Bernardino County. In the late 1880s, the town operated as a major hub for the Santa Fe Railway and served as an icing station for fruits and vegetables that were shipped from inland valley farms in California. In the 1930s, Needles became a welcome haven for Dust Bowl and Depression-era transplants escaping poverty, signifying they had made it to the "land of opportunity."

The town's most famous resident might be Charles Shultz, the creator of the *Peanuts* comic strip. Shultz lived in Needles from 1928 to 1930. His short stint here inspired the creation of Snoopy's brother Spike, a loner beagle who lived in the Mojave Desert. Several murals in Needles pay homage to Spike, one of Shultz's most offbeat characters.

◈ Route 66 Through Needles

The original 1926-1947 alignment is not intact through Needles; it dead-ends into a sandy wash. However, the 1947-1966 alignment is drivable via Broadway Street.

1947-1966 Alignment

From I-40, take Exit 144 for U.S. 95 and make a slight right onto East Broadway Street (Historic Route 66). Broadway goes left past Quivera Street to become West Broadway Street as it continues through town. Turn left (west) onto Business I-40/Needles Highway for food and lodging.

1926-1947 Alignment

To drive part of the original 1926-1947 alignment, continue straight past Quivera Street onto Front Street. Turn left (south) onto F Street, then right (west) onto Quinn Court. At G Street, turn right (north) and then make the next left (west) onto Front Street. The El Garces Harvey House will be on the north side of Front Street.

Sights

El Garces Harvey House

In 1908, Frances Wilson built the **El Garces Harvey House** (950 Front St. at G St.) to resemble a Greek temple. Today, you can still admire the Grecian columns and fan palms that surround the sprawling structure. Named after the Spanish missionary and explorer Father Francisco Garcés, it originally operated as a freight and passenger depot with a hotel and restaurant. As one of the Harvey Houses that were established along the railroad in the western United States, El Garces was known as the "crown jewel" for its distinctive china, linens, silver, and quality service. For the waitresses who worked in Harvey Houses, getting assigned to El Garces was a coveted position.

El Garces closed as a Harvey House in 1949 and was under the threat of demolition until a group of local residents petitioned to save it in 1993. In 2002, the National Park Service listed El Garces on the National Register of Historic Places. Although the building is not open to the

Top to bottom: welcome sign in Needles; Pirate Cove Resort in Park Moabi; El Garces Harvey House

Needles to Barstow

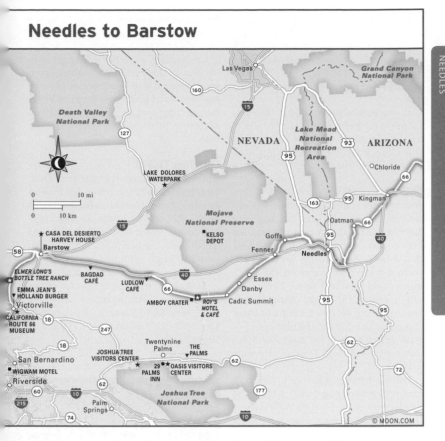

public, you can still wander the grounds to explore the exterior, fully renovated to its former glory.

From I-40 west, take Exit 148 for Five Mile Road, which becomes East Broadway Street (Route 66). Stay on Broadway Street as it bears left through downtown. Turn right (north) onto G Street and drive straight to Front Street. El Garces Harvey House sits alongside the Santa Fe Railway tracks.

Havasu National Wildlife Refuge

Havasu National Wildlife Refuge (www. fws.gov/refuge/havasu, free) is a riparian zone on the California-Arizona border. The refuge provides habitat for 318 species of birds and more than 25 types of dragonflies; desert bighorn sheep scale steep rock faces while coyotes, bobcats, and foxes forage for food. There are multiple ways to get into the refuge, but the **park headquarters** (317 Mesquite Ave., Needles, 760/326-3853, 7am-3:30pm Mon.-Fri.) is in Needles. Make this your first stop for maps and information.

From I-40 in Needles, take the J Street exit (Exit 142) and turn left (southwest). Continue 0.6 mile (1 km), then turn right at the refuge entrance sign. Follow the signs to the administrative office.

Food and Accommodations

The designs on the menu at **The Wagon Wheel** (2420 Needles Hwy., 760/326-4305, www.wagonwheelneedles.com,

6:30am-9:30pm daily, $8-16) are the work of famed Route 66 artist Bob Waldmire. Beyond admiring the art, you can tuck into a savory, slow-cooked pot roast amid authentic 1970s-era digs. You'll find fun Mother Road souvenirs in the gift shop, too.

If you need a place to stay, **Rio Del Sol Inn** (1111 Pashard St., 760/326-5660, www.riodelsolinn.com, $96) is a bright and clean hotel with well-appointed rooms at good prices.

❖ Back on 66

Route 66 from Needles to Barstow is notorious for road closures due to fierce desert storms and monsoons. If you see a temporary sign alerting you to danger ahead, heed the warning. To stay safe, avoid driving over water on the road, which could be a flash flood. These happen in seconds and can be deadly. Before venturing off I-40, check **Cal Trans Road Closures** (http://www.sbcounty.gov) to make sure the roads are clear. For areas that are closed, I-40 is your alternate route.

Follow Broadway through Needles, turning left (west) on Needles Highway (aka Historic Route 66, then W. Broadway St.). The road quickly changes names again, becoming River Road. Stay in the left lane to take National Trails Highway, which splits left after crossing over I-40. Turn left at West Park Road and take I-40 west for 6 miles (9.7 km). Take Exit 133 onto U.S. 95 north (right). Follow Highway 95 north for 6 miles (9.7 km) and turn left onto Goffs Road to follow the pre-1931 alignment.

❖ Side Trip: Las Vegas, Nevada

The only thing Las Vegas and Route 66 have in common is a fun-filled approach to kitsch, which is a good thing. That being said, the glitz and glitter of Las Vegas can be a jarring change from the open-road, small-town, slow and steady vibe of a Route 66 journey.

Las Vegas is a worthy side trip if you won't be in this part of the country again soon, since it's only a few hours from Needles. But if you're able to make Vegas its own trip, separate from your Route 66 adventure, then continue westward to the coast.

Getting There

Las Vegas is about a two-hour drive from Needles and a three-hour drive from Barstow. From Needles, take I-40 west to U.S. 95 north and drive 80 miles (129 km) north. At the U.S. 95 North/U.S. 93 North ramp, continue onto U.S. 93 North into Las Vegas. Follow I-515 North to I-215 West and then to I-15 North, the main freeway through the center of Las Vegas. If you're staying on the Strip, take I-215 West to I-15 North; if you're not, stay on I-515 and take Exit 75 for Las Vegas Boulevard.

Sights
South Strip

In front of the **Bellagio** (3600 Las Vegas Blvd. S., 702/693-7111, www.bellagio.com) choreographed fountains dance to music and lights; the website has the schedule. Crowds gather for the free show, so you might have to angle for a good spot. In the lobby, the **Conservatory and Botanical Garden** exhibits flower-draped gazebos and bridges. The Bellagio is also the home of **Cirque du Soleil's O** (7pm and 9:30pm daily, from $99).

The Cosmopolitan (3708 Las Vegas Blvd. S., 702/698-7000, www.cosmopolitanlasvegas.com) is all glass, crystal, chrome, and sleek chic. Head straight to the glittering **Chandelier** bar and order the secret, off-menu Verbena cocktail.

Mandalay Bay (3950 Las Vegas Blvd. S., 877/632-7700, www.mandalaybay.com) has the **Shark Reef Aquarium,** which showcases 2,000 sea creatures; it also has an 8-foot (2.4-m) Komodo dragon. You can also catch the critically acclaimed **Cirque du Soleil's *Michael Jackson One*** (7pm and 9:30pm Thurs.-Mon., from $69).

About a 10-minute walk south of Mandalay Bay is the iconic **Welcome to Las Vegas** sign. This 1959 landmark glows in all its neon glory in the middle of Las Vegas Boulevard.

Sample sweet confections at the two-story **Hershey's Chocolate World** (3790 Las Vegas Blvd., 702/437-7439, www.hersheyschocolateworldlasvegas.com), shop for goodies, and even customize candy wrappers.

Get big thrills—and views of the New York City skyline—on the **Big Apple Coaster** at **New York-New York Hotel & Casino** (3790 Las Vegas Blvd., 702/740-6616, www.newyorknewyork.com, $17). The roller coaster whisks you past replicas of the Chrysler Building, Statue of Liberty, and other famed NYC sights.

Luxor Hotel & Casino (3990 Las Vegas Blvd. S., 702/262-4000, www.luxor.com)

Las Vegas

is the home of the **Blue Man Group** (7pm and 9:30pm daily, from $59), a captivating show that has entertained more than 25 million people.

Go to the top of the Eiffel Tower at **Paris Las Vegas** (3655 Las Vegas Blvd. S., 877/796-2096, www.caesars.com/paris-las-vegas) or dine at delightful Parisian-themed cafés.

Mid-Strip

The Linq Hotel + Experience (3535 Las Vegas Blvd. S., 800/634-6441, www.caesars.com/linq) is home to **High Roller,** the world's tallest observation wheel. For live music, there's **Brooklyn Bowl,** which combines top musical acts with 32 lanes of bowling.

The Mirage (3400 Las Vegas Blvd. S., 702/791-7111, www.mirage.com) hosts Siegfried and Roy's **Secret Garden and Dolphin Habitat,** a lush tropical garden with dolphins, lions, tigers, and leopards. If you can snag tickets, don't miss **Cirque du Soleil's** *Beatles Love* (7pm and 9:30pm Tues.-Sat., from $79).

Step into Old World Italy with a **gondola ride** ($29/person) through a vibrant Venetian street scene at **The Palazzo** (3325 Las Vegas Blvd. S., 702/607-7777, www.palazzo.com).

Mystère at **Treasure Island Casino** (3300 Las Vegas Blvd. S., 702/894-7111, www.treasureisland.com, 7pm and 9:30pm Fri.-Tues., from $64) set the standard for Cirque du Soleil in Vegas. This high-energy performance is filled with the drama of Shakespeare and the surrealism of Salvador Dali.

Absinthe at **Caesars Palace** (3570 Las Vegas Blvd. S., 855/234-7469, www.caesars.com, 7pm, 8pm, 9pm, 10pm, and 11pm daily, from $99) is a provocative and uncensored circus-style act with raunchy burlesque performers, tightrope walkers, and aerialists.

XS Nightclub at **Wynn Casino** (3131 Las Vegas Blvd. S., 702/770-7000, www.wynnlasvegas.com) is the hottest nightspot in Vegas. Book a cabana near the pool, request bottle service at a table on the dance floor, or soak up the sounds of popular DJs such as Diplo and The Chainsmokers.

The National Atomic Testing Museum (755 E. Flamingo Rd., 702/409-7366, http://nationalatomictestingmuseum.org, 10am-3pm Thurs.-Sun., $22) chronicles the story of our country's nuclear weapons program at the Nevada Test Site, and the cultural impact of the Cold War, with more than 12,000 rare photographs, reports, videos, and artifacts.

Downtown and Fremont Street

Goodfellas and *Casino* fans—and anyone who has a fascination with the Mafia—shouldn't miss the **The Mob Museum** (300 Stewart Ave., 702/229-2734, www.themobmuseum.org, 9am-9pm daily, $29.95). Things you'll see: an underground, re-created Prohibition-era world; Al Capone's personal items; and relics from the 1929 St. Valentine's Day Massacre in Chicago.

Get your neon-sign fix at **The Neon Museum** (770 Las Vegas Blvd. N., 702/387-6366, www.neonmuseum.org, 4pm-midnight daily, $20). Peruse this outdoor museum housing more than 250 vintage signs from the 1930s through the 1990s. A general admission ticket lets you explore at your leisure, or you can take a 45-minute **guided tour** ($28).

Located in the center of the Las Vegas Arts District, **The Arts Factory** (107 E. Charleston Blvd., 702/383-3133, www.dtlvarts.com) is a collective of contemporary artists, photographers, and galleries. The space hosts concerts, poetry readings, and theatrical performances.

Old shipping containers have been converted into a quirky venue at the **Downtown Container Park** (707 Freemont St., 702/359-9982, http://downtowncontainerpark.com). Browse boutique shops, eat and drink at one of dozens of restaurants, and let the kids frolic at the interactive playground. When the sun goes down, be wowed by

The Dome, a high-definition, 360-degree music and light show featuring 14 million pixels.

Food and Drinks
South Strip
America (New York-New York Hotel & Casino, 3790 Las Vegas Blvd., 702/740-6451, www.newyorknewyork.com, 7am-10pm daily, $10-15) is an affordable spot for a quick bite. Check out the giant U.S. wall map highlighting each state's iconic landmarks.

Famed chef Michael Mina offers classic French cuisine at **Bardot Brasserie** (Aria, 3730 Las Vegas Blvd. S., 702/590-7711, www.aria.com, 5pm-10pm Wed.-Sun., 9am-1:30pm Sat.-Sun., $18-45).

Open for breakfast and lunch, **Della's Kitchen** (Delano, 3940 Las Vegas Blvd. S., 702/632-9250, www.delanolasvegas.com, 6:30am-2pm daily, $10-18) is a farmhouse-chic restaurant that serves hormone- and antibiotic-free comfort food using locally sourced ingredients.

You might recognize the **Peppermill Restaurant and Fireside Lounge** (2985 Las Vegas Blvd., 702/735-4177, www.peppermilllasvegas.com, 7am-11pm Sun.-Wed., 7am-2am Thurs.-Sat., $9-35) from famous films. It's been a staple on the Strip since it opened in the 1970s.

Mid-Strip
Bobby Flay's award-winning **Mesa Grill** (Caesars Palace, 3570 Las Vegas Blvd. S., 877/346-4642, www.mesagrill.com, 5pm-11:30pm Wed.-Sun., $15-60) serves zesty southwestern dishes for brunch, lunch, and dinner.

Enjoy Italian fare and brick-oven pizza at **Trevi** (Forum Shops at Caesars Palace, 3500 Las Vegas Blvd. S., 702/735-4663, www.trevi-italian.com, 11am-11pm Sun.-Thurs., 11am-midnight Fri.-Sat., $10-36).

At the **Yardbird Southern Table & Bar** (The Venetian, 3355 Las Vegas Blvd. S., 702/297-6541, www.venetian.com, 11am-11pm Sun.-Thurs., 11am-midnight Fri.-Sat., $10-36), you'll find shared plates, craft cocktails, and inventive takes on down-home cooking.

Sushisamba (The Venetian, 3355 Las Vegas Blvd. S., 702/607-0700, www.venetian.com, noon-11pm Mon.-Thurs., noon-midnight Fri.-Sat., $17-55) serves imaginative dishes that blend Japanese, Peruvian, and Brazilian cuisine.

Lotus of Siam (620 E. Flamingo Rd., 702/735-3033, http://lotusofsiamlv.com, 5:30pm-10pm Mon.-Sun., $15) dishes out the best Thai food in Vegas. Make reservations or arrive early; waits can take up to an hour.

Downtown and Fremont Street
Get authentic Mexican tacos with your choice of tangy sauces at **Tacos El Gordo** (1724 E. Charleston Blvd., 702/251-8226, http://tacoselgordobc.com, 10am-2am Sun.-Thurs., 10am-4am Fri.-Sat., $7-10).

The vegan- and vegetarian-friendly **Bronze Café** (611 Fremont St., 702/586-3401, 7:30am-11pm daily, $10) offers primo coffee and espresso, plus health-conscious sandwiches, salads, smoothies, and sweet treats.

Gastropub cuisine pairs with craft beer at **The Smashed Pig** (509 Fremont St., 702/444-7816, www.thesmashedpig.com, 4pm-9pm Wed.-Thurs., 4pm-11pm Fri., 10am-11pm Sat., 10am-10pm Sun., $8-19).

Accommodations
South Strip
At the luxurious **Aria** (3730 Las Vegas Blvd. S., 702/590-7711, www.aria.com), every guest is treated like a VIP. Each of the tastefully appointed rooms boasts corner views and tablet-controlled temperature, lights, drapes, and sound systems.

The Cosmopolitan (3708 Las Vegas Blvd. S., 702/698-7575, www.cosmopolitanlasvegas.com) is a sophisticated, ultra-glam property with a blend of bold art, hot music, and cool technology.

Waldorf Astoria Las Vegas (3752 Las Vegas Blvd. S. 702/590-8888, www.waldorfastorialasvegas.com) offers the ultimate in comfort and serenity with beautiful accommodations and restaurants helmed by Michelin-starred chefs.

Platinum Hotel & Spa (211 E. Flamingo Rd., 702/365-5000, www.theplatinumhotel.com) is a non-gaming, smoke-free hotel a block from the Strip. Spacious rooms come with balconies, free Wi-Fi, and no resort fees. Pets are welcome.

The accommodations at the non-gaming and smoke-free **Vdara Hotel & Spa** (2600 W. Harmon Ave., 702/590-2111, www.vdara.com) range from studio suites to two-bedroom lofts and penthouses.

Mid-Strip

Artisan Hotel Boutique (1501 W. Sahara Ave., 702/214-4000, www.artisanhotel.com) is an art deco boutique hotel with an impressive collection of art—hence the property's name—on nearly every wall, as well as the ceilings.

The Linq Hotel + Experience (3535 Las Vegas Blvd. S., 800/634-6441, www.caesars.com/linq) is a bright and modern hotel with all of the high-tech, digital amenities you could dream of.

Famed sushi chef Nobu Matsuhisa created **Nobu Hotel** (Caesars Palace, 3570 Las Vegas Blvd. S., 800/727-4923, www.nobucaesarspalace.com), a boutique property with Japanese-inspired decor; hot tea is served in the rooms.

Downtown and Fremont Street

The D (301 Fremont St., 702/388-2400, www.thed.com) has plenty of juicy mob history; it opened in 1980 as The Sundance Hotel and was owned by organized crime gangster Moe Dalitz, also known as "Mr. Las Vegas."

The **Downtown Grand** (206 N. 3rd St., 855/384-7263, www.downtowngrand.com), located across the street from The Mob Museum, has a rooftop pool with a restaurant and full bar.

Once owned by Bugsy Siegel, the **El**

Cortez Hotel & Casino (600 E. Fremont St., 800/634-6703, http://elcortezhotelcasino.com) opened in 1941 and is the longest continuously operating hotel in Vegas. Room styles range from vintage Vegas and 1950s glam to contemporary.

Oasis at Gold Spike (217 Las Vegas Blvd. N., 702/768-9823, www.oasisatgoldspike.com) is a playfully styled hotel for the urban, mid-century-loving adventurer, with bike rentals, a library, and a turntable lounge to spin your favorite vinyl.

The Strat Hotel and Casino (2000 Las Vegas Blvd. S., 702/380-7777, https://thestrat.com) is north of the Strip and towers 1,149 feet (350 m) over the bustling scene—you're nearly guaranteed to get a room with a breathtaking view of the Las Vegas skyline.

Goffs and Fenner

Goffs Road travels 13.5 miles (21.7 km) along the pre-1931 alignment of Route 66, which leads to the ghost town of **Goffs.** Because Goffs sits at a slightly higher elevation than Needles, residents used to go to Goffs to beat the 120°F (49°C) heat.

Originally, Goffs was home to employees of the Santa Fe Railway and was a popular stop on Route 66 until 1931, when the Mother Road was realigned to follow a more direct route from Needles to Essex. As you enter Goffs today, look for the abandoned **General Store** on the north side of the highway. In better condition is the Spanish Mission-style **Goffs Schoolhouse** (37198 Lanfair Rd., 9am-4pm Sat.-Mon. Oct.-June, free), built in 1914. Sitting unused for decades, by 1982 it was in ruins; the **Mojave Desert Heritage and Cultural Association** (www.mdhca.org) restored it to its original condition.

From Goffs, continue west on Route 66 for 10 miles (16.1 km) as it dips south to Fenner.

Fenner is one of many forgotten towns that dot the Mojave Desert. Established in 1883, the town operated as a watering station for steam trains. Today, Fenner has gas and limited services along I-40. If you're low on **gas,** get it here because the next service station is 55 miles (89 km) away.

✦ Back on 66

Leave Fenner heading south on Route 66 for 4.5 miles (7.2 km), then join the National Trails Highway (Route 66) for 28 miles (45 km), crossing Kelbaker Road. For the side trip to Mojave National Preserve (about 30 mi/48 km away), turn right (north) on Kelbaker Road or continue heading west on Route 66.

✦ Side Trip: Mojave National Preserve

From I-40 at the junction to Amboy, turn north on Kelbaker Road to explore the **Mojave National Preserve** (90942 Kelso Cima Rd., www.nps.gov/moja, 24 hours daily, free). The road stretches through an otherworldly landscape of desert dunes created from ancient volcanic activity. In 22 miles (35 km) along Kelbaker Road, you'll reach the **Kelso Depot,** a beautifully restored 1920s-era railroad depot. The Mission Revival and Spanish Colonial architecture was designed to resemble the Harvey Houses along the Santa Fe Railway. The interior has been repurposed into the **visitors center** (Kelso Cima Rd., 760/252-6108, 10am-5pm Thurs.-Mon.), with exhibits, films, an art gallery, bookstore, restrooms, and a picnic area. As you walk toward the depot from the parking lot, look for two tan cages in front of the railroad tracks. In the 1940s, this was the Kelso Jail, which housed unruly drunks from the nearby Kaiser mine and Union Pacific Railroad.

Top to bottom: an abandoned building in the Mojave Desert; Mojave National Preserve; motel sign near Fenner

Kelbaker Road terminates at I-15 in 56 miles (90 km), passing cinder cones and lava beds from millions of years ago. This short stretch offers just a glimpse into the 1.6-million-acre (647,497-hectare) park. Primitive campgrounds are available via a north turn on Essex Road, just west of Fenner.

Essex, Danby, and Cadiz Summit

The former railroad water stations and towns along this portion of Route 66 were named in alphabetical order—Amboy, Bristol, Cadiz, Danby, Essex, Fenner, and Goffs. From I-40 near Fenner, head south on Route 66 for 6 miles (9.7 km) to the nearly nonexistent town of **Essex**. This was once a happening stop with cafés and auto garages staffed with mechanics who rescued stranded travelers who underestimated the severity of the desert weather. Today, the post office is pretty much the only operational business.

Continue west on Route 66 for 9 miles (14.5 km) to **Danby,** now abandoned except for dilapidated ruins and fenced-off buildings. About 12 miles (19.3 km) west, the next "town" is Chambless, near the **Cadiz Summit.** After I-40 opened in 1973, Chambless withered away into nothing, today marked by graffiti-covered rubble.

✥ Back on 66

From Chambless, continue 11 miles (17.7 km) west to Amboy.

Amboy

Route 66 helped put Amboy on the map. By the time Roy's opened in 1938, this desert spot had a population of around 65 people.

Sights
★ Roy's Motel & Café
On the north side of the National Trails

Highway (Route 66) is the dusty town of Amboy, home to the iconic **Roy's Motel & Café** (87520 National Trails Hwy., 760/733-1066, https://visitamboy.com). Opened in 1938, Roy's was the only spot in the area for gas, food, and lodging. Though the motel is closed now, gas is available, and the café sells drinks and souvenirs. Don't miss the chance to get pictures of the Roy's sign—it's in the mid-century Googie style, a type of futuristic architecture influenced by the Space Age and car culture. Perhaps it's that very architecture set against a bright desert sky that attracts Hollywood—Roy's has been the sight of films, music videos, and commercials over the years.

In 2003, the entire town was on sale on eBay for $1.9 million, but the highest offer ($995,000) was not accepted. In 2005, Albert Okura, owner of the Juan Pollo restaurant chain, bought the town (all 490 acres/198 hectares) for $425,000. Okura is hoping to resuscitate Amboy, but it's a venture that could easily cost more than $1 million.

Amboy Crater
About 3 miles (4.8 km) west of Roy's, on the south side of National Trails Highway, is **Amboy Crater** (BLM Needles Field Office, 1303 S. U.S. 95, Needles, 760/326-7000, www.blm.gov, dawn-dusk daily, free). The 250-foot (76-m) crater, a volcanic cinder cone, formed roughly 6,000 years ago; a moderate hiking trail (1.7 mi/2.7 km) leads to the top. Hiking to the rim is not recommended during summer or in windy conditions. Avoid pathways where people tried to drive ATVs up to the crater; these are not trails and can be dangerous.

✥ Back on 66

To stay on Route 66, continue driving west. To reach Joshua Tree, head west on National Trails Highway, then turn left onto Amboy Road and continue 40 miles (64 km) south.

Women of the Mother Road

The story of Route 66 isn't complete without the illustrious women who've contributed greatly to the road's growth, success, and preservation. Here, celebrate the Californian women who made a profound impact on the Mother Road.

♦ **Minerva Hoyt:** The preservation of California's deserts owes much to Minerva Hoyt. She was raised in Mississippi, but after marrying, she and her husband moved to Pasadena. She loved the desert environs and took up gardening to learn more about the local flora. As automobile traffic encroached on wild areas, Minerva began to exhibit her plants and educate the public on the dangers of losing green spaces. In 1930, she founded the International Desert Conservation League; and by 1936, her tireless preservation efforts resulted in the U.S. government officially designating 800,000 acres (323,749 hectares) of Joshua Tree as a national monument.

♦ **Lucia Rodriguez:** In the 1930s, Lucia Rodriguez and her husband were Mexican Americans living in San Bernardino. At the time, Route 66 ran through the heart of the Mexican American community. Lucia—looking for ways to cater to Mother Road travelers—opened **Mitla Café** (page 325). San Bernardino was a segregated city; in order to foster a sense of community among Mexican American residents, Mitla Café hosted local events and fiestas, and even sponsored a neighborhood baseball team. All of these grassroots efforts paved the way for the establishment of the Mexican American Defense Committee, an organization that helped desegregate California schools.

♦ **Cynthia Hare Troup:** Bobby Troup is known as the writer of the famous "(Get Your Kicks on) Route 66" tune, but it was his wife, Cynthia, who came up with the catchy title on their road trip from the East Coast to Hollywood.

⚑ Side Trip: Joshua Tree National Park

Joshua Tree National Park (760/367-5500, www.nps.gov/jotr, $30 for a 7-day pass) is an 800,000-acre (323,749-hectare) wilderness wonderland comprising the two very distinct ecosystems of the Mojave and Colorado Deserts; the latter is part of the Sonoran Desert. Molded by eons of wind and rain, the landscape of craggy boulders and rugged rock formations morphs into the stark desert and into seas of the namesake Joshua tree—not a tree at all, actually, but a flowering agave plant.

Getting There

From Amboy and the National Trails Highway (Route 66), turn left (south) on Amboy Road. Drive 40 miles (64 km) south, passing through the unincorporated town of **Wonder Valley,** where empty homestead cabins are slowly decomposing in the middle of the desert. At the junction with Godwin Road, turn left to reach SR-62 in 2 miles (3.2 km). In **Twentynine Palms,** turn left (south) onto Utah Trail, which turns into Park Boulevard after crossing SR-62 (Twentynine Palms Hwy.). Park Boulevard continues south to the east entrance of Joshua Tree National Park.

Visitors Centers

At the junction of SR-62 (Twentynine Palms Hwy.) and Utah Trail is the **Oasis Visitors Center** (74485 National Park Dr., Twentynine Palms, 760/367-5500, 8:30am-5pm daily). A bookstore is on-site, and facilities include drinking water, flush toilets, and picnic tables. The larger **Joshua Tree Visitors Center** (6554 Park Blvd., Joshua Tree, 760/366-1855,

Joshua Tree National Park

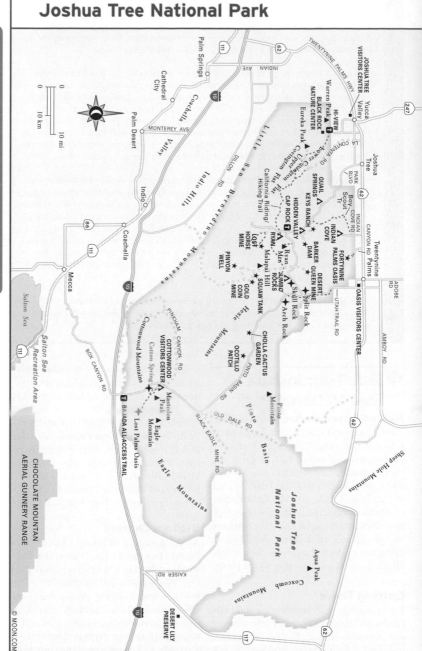

7:30am-5pm daily) is located farther west in the town of Joshua Tree.

Sights
Oasis of Mara

The best-known oasis in Joshua Tree is the 9,000-year-old **Oasis of Mara** (SR-62 and Utah Trail). A number of small springs well out of the ground along the Pinto Mountain fault, providing the life-giving water that supports a large and surprisingly lush ecosystem. Though the oasis sits outside the park boundaries, it's still treated as part of the park. A lovely wheelchair-accessible nature trail loops 0.5 mile (0.8 km) and includes a variety of informative signs about the natural features of the area. You'll see the palm trees, hardy grasses, and huge boulders that characterize the region and hint at the beauty you'll find elsewhere in Joshua Tree.

Skull Rock and Cap Rock

Among the wonders of Joshua Tree are the sculpted rock formations that rise up from the earth. Geologists date the rocks back nearly 2 billion years. As you drive or hike, you'll have a hard time missing these nature-made works of art.

To see two exceptionally distinctive formations, take the east-west connecting road from Pinto Basin Road (the main north-south corridor) to Keys View and Hidden Valley. You'll first pass **Skull Rock** (Park Blvd., 7 mi/11.3 km east of Hidden Valley), one of the many giant stones that provide shade at the aptly named Jumbo Rocks campground. Just past the intersection toward Hidden Valley, **Cap Rock** and its buddies are showpieces of fascinating geology. Here, you'll find a small picnic area and a good spot for rock climbing, if that's your thing.

Hidden Valley

One of the centerpieces of Joshua Tree, **Hidden Valley** (Park Blvd., 10 mi/16.1 km south of West Entrance) is a popular spot for hikes, wildlife viewing, rock climbing, and camping. It also offers a rare glimpse of a tiny micro-habitat of plants and animals not found together in other parts of the park. On a trail to the right of the parking lot, you can scramble up the massive boulders for a close-up view of the granite mineral content of the rocks. Emerge from the rocky trail into a small meadow-like area, which includes informational signs describing the natural features.

Keys Ranch

William and Frances Keys were among the rugged settlers of the Mojave Desert. They ranched on the sparse desert grasses and raised five children on this patch that would become part of Joshua Tree National Park. Today, visitors can see the weathered pine buildings that housed the original ranch house, the schoolhouse that educated the few local children, the general store, and a workshop. The orchard and landscaping have been replanted, and a collection of old mining and farm equipment sits in the dry desert air.

The only way to explore **Keys Ranch** (760/367-5522, tours offered Oct.-May, $10) is to take a docent-guided tour of the buildings and property. Reservations are required; call between 9am and 4:30pm or purchase tickets on-site at one of the visitors centers. The tour covers 0.5 mile (0.8 km), lasts about 1.5 hours, and requires sturdy walking shoes.

Keys View

One of the best photo ops in all of Joshua Tree is the vista as seen from **Keys View** (end of Keys View Rd., bear right off Park Blvd. past Cap Rock). On a clear day, the view redefines the term "panoramic," letting you soak up the sights of Palm Springs, the Coachella Valley farmland, the San Andreas Fault, and even the Salton Sea (a saline lake) many miles to the southeast. Drive to the end of the road out of the West Ranger Station, up to about 5,000 feet (1,524 m) elevation, and the parking lot. Get out of your car and climb a brief paved trail to the vantage point at the top of the ridge. For a truly breathtaking picture from Keys View, arrive in the early morning hours, around sunrise.

Black Rock Canyon

Follow Park Boulevard west to exit the park at the Joshua Tree Visitors Center. West of the main entrance, and just south of the small town of Yucca Valley, is **Black Rock Canyon** (SR-247 at the northwest corner of the park), with a developed campground, nature and ranger center, and hiking trails surrounded by Joshua trees, which begin the spring bloom late each February. Visitors often walk the **Hi-View Nature Trail** (1.3 mi/2.1 km), a pleasant interpretive stroll that points out and describes the plants, wildlife, and geological features that characterize the northern Mojave Desert region.

Hiking

There are several self-guided nature trails in the park. Before you take a hike—even a short 2- or 3-mile (3.2- or 4.8-km) jaunt—be sure you're properly prepared. Joshua Tree is a harsh and unforgiving desert. Bring lots of water (at least 1 gallon/3.8 liters per person), maps, first-aid, and sun protection.

Five miles (8 km) from the Oasis Visitors Center, the trail to the **49 Palms Oasis** weaves 1.5 miles (2.4 km) south to pools of water surrounded by fan palms. Look for the trailhead 2 miles (3.2 km) south of SR-62 off Canyon Road.

The popular **Barker Dam Loop** circles 1.3 miles (2.1 km) around a water tank built by early cattle ranchers. Note that the tank may be empty in times of drought, but the walk is still an enjoyable entry into the desert. The trailhead is located near the parking area for Keys Ranch.

Joshua Tree National Park

Located on Park Boulevard near Cap Rock, the strenuous trail to **Ryan Mountain** (2.8 mi/4.5 km round-trip) climbs to the 5,461-foot (1,665-m) summit with views of the surrounding valleys below.

If you're looking to stretch your legs after the drive to Keys View, consider hiking the **Lost Horse Mine Loop** (6.2 mi/9.9 km round-trip), which passes by the site of an abandoned 10-stamp mill as the trail climbs above 5,000 feet (1,524 m).

Food and Accommodations

There are nine **campgrounds** in Joshua Tree National Park, and many do not have water and are primitive. Bring everything you think you'll need. Sites are first-come, first-served, but reservations are accepted (www.recreation.gov, 877/444-6777, $20-25) from September through May.

Twentynine Palms

Near the east entrance of Joshua Tree National Park is **The Palms** (83131 Amboy Rd., Twentynine Palms, 760/361-2810, 3pm-6pm Thurs., 3pm-9:30pm Fri., 3pm-8pm Sat., 9am-6pm Sun., $5-10), a restaurant and bar with live music that runs the gamut from indie to bluegrass. An eclectic but friendly mix of locals, desert rats, and visiting urbanites populate this odd little place way out in the middle of nowhere.

Just 0.5 mile (0.8 km) from the Oasis Visitors Center is the **29 Palms Inn** (73950 Inn Ave., Twentynine Palms, 760/367-3505, www.29palmsinn.com, $117-287), which sits on 70 acres (28 hectares) in the Oasis of Mara. Bed down in one of the 1930s adobe bungalows and cabins—they come with wood-burning fireplaces and private sun patios. Dogs are welcome, too. The on-site restaurant overlooks the pool and serves delicious meals with produce from the adjacent organic garden.

Joshua Tree

In Joshua Tree, there are several places to eat. **Crossroads Café** (61715 Twentynine Palms Hwy., Joshua Tree, 760/366-5414, http://crossroadscafejtree.com, 7am-9pm daily, $6-13) offers a range of breakfast and lunch dishes, from salads and tacos to burgers and sandwiches, including good vegetarian options.

For a quick slice, hit up **Pie for the People** (61740 Twentynine Palms Hwy., Joshua Tree, 760/366-0400, www.pieforthepeople.com, 11am-9pm Sun.-Tues., 11am-10pm Wed.-Sat., $8-18). Order from a menu of thin-crust pizzas with gourmet toppings. They also offer choices for vegan and gluten-free customers.

Royal Siam Cuisine (61599 Twentynine Palms Hwy., Joshua Tree, 760/366-2923, 11am-2pm and 4pm-7pm Mon. and Wed.-Sat., noon-2pm and 4pm-7pm Sun., $5-10) has tasty but very spicy Thai dishes. Don't let the strip-mall setting deter you; the service is friendly and the prices are right for how good the food is.

Joshua Tree Inn (61259 Twentynine Palms Hwy., 760/366-1188, www. joshuatreeinn.com, $125-135) offers hacienda-style lodging, complete with Spanish architectural touches—Saltillo tile and wood-beamed ceilings—and a large palm tree-shaded pool. The grounds also include a zen garden and fish pond, plus a gift shop selling candles, clothes, and vintage motel keys.

The outdoorsy camper who's game to try something other than a traditional tent can reserve a "pod" at the **Bonita Domes** (www.airbnb.com, $89). These sustainable geometric domes were built with Earthbag Technology; the 18-inch (46-cm) walls produce a thermal mass enabling the structures to maintain a comfortable temperature. The domes sleep 1-2 people and come with a shower, outhouse with sink and flush toilet, and a shaded outdoor kitchen.

✪ Back on 66

To head back to Route 66, drive 16 miles (26 km) east on Twentynine Palms Highway (SR-62). Turn left (north) on Utah Trail. In less than 2 miles (3.2 km), turn right (east) on Amboy Road. Follow Amboy Road for 17 miles (27 km) until it heads north and climbs 28 miles (45 km); the road dead-ends into Route 66 (National Trail Hwy.). Turn left (west) and drive 5 miles (8 km) to the silent, eerie town of **Bagdad.**

Bagdad was once a bustling place, considering it's in the middle of the desert. After Route 66 was rerouted in 1973, the town floundered. By 1991, the remaining buildings were razed, leaving little more than rusted-out cars and creosote. The Bagdad Café, which inspired the Academy Award-nominated 1987 German film of the same name, was originally located here, but the actual filming took place farther west in Newberry Springs.

Continue west on National Trails Highway (Route 66) for 20 miles (32 km) to the town of Ludlow.

Ludlow

In 1882, Ludlow was a regular water stop for the Atlantic and Pacific Railroad. It was also a prosperous mining town after ore was discovered in the nearby hills.

In the 1940s, Ludlow boasted a motor court (still in operation today), cabins, and the **Ludlow Café** (68315 National Trails Hwy., 760/733-4501, 6am-6pm daily, $5-10). The gabled-roof building showcases a modernist facade, and the menu has everything you'd want in a roadside diner experience: pancakes, biscuits and gravy, and all-day breakfast. Walk off your meal by wandering over to see the vintage trucks on display next door.

If you need **gas,** there is a Chevron station on the north side of National Trails Highway. A 76 station is found north of I-40 on Crucero Road.

✪ Back on 66

Continue driving west on Route 66 for 28 miles (45 km) to Newberry Springs.

Newberry Springs

Although the original Bagdad Café was located in Bagdad about 50 miles (81 km) east, today the ★ **Bagdad Café** (46548 National Trails Hwy., 760/257-3101, 7am-7pm daily, $6-11) lives on in Newberry Springs. The café was used in the 1987 German film of the same name directed by Percy Adlon. Decent burgers, good service, and plenty of ambience and filmic history make it a worthwhile stop for a cold drink on a 120°F (49°C) day.

✪ Back on 66

Keep heading west on Route 66 (National Trails Hwy.) for 11 miles (17.7 km) to Daggett.

◈ Side Trip: North to I-15

Lake Dolores Waterpark

There's nothing creepier—or cooler—than an abandoned water park. **Lake Dolores Waterpark** (which also operated under the names Rock-a-Hoola and Discover Waterpark) sits crumbling under the desert sun about 20 minutes north of Bagdad Café and Newberry Springs. Despite the "No Trespassing" signs, the park is easy to access and an interesting stop for adventurous urban explorers.

Lake Dolores Waterpark opened in the late 1950s as a playground and campground, with a 273-acre (110-hectare) artificial lake. The owners added rides and attractions over the next 25 years, with the park reaching peak popularity in the 1970s. Rides included waterslides, trapeze-like swings, and river rafts. But dwindling attendance in the 1980s caused the park to close in 1990. After the park had a renovation and reopening in 1998, an employee injury—and subsequent lawsuit—bankrupted the park, forcing it to shut down again in 2004.

Today, slides cracked by the desert air line a hillside, graffiti-covered pools sit empty, a concrete riverbed, once filled with sparkling water for the raft ride, is dry, and chunks of concrete lie strewn about. Murals painted over billboards (one is of a couple sitting in a 1950s convertible; above them is the phrase: "The Future is Blight") overlook the park.

Getting There

From Newberry Springs, take Newberry Road north for 6 miles (9.7 km), turning east as it becomes Palma Vista Road. In 1 mile (1.6 km), turn left (north) on Harvard Road. Follow Harvard Road

Top to bottom: Ludlow Café; Ludlow fire truck; Bagdad Café in Newberry Springs

north for 3 miles (4.8 km) to I-15 and turn west onto Hacienda Road. Drive 2.5 miles (4 km) west on Hacienda Road to the water park on the north side of the road.

✤ Back on 66
Continue south on Hacienda Road for about 2.5 miles (4 km). Turn right onto Yermo Road and drive 5.5 miles (8.9 km) west. At a T junction, turn left (west) to continue on East Yermo Road and the town of Yermo.

Yermo
Peggy Sue's Diner (35654 W. Yermo Rd., 760/254-3370, www.peggysuesdiner.com, 6am-10pm daily, $8-15) is a Hollywood version of the 1950s, with black-and-white checkered floors, pictures of Marilyn and Elvis on the walls, and a life-size sculpture of Betty Boop dressed as a waitress. Pick up retro candies and classic-movie memorabilia in the gift shop. For food, skip lunch and go straight for a cherry, strawberry, or chocolate milk shake.

✤ Back on 66
To return to Route 66, head west on Yermo Road and turn left (south) on Dagget-Yermo Road. In 2.5 miles (4 km), turn right (west) on National Trails Highway (Route 66).

Dagget

Daggett was named after California Lieutenant Governor John Daggett. In the late 1800s, the town was a supply center that accommodated the nearby silver mines in Calico. It took teams of mules to haul water and ore from Daggett to Calico. By 1902, Daggett was supported by three borax mines; more than $90 million worth of silver was removed from the Calico Hills. Dagget was also the California inspection station mentioned in Steinbeck's *Grapes of Wrath*.

Some of the buildings still standing date back more than 100 years.

If you want to stock up on soda and snacks, stop by **Desert Market** (35596 Santa Fe Ave., 760/254-2774, 8am-8pm Mon.-Sat., 9am-6pm Sun.), a family-owned convenience store and local gathering spot.

To get there from Route 66 (National Trails Hwy.), turn right (north) on Daggett-Yermo Road. Cross the tracks and take the first right (east) on Santa Fe Street. The market is two blocks on the north side, across the street from an old garage that used to repair mining equipment.

✤ Back on 66
Drive west on National Trails Highway for 2.5 miles (4 km). Turn left (south) on Nebo Street and take the next right to join I-40 west. Continue 2.5 miles (4 km) on I-40 to take Exit 2. Turn left, go under I-40, and then turn right to take the South Frontage Road for about 1 mile (1.6 km). Turn right (north) to follow East Main Street into Barstow.

Barstow

As the mining boom busted in the nearby Calico and Daggett mines, Barstow became an important railway hub and stopping point for travelers entering California via Route 66. In the 1950s, car transportation became more prevalent, and Barstow's main drag turned into a popular place to stop along the Mother Road.

Sights
Casa del Desierto Harvey House
Casa del Desierto Harvey House (681 N. 1st Ave., 760/818-4400, www.barstowharveyhouse.com, 8:30am-5pm Mon.-Sat.) was built in 1885 as a restaurant and hotel for Santa Fe Railway passengers. After it burned down in 1908, famed architect Mary Colter rebuilt it in

1913 in a style that fuses 16th-century Spanish and Classical Revival architecture. In 1999, the city of Barstow renovated and reopened Casa del Desierto. Today, it houses the **Route 66 Mother Road Museum** (760/255-1890, www. route66museum.org, 10am-4pm Fri.-Sun., free).

From Route 66, turn right (north) onto 1st Avenue. Drive 0.4 mile (0.6 km) and the road will curve to the right (east). Casa del Desierto Harvey House is on the right.

Food and Accommodations

Unfortunately, decent food and lodging options in Barstow are limited. **Lola's Kitchen** (1244 E. Main St., 760/255-1007, 4am-7:30pm Mon.-Sat., $5-12) is hidden away in a strip mall. It's easy to miss, but if you want good Mexican food, make a point to visit—the chile relleno is near perfection.

The 1922 **Route 66 Motel** (195 W. Main St., 760/256-7866, www. route66motelbarstow.com, $55-70) offers an acceptable choice, with a retro neon sign and vintage cars parked out front, plus funky Route 66 memorabilia throughout the property. Guest rooms don't offer much in the way of amenities or style, but the price is cheap.

◆ Back on 66

Drive west on Main Street (Route 66/ National Trails Hwy.) through Barstow for 23 miles (37 km) past Hinkley Road and through Helendale to Oro Grande.

Top to bottom: Route 66 Motel in Barstow; mural in Barstow; Casa del Desierto Harvey House in Barstow

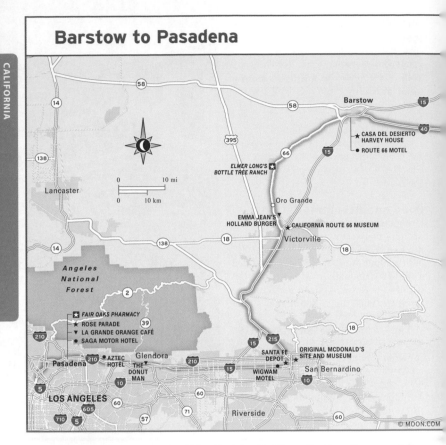

Barstow to Pasadena

Oro Grande

Sights
★ Elmer Long's Bottle Tree Ranch

After passing through Helendale, keep an eye out for **Elmer Long's Bottle Tree Ranch** (24266 National Trails Hwy., dawn-dusk daily, free) in less than 2 miles (3.2 km). You don't want to skip this place.

Since he was a kid camping with his father in the 1950s, Elmer Long has collected treasures from trash heaps in the desert. They found stuff from as far back as the 1800s. Elmer's father started collecting glass bottles from these father-son treasure hunts, and after he died, Elmer inherited the collection. To memorialize his father—and show off the astounding and odd collection of found objects—Elmer turned "one man's trash, another man's treasure" into an art installation of nearly 200 bottles. When the sun shines through them, they glimmer in hues of amber, sapphire, and emerald. Wander the "forest" of glass trees, and you'll come across other sculptures made from antique signs, vintage gas pumps, old cars, toys, wind chimes, wheel wells, teapots, and more. If you leave a donation, you can take a piece of glass as a souvenir.

⬥ Back on 66

From Oro Grande, head south on National Trails Highway for 4 miles (6.4

The Green Book in California

California offered plentiful resources—from lodging and dining to car service stations—for Black travelers, with most of these businesses listed in the *Negro Motorist Green Book.* The majority of these were located in Los Angeles. Among those businesses still in operation today are **El Garces Harvey House** in Needles, Barstow's **Casa del Desierto Harvey House,** and **Union Station** and **Clifton's,** both in Los Angeles.

km). Crossing under the I-15 overpass brings you into Victorville. Continue 1 mile (1.6 km) south on D Street.

Victorville

Mormons made their way to Victorville in the 1860s and established a telegraph station. When Route 66 arrived in 1926, it passed through the center of what is today considered "Old Town" Victorville. During the peak of Route 66, Victorville's dude ranches and apple orchards were the perfect site for movie producers to film several Hollywood B films, including *It Came from Outer Space.* In 1940, Herman J. Mankiewicz penned the first two drafts of *Citizen Kane* at the Green Spot Motel on Route 66.

Sights
California Route 66 Museum
To see the Green Spot Motel's green neon sign, as well as other iconic Route 66 memorabilia, visit the **California Route 66 Museum** (16825 S. D St., 760/951-0436, http://califrt66museum. org, 10am-4pm Mon. and Thurs.-Sat., 11am-3pm Sun., $2). Explore more than 4,500 square feet (418 sq m) of photographs, artifacts from now-defunct Route 66 businesses, antique radios, and a Ford Model T from 1917. Be sure to ask questions of the friendly, knowledgeable staff.

Food
Juicy burgers and crispy chicken-fried steak come with a side of history and fame at ★ **Emma Jean's Holland Burger** (17143 N. D St., 760/243-9938, www.hollandburger.com, 5am-3pm Mon.-Fri., 6am-12:30pm Sat., cash only, $6-10). Inside these mint-green walls, Emma Jean's has been serving Route 66ers since 1947. In fact, it has been around longer than any other restaurant in the area. It was also the restaurant that Uma Thurman walked into after being buried alive in Quentin Tarantino's cult classic *Kill Bill 2.* The milkshakes are the big winners here, as are the burgers. The Brian Burger comes topped with Ortega chili and melted swiss cheese and sits between slices of thick, parmesan-crusted garlic bread. The portions are huge, so split a sandwich or leave your diet outside where it belongs.

⬆ Back on 66
Leaving Victorville, the southbound lanes of I-15 cover Route 66, so take I-15 south for about 20 miles (32 km) through the Cajon Pass.

Cajon Pass

On I-15, take the Cleghorn Road (Exit 129) and turn right onto Cajon Boulevard to drive through the Cajon Pass. This mountain pass is between the San Bernardino and San Gabriel Mountains, a rift formed by the shifting of the San Andreas Fault. Popular with trainspotters, Cajon Pass is often photographed and featured in books and magazines.

The 1952 **Summit Inn** got its name from the original Summit Inn (now closed) built in 1928 to serve Route 66 travelers. This iconic landmark for travelers boasted an interior decked out with vintage gas company signs, a homey diner serving odd-but-yummy dishes like ostrich-egg omelets, and a small gift shop. Sadly, the Blue Cut Fire, a 2016 wildfire that swept through the area, obliterated the inn. The owners have plans to rebuild, hoping to restore the beloved destination to its former glory.

The Summit Inn was on the east side of I-15. Traveling west on I-15, take Exit 138 and turn left (east) to cross the freeway. Take the first right (south) to the restaurant site.

Back on 66

From the Cajon Pass, the road begins to run parallel to I-15. In less than 2 miles (3.2 km), turn left on Kenwood Avenue and join I-15 south. Immediately after entering the freeway, get into the middle/left lanes toward Riverside/San Bernardino I-215. Bear left to follow I-215. Drive 3.5 miles (5.6 km) to Exit 50 and turn right. In about 1,000 feet (305 meters), cross the railroad tracks and take an immediate left (south) on Cajon Boulevard. Drive 4.5 miles (7.2 km) to 21st Street. Make a right (west) and then an immediate left to follow North Mt. Vernon Avenue as it heads south into San Bernardino. In 1.5 miles (2.4 km), turn right (west) on West 5th Street, which soon turns into Foothill Boulevard.

Elmer Long's Bottle Tree Ranch

San Bernardino

Rugged mountain ranges encircle the San Bernardino Valley. However, driving through on Foothill Boulevard (Route 66), you'll see little more than a concrete slab of suburbia and a gateway to the sprawling metropolis of Los Angeles.

Sights
Santa Fe Depot
Built in 1918, the **Santa Fe Depot** (1170 W. 3rd St., www.sbdepotmuseum.com, 9am-noon Wed., 10am-3pm Sat., free) is an architectural beauty that sports Mission Revival, Moorish Revival, and Spanish Colonial Revival styles. It's also home to a museum of automobile and train artifacts, including 19th-century horse-drawn buggies. A former Harvey House, the depot is listed on the National Register of Historic Places. Today, it functions as the San Bernardino Amtrak station.

To get here from the Cajon Pass, take I-15 south, keep left at the fork, and continue on I-215 south. Take the West 3rd Street/West 2nd Street exit and turn right onto West 5th Street, which is Route 66.

Original McDonald's Site and Museum
In San Bernardino, you can visit the home of the first McDonald's restaurant at the **Original McDonald's Site and Museum** (1398 N. E St., west of I-215, 909/885-6324, 9am-5pm Mon.-Fri., 10am-5pm Sat.-Sun., free). It's not the original building, unfortunately (that was torn down in 1972), but you can browse a fascinating collection of toys—some from the 1940s—old packaging, the first Happy Meal boxes, even classic Route 66 road signs. To get here from I-215, take the West Baseline Road exit and turn left onto North E Street.

Food and Accommodations
Opened by Lucia Rodriguez, ★ **Mitla Café** (602 N. Mt. Vernon Ave., 909/888-0460, www.mitlacafesb.com, 9am-8pm Tues.-Sun., $8-20) has been owned and operated by Lucia's family since the day she served the restaurant's first meal in 1937. Not only does Mitla Café serve up excellent Mexican fare—chile rellenos, carne asada, bean burritos—but it also acts as a hub for the Mexican-American community in San Bernardino. It's also the restaurant known for inspiring Taco Bell founder Glen Bell.

The historic 1848 **Sycamore Inn** (8318 Foothill Blvd., Rancho Cucamonga, 909/982-1104, www.thesycamoreinn. com, 5pm-9pm Mon.-Thurs., 5pm-10pm Fri.-Sat., 4pm-8:30pm Sun., $13-60) opened almost 70 years before Route 66 came through. The restaurant serves old-school fine-dining fare like buttery prime rib, creamy mashed potatoes, and stuffed-mushrooms capped with blue cheese.

The ★ **Wigwam Motel** (2728 E. Foothill Blvd., 909/875-3005, www.

Road Trip Playlist

Curating your road trip playlist is almost as important as mapping the route or booking hotels. Route 66 takes you through vastly different regions of the country, each with its own distinct culture and, yes, music. These song suggestions are tailored to the state you're in.

♦ **"California Love" by 2Pac:** The late, great, gone-too-soon rapper 2Pac pairs up with Dr. Dre for a song that topped charts in 1996.

♦ **"Cycles of Existential Rhyme" by Chicano Batman:** Considered the leader of the Latin soul revival, this four-man band from Los Angeles brings the funk—and the fun—to its songs, including this groovy song.

♦ **"Gasoline" by Haim:** The three sisters who comprise pop rock band Haim hail from Los Angeles. This song about kicking back in the passenger seat is the highlight of their 2020 album *Women in Music Pt. III*.

♦ **"Kokomo" by The Beach Boys:** Including The Beach Boys on a playlist about California? Obvious. Picking the 1989 track "Kokomo"? Surprise move!

♦ **"California Girl" by Cayucas:** This indie band is from Santa Monica, the end of Route 66's epic journey. Play this breezy song as you roll up the coast to the Santa Monica Pier.

wigwammotel.com, $75-90) is all roadside kitsch. At this 1949 motor court, each guest room takes the shape of a 20-foot-tall (6-m) tepee (not a wigwam, despite the property's name). The teepees fit a bed, flat-screen TV, and a mini fridge. When you're not in your tepee, enjoy the motel's amenities, such as free Wi-Fi, an outdoor firepit, swimming pool, and gift shop.

◆ Back on 66

If you're not pressed for time, continue west on Foothill Boulevard for 11 miles (17.7 km) through Claremont, Pomona, Laverne, and San Dimas to Glendora. If time is an issue, turn north on Euclid Avenue and make a right (west) on West 16th Street. From here, you can jump on I-210 west (Foothill Freeway) and exit at South Lone Hill Avenue (Exit 44) in Glendora. Turn right (north) and after 0.25 mile (0.4 km) make a left on East Route 66.

Glendora

Even if you don't love doughnuts (but really, who doesn't love doughnuts?), make it a point to stop at **The Donut Man** (915 E. Route 66, 626/335-9111, www. thedonutmanca.com, 24 hours daily) in Glendora. Since 1972, people have been flocking to this place for its delectable morsels of fried dough. Try one of the famous fresh peach- and strawberry-stuffed doughnuts, then order a maple-frosted cruller for the road.

◆ Back on 66

Drive 10 miles (16.1 km) west to Monrovia; as you reach Duarte, Foothill Boulevard turns into Huntington Drive. In 3 miles (4.8 km), turn right (north) on Shamrock Avenue to follow the 1926 alignment. After 1 mile (1.6 km), turn left (west) on East Foothill Boulevard into Monrovia.

Monrovia and Duarte

The **Aztec Hotel** (305 W. Foothill Blvd., Monrovia) is one of the few remaining examples of Mayan Revival architecture in the entire country. In 1925, architect Robert Stacy-Judd merged art deco sensibilities with Mayan script, known as glyphs. This rare historical landmark has faced foreclosure and is currently undergoing renovations.

Le Roy's The Original (523 W. Huntington Dr., Monrovia, 626/357-5076, 6am-3pm daily, $5-11) is a warm and welcoming eatery that serves breakfast all day and has a lunch menu featuring more than 20 sandwiches.

⬥ Back on 66

Follow Huntington Drive west for about 10 miles (16.1 km) through San Marino and Arcadia. Huntington Drive turns into East Colorado Boulevard in Pasadena. Along the way, consider a side trip to the Huntington Library.

⬥ Side Trip: The Huntington

If the weather is nice and you have extra time, visit **The Huntington** (1151 Oxford Rd., San Marino, 626/405-2100, www.huntington.org, 10am-5pm Wed.-Mon., $25-29). You'll find a library housing nearly a half-million rare books; an impressive art museum featuring European and American works; and 120 acres (49 hectares) of botanical gardens. It's not on Route 66, but it's very close and offers an ideal way to stretch your legs.

To get there from Huntington Drive, turn right on East California Boulevard and make a left on South Allen Avenue.

Top to bottom: Wigwam Motel in San Bernardino; The Huntington; Fair Oaks Pharmacy in Pasadena

Pasadena to Santa Monica

You'll make a second right on Orlando Road, then another right onto Oxford Road.

Pasadena

Sights
★ Fair Oaks Pharmacy
Fair Oaks Pharmacy (1526 Mission St., South Pasadena, 626/799-1414, www. fairoakspharmacy.net, 9am-4pm Mon.-Fri., 9am-1pm Sat.) is a 1915 landmark, a corner drugstore where soda jerks pour floats, egg creams, and lime rickeys. The soda fountain has a food menu of melts, burgers, hot dogs, and sandwiches, too. While you wait for your meal, walk around the store to look at the collection of antique toys, rare and classic candies, vintage advertisements, and Route 66 memorabilia. There's also a fully functional pharmacy where you can consult with a clinical pharmacist about anything that ails you.

Festivals and Events
Rose Parade
Traversing a segment of Route 66, the **Rose Parade** (Colorado Blvd., www. tournamentofroses.com/rose-parade) has taken place every New Year's Day since 1890. When it originally launched, the parade was intended as a celebration of California's mild winters, a time of year when flowers bloom and citrus

trees bear fruit. Since its start, the parade has blossomed into a spectacular event watched by hundreds of thousands of spectators and broadcast nationwide. It boasts nearly 50 flower-draped floats and over 20 marching bands, and showcases equestrian teams. It also acts as a prelude to the Rose Bowl, a college football playoff game. If you're in town on January 1, don't miss this historic event; it's free to watch and you don't need tickets.

Food and Accommodations

La Grande Orange Café (260 S. Raymond Ave., 626/356-4444, www.lgostationcafe. com, 11am-10pm Mon.-Thurs., 11am-11pm Fri., 10am-11pm Sat., 9am-9pm Sun., $13-29) is a spunky little spot in the restored 1934 Del Mar railroad station. Regional and seasonal American dishes grace the menu at LGO (as it's colloquially called).

The egg-salad sandwich at **Euro Pane Bakery** (950 E. Colorado Blvd., 626/577-1828, http://europanebakery.juisyfood. com, 7am-4:30pm Mon.-Sat., 9am-3pm Sun., $4-8) is a local fave. But it's the sweets that bring the crowds to this bakery. Try to choose just one type of macaroon from flavors such as blackberry, hazelnut, mocha, passion fruit, pistachio, raspberry, and sea salt caramel. There are also pound cakes (pear spice, orange) and tarts (lemon, brown butter, custard) to tempt you.

Located right on the Rose Parade route, the **Saga Motor Hotel** (1633 E. Colorado Blvd., 626/795-0431, www. thesagamotorhotel.com, $113-185) offers guests free breakfast, free Wi-Fi, dog-friendly rooms, and a heated pool. It's a clean and affordable option in a great location.

◆ Route 66: First End Point

To follow the original Route 66 from Pasadena into Los Angeles, drive south on Fair Oaks Avenue to where it dead-ends at Huntington Drive. Turn right (west) and drive 3.5 miles (5.6 km) on

Huntington Drive. Continue on North Mission Road for about 0.3 mile (0.5 km), then take a right (west) onto North Broadway. In 1.5 miles (2.4 km), stay right (don't follow Spring St.) to continue on Broadway. Drive 2.5 miles (4 km) down Broadway to 7th Street and you've done it! This is the **first end point** of the original Route 66!

There were actually three endings on Route 66 in Los Angeles. The first terminus at 7th and Broadway Streets existed between 1926 and 1936. Later, the second terminus was extended farther west to Santa Monica at the intersection of Olympic and Lincoln Boulevards. In 2009, the terminus was moved a third time to the Santa Monica Pier, where the Mother Road ends within steps of the vast Pacific Ocean.

Los Angeles

Los Angeles is a sprawling metropolis of more than 10 million people living within 400 square miles (1,036 sq km). It's the second-largest city in the country, after New York.

Welcome to the "City of Angels." It's one of the most diverse places in the United States, a beautifully woven fabric of culture, food, art, and architecture.

◆ Route 66 Through Los Angeles

The major freeways into Los Angeles are I-405 and I-5, both of which run north-south, while I-10, another major artery, runs east-west. Traffic is practically unavoidable in Los Angeles, but life will be easier if you stay off the freeways 7am-10am and 3pm-7pm Monday-Friday. We'll pick up Route 66 in downtown Los Angeles at the first terminus (S. Broadway and 7th Sts.).

Sights
Bradbury Building

The first Route 66 terminus is located in

a historic theater district with old movie palaces that span seven blocks along South Broadway, between 2nd Street and 9th Street. Check out the **Bradbury Building** (304 S. Broadway, 213/626-1893, www.laconservancy.org). Its modest exterior belies the grandeur inside. This five-story cathedral of wrought iron, glass, and light has been featured in many sci-fi and noir films, most notably in the climactic scene in Ridley Scott's 1982 film *Blade Runner*.

Grand Central Market

Grand Central Market (317 S. Broadway, www.grandcentralmarket.com, 8am-10pm daily), located across the street from the Bradbury Building, merges the cuisines and cultures of Los Angeles in one delightful place. Open since 1917, the market occupies 30,000 square feet (2,787 sq m) and includes dozens of vendors selling meats, cheeses, fish, baked goods, coffee, ice cream, fruit, vegetables, flowers, and more.

El Pueblo de Los Angeles

El Pueblo de Los Angeles (125 Paseo de la Plaza, 213/628-1274, http://elpueblo.lacity.org) is a 44-acre (18-hectare) district that celebrates the history, culture, and ethnicities that make LA different from any other place on the planet. It's located in the oldest section of the city and consists of 27 historic buildings, including **Avila Adobe** (10 Olvera St.), the oldest surviving residence in Los Angeles. Also at the Pueblo are two outdoor plazas, museums, and a Mexican marketplace.

J. Paul Getty Museum

The **J. Paul Getty Museum** (1200 Getty Center Dr., 310/440-7300, www.getty.edu, 10am-5:30pm Sun. and Tues.-Thurs., 10am-9pm Fri.-Sat., free) sits on top of a hill overlooking Los Angeles. In fact, half of the fun of visiting this art repository

Top to bottom: Bradbury Building; Grand Central Market; Union Station

Downtown Los Angeles

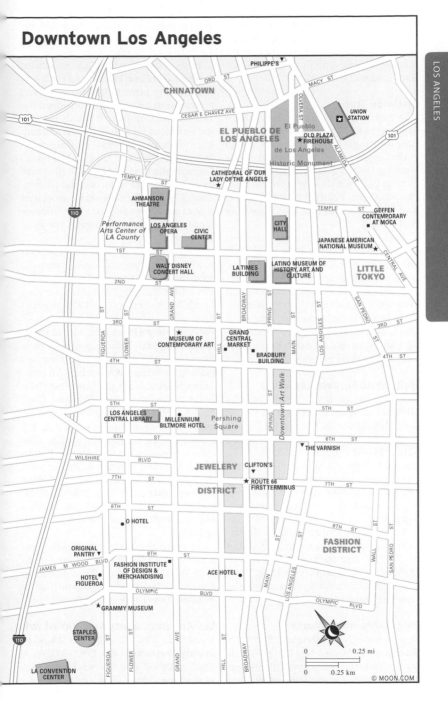

PHILIPPE'S ▼

CHINATOWN

ORD ST
MACY ST

CESAR E CHAVEZ AVE

UNION STATION

101

El Pueblo

EL PUEBLO DE LOS ANGELES
OLD PLAZA ★ FIREHOUSE

de Los Angeles

Historic Monument

CATHEDRAL OF OUR
LADY OF THE ANGELS ★

TEMPLE ST

AHMANSON THEATRE

TEMPLE ST GEFFEN CONTEMPORARY AT MOCA

Performance Arts Center of LA County

LOS ANGELES OPERA
CIVIC CENTER

CITY HALL

JAPANESE AMERICAN NATIONAL MUSEUM ★

1ST ST

110

WALT DISNEY CONCERT HALL

LA TIMES BUILDING

LATINO MUSEUM OF HISTORY, ART, AND CULTURE

LITTLE TOKYO

2ND ST

GRAND AVE

BROADWAY

SPRING ST

SAN PEDRO

CENTRAL AVE

FIGUEROA ST

FLOWER

3RD ST

MUSEUM OF CONTEMPORARY ART ★

GRAND CENTRAL MARKET

HILL

MAIN

LOS ANGELES

3RD ST

BRADBURY BUILDING

4TH ST

4TH ST

Downtown Art Walk

5TH ST

LOS ANGELES CENTRAL LIBRARY

MILLENNIUM BILTMORE HOTEL

Pershing Square

SPRING

5TH ST

6TH ST

6TH ST

WILSHIRE BLVD

▼ THE VARNISH

JEWELERY
CLIFTON'S ▼

7TH ST

★ ROUTE 66 FIRST TERMINUS

7TH ST

DISTRICT

8TH ST

8TH ST

● O HOTEL

FASHION DISTRICT

WALL

SAN PEDRO

ORIGINAL PANTRY ▼

9TH ST

JAMES M WOOD BLVD

HOTEL FIGUEROA ●

FASHION INSTITUTE OF DESIGN & MERCHANDISING

ACE HOTEL ●

MAIN

LOS ANGELES

OLYMPIC

BLVD

OLYMPIC BLVD

★ GRAMMY MUSEUM

110

STAPLES CENTER

FIGUEROA ST

FLOWER ST

GRAND AVE

HILL ST

BROADWAY

0   0.25 mi

LA CONVENTION CENTER

0   0.25 km

© MOON.COM

is taking the tram from the parking lot at the base of the hill to the top. Explore the museum's renowned collection of art, then stroll the beautifully manicured outdoor gardens.

★ Union Station

The architecturally impressive **Union Station** (800 N. Alameda St., www.unionstationla.com, 4am-1am daily) is the largest passenger terminal in the western United States. It was built in 1939 as part of a joint venture between the Southern Pacific, Union Pacific, and Atchison, Topeka, and Santa Fe Railroads.

Even if you're not catching a train, this 1939 Mission Moderne-style building is still a must-visit. Considered one of the last great rail stations, it's filled with restaurants and coffee shops, commissioned artwork, and a bike hub where you can rent a bicycle to tool around downtown. It also hosts a rotating calendar of live performances, music, art exhibitions, festivals, and cultural programming.

Hollywood Forever Cemetery

Skip the throngs of tourists on the Hollywood Walk of Fame and honor the celebrities who have passed on at the **Hollywood Forever Cemetery** (6000 Santa Monica Blvd., 323/469-1181). Tour 62 acres (25 hectares) of manicured lawns, complete with peacocks and swans, and discover the final resting place of film icons and Hollywood legends.

To reach the cemetery from downtown, hop on U.S. 101 north near Union Station and drive 4.5 miles (7.2 km) north to the Santa Monica Boulevard exit. Head west on Santa Monica Boulevard, and the cemetery will be on the left.

Original Farmer's Market

Stroll through the **Original Farmer's Market** (6333 W. 3rd St., 323/933-9211, www.farmersmarketla.com, 10am-6pm daily) to see the wares from more than 100 vendors from all over the world, including Brazilian, Greek, French, and German food stands.

In the 1880s, Arthur Gilmore settled the land at 3rd and Fairfax and ran a successful dairy farm. Gilmore and his son struck oil in 1900 and his business, the Gilmore Oil Company, had a sly marketing technique for selling their trademark blue-green gas. By 1934, drilling regulations changed and they had to move. Gilmore decided to turn the property into a place where farmers could sell produce. Eighteen farmers set up shop, and it became a huge success. The Gilmore family still owns and operates the market today.

Magee's Kitchen (stall 218, 323/938-4127, www.mageesnuts.com) was the first restaurant to open in the market after Blanche Magee started serving lunch to the farmers in 1917. It's still here today and run by the same family. **Patsy d'Amore's Pizza** (stall 448, 323/938-4938, www.patsydamore.com) has been here since 1949 and was the first operation to bring pizza to Los Angeles. Frank Sinatra, Nat King Cole, and Dean Martin were fans. **Kip's Toyland** (stall 720, 323/939-8334, http://kipstoyland.com) is the oldest toy store in LA. It's been here since 1956 and sells old-school toys and games like Mr. Potato Head, Life, and Operation. Before leaving the market, stock up on **Bob's Coffee & Doughnuts** (stall 450, 323/933-8929, www.bobscoffeeanddoughnuts.com), a well-deserved treat in case you get stuck in traffic.

To reach the Farmer's Market, continue west on Santa Monica Boulevard into West Hollywood. Turn left onto North Fairfax Avenue and continue to West 3rd Street.

Los Angeles County Museum of Art

Known as LACMA, the **Los Angeles County Museum of Art** (5905 Wilshire Blvd., 323/857-6000, www.lacma.org, 11am-5pm Mon.-Tues. and Thurs.,

Hollywood

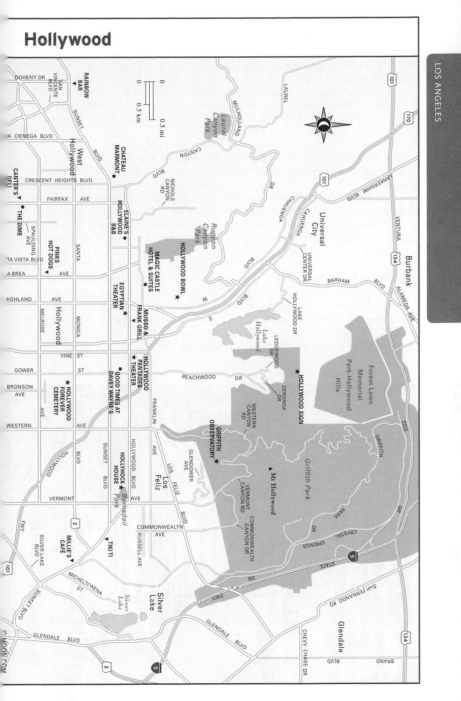

11am-8pm Fri., 10am-7pm Sat.-Sun., $25) features some of the most compelling modern art exhibitions in the country. In addition to offering art classes, film screenings, live music, and tours, LACMA is the largest art museum in the western United States. Outside the museum, walk through Chris Burden's *Urban Light* installation—made insanely popular by Instagram and recent Hollywood films—which comprises 202 antique cast-iron street lamps lined up in neat rows.

LACMA is located eight blocks south of the Farmer's Market off South Fairfax Avenue. Turn right on West 6th Street to access the Pritzker parking garage ($16 for 2 hours).

La Brea Tar Pits & Museum

Located next door to the Los Angeles County Museum of Art, **La Brea Tar Pits & Museum** (5801 Wilshire Blvd., 213/763-3499, http://tarpits.org, 9:30am-5pm daily, $15 adults, $7 children) is a family-friendly destination where you can see more than 5.5 million fossils from the most recent ice age in the collection, including a full skeleton of a mastodon. It's the only active urban paleontological excavation site in the country. Watch the excavators unearth fossils in a pit that's been active for more than 100 years.

Greystone Mansion

Greystone Mansion (905 Loma Vista Dr., Beverly Hills, 310/286-0119, www.greystonemansion.org, 10am-5pm daily, free) is an elegant Tudor Revival mansion with 18 acres (7 hectares) of English gardens. The mansion was built in 1927 by Edward L. Doheny, an oil tycoon, and has been featured in the films *The Big Lebowski, The Dark Knight, The Social Network, Ghostbusters,* and *There Will Be Blood.* Outside areas are open to the public via self-guided tours. There's no access to the interior spaces, except for special events. No pets or picnicking is allowed.

Los Angeles County Museum of Art

Griffith Observatory

See the stars—the cosmic kind—at **Griffith Observatory** (2800 E. Observatory Rd., 213/473-0800, http://griffithobservatory.org, noon-10pm Tues.-Fri., 10am-10pm Sat.-Sun., free). Since opening in 1935, Griffith Observatory has been an iconic landmark and favored destination for locals and visitors alike. Explore exhibits, look through telescopes, see planetarium shows, and enjoy unobstructed views of the Hollywood sign.

Grammy Museum

The **Grammy Museum** (800 W. Olympic Blvd., 213/765-6800, www.grammymuseum.org, 10:30am-6:30pm Sun.-Thurs., 10am-8pm Fri.-Sat., $15) dedicates four floors of interactive exhibits to all things music. From the Songwriters Hall of Fame gallery to footage from concerts and interviews with musicians, this museum showcases how the power of music has influenced, inspired, and revolutionized American culture.

From 7th Street and Broadway in downtown Los Angeles, drive southwest on Broadway for three blocks to Olympic. Turn right (northwest) and the Grammy Museum will be 0.5 mile (0.8 km) near the corner of Figueroa Street.

Hollywood Bowl

Live music venue the **Hollywood Bowl** (2301 N. Highland Ave., 323/850-2000, www.hollywoodbowl.com) may be known more for its unique architecture and dramatic outdoor setting—the stage sits under a band shell of concentric arches set against the backdrop of the Hollywood Hills—but it boasts a rich history, too. For more than 100 years, the Hollywood Bowl has played host to the likes of The Beatles, The Doors, Billie Holiday, and Prince, as well as acting as the summer home of the Los Angeles Philharmonic since 1922.

Entertainment

The stately **Chateau Marmont** (8221 Sunset Blvd., 323/656-1010, www.chateaumarmont.com, bar 6pm-2am daily) is like a gothic castle looming over Sunset Boulevard. It's the perfect place for classy drink in a dark bar. Keep your eyes out for celebrities lurking around trying to keep a low profile.

Rainbow Bar (9015 Sunset Blvd., 310/278-4232, www.rainbowbarandgrill.com, 11am-2am daily) is one of LA's most famous rock bars. Alice Cooper, Led Zeppelin, Guns & Roses, Ringo Starr, John Lennon, and Keith Moon are rumored to have hung out upstairs. Slash's favorite booth is under his picture, and his guitar is on the wall.

R Bar (3331 W. 8th St., 213/387-7227, 4pm-11pm Wed.-Sun.) is a hip Koreatown dive with crazy karaoke nights, DJs, and special events. To get in, check their Twitter feed (@Rbarla) for the password, which changes every two weeks.

Tiki Ti (4427 Sunset Blvd., 323/669-9381, www.tiki-ti.com, 4pm-2am Wed.-Sat.) is a tiny, tiki-themed tavern and a Los Feliz favorite that's been serving 100 different kinds of tropical drinks since 1961. The Blood and Sand cocktail, created for a Tyrone Power movie, is mixed with tequila, cherry, and orange juice. Order it and watch a motorized bull parade down the bar while locals chant, *"Toro! Toro! Olé! Olé!"*

The Varnish (118 E. 6th St., 213/265-7089, www.pouringwithheart.com/the-varnish, 6pm-midnight Sun.-Thurs., 6pm-1am Fri.-Sat.) is a 1920s speakeasy hidden behind the legendary Coles restaurant. Meticulously crafted drinks from the 1890s are served in frozen glassware with block ice and fresh juices, while a standup bassist and pianist play tunes. During Prohibition, gangster Mikey Cohen held meetings in the back, where The Varnish is located now.

Good Times at Davey Wayne's (1611 N. El Centro Ave., Hollywood, 323/498-0859, www.goodtimesatdaveywaynes.com, 8pm-2am Thurs.-Sat., 2pm-2am Sun.) is a retro 1970s bar with era-appropriate decor and a super fun vibe. Go to the back of the garage to enter via a secret "refrigerator door." Inside, drinks are named after '70s songs, Coors is served in coffee mugs, and liquor-spiked snow cones keep you cool on a warm California day.

The Wiltern (3790 Wilshire Blvd., Koreatown, 213/388-1400, www.wiltern.com) is an intimate art deco theater with great acoustics. Everyone from Tony Bennett to Bastille has played here. With fewer than 2,000 seats, the venue sells out quickly.

The Dime (442 N. Fairfax Ave., West Hollywood, 323/272-3397, 7pm-1:30am Tues.-Sat., 6pm-1:30am Sun.-Mon.) spins old-school hip-hop in a cool dive setting.

Hollywood Pantages Theatre (6233 Hollywood Blvd., Hollywood, 323/468-1770, www.hollywoodpantages.com) is an art deco hall featuring Broadway productions, music, and live entertainment.

See a movie at the restored 1922 **Grauman's Egyptian Theater** (6712 Hollywood Blvd., Hollywood, 323/461-2020, www.americancinemathequecalendar.com), an early example of a majestic movie house, located on Hollywood's Walk of Fame.

During the height of Route 66's popularity, **Barney's Beanery** (8447 Santa Monica Blvd., West Hollywood, 323/654-2287, www.barneysbeanery.com, 11am-2am Mon.-Fri., 9am-2am Sat.-Sun.) would take customers' license plates as collateral for food. Some paid their bill and got their license plates back—some didn't. The owner decorated the ceiling with the leftover license plates, and you can still see them in the bar today.

Shopping

The downtown **LA Fashion District** (https://fashiondistrict.org) spans 90 blocks with more than 1,000 stores. The Fashion District acts as a design hub for the clothing, accessories, and fabric industry. The best day to go is on Saturday, when wholesale stores sell to the public. Samples go for up to 70 percent off retail prices. Stores marked "Solo Mayoreo" means they are not open to the public.

For knockoff designer labels, go to **The Santee Alley** (Olympic Blvd. between Santee St. and Maple Ave., www.thesanteealley.com), which takes up two blocks of the Fashion District and is home to 150 stores selling clothes, shoes, accessories, and beauty supplies.

Olvera Street (125 Paseo de la Plaza, downtown, www.olvera-street.com, 10am-7pm daily) is a world-renowned Mexican marketplace that has been going strong since the 1940s. Browse vendor stalls selling everything from leather goods and art to clothing, imported crafts, candles, and traditional Mexican goods.

The Last Bookstore (453 S. Spring St., downtown, 213/488-0599, http://lastbookstorela.com, 11am-8pm daily) is a bibliophile's dream. LA's largest store for new and used records and books, this place is packed with treasures. Wander the aisles stacked with used books, new releases, and classic vinyl. Don't miss the Labyrinth on the mezzanine level, with hundreds of thousands of books priced at $1 each.

Bar Keeper (614 N. Hoover St., Silver Lake, 323/669-1675, www.barkeepersilverlake.com, noon-6pm Sun.-Thurs., noon-7pm Fri.-Sat.) offers bar tools, rare liquors, mid-century glassware, and more than 100 aromatic bitters. It's a candy store for boozehounds and a mecca for mixologists.

For comics, go to **Secret Headquarters** (3817 Sunset Blvd., Silver Lake, 323/666-2228, www.thesecretheadquarters.com, 11am-9pm Mon.-Sat., noon-7pm Sun.). You'll find a great selection of graphic novels and indie comics, plus a knowledgeable staff.

Soap Plant + Wacko (4633 Hollywood Blvd., Los Feliz, 323/663-0122, http://soapplant.com, 11am-7pm Mon.-Wed., 11am-9pm Thurs.-Sat., noon-7pm Sun.) brings good pop-culture game. This bold and zany shop offers hard-to-find toys, vintage auto decals, posters and prints, gag gifts, T-shirts, rare movies, and books.

It's a Wrap (3315 W. Magnolia Blvd., Burbank, 818/567-7366, www.itsawraphollywood.com, 10am-8pm Mon.-Fri., 11am-6pm Sat.-Sun.) is technically a thrift shop, but that's in an "only in LA" kind of way. They sell clothing, furniture, props, and collectibles used in film and TV productions.

The Grove (189 The Grove Dr., 323/900-8080, www.thegrovela.com, 10am-8pm Sun.-Thurs., 10am-9pm Fri.-Sat.) adjoins the Original Farmer's Market. Take the trolley around this upscale outdoor mall to visit 38 stores, 21 restaurants, and a 12-screen movie theater.

Recreation

The **Los Angeles Conservancy** (523 W. 6th St., Ste. 826, 213/623-2489, www.laconservancy.org/walking-tours, $15) offers several walking tours, each of which covers a specific aspect of LA—from architecture to history. Tours vary in length, so check the website for detailed descriptions.

Lounge, picnic, or take a 2-mile (3.2-km) stroll around the **Silver Lake Reservoir** (1854 Silver Lake Blvd.). The views are great; see if you can spot a Richard Neutra house or two perched above the lake in the hills.

If you're a fan of Laurel and Hardy, keep in mind that the steep **Music Box Steps** (936 N. Vendome St., Silver Lake) are the actual staircase up which they attempted to carry a piano. It's a secluded but public staircase with about 130 steps in the hills of Silver Lake.

Runyon Canyon (2000 N. Fuller Ave., Hollywood, 323/644-6661, www.laparks.org/park/runyon-canyon, sunrise-sunset daily) is a 160-acre (65-hectare) park with plenty of hiking trails that offer spectacular views of the Hollywood sign, Griffith Observatory, and downtown Los Angeles. Parking is difficult, so you might want to leave extra time or plan to park farther away and walk to the canyon.

Food

★ **Clifton's** (648 S. Broadway St., 213/627-1673, https://theneverlands.com/cliftons-republic, $15-35) is full of atmosphere, intrigue, history, and yes, taxidermy. This cafeteria-style restaurant opened in 1935, closed in 2011, and underwent a renovation, reopening in 2015. Owner Clifford Clinton followed what he called the "The Cafeteria Golden Rule;" he never turned away anyone who was hungry, allowing customers to pay what they could afford. Today, the large, unusual space spans five floors and boasts a giant fake redwood tree rising through the middle. Come here to dine, drink, and soak up the nightlife. After 9pm, there is a dress code.

Classic LA Drives

Mulholland Drive winds 24 miles (39 km) through the Santa Monica Mountains along the crest of the Hollywood Hills. And it offers some of the best, and most iconic, views of the city. Jack Nicholson and Warren Beatty live on this road, which inspired the 2001 David Lynch film of the same name. From U.S. 101, take the Cahuenga exit and follow the signs. Drive west until you get to I-405 (San Diego Freeway) and go south to head back to Los Angeles. Allow an hour for the drive.

The **Pacific Coast Highway** (or the PCH) is a signature LA drive that parallels the Pacific coastline with soul-stirring ocean views. Take Santa Monica Boulevard (Route 66) to Ocean Avenue, turn right (north), and merge left onto the Pacific Coast Highway (SR-1). If you're short on time, Malibu is a good place to stop for lunch and turn around.

Clifton's main branch (618 Olive St.) is located at 7th and Broadway, the original terminus of Route 66, making it the perfect place to celebrate the end of a long and wonderfully strange trip.

Philippe's (1001 N. Alameda St., downtown, 213/628-3781, www.philippes.com, 10am-8pm daily, $5-10, cash only) serves French dip sandwiches, kosher pickles, soups, coleslaw, homemade spicy mustard, and pickled eggs; it's been doing so since 1908. To place your order, jump in any of the 10 lines, and sit where you like.

The front door at the **Original Pantry** (877 S. Figueroa St., downtown, 213/972-9279, www.pantrycafe.com, 7am-7pm daily, $5-29, cash only) used to have no key because the place had not closed since it opened in 1924. Today, it's open daily, just not for 24 straight hours. This Los Angeles landmark has been serving hash browns, bacon, and griddled pancakes. There's usually a line on the weekends and at lunchtime. Once you sit down, don't wait for a menu; everything you need to know is on the wall.

Millie's Café (3524 W. Sunset Blvd., Silver Lake, 323/664-0404, www.milliescafe.net, 8am-3pm daily, $9-16) opened in 1926, the same year Route 66 was born. The bread is baked fresh every day; they use real butter and hormone-free dairy products and grind each pot of French-roast coffee to perfection.

Sip sublime martinis at ★ **Musso & Frank Grill** (6667 Hollywood Blvd., Hollywood, 323/467-7788, www.mussoandfrank.com, 11am-11pm Tues.-Sat., $21-55). They have been serving Hollywood's A list since 1919. Chaplin, Garbo, Bogart, and Bacall lounged in the red leather booths and hobnobbed with literary legends like F. Scott Fitzgerald and William Faulkner, who mixed his own mint juleps behind the mahogany bar. Today, it's still a place to see and be seen. *Mad Men* filmed an episode and also celebrated its premiere party here.

In 1930, **Pinks Hot Dogs** (709 N. La Brea Ave., 323/931-4223, www.pinkshollywood.com, 9:30am-2am Sun.-Thurs., 9:30am-3am Fri.-Sat., $5-13) opened as a pushcart back before food trucks were trendy. Today, people drive from all over Southern California to eat one of the more than 30 different types of hot dogs on offer (you can't go wrong with the chili cheese). It's busy day and night.

An impressive collection of **food trucks** lines up on Wilshire Boulevard near Fairfax Avenue, outside the Los Angeles County Museum of Art. From the Thai fusion Arroy truck to Poutine Brothers and Kings Road Coffee, it's the most eclectic roundup of food in one block. To find other food trucks in the city (like Kogi, LA's best Korean taco truck), check www.roaminghunger.com for schedules and locations.

You won't get better pastrami and corned beef sandwiches than the ones

Local Eats

You've had **guacamole** before. But in California, where avocados are abundant and locally grown, the guac might just be the best on Earth. And it pairs with everything. Good guacamole is simple: usually just mashed avocados, a little lemon juice, a clove of garlic, and finely chopped tomatoes and onions.

California boasts the largest population of Korean residents in the country, and it's here that you'll find some of the best **Korean barbecue** outside of Korea. What it is: thinly sliced meat marinated in soy sauce, sugar, sesame oil, garlic, and pepper, and then grilled. Side dishes like green onion salad are popular, as is wrapping the meat in lettuce and topping it with a spicy paste or a spicy scallion salad.

Thanks to the nearby Pacific Ocean, in California you can find fresh **fish tacos** practically everywhere. This dish originated in Baja California, Mexico, and a traditional take on it means deep-fried white fish, shredded cabbage (for a nice crunch), and a zesty white sauce, served in corn tortillas. Anything else and it ain't the real deal.

at **Canter's Deli** (419 N. Fairfax Ave., 323/651-2030, www.cantersdeli.com, 24 hours daily, $8-25). This third-generation family-owned business has been attracting famous politicians, rock stars, and regular folks since 1931.

Accommodations

Elaine's Hollywood B&B (1616 N. Sierra Bonita Ave., Hollywood, 323/850-0766, www.elaineshollywoodbedandbreakfast. com, $120-140, cash only) is a renovated 1910 bungalow on a palm tree-lined street that's within walking distance of the Hollywood Walk of Fame. Some rooms have a private sundeck.

The **Ace Hotel** (929 S. Broadway, downtown, 213/623-3233, www.acehotel. com/losangeles, $201-525) is a boutique hotel in the historic 1927 United Artists building. Rooms have an industrial-chic style with exposed wood-beam ceilings, low-slung beds, and custom Revo radios. It's within walking distance of the original terminus of Route 66.

Magic Castle Hotel & Suites (7025 Franklin Ave., Hollywood, 323/851-0800, www.magiccastlehotel.com, $190-350) offers apartment-style suites with kitchens. Rooms are spacious and modern, with crisp white walls and well-stocked kitchens. It's walking distance to grocery stores and includes lots of free stuff, such

as movies, Wi-Fi, snacks, and continental breakfast.

★ **Hotel Figueroa** (939 S. Figueroa St., downtown, 866/723-9381, www. hotelfigueroa.com, $169-204) is a 1920s Spanish Colonial hotel with eclectic accents, bold, rich colors, tile floors, unusual textiles, and ornate chandeliers. There are 268 rooms and suites, plus a swimming pool tucked inside a lush botanical garden. The stylish rooms come with luxury bed linens, high-end bath products, and free Wi-Fi.

Farmer's Daughter (115 S. Fairfax Ave., 800/334-1658, www. farmersdaughterhotel.com, $220-325) is an adorable 1950s-inspired motel. Rooms have hardwood floors and are decked out in denim fabric, gingham curtains, and country-style rugs. Some have rocking chairs and rain showerheads. It's across the street from the Original Farmer's Market and The Grove.

★ **The Line** (3515 Wilshire Blvd., Koreatown, 213/381-7411, www. thelinehotel.com, $209-450) is a slickly modern hotel with concrete walls, plush textiles, original artwork, and rooms with views of the Hollywood Hills. Onsite restaurants include Openaire, run by talented chef Josiah Citrin. It's centrally located between downtown and Beverly Hills, right in the heart of Koreatown.

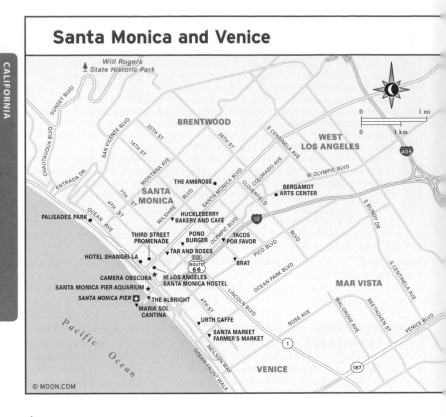

Santa Monica and Venice

© MOON.COM

⬥ Back on 66

While Santa Monica Boulevard technically follows Route 66, it's also one of the most congested roads in the city. From Los Angeles, I-10 is the quickest way to get to Santa Monica and the next terminus of Route 66. Avoid the rush hours of 7am-10am and 3pm-7pm Monday-Friday. If your travel falls during these times, take Olympic Boulevard instead.

Take I-10 heading west. Cross under I-405, and in approximately 3 miles (4.8 km), turn right (northwest) onto 4th Street. Turn left (southwest) at the next street, which is Colorado Avenue. The entrance to the Santa Monica Pier is a few blocks straight ahead.

Santa Monica

⬥ Route 66 Ends

The second "official" ending point of Route 66, at the corner of Lincoln Boulevard and Olympic Boulevard, isn't the most exciting place, but for purists who want to know where it ended, this is it.

Sights
★ Santa Monica Pier

As they say, everything must come to an end. Could there be a more thrilling conclusion to Route 66 than arriving at the land's edge, with the sparkling Pacific Ocean stretching before you? The historic 1909 **Santa Monica Pier** (200

Santa Monica Pier, 310/458-8901, www.santamonicapier.org, daily, hours of businesses vary) lets you linger a little longer on the Mother Road. Walk the pier to its edge jutting over the ocean, stopping first to snap a picture of the famous "End of the Trail" sign—a must-do for Route 66ers. At the end of the pier, pick up a Route 66 souvenir at **The Last Stop Shop.** It's literally the last store on Route 66.

You can spend a few hours here: dining, shopping, people-watching, and riding the Ferris wheel at the floating carnival that is **Pacific Park.** Before you leave, stop at the End of the Trail information booth to sign your name in the log of travelers who've successfully completed Route 66. The friendly staff will offer a much-deserved "congratulations" and will chat with you about your favorite Mother Road stops.

There is parking on the pier deck, accessible via the ramp at Ocean Avenue and Colorado Avenue.

Camera Obscura

The camera obscura is believed to date back to the ancient Greeks, and may have been used by Renaissance painters to project images onto their canvases as a guide. There are only a handful of these devices left in North America. This **Camera Obscura** (1450 Ocean Ave., 310/458-2239, www.santamonica.gov, 9am-3pm Mon.-Fri., 11am-4pm Sat., free) was built in 1898 and donated to the city in 1907. It's been used to capture images of Santa Monica beach life for decades. You can find it at the mid-century Senior Recreation Center, near the Santa Monica Pier. If the door is locked, simply knock and someone will let you in.

Bergamot Arts Center

Bergamot Arts Center (2525 Michigan Ave., http://visitbergamot.com, hours vary by gallery, free) is the largest art

Top to bottom: Santa Monica beach; Route 66 End of the Trail, Santa Monica Pier; Pacific Park

gallery complex and cultural center in Southern California. The Santa Monica Museum of Art, several architecture and design firms, and a café are on-site.

Palisades Park

Ocean breezes, excellent people-watching, and good eats from nearby food trucks; you'll find all of that and more at **Palisades Park** (Ocean Ave. and Washington Ave.), along with Pacific Ocean vistas.

Food

Dine on the Santa Monica Pier at **The Albright** (Santa Monica Pier, 310/394-9683, http://thealbright.com, 11am-8pm daily, $10-25). The menu features fresh seafood (lobster, crab, oysters), poke, ceviche, and beach fare like fish and chips and mussels and fries.

Also on the pier, at the end with the Pacific Ocean as a backdrop, is **Maria Sol Cantina** (Santa Monica Pier, 310/917-5050, www.mariasol.com, 11am-7pm Mon.-Fri., 10am-8pm Sat.-Sun., $10-30). The restaurant highlights the cuisine of Mexican beach towns like Cabo San Lucas and Puerto Vallarta. Closing hours are subject to change depending on weather.

Pono Burger (829 Broadway, 310/584-7005, www.ponoburger.com, 11:30am-8pm daily, $10-13) is one of the best burger joints in town. All beef patties are organic and come topped with amazing cheeses (brie, oak-smoked cheddar, aged blue) and house-made sauces. Free parking is available in an underground lot through the alley off Broadway between 8th and 9th Streets.

There's almost always a line at **Huckleberry Bakery and Café** (1014 Wilshire Blvd., 310/451-2311, www.huckleberrycafe.com, 8am-3pm daily, $12-17), but the maple bacon biscuits and green eggs and ham are worth the wait.

Tacos Por Favor (1408 Olympic Blvd., 310/392-5768, http://tacosporfavor.net, 8am-8pm daily, $3-14) serves Mexican

Palisades Park, Santa Monica

breakfast, lunch, and dinner at cheap prices. Order the shrimp fajitas or the carne asada sopes.

Urth Caffé (2327 Main St., 310/314-7040, www.urthcaffe.com, 7am-10pm Sun.-Thurs., 7am-11pm Fri.-Sat., $7-15) serves fresh, healthy, organic dishes, along with smoothies, coffee, and teas.

The buzzy **Tar and Roses** (602 Santa Monica Blvd., 310/587-0700, www.tarandroses.com, 5:30pm-10:30pm Mon.-Sat., 5:30pm-9:30pm Sun., $10-35) offers shared plates of seasonal American fare. A touch of mint and a pinch of sea salt top wood-roasted English peas—perfect for a starter—and kumquat chutney sweetens the duck entrée.

Accommodations

★ **Hotel Shangri-La** (1301 Ocean Ave., 310/394-2791, www.shangrila-hotel.com, $369-500) is a Streamline Moderne hotel shaped like an ocean liner. Rooms are tastefully decorated with jewel-toned comforters, and ocean-facing windows let in the Pacific air. A pool, hot tub, spa, and rooftop bar with views of the Pacific Ocean round out the amenities.

The Georgian Hotel (1415 Ocean Ave., 310/395-9945, www.georgianhotel.com, $275-425) is a timeless Santa Monica landmark that blends vintage glamour with modern amenities. An evening turn-down service spoils guests, while a special treat, water bowl, or toy will spoil your pet.

The Ambrose (1255 20th St., 310/315-1555, www.ambrosehotel.com, $250-389) is a relaxing, eco-friendly boutique hotel. Rooms feature hardwood floors, spacious bathrooms, and balconies. Amenities include a complimentary continental breakfast, bicycles available for guests' use, and Tesla car service within a 3-mile (4.8-km) radius of the hotel.

Lodging is expensive in Santa Monica, so if you're on a budget, try the **HI Los Angeles Santa Monica Hostel** (1436 2nd St., 310/393-9913, www.hiusa.org, from $90). Natural sunlight pours into the guest rooms, the mattresses are comfortable, and the shared bathrooms are clean. Amenities include free Wi-Fi, free breakfast, laundry facilities, and an outdoor courtyard—plus it's only two blocks from the beach.

Essentials

ROY'S
VACANCY
MOTEL
CAFE

ROUTE
66

Getting There

Air

Chicago, Illinois

This road trip begins Route 66 in Chicago, Illinois, and heads west for 2,448 miles (3,939 km) to Los Angeles, California. There are two major airports in Chicago. **O'Hare International Airport** (ORD, 10000 W. O'Hare Ave., 800/832-6352, www.flychicago.com) hosts nearly all of the major airlines, including American, British Airways, JetBlue, and United. **Midway International Airport** (MDW, 5700 S. Cicero Ave., 773/838-0600, www.flychicago.com) is a smaller, more manageable airport hosting Allegiant, Delta, North Country, Porter, Southwest, and Volaris airlines.

Los Angeles, California

If you choose to launch the road trip from the West Coast, you have two airport options. **Los Angeles International Airport** (LAX, 1 World Way, Los Angeles, 855/463-5252, www.flylax.com) is the second-busiest airport in the country, so flying into **Hollywood Burbank Airport** (BUR, 2627 N. Hollywood Way, Burbank, 818/840-8840, www. hollywoodburbankairport.com) may be easier.

Phoenix, Arizona

Phoenix Sky Harbor International Airport (PHX, 3400 E. Sky Harbor Blvd., 602/273-3300, www.skyharbor. com) offers service from about 20 airlines—American, British Airways, Delta, Southwest, and United, to name a few—including nonstop service from London. Phoenix is about a two-hour drive south of Flagstaff, Arizona.

Las Vegas, Nevada

McCarran International Airport (LAS, 5757 Wayne Newton Blvd., 702/261-5211, www.mccarran.com) hosts American, Delta, JetBlue, Southwest, United, and 10 others. Las Vegas is about a two-hour drive north of Needles, California, and about 100 miles (161 km) west of Kingman, Arizona.

Albuquerque, New Mexico

Albuquerque International Sunport (ABQ, 2200 Sunport Blvd. SE, 505/244-7700, https://abqsunport.com) is located just a few miles from Route 66 and has nonstop service to 20 cities via American, Delta, JetBlue, Southwest, and United airlines.

Train

Since part of Route 66 parallels the Santa Fe train route, **Amtrak** (800/872-7245, www.amtrak.com) offers easy access to the Mother Road. **Chicago's Union Station** (210 S. Canal St., 5am-1am daily) is the third-busiest rail station in the United States and operates as a major hub for Amtrak with service to cities throughout country. Amtrak's California stations are located along Route 66 in **Needles** (950 Front St.), **Barstow** (685 N. 1st Ave.), **Victorville** (16858 S. D. St.), **San Bernardino** (1170 W. 3rd St.), and **Los Angeles** (800 N. Alameda St.).

The *Southwest Chief* route travels west from Chicago to Los Angeles with stops in **Albuquerque** (320 1st St. SW) and **Gallup** (201 E. Hwy. 66), New Mexico; through **Winslow** (303 E. 2nd St.), **Flagstaff** (1 E. Rte. 66), and **Kingman** (402 Andy Devine Ave.), Arizona; and ending at **Union Station** (800 N. Alameda St.) in Los Angeles.

The *Texas Eagle* route travels south from Chicago to St. Louis, Missouri, with stops in **Joliet, Pontiac, Bloomington, Lincoln,** and **Springfield.**

Amtrak also offers a 14-day **Route 66 by Rail tour** (800/268-7252, www. amtrakvacations.com, from $2,349) that starts in Chicago, with stops in St. Louis, Albuquerque, Williams, the Grand Canyon, and Los Angeles.

The *Heartland Flyer* makes daily trips

from **Oklahoma City** (100 South E. K. Gaylord Blvd.), Oklahoma, to **Fort Worth,** Texas (1001 Jones St.).

Bus

Greyhound Bus (www.greyhound.com) lines don't follow Route 66 exactly, but there are stations located along the way. The Greyhound station in **Chicago** (630 W. Harrison St., 312/408-5821) offers service to all major U.S. cities. California stations are located in **San Bernardino** (596 N. G St., 909/884-4796) and **Los Angeles** (1716 E. 7th St., 213/629-8401). Other stations include:

* **Oklahoma:** Oklahoma City (1948 E. Reno Ave., 405/606-4382) and Tulsa (317 S. Detroit Ave., 918/584-4428)

* **New Mexico:** Tucumcari (McDonald's, 2608 S. 1st. St., 575/461-1350), Albuquerque (320 1st St. SW, 505/243-4435), and Gallup (3405 W. Rte. 66, 505/863-9078)

* **Arizona:** Holbrook (101 Mission Ln., 928/524-3832), Flagstaff (880 E. Butler Ave., 928/774-4573), and Kingman (2770 W. Rte. 66, 800/231-2222)

Car Rental

Route 66 travels through a lot of remote areas. If you decide to rent a car, it's best to rent from one of these major chains. All of them have locations throughout the United States, which is good news in case you need roadside assistance or have to switch cars.

To rent a car, you must have a valid driver's license and be at least 25 years old. Some companies will rent to drivers under the age of 25 as long as they pay the underage driver fee and meet all of the requirements. Multiple drivers may incur an additional charge of $5-7 per day. Airport locations usually have the largest fleet to choose from and often offer unlimited mileage. Most importantly, shop around for the best drop-off rate if you're going to rent a car in one state but return it in another.

Car rental fees may change drastically with seemingly no rhyme or reason. To save money, consider renting a hybrid vehicle, which can cut the gas bill in half. An electric vehicle is not recommended since charging stations are scarce. A 4WD vehicle is not needed for this road trip, and is not recommended due to high gas consumption.

Road Rules

Since there are so many alignments of Route 66, it's possible to drive any type of vehicle on it. However, with 15 percent of the road gone, many old alignments have been reduced to dirt and gravel. Jerry McClanahan's *EZ66 Guide for Travelers* offers helpful tips on taking some of the older dirt alignments.

Since Route 66 passes through cities and along tight, winding roads, RVs are not recommended for the complete route, as motor homes can make driving and parking more of an endurance test than a fun road trip. In addition, much of the fun of driving Route 66 includes eating in roadside diners and staying in quirky motels.

For experienced motorcyclists, driving Route 66 on a bike can be an exciting way to see the United States. Thousands of motorcyclists have taken to the Mother Road, and there are several motorcycle tours that travel Route 66. A large community of bikers often meets up at points along the way. **Eagle Riders** (877/557-3541, www.eaglerider.com) offers 15-day tours and also rents Harleys, Indians, Hondas, and BMWs.

Adventure Cycling Association (www.adventurecycling.org, $88.50 for the full set of six maps or $15.75 per map) created one of the first comprehensive Route 66 bicycle maps. Six cartographers, four researchers, and cooperation from state tourism bureaus contributed to the waterproof map, which includes turn-by-turn directions and lodging information,

A Timeline of Route 66

♦ **November 11, 1926:** Route 66 was born, just before the Great Depression and the Dust Bowl. At the time, only 800 miles (1,290 km) of the 2,448-mile (3,939-km) road were paved. The other 1,500 miles (2,414 km): gravel, dirt, bricks, and wood planks.

♦ **1920s and 1930s:** Route 66's diagonal trajectory across the country offered access to California, transforming it into a "road of dreams." Because of the hardships caused by the Great Depression and the Dust Bowl, Route 66 symbolized a pathway to easier times, a gateway to freedom. Thousands of emigrants—with few resources and a lot of hope—motored west in search of a better life.

♦ **1937:** Paving the entirety of Route 66 was completed. And it couldn't have happened fast enough. In 1921, there were 9 million cars on the road. By 1929, there were more than 26 million cars.

♦ **1940s:** The asphalt was thickened along parts of Route 66 in Illinois and Missouri to handle military convoys during World War II. After the war, Route 66 became a popular tourist route, with vacationers cruising the highway to stay at kitschy tepee motels, shop the trading posts, and explore the "Wild West."

♦ **1959:** President Eisenhower's Federal Highway Act changed everything. The bigger, faster four-lane interstate highway system bypassed Route 66 and marked the beginning of its demise.

♦ **1985:** Route 66 was decommissioned. Businesses closed and towns were abandoned.

♦ **Today:** After its decommission, the Mother Road could have become a forgotten footnote. But the spirit of Route 66 lives on, thanks to the tireless and impassioned efforts of those who live and work along the road. Revitalization projects, like the National Park Service Route 66 Corridor Preservation Program, breathe new life into this beloved and historic highway.

hardware stores, grocery stores, and libraries with free Internet access.

Driving and Highway Safety

Always be a courteous, considerate driver. When driving on highways, stay to the right and use the left lane for passing. Earlier alignments of Route 66 have tight turns and slower speed limits, and require more effort and attention to the road.

Take special care when driving on American Indian lands; each community has its own guidelines, rules, and judicial system. In addition, many people walk along roads in these communities, so drive carefully and pay close attention to the speed limits.

If driving your own car, have a mechanic examine the belts, lights, and turn signals before you travel. Check all fluid levels, including oil, brakes, coolant (you'll need this driving through the desert), and power steering. Tires should have at least 2/32-inch (0.2-cm) tread, and check the tire pressure before and during your trip. Check the tire pressure when cold, as hot tires expand and can yield a false PSI reading.

If your car breaks down in a remote area, pull off to the right side of the road; if the car stalls on the road, put the car in neutral and coast or push it off to the right side of the highway. If you have cell service, contact **AAA** (800/222-4357, www.aaa.com) or the rental car company

Desert Driving Tips

With extreme hot and cold temperatures, unflinching sun, poisonous critters, spiny plants, and towns spaced few and far between, the desert can be deadly. It's best to come prepared.

♦ Bring plenty of water, ideally 1 gallon (4 liters) per every passenger in the vehicle.

♦ Stow an additional 5 gallons (19 liters) of water in case your car radiator needs cooling; engines run hot in the desert.

♦ Use caution when driving on dirt roads and avoid driving on soft sand as it's easy to get stuck.

♦ Watch for flash floods and do not drive through flooded areas.

♦ Do not rely on GPS in remote desert areas, as directions are notoriously unreliable. Always have a print map on hand as a backup.

♦ Fill up with gas whenever you can. There are few service stations in the desert.

♦ The desert sun is bright, even through car windows. Wear sunscreen and sunglasses.

♦ Pack layers of clothing or a blanket. A sunny 70°F (21°C) day can easily drop to 20°F (-7°C) at night.

♦ If you see wildlife—rattlesnakes, coyotes, javelinas, scorpions—let them be. Do not approach or engage them.

emergency number. Put on your hazard lights while waiting for help; if it's night, turn on the inside ceiling light and keep the car running to avoid draining the battery while you wait for help to arrive.

In the event that you are stranded, be prepared for any kind of weather or situation. Always travel with water, a flashlight, batteries, cell phone charger, blankets, jumper cables, flares, waterproof matches, a first-aid kit, and nonperishable food items such as protein bars or jerky.

Plan ahead. You don't have to book lodging weeks or even days in advance. But try to call ahead to make same-day reservations so when you're pulling into a town after dark, you don't have to hunt for a hotel room.

Gas

When driving Route 66, keep the gas tank level above the half-full line, and fuel up in major towns whenever possible. Illinois, Missouri, and Oklahoma have several small towns on Route 66 with gas stations, but in Texas, New Mexico, Arizona, and California, there are long stretches of Route 66 with limited or no services. Keep an eye on the gas gauge.

Visas and Officialdom

Passports and Visas

Visitors from other countries must have a **valid passport** and a **visa.**

Visitors from certain countries may qualify for **visa waivers.** Visit the U.S. Customs and Border Protection website (www.cbp.gov) to see the complete list. Travelers from these countries must apply online with the Electronic System for Travel Authorization and hold a **return plane ticket** to their home countries less than 90 days from the time of entry.

Holders of **Canadian passports** don't need visas or waivers. In most countries, the local U.S. embassy can provide a **tourist visa.** Plan for at least two weeks for visa processing, longer during the busy summer season (June-Aug.). More information is available online at http://travel.state.gov.

If you lose your passport, visit the **U.S. Department of State** (www.usembassy.gov) to find an embassy from your home country to help.

When you drive across the state line into California, there is an agricultural checkpoint; do not bring any fresh fruit or plants into the state.

Customs

U.S. citizens age 21 or older may import (free of duty) the following: 1 liter of alcohol; 200 cigarettes (one carton); 100 cigars (non-Cuban); and $800 worth of gifts.

International travelers must declare amounts that exceed $10,000 in cash (U.S. or foreign), traveler's checks, or money orders. Meat products, fruits, and vegetables are prohibited due to health and safety regulations.

Drivers entering California must stop at **Agricultural Inspection Stations.** They don't need to present a passport, visa, or even a driver's license, but should be prepared to present fruits and vegetables, even those purchased within neighboring states just over the border. If you have produce, it could be infected by a problem pest or disease; expect it to be confiscated on the spot.

International Driver's Licenses

International visitors need to secure an **International Driving Permit** from their home country before coming to the United States. They should also bring the government-issued driving permit from their home country. They are also expected to be familiar with the driving regulations of the states they will visit. More information is available online at www.aaa.com/International.

Travel Tips

Wi-Fi is available at most hotels, motels, libraries, and visitors centers along Route 66. Cell phone service is widely available, with the exception of remote areas in northern New Mexico, parts of northern Arizona, and the Mojave Desert in California. Always have a printed map on hand as a backup.

Budget

Traveling on Route 66 can be done on a budget, but if you have the means, there are definitely worthy opportunities to splurge. The moderate traveler should plan $125 per night for lodging, and about $50 per day for modest meals. Fuel costs vary depending on your vehicle's mileage and the current prices. To save money, fill up your tank in large towns or cities, as prices in rural locations can cost up to $1 more per gallon (4 liters).

On a budget? **Hotel Tonight** (www.hoteltonight.com) offers great last-minute lodging deals. When hotels have empty guest rooms, they release them at discounted prices. Hotel Tonight collates these options in one place—their website and mobile app—and you can search for what you're looking by location or amenities.

Accommodations that include a free continental breakfast, and dining at restaurants only once per day, can add up to a savings of at least $600 for a family of four on a two-week trip. Avoid larger museums or attractions with high entrance fees; these places are not unique to Route 66, and the smaller, quirky museums generally charge less than $5 in entry fees. There are also many free things to do on Route 66. So as long as you can cover your gas, lodging, and food, you'll have a fulfilling and memorable time.

For most trip expenses—gas, lodging, attractions, and restaurants—you can use a **credit** or **debit card**. However, there are a handful of businesses on Route 66 that don't accept cards as payment; for these businesses, as well as for tips, souvenirs, and miscellaneous purchases, bring **cash.** Plan for $100-150 per week. You'll find **bank ATMs** located in cities and mid- to large-size towns.

If you're traveling to the United States from a foreign country, you'll need to exchange your currency at the airport, bank, or currency exchange. Businesses within the United States only accept U.S. currency.

Time Zones

Route 66 passes through eight states and three time zones. As you travel west, it is an hour earlier as you cross into each time zone.

Illinois, Missouri, Kansas, Oklahoma, and Texas are in the central time zone (CST). New Mexico is in the mountain time zone (MST). Arizona does not observe daylight savings time (except for the Navajo Nation). This means that from the beginning of November to the beginning of March, Arizona is in the mountain time zone, but from March through October, Arizona is in the Pacific time zone (PST). California is in the Pacific time zone.

Solo Travelers

Most, if not all, of the cities and towns along Route 66 are safe for solo travelers. However, there are general road-trip precautions to take if you're traveling alone:

- **Know your limits.** Driving long distances can take a physical and mental toll. Before you set out, have an idea of how long you're comfortable driving each day.

- **Set a schedule.** It helps to have a list of must-see highlights for each day.

- **Book accommodations in advance.** This saves you the hassle of booking while on the road.

- **Get a membership to AAA.** The automobile association provides roadside assistance, maps, travel tips, discounts, and itineraries.

- **Start each day's drive early.** This helps to ensure you arrive at your destination before dark.

- **Lock your vehicle doors.** Even if it seems like you're in a safe spot, lock up anyway.

- **Stay in touch.** A quick text or email to let trusted friends or family know where you are and where you plan to be goes a long way.

- **Don't pick up strangers or hitchhikers.** Also, don't stop for someone stranded on the side of the road. Instead, find a safe place and then dial 911 for them.

There are some specific resources for **women traveling alone.** To meet other solo travelers along the way, the free app **Tourlina** connects women with travel companions matched by interest or itinerary. Another free app, **Alix,** curates restaurant recommendations for solo female travelers. For emergencies, there's **TripWhistle,** an app that links you to local emergency services via GPS. And **Smart Traveler,** an app from the U.S.

Coronavirus along Route 66

At the time of writing in early 2021, most cities and towns along Route 66 had been significantly affected by the coronavirus pandemic. Most, if not all, required that face coverings be worn indoors and that people maintained a distance of six feet from each another. However, the situation was constantly evolving.

Now more than ever, Moon encourages its readers to be courteous and ethical in their travel. We ask travelers to be respectful to residents, and mindful of the evolving situation in their chosen destination when planning their trip.

Before You Go

♦ Check relevant websites (listed below) for updated local restrictions and the overall health status of the destination.

♦ If you plan to fly, check with your airline and the destination's health authority for updated recommendation requirements.

♦ Check the website of any museums and other venues you wish to patronize to confirm that they're open, if their hours have been adjusted, and to learn about any specific visitation requirements, such as mandatory reservations.

♦ Pack hand sanitizer, a thermometer, and plenty of face masks. Road trippers may want to bring a cooler to limit the number of stops along their route.

♦ Assess the risk of entering crowded spaces, joining tours, and taking public transit.

♦ Expect general disruptions. Events may be postponed or cancelled, and some tours and venues may require reservations, enforce limits on the number of guests, be operating during different hours than the ones listed, or be closed entirely.

Resources

♦ Centers for Disease Control and Prevention (www.cdc.gov)

♦ National Park Service (www.nps.gov)

ILLINOIS

♦ Illinois Department of Public Health (www.dph.illinois.gov/covid19)

♦ Illinois Office of Tourism (www.enjoyillinois.com)

KANSAS

♦ Kansas Department of Health and Environment (www.coronavirus.kdheks.gov)

♦ Kansas Department of Wildlife, Parks and Tourism (www.travelks.com)

MISSOURI

♦ Missouri Department of Health and Senior Services (https://health.mo.gov)

♦ Missouri Division of Tourism (www.visitmo.com)

the iconic *Golden Driller* statue near Route 66 in Oklahoma

OKLAHOMA

♦ Oklahoma State Department of Health (https://oklahoma.gov/covid19.html)

♦ Travel Oklahoma (www.travelok.com)

TEXAS

♦ Texas Department of State Health Services (www.dshs.texas.gov/coronavirus)

♦ Travel Texas (www.traveltexas.com)

NEW MEXICO

♦ New Mexico Department of Health (https://cv.nmhealth.org)

♦ New Mexico Tourism Department (www.newmexico.org)

ARIZONA

♦ Arizona Department of Health Services (www.azdhs.gov)

♦ American Indian Tribal Lands: Hopi (www.hopi-nsn.gov), Navajo (www.navajo-nsn.gov)

♦ Visit Arizona (www.visitarizona.com)

CALIFORNIA

♦ California Department of Public Health (www.cdph.ca.gov)

♦ County of Los Angeles Public Health (http://publichealth.lacounty.gov)

♦ Visit California (www.visitcalifornia.com)

Department of State, lists current travel advisories and information about your destination.

Black Travelers

Route 66 runs through parts of the United States that were once home to "sundown towns," all-white cities and counties that practiced racial segregation by excluding people of color through discriminatory local laws (Jim Crow laws), intimidation, and in some cases, violence.

The term "sundown town" came from signs telling non-whites they had to leave by sunset. From 1936 to 1966, Victor Hugo Green published the *Negro Motorist Green Book,* a road-trip guide for Black travelers listing all of the businesses throughout the country that welcomed Black Americans.

Even though Jim Crow laws stopped being enforced in 1965, there are still some regions of the United States where people of color experience unequal treatment and racism. In 2017, the National Association for the Advancement of Colored People (NAACP) issued a travel advisory for Missouri. It calls for Black travelers to pay special attention and exercise caution when traveling throughout the state due to several race-based incidents that occurred.

Major cities along Route 66 are diverse, with significant Black populations. When traveling through less-diverse rural areas, racial discrimination and its practices still exist. Exercise caution, follow road rules, don't drive late at night, and avoid empty gas stations or empty businesses.

Helpful resources include **Travel Noire** (https://travelnoire.com), **Soul of America** (www.soulofamerica.com), **Innclusive** (www.innclusive.com), and **Nomadness** (www.nomadnesstv.com).

LGBTQIA Travelers

LGBTQIA travelers will feel perfectly comfortable in major cities along Route 66: Chicago, St. Louis, Santa Fe, Flagstaff, and Los Angeles. However, when driving through smaller rural towns, travelers will find a dearth of establishments that cater to the LGBTQIA visitor. A few good LGBTQIA travel resources are **Advocate** (www.advocate.com/travel), **Mister B&B** (www.misterbandb.com), **Out Traveler** (www.outtraveler.com), and **Purple Roofs** (www.purpleroofs.com).

Travelers with Disabilities

The Americans with Disabilities Act (ADA), enacted in 1990, requires public places to provide facilities to accommodate disabled patrons. Most museums and restaurants are wheelchair accessible, but small mom-and-pop motels located in older properties built before 1991, or not renovated since 1991, don't have to abide by current ADA standards. Chain motels generally have rooms with larger doors for wheelchair access, but it's best to call ahead and reserve the room you need.

Before you pay entrance fees to national parks, note that U.S. citizens with permanent disabilities are eligible for a lifetime **Access Pass** (http://store.usgs.gov/access-pass) with free entry to 2,000 national parks and federal recreation sites. You can obtain an Access Pass in person at any federal recreation site or by submitting a completed application (www.nps.gov/findapark/passes.htm, $10 processing fee may apply) online or by mail. The pass does not provide benefits for special recreation permits or concessionaire fees. Passes take 3-5 days to process and about one week to ship.

Traveling with Children

Assuming your kiddos are happy car travelers, Route 66 can be a fun trip with the little ones. There are plenty of family-friendly attractions, interactive museums, restaurants with children's menus, and lodgings with swimming pools. One of the best things about Route 66 is that each day you'll encounter a new topography, a big city, a small town, and a rich piece of American history. You'll drive through farmland, city streets, natural wonders, urban neighborhoods, and national monuments, all of which offer great fodder for discovery and discussion.

Traveling with Pets

It's more common than ever to bring your four-legged friend on vacation, a trend that has encouraged lodging, restaurants, and tourist attractions to welcome travelers with pets. If your dog is a good road companion, then Route 66 is an ideal trip. Just make sure to schedule your journey for the cooler months of spring or fall to avoid the extreme heat of the Southwest during the summer. Most national parks and monuments along Route 66 allow leashed animals, and many major motel and hotel chains (Red Roof Inn, La Quinta, Kimpton, Best Western), as well as independently owned hotels and motor courts, welcome dogs. Pet-friendly travel resources include **Go Pet Friendly** (www. gopetfriendly.com) and **Bring Fido** (www. bringfido.com).

Resources

Suggested Reading

No other road has captured the essence of the American Dream than Route 66. It inspired John Steinbeck's *The Grapes of Wrath,* Pixar's film *Cars,* and even the video game Grand Theft Auto.

Hinckley, Jim. *The Illustrated Route 66 Historical Atlas.* Minneapolis, MN: Voyager Press, 2014. A state-by-state illustrated guide.

Jakle, John A. and Keith A. Sculle. *The Gas Station in America.* Baltimore, MD: The Johns Hopkins University Press, 1994. A comprehensive history of the gas station and its role in American roadside culture.

Krim, Arthur. *Route 66: Iconography of the American Highway.* Staunton, VA: George F. Thompson Publishing, 2014. A meticulously researched cultural geography of the symbolism of Route 66.

Mahar-Keplinger, Lisa. *American Signs: Form and Meaning on Route. 66.* The Monacelli Press, 2002. Examines the iconography of roadside signage, offering a different way to see Route 66.

Mangum, Richard K. and Sherry G. Mangum. *Route 66 Across Arizona: A Comprehensive Two-Way Guide for Touring Route 66.* Flagstaff, AZ: Hexagon Press, Inc., 2001. Illustrations, color maps, photos, hikes, bike rides, and tours along Route 66 in Arizona.

Olsen, Russell A. *The Complete Route 66 Lost & Found,* St. Paul, MN: MBI Publishing Company, 2008. Filled with 150 side-by-side photos of modern and mid-century-era filling stations, motor courts, cafés and truck stops.

Steinbeck, John. *The Grapes of Wrath: 50th Anniversary Edition.* New York, NY: Viking, 1989. This Pulitzer Prize-winning novel traces the Joad family fleeing the Dust Bowl during the Great Depression. Steinbeck was the first to call Route 66 the "Mother Road."

Taylor, Candacy A. *Overground Railroad: The Green Book and the Roots of Black Travel in America.* New York, NY: Abrams Press, 2020. This book celebrates the stories of th people that stood up against segregation by listing their businesses in the *Negro Motorist Green Book.*

Wallis, Michael. *Route 66: The Mother Road, 75th Anniversary Edition.* New York, NY: St. Martin's Griffin, 2001. A richly illustrated cultural history book, filled with compelling stories from people who have lived and worked on the Mother Road.

Internet Resources

National Historic Route 66 Federation
www.national66.org
A nonprofit dedicated to documenting the cultural heritage, preserving the landmarks, and revitalizing the economy along Route 66.

National Park Service
www.nps.gov/subjects/travelroute66/index.htm
A comprehensive site with detailed histories of sights along Route 66, including many that are listed on the National Register of Historic Places.

National Park Service Route 66 Corridor Preservation Program
http://ncptt.nps.gov/rt66
This site features information about the preservation efforts taking place on Route 66 and the cost-share grants that are keeping historic businesses alive.

Illinois
www.illinoisroute66.org
A mile-by-mile exploration of Route 66 in Illinois.

Missouri
www.missouri66.org
A state resource featuring Route 66-related activities happening in Missouri.

Oklahoma
www.travelok.com/route_66
A guide to the cultural heritage of Oklahoma and Route 66.

New Mexico
www.rt66nm.org
A site dedicated to promoting, preserving, and educating people about Route 66 in New Mexico.

Arizona
www.azrt66.com
A site outlining activities, attractions, and history along Route 66 counties in Arizona.

California
www.route66ca.org
A nonprofit dedicated to preserving and promoting Route 66, including brief histories of the desert towns and communities along Route 66.

INDEX

364

INDEX

LIST OF MAPS

PHOTO CREDITS

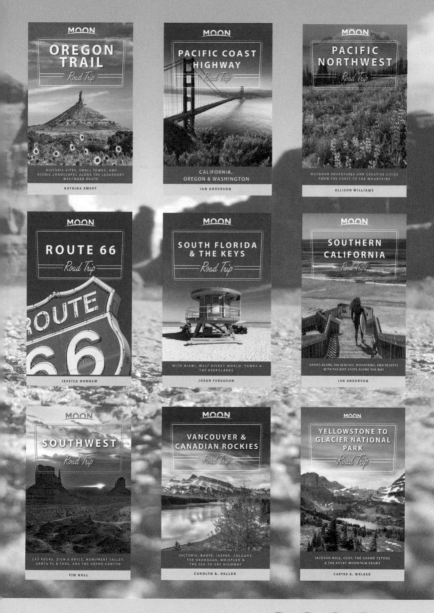

...to Beachy Getaways Around the Globe

MOON
AMALFI COAST

MOON
ARUBA

MOON
BAHAMAS

MOON
BAJA

MOON
BELIZE

MOON
CARTAGENA & COLOMBIA'S CARIBBEAN COAST

MOON
COSTA RICA

MOON
DOMINICAN REPUBLIC

MOON
FIJI

MOON
JAMAICA

MOON
MAUI
With Moloka'i & Lāna'i
GREG ARCHER

MOON
PUERTO RICO
SUZANNE VAN ATTEN

Craft a personalized journey through the top National Parks in the U.S. and Canada with Moon!

In these books:

Coverage of gateway cities and towns

Suggested itineraries from one day to multiple weeks

Advice on where to stay (or camp) in and around the parks

MOON

GREAT SMOKY MOUNTAINS
NATIONAL PARK

HIKING · CAMPING
SCENIC DRIVES

JASON FRYE

MOON

JOSHUA TREE & PALM SPRINGS

JENNA BLOUGH

MOON

YELLOWSTONE & GRAND TETON

HIKE, CAMP,
SEE WILDLIFE

BECKY LOMAX

MOON

YOSEMITE
SEQUOIA & KINGS CANYON

ANN MARIE BROWN

MOON

ZION & BRYCE

Including Arches, Canyonlands,
Capitol Reef, Grand Staircase-
Escalante & Moab

W. C. McRAE & JUDY JEWELL

Get inspired for your next adventure

Follow **@moonguides** on Instagram or subscribe to our newsletter at **moon.com**

#TravelWithMoon

MAP SYMBOLS

═══	Expressway	○	City/Town	ⓘ	Information Center	♠	Park
───	Primary Road	◉	State Capital	🅿	Parking Area	⚲	Golf Course
───	Secondary Road	⊛	National Capital	♦	Church	✛	Unique Feature
- - - -	Unpaved Road	✪	Highlight	🍇	Winery/Vineyard	✎	Waterfall
··········	Trail	★	Point of Interest	🚩	Trailhead	⋀	Camping
··········	Ferry	•	Accommodation	🚉	Train Station	▲	Mountain
⊣⊢⊣⊢	Railroad	▼	Restaurant/Bar	✈	Airport	⚡	Ski Area
▦	Pedestrian Walkway	■	Other Location	✕	Airfield	⬭	Glacier
▦▦▦	Stairs						

CONVERSION TABLES

°C = (°F − 32) / 1.8
°F = (°C x 1.8) + 32
1 inch = 2.54 centimeters (cm)
1 foot = 0.304 meters (m)
1 yard = 0.914 meters
1 mile = 1.6093 kilometers (km)
1 km = 0.6214 miles
1 fathom = 1.8288 m
1 chain = 20.1168 m
1 furlong = 201.168 m
1 acre = 0.4047 hectares
1 sq km = 100 hectares
1 sq mile = 2.59 square km
1 ounce = 28.35 grams
1 pound = 0.4536 kilograms
1 short ton = 0.90718 metric ton
1 short ton = 2,000 pounds
1 long ton = 1.016 metric tons
1 long ton = 2,240 pounds
1 metric ton = 1,000 kilograms
1 quart = 0.94635 liters
1 US gallon = 3.7854 liters
1 Imperial gallon = 4.5459 liters
1 nautical mile = 1.852 km

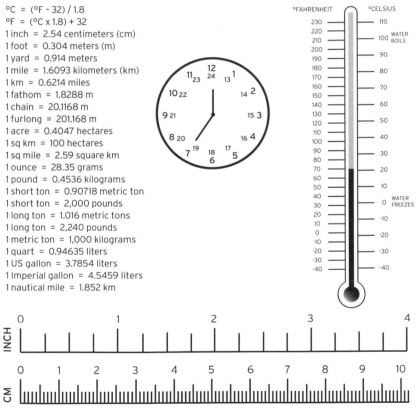

MOON ROUTE 66 ROAD TRIP

Avalon Travel
Hachette Book Group
1700 Fourth Street
Berkeley, CA 94710, USA
www.moon.com

Editor: Rachael Sablik
Acquiring Editor: Nikki Ioakimedes
Graphics Coordinator: Rue Flaherty
Production Coordinator: Rue Flaherty
Cover Design: Erin Seaward-Hiatt
Interior Design: Darren Alessi
Moon Logo: Tim McGrath
Map Editor: Mike Morgenfeld
Cartographer: Karin Dahl
Indexer: Rachel Kuhn

ISBN-13: 9781640494978

Printing History
1st Edition — 2016
3rd Edition — September 2021
5 4 3 2 1

Text © 2021 by Avalon Travel.
Maps © 2021 by Avalon Travel.
Some photos and illustrations are used by permission and are the property of the original copyright owners.